CALL THE MIDDLE WATCH

Call the Middle Watch

An Account of Life at Sea in the Royal Navy 1905 to 1963

P.F.R.CORSON

The Pentland Press
Edinburgh – Cambridge – Durham – USA

First published in 1997 by
The Pentland Press Ltd
1 Hutton Close
South Church
Bishop Auckland
Durham

Typeset by Carnegie Publishing, 18 Maynard St, Preston
Printed in Great Britain by Antony Rowe Ltd, Chippenham, Wiltshire

Acknowledgements

The Hydrographer's 1953 Review Print on the jacket, a copy of the whole print is available from the Hydrographer. © Crown Copyright. Reproduced by permission of the Controller of HMSO and the UK Hydrographic Office.

Imperial War Museum – photographs of HMS *Valiant* and HMS *Norman*

The Times On This Day cutting – Christmas 1868

Details of ships – Reprinted with permission of Jane's Information Group from editions of *Jane's Fighting Ships 1905–1963*. All rights reserved

Contents

Acknowledgements v

Contents vii

Illustrations ix

Preface xi

Part One

1 A Letter from Port Arthur – 1905 3

2 The West Indies – 1910 15

3 The Persian Gulf – 1913/14 37

4 The Grand Fleet – 1916 63

5 A Return to Wester Ross 73

6 Between the Wars 81

Part Two

1 Another Beginning 89

2 Eastern Fleet 96

3 Durban and Back 106

4 To the Pacific 114

5 Return to the East Indies 124

6 A Frigate in the Persian Gulf 132

7 The Persian Dawn 141

8 Tales from the Hills and the Islands 150

9	Singapore for Christmas	157
10	Station Safari	163
11	By Whaler to Kiltan	171
12	Malayan Emergency	178
13	A Visit to Pekan	187
14	Home Fleet Destroyer	194
15	A Magic Cruise	202
16	"Are we seamen or aren't we?"	209
17	Norfolk, Virginia; Nelson's Shirt and a Lost Anchor Cable	215
18	A Voyage to Dundee	226
19	West Coast	235
20	A Family Affair	240
21	Cyprus Wedding	247
22	Cod War	251
23	A Near Thing	262
24	*Barrosa* – Devonport to Kuwait	270
25	Seychelles and Aden to Singapore	279
26	Confrontation in Borneo	284
27	To Hong Kong	295
28	Pirates	300
29	A Black Mark – and a Typhoon Avoided	308
30	Last Lap	317
	Outline Particulars of Principal Ships mentioned in the text	327

Illustrations

North-East China, Korea and Japan   4

Sketches of a Fort at Port Arthur   8&10

The West Indies and Central America   16

Sketch of the Coast – Greytown, Nicaragua   31

Sketch of the Coast – Blewfields, Nicaragua   33

The Persian Gulf   39

HMS *Valiant* 1943   97

HMS *Norman*, 1944   115

Christmas 1868 – A cutting from *The Times*   159

The Tindal's letter   168

Malaya – East Coast   179

HMS *Broadsword*   197

HMS *Largo Bay* Boys Training Squadron entering the
    Solent for the 1953 Coronation Review   227

HMS *Virago*, 6th Frigate Squadron, Home Fleet 1955   241

HMS *Russell*, Fishery Protection Squadron 1958   252

HMS *Barrosa*   271

South-East Asia and North-East Borneo   285

Preface

The book sets out to describe life at sea in the Royal Navy during the first half of the twentieth century. It begins in 1905, about the time that the steam turbine was replacing the reciprocating steam engine as the main power-plant in ships and naval gunnery was beginning to benefit from the improving effectiveness of the rifled gun. It ends in 1963 as steam is being ousted by gas turbine and the gun is giving way to the guided missile as the main surface and above surface weapon. These years thus encompass a clearly definable period which might perhaps be called the 'Steam Turbine – Rifled Gun era'.

Two events suggested to me that an account of it might be worthwhile. My Father went to sea as a Midshipman in 1904 and some years after he died I came across a bundle of letters which he had written to his Mother between 1905 and 1916. In them he describes experiences on the China Station (1905), in the West Indies (1908), the Persian Gulf (1913/14) and during the Battle of Jutland (1916). They seemed to me to give a fascinating picture of life at sea nearly a century ago and they form Part I of this book. I have added short descriptive passages where it appeared helpful to have a background to the events described.

Part II stems from my own experience at sea 1943–63. Here the spur to write was a chance remark made to me when buying some rope a year or two back. The store only had two short lengths instead of the one long one that I had asked for. 'I'll take those' I said. 'I can easily splice them together.' 'A Boy Scout, then?' asked the storeman. 'No' I said, 'Royal Navy'. 'Sailors can't splice any more' came the riposte. 'All they can do now is programme computers'. He did seem to have a point, and I came to feel that perhaps the years when sailors could still splice – just, when they still got a daily tot, still slept in hammocks and the women in their lives remained safely tucked up ashore – that those years also had something worth telling.

I have tried to give some account of what life at sea was about in a fairly uncomplicated age – of what the Navy was required to do. It has been difficult to get a balance between the story being just personal memories or on the other hand turning into something of an essay on the exercise of sea power. I am not sure that I have succeeded, but here it is.

PART ONE

Chapter 1

A Letter
from Port Arthur – 1905

My Father's first letter in the collection was written from HMS *Sutlej*, an armoured cruiser in which he was serving as Midshipman on the China Station. He describes a visit to Port Arthur, the erstwhile Russian base on the North China coast, shortly after the end of the Russo-Japanese War of 1904–5.

A cruiser's historic function was the protection of maritime trade, imperial policing, and scouting ahead of the battle-fleet in the event of an action between battleships. *Sutlej* displaced 12,000 tons and her armament comprised two 9.2-inch guns and twelve 6-inch guns. By comparison the battleship *Empress of India* in which my Father first went to sea displaced only two thousand tons more and was a shorter and slower ship though more heavily armoured and with a heavier armament. Armoured cruisers were often considered able to take part in battleship actions themselves, and they in fact did so, on both sides, at the battle of Tsushima mentioned below. A few years later the term 'armoured' was dropped from the cruiser designation. The larger ships were known merely as 'cruisers' and the smaller ones were christened 'light cruisers'.

Sutlej reached Port Arthur in the summer of 1905. It must have been about six months after its capture by the Japanese. The war had begun in February the previous year with a pre-emptive strike by the Japanese two days before they declared hostilities. They were of course to repeat the tactic thirty-seven years later at Pearl Harbour.

The origins of the war lay in the simultaneous determination of Russia and Japan to develop zones of influence in the Far East, mainly at the expense of China. Japan had an alliance with Great Britain. Many of her naval officers had received training in this country and most of her larger naval vessels were Tyne- or Clyde-built. The friendly ties which she had with Britain at the time are evident throughout my Father's letter. Her army on the other hand was modelled on that of the Prussians. The backbone of her fleet in 1904 consisted of six modern battleships and six

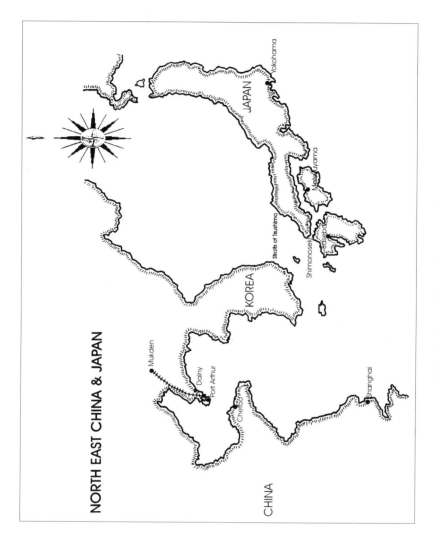

North-East China, Korea and Japan

armoured cruisers. At the start of the war the Russian navy was stronger, on paper at least, than the Japanese but of course only part of it was stationed in the Far East.

On the night of 9 February 1904 the Russian Far East Squadron comprising five battleships and a number of cruisers and smaller craft was attacked by Japanese torpedo boats as it lay at anchor outside Port Arthur. War had not yet been declared. Two battleships and a cruiser were damaged. Next day the attack was continued by the Japanese battle-fleet of four battleships and all the Russian ships were effectively disabled. In twenty-four hours the Japanese had seriously dented Russian morale and had achieved naval superiority.

To retrieve the position the Russians determined to send reinforcements. These could only come from the Baltic or Black Sea Fleets. The latter was ruled out, being bound by treaty not to sail outside the Bosphorus. The onus was on the Baltic ships.

It was not until 11 October 1904 that the Baltic Squadron was ready to sail. By then it had been much strengthened by the addition of four newly-completed battleships making seven in all. Together with its cruisers, smaller warships, supply ships and colliers the Squadron totalled 42 vessels. Its departure for the Far East was hardly auspicious. On passage through the North Sea and in the vicinity of the Dogger Bank it came upon a number of trawlers fishing out of Hull, took them, unbelievably, for Japanese torpedo boats, and opened fire on them, hitting several and causing considerable casualties. It was not to reach Singapore for another six months.

Meanwhile on 2 January 1905 Port Arthur, which had been under siege for many months, was finally occupied by the Japanese; and in March the Japanese also took Mukden, some 200 miles away to the north-east. This marked the virtual end of the war on land.

By now the Japanese war effort was beginning to show signs of strain. Their casualties for instance in front of Port Arthur had been double those of the Russians; and the war was costing over half the national budget. The Russians however, despite their disasters at sea and indifferent performance on land, were certainly not beaten and probably never would be. There was a growing feeling in Japan that if peace could be made now it ought to be possible to secure very favourable terms, and the United States was anxious to mediate. They had supported Japan at the beginning of the war but each Japanese success had made them more aware of that country's growing impact on the international scene, particularly in the

West Pacific: judicious peace negotiations might be used to redress the balance of power between the two adversaries and this could do no harm to US interests in the area.

The war dragged on however for another two months until on 27 May 1905 the Russian ships from the Baltic, joined recently by the remnants of their Pacific fleet, came up with the Japanese navy in the Straits of Tsushima between Korea and Japan. It was the first encounter between fleets of heavy ships since Trafalgar and the first fought with modern weapons. The Russians were once again decimated and Japan emerged as a maritime power to be taken seriously.

The subsequent peace negotiations did not however reflect the completeness of the Japanese naval and military successes. The Russians by careful diplomacy managed to secure a reasonably favourable settlement whilst the Japanese by overplaying their hand were left more than a little disappointed.

My Father's letter from Port Arthur bears no date other than 1905 but *Sutlej* must have visited the port while peace negotiations were under way. The meticulous description of every aspect of the visit reflects no doubt the requirements of his Midshipman's 'Log'. These handsomely bound and weighty works were required to be kept by all Midshipmen as a contribution towards developing a habit of accurate observation and clear expression. Often tedious and sometimes meretricious to reread in later years these Journals did at least epitomise a recognition that life at sea across the world needed more than just technical efficiency.

Since 1905 a number of the place names mentioned have changed: Port Arthur is now Lushun, Chefoo is Yentai and Mukden is Shenyang.

The letter mentions a number of damaged or half-sunk warships. Those that are Japanese are self-evident from the text. The Russian *Petropavlosk* and *Retvisan* were battleships and *Pobieda* and *Pallada* cruisers.

HMS Sutlej
China Station, 1905

At Chefoo there was nothng to see except flagstaffs on the hills around and a tall wireless mast. Then on Tuesday morning we sailed for Dalny, arriving there at 5 p.m. the same night. We had to lie about two and a half miles from the town as the water is too shallow to go in close.

The place is a straggling town of modern brick villas in gardens which have been overrun with weeds and so on. The roads as usual are execrable, ruts and mud abounding. Naturally the houses are only partially occupied, and those that are have soldiers in them as the Town is in military occupation and no one except the Japanese and Chinese coolies are allowed. The glass of most of the houses is shattered by concussion but I did not see a single place damaged by shellfire.

There was one old Japanese ship, a few gunboats and two torpedo boats in the harbour. Many transports and launches lay alongside the wharves. There were two raised merchant ships which had been towed round from Port Arthur, one in the dock and one alongside the wharf. Two Red Cross ships were lying at anchor.

The first day we were there they gave us a garden party. They said it was a fine show. We rubbed up against the Japanese Admiral who had gone down in the *Hatsuse*, Lieutenants who had torpedoed battleships from torpedo boats and all sorts of celebrities.

Next morning I was roused out of my blankets by Wilson telling me to get into my clothes, as we had got leave to go to Port Arthur and the boat was leaving at 6.45, that was in half an hour's time. No bath, no wash, jump into a clean tunic and trousers, cram a shirt, mess jacket and collars into a bag, bolt a grape or two and so into the boat. The Commander asked Bevan if he'd had any breakfast and, as he said, 'No', he went down and got him a box of biscuits. We went ashore eating biscuits and getting soaked by sheets of water flying over the boat. (I am going to turn in. Good night!)

Next day

Inside the breakwater were the Jap cruiser *Chiyoda* and a few gunboats. We landed and walked up to the station carrying our bags, passing beneath a large arch with 'Welcome' in red on white canvas. Unluckily there had been rain the night before so it presented a rather washed out appearance. We got to the station at last and found that the one and only train of the day had gone a good hour ago!!!

What were we to do? I gave it up and looked about me. There were a great many trucks and engines but hardly any passenger coaches. The offices were in a small wooden hut at the side. A large shed, just to the left of the platform, was used as a receiving hospital, and whilst we were there, wounded men were coming down from another hospital a few hundred yards away in rickshaws and on stretchers, a long never-ending stream of them.

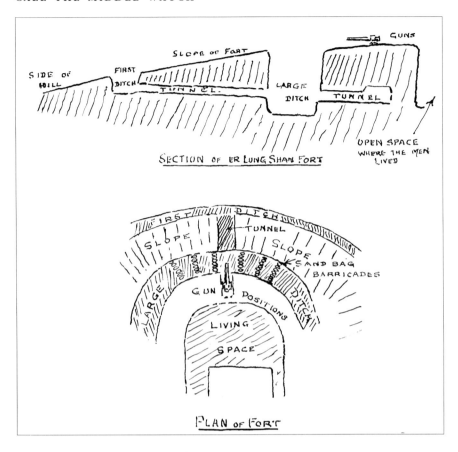

Sketches of a Fort at Port Arthur

We got hold of an official and bombarded him with questions, but all we could get out of him was that 'Tomorrow another train go; only one each day.' In the end however a Japanese officer was got hold of by Lieutenant Grant who could speak Japanese, and he conducted us to a Naval club to wait there while he found out if there was a transport going round to Port Arthur that day. It had evidently been a Russian place for it contained two billiard tables which afforded amusement to some of the company. For the others there were copies of 'Black and White', cigarettes and so on.

The reason we had missed the train was that Japanese time is just one hour in advance of ours so the train departed at 6.30 (our time) and 7.30 (Jap time) while we arrived at 7.25 (our time). About 10.30, after having

8

written all our names on a piece of paper, our bags were piled on a hand-cart and taken down to the jetty where a small tug was waiting. They put the bags on board so we went too. A few minutes afterwards the rest of the party came down with a Japanese officer who turned out to be the Commodore, late Captain of the *Yashima* when she struck a mine and went down. He saw us onboard, bowed and smiled and so on, and we departed.

The tug took us to a small transport of about 400 tons, which had got up steam for our especial benefit. I was fearfully hungry and ate some of the raw rice which was in a basket in the pantry. The skipper of the packet showed us some fragments of shell, wire entanglements and a Russian cap which he had picked up on the battlefield. We had a lovely passage and about 12.30 came in sight of the Golden Hill fort at the eastern end of Port Arthur.

I went up on the Bridge to see things better, and the skipper pointed out the place where the *Petropavlosk* sank, marked by a buoy. Then the sunken merchant ships, used to block the entrance, came in view. There were fourteen of them altogether besides two which had been raised and taken to Dalny and two which were inside Port Arthur. Some were right under water with just the tops of their davits showing. A Japanese mail steamer had piled up on one of the sunken ships two or three days ago trying to get in. There was just room for us to get in between the two buoys which marked the passage.

The next thing that met our gaze was the *Pobieda* in mid-channel, lying over on her starboard side at an angle of 15° as I afterwards found out. As we got in, a steam launch came alongside for us and landed us at some steps in the dockyard.

Now the next incident completely won my heart over to the Japanese. As I have mentioned before I had had no breakfast and I was so hungry. Well, on getting to the top of the steps a Japanese officer (army) met us and said, 'Good morning. I have had a telegram from the Commodore at Dalny to say you have had no breakfast, so please come with me and have some tiffin.' Wasn't it thoughtful of them?

We left our bags down there, where they were taken charge of by some sailors and taken up to Admiralty House for us. We followed this officer out of the dockyard for about half a mile to a large building standing in its own grounds and surrounded with high railings. A broad cement drive led up to the porch. This was Admiralty House, late Viceroy Alexieff's, as we found out afterwards. We were met in the vestibule by the Chief

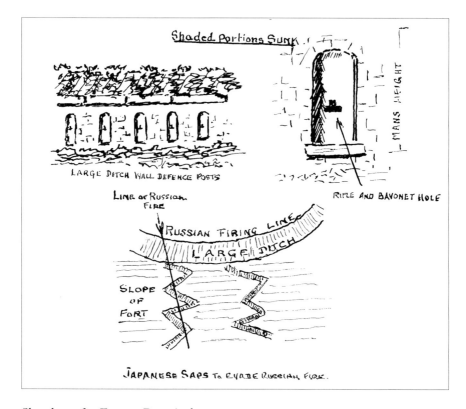

Sketches of a Fort at Port Arthur

of Staff, a Captain (Naval) and some other officers who at once conducted us into a long room, one half curtained off from the other with a long table down the centre (no chairs) covered with eating utensils. There was a huge stove right up to the ceiling and about four feet square with a door near the bottom. This was covered with white glazed tiles like the one at Lausanne. The ceiling had plaster mouldings all over it and the floors were all waxed wood, so I suppose it was Alexieff's ball-room. Soup, chops and beefsteak were the *pièces de résistance* and never did soup taste so good.

After lunch they told us that rooms had been engaged in four hotels for us, and we were told off for our respective dwellings. I went to the 'Honodekwan', a Japanese place (more of that anon). This item over, we split up into parties, each under the guidance of a Japanese officer, and were told we were going to 203 Metre Hill.

So off we started and walked past the railway station and long lines of

10

trucks and a couple of Russian engines distinguishable by their funnels. The Japs have changed the gauge of the line, that is the distance between the lines, making it smaller so that their own engines could use it. They then chopped the sleepers off so that the Russians could not change it back again! We walked on for about five miles until we came to 203 Metre Hill, a two-humped thing about 203 metres high. This was central to the defence of Port Arthur. It was resolutely defended by the Russians and the Japanese only managed to take it after suffering huge casualties.

We went up the road on the right, which had once been a road but was now covered by flints, having been badly cut up by shellfire. The top was covered with graves of Russian and Japanese soldiers; each had a wooden cross on it with Japanese characters. Round the hill, by the side of the road by which we came up, we were told that there was a huge Russian and Japanese grave. It had been a Russian trench. All the corpses were placed in and stones then piled up on top. Wooden crosses at intervals marked some particular personages. There was a good breeze at the time but that was not sufficient to carry away the odours.

An artillery officer who had been there explained all the fighting to us. He mentioned that 20,000 tons of iron had been fired into the hill by both sides. There are two humps on the hill as I have said before and he told us that the Russians held one hump and the Japanese the other and it was <u>two days</u> before the Japs could drive them out.

I went round and collected some relics of the fight to carry home and show with pride as 'found on my first battlefield'. There was a sackful of bombs on one side of the hill and I took one and opened it to find out what was inside. There were four sticks of dynamite wrapped up in paper, one of them being connected to the fuse coming out of it. You are supposed to light the fuse, count three, and hurl it at your enemy but if you are excited you forget to count three, so when you chuck it at him, he usually picks it up and chucks it back at you, so it cuts both ways. I carried one of these back but when I got to the ship the dynamite was taken out so it is quite harmless.

We then returned by the way we had come and repaired to our various hostelries for the night. Ours, the 'Honodekwan', had been a Russian place and was now run by a Jap and his wife. We managed to get a bed each but that was about all. They gave us supper; margarine, coffee, greasy cutlets and some fish, bread and so on. Hyde-Smith and I were rather late so found all our supper was cold as it is all 'dished' and put on a side table to wait for you, no matter how long you are going to be.

The cause of our lateness was that he and I went over the *Retvizan*, a battleship, which was lying alongside the wharf and had just been raised. We went aboard in pitch darkness and seeing a light went towards it, and found a couple of workmen just leaving. They gave us a candle and left us to our own devices. We went round the upper deck and then crawled down into the Admiral's cabin by the skylight, getting very dirty doing so. Everything was covered with mud and a great smell arose from it but we found a few papers from an old Russian seamanship manual and collared them. Then on our way out we found the night watchman with a lantern at the top of the skylight waiting for us, but he was quite polite and bowed us out and we bowed back to him. Everyone bows to everyone else here, quite a nice custom I think. Then we went back to our cold supper as you have heard.

I had quite a comfortable night despite the only bedclothes being a quilt and a long towel but I woke up in the morning in pitch darkness and very cold. After breakfast we went to the dry dock where the *Amur* was. She is a torpedo-craft depot ship (Russian). The Russians placed her in the dock, pumped out the water, and then knocked away the chocks from underneath her so that she fell heavily onto the port side, her funnels resting on the dock. They then floated out the caisson and sank it in the middle of the harbour. Now, the Japs have raised the caisson and it has been repaired. Divers are working on the vessel and it is expected she will be raised in a month or so. Further on we came to the *Pallada*, a cruiser which had been raised and was now perfectly clean and in commission being practically on her way to Japan. A Lieutenant very kindly asked us to come aboard and showed us round. All the shot-holes had been patched up with boards and she was wonderfully clean for a ship which had been in the mud for a long time.

After tiffin, at which coffee was the only thing eatable, or rather drinkable, they took us to visit a museum which they had made of all the things that had been used in the war. Suffice to say that every imaginable kind of warlike instrument that science & ingenuity could devise was there.

After seeing this Wilson and I hurried back to the hotel, got our bags and made for the train, but when we got there we found that we could stay another day if we wished. Wilson didn't want to but I talked him round after a bit and we went back to the hotel again where we got a drosky to take us out to Er Lung Shan fort.

The first fort you come to is Sung Shui Shan on a hill and to get to the other you have to dip into a valley and up the next hill at the top of which is the fort. So we left our drosky on the near hill and did the rest on foot. Lining the back of the near hill could be seen the bomb-proof shelters and living trenches of the Russians, some completely destroyed by shellfire and others quite intact. On the way down the valley we came across Russian trenches, ammunition boxes and so on. In the valley I came upon a shell with a fuse in the head. Hyde-Smith, who was with us, and I hammered away at this fuse to unscrew it but could not move it so proceeded on our way.

On entering the fort on one side we found everything in a jumble of broken stones etc. An old traction-engine smashed up by shells was squatting by part of the wall. Then we made our way along over this broken stone into the living space. This is what we saw. A long line of niches in a wall with shields exactly fitting the holes and slits to fire through. On crawling through here we found ourselves in a long gallery with all sorts of debris lying about, caps, bits of clothes, etc. We were told afterwards that the Russians were all buried here where they fell. Going back from this was an ascending gallery which led out into the gun positions. This was all a jumble of broken stone, bits of concrete and so on.

Just past this was a huge ditch about thirty or forty feet deep, half filled with bits of stone, rock etc. Climbing up over this I found on the other side a shell with a nose fuse which I unscrewed and took back with me. On the other side of the ditch were lines of 'saps' or trenches dug zigzag towards the Russian firing lines. These were dug by the Japanese under fire using iron shields on wheels which were scattered here and there. The idea of making them zigzag is so that the Russians could not fire down any of the lines of trenches.

The Japs sapped up the hill to the first ditch from which they drove the Russians. Then as they found they couldn't carry the fort by assault they tunnelled right under to the large ditch. Now when they got to this they had to rush across it to the other side for about twenty yards right under the enemy's nose. So they built barricades of sandbags across the ditch, three on each side of the tunnel, and kept these continually manned to repulse the Russians that came round along the trench from each side. Then they started to tunnel on the other side and eventually got underneath where the guns were. Here they made a sort of chamber and collected dynamite, etc. for some time. Then when all was ready they blew it up. It took two months to make that tunnel. In no place is it more than three to four feet high and it is only about eighty yards long in all.

When we had seen all this we had to return to catch our train. We got seats in a compartment with a Lt.-Colonel, a Captain, another Lt.-Colonel and his orderly. They were very nice on the journey down pointing out all the places to us – one of them had been in the attack – including General Nogi's headquarters in a farmhouse five miles away from Port Arthur. It made the journey pass very quickly. Just before we left Usher had a shell which he was showing us. One of the officers asked to see it so he handed it over. To his surprise and dismay it was then given to another officer outside in a very gorgeous uniform (he was a Colonel I think), who put it carefully on the ground and explained to the wrathful Usher that it was most dangerous as they had had any amount of deaths from their men taking such things as curios.

On the way back from the fort I had another go at the shell I had left and after hammering away for ten minutes with a stone succeeded in getting out part of the fuse but not all as it was rusted in. We got back to Dalny and found a boat waiting for us. On arrival on board all our fuses, etc. were examined and the dangerous part taken out, or if that could not be done, chucked overboard. One chap had a tin bomb full of guncotton and <u>Fulminate of Mercury</u>, the most deadly of all explosives. One of my fuses was, to my chagrin, thrown overboard.

I have put the rest in a letter to Father from Kyoto.

14

Chapter 2

The West Indies – 1910

The next letters come from HMS *Scylla*, a second-class light cruiser attached to the Fourth Cruiser Squadron on the America and West Indies Station. For a cruiser the ship was tiny, no longer than a frigate in the 1950s, though rather more beamy. My Father joined her in 1909. He was twenty-two at the time. He was evidently detailed off as the ship's Navigating Officer although I doubt that he would by then have done the specialist Long Navigation Course. His expertise in the subject would thus have been no more than that of any other junior Lieutenant. Despite this he appears to have avoided the lurking navigational hazards of the West Indies.

Besides *Scylla* there were three other ships in the Squadron. Their role was the protection of British interests and nationals throughout the Caribbean and along both seaboards of North and South America. *Scylla* had completed building in 1891. Her early years of service were not remarkable but in 1898 a Captain Percy Scott was appointed in command whilst the ship was serving in the Mediterranean. Scott was a gunnery specialist. Gunnery at the time was unpopular. There was nothing much wrong with the guns themselves but for reasons of fuel economy ships spent weeks in harbour and opportunities for gunnery practice with ships rolling and heaving in a seaway were limited. In any case firing guns tended to dirty the paintwork! Scott however was of an inventive turn of mind and developed a training aid to give practice to gun-aimers in harbour, and he tried it out first in his ship, *Scylla*. It was so successful that by the end of his time in command *Scylla* was averaging 80 per cent hits in gunnery practices compared with the Fleet average of 20–40 per cent.

Scott was not apparently an easy man to work with but he continued to develop and promote his ideas and came to be known in his time as the father of modern naval gunnery. His next appointment after *Scylla* was in command of HMS *Terrible*, an armoured cruiser. The ship was on passage to China when the South African War broke out and she was diverted to Capetown. There the 4.7-inch guns were landed on mountings devised by Scott and were sent to help in the defence of Ladysmith. This

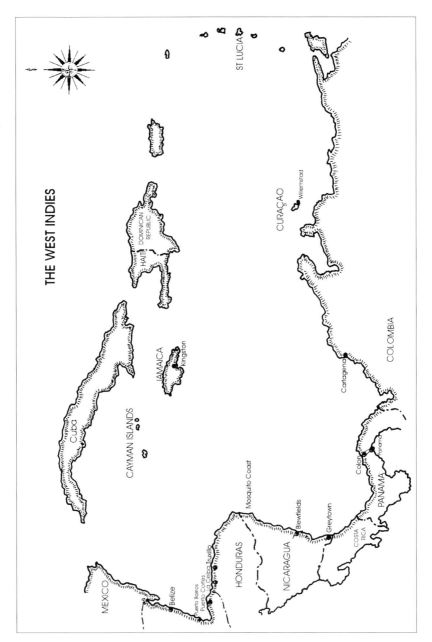

The West Indies and Central America

improvised and very successful operation was the origin of the present-day Royal Naval Field Gun Competition in the Royal Tournament each year in London.

By 1910 the old *Scylla* was beginning to feel her age and her original design speed of twenty knots had reduced by nearly a quarter. The following letters, written some five years after the one from *Sutlej*, reflect my Father's new responsibilities. Two, those describing a visit to the construction site of the Panama Canal and to the then almost unknown Cayman Islands, might almost rank as historical sources.

HMS Scylla at sea, 4th Cruiser Squadron–
Puerto Barrios to Puerto Cortez, Gulf of Honduras.
Sunday 3 April 1910

I am feeling very done up today after a flying visit to Guatemala City. The Captain and Warner, the Engineer Commander, the Paymaster and myself were the party, the first two being the official part and the remainder unofficial.

We left Belize on Tuesday and arrived off Puerto Barrios the same night. Anchored for the night we went right into the harbour next morning. This place is solely of importance in connection with the banana trade. There is an enormous company which grows and deals in bananas all the way round the coast from Belize to Colon. They own miles and miles of plantations, railways and the best line of steamers on the coast. Well, in Guatemala they got a strip of land about eighteen miles long and one to two miles broad on condition that they built a railway through it to connect with the Government railway to the capital. This they did, and at Puerto Barrios is a large pier, railway houses, one second-class hotel and several native shacks. These stand in a clearing about a mile square and all the rest is impenetrable virgin forest. You can see more or less what it looks like from the postcards coming by the same mail.

Well, at 6.30 a.m. we were on the pier and were received at the train by a General and the President's ADC who had travelled down the day before to take us up. A special car was at the end of the train with a large platform to stretch one's legs on. For the first eight or ten miles the line ran through jungle. On each side the trees towered up, covered with tendrils and almost meeting overhead. The undergrowth was so thick and luxuriant that nothing short of axes and machetes could force a way through it. Palms here and there in clusters added to the general beauty of the whole scene. Enormous clumps of bamboo spread themselves gracefully at the side of the track. It was a single line of narrow gauge and very badly laid, twisting and turning round sharp curves with a jerk which nearly sent one's chair off the platform. We all sat outside, at first anyway, the scenery being so glorious, although one's range of vision was limited to up-and-down the track. At one corner we came across a fruit train which had left the track and was in a higgledy-piggledy mess on the bank – five fruit vans and one engine. Four men had been killed in the accident about a fortnight ago.

Eventually the forest thinned out a little where the fruit company had started their clearing work and soon we came to the banana plantations. Miles and miles of them stretched as far as the eye could see along the line, the breadth of the cleared strip being only a mile or so. At every four or five miles one came to a station with a nice plank hut being erected, a store belonging to the fruit company. Further back were two other huts, one for the overseer and one for the work people who were all Jamaicans. At one station was a hospital for the employees. Across a river and up along its left bank until we got to a junction called Zacap at about 12.30 p.m. Here the train stopped and we got out for luncheon, heralded by a band and received by the Governor. After quite a good meal we went on and on, the country being hilly and by now very parched and monotonous. Most of us I think slept. Eventually about 4.0 p.m. the train started to climb and we got colder and colder. Then at 7.15 p.m. the glare of Guatemala City was pointed out. Across a very high bridge and we were on the plateau in the middle of which it stands.

Some of the Legation people met us and the official party drove to the Minister's place while we three went to the hotel. After a wash and brush-up the 'English Colony' dined us, the official party being on their own entirely. One was very tired, but food bucked one up and after dinner we had a sing-song in the Club until closing time.

Next morning up at 9.0 a.m. coffee, eggs and so on, and at 10.30 we went out to the race course to see a marvellous map which they have, in relief, of the country. It is about fifty yards from corner to corner and shows all the rivers, towns and villages – all the rays of Belize volcanoes, etc., and if one pays a shilling water will run down the rivers. One of the postcards shows the Pacific side. The mountains are exaggerated in height so as to show up better but the rest is all to scale. An English engineer made it some years ago and it really is most instructive. We followed up our route in the train, even bridges being built in detail. As to the town itself, it is merely a moderate sized Spanish town, streets badly paved, tram-lines shockingly laid and little mule trams; one large square with a fine statue of Columbus and a large church, moderately dirty. After Vera Cruz and accounts of Mexico City, a great comedown.

We went back to the hotel, meeting the official party on their way back from calling on the President. The 'English Colony' entertained us to lunch. A little shopping took us till 3.45 and then we drove out to the Embassy where Mrs Carden, the Minister's wife, was giving a garden party. They have distinctly the nicest house in the city and plenty of grounds. Many fair charmers were gathered there and we drank tea, walked and talked, played croquet, badminton and all sorts of weird games. There was a musical instrument called a 'marimba' (I fancy that is the name), native to Guatemala and played by four men. It is a type of xylophone, being an arrangement of flat slats of wood, horizontally arranged on a frame, some of them being directly over square wooden pipes hanging vertically, so that when a particular slat was hit, the sound reverberated like a violin string. Delightful music was played on this all through the afternoon.

We had to leave about six and went to dress for a banquet being given by the Government. We drove up in fine style and met the official party. We were received by 'God Save the King' played better than I have ever heard it before. The President was not there. He lives in danger of his life and never leaves his house but he sent a message which was read out to us all. It was rather weird but very nice. I had two people who couldn't talk English on either side of me, and another opposite. The GOC, Guatemala Army, the Mayor of Guatemala and Minister of Foreign Affairs. The hall was at the back of a courtyard and all the stone part of the floor and of the walks outside was strewn with long grass. It certainly kept one's feet warm. They had two most delightful bands and kept them going alternately so there was no real excuse for conversation and we got on swimmingly. After the speeches (the Captain made rather a good one), the party broke up and I had a yarn with the English clergyman in charge. I don't know what his rank was but he said that he had the whole of Guatemala to look after.

After the élite had gone back to Government House, the unofficial party crossed over the road to the house of one Bellinger, clerk to the Legation, where all the fair charmers we had met during the afternoon

19

were gathered and we had a small dance. This was kept going till 2.0 a.m., when we retired to snatch a few minutes snooze. Awakened at 4.0 a.m. (the silly porter had made a mistake of an hour). Snooze till 5.0 a.m., then got up in cold and dismal surroundings – no bath. Down at 5.45, ordered coffee and eggs, when Bellinger arrives not having been to bed at all, then two others who had not either, being still in evening dress. We swallowed what we could and rushed off. They would not let us pay the bill. It was down to the President.

It was raining when we left, cold and cheerless, but the three of them who saw us off managed to raise a healthy cheer when we started to move. The way down was just like the way up only we slept more. At about midday they telegraphed that a fruit train had gone off the rails about eight miles from Puerto Barrios. When we got down there we had to stop four or five miles this side of the point as the line had not been quite cleared. At last we went on, the line being clear. It was pitch dark by now, the track running between huge walls of jungle, stars blazing overhead in the strip one could see, fireflies winking all round one. Then at a corner we slowed down and went very cautiously. 'This must be the place,' we all thought. Then G-r-r- stop! We backed away. The guard and General got out with lights and went up to the head of the train. Shortly the Captain and Warner followed. I was trying to sleep, wishing we would get a move on. The Captain came back telling us there was an engine off the line but overhanging it so as to block our passage; so then I got out to have a look. It was rather a unique sight. As we tried to pass, an iron projection under the foremost coach hit up against one of the wheels of the overturned engine and would have been torn off. This overturned johnny had been just off the line, standing upright, and whilst jacking him back on they jacked too far and over he went. It was very lucky he stopped when he did, being two yards from the brink of a hill which descended into undergrowth and jungle and stopped I don't know where.

Well, to get us past they decided to shift the track, and sent down the line for a gang to do it. Eventually they came up and did the job. It was on a curve and the line needed to go out, so they levered the whole – rails, sleepers and all – by sheer force, bending the rails ever so slightly. There were seven of them and each planted his huge iron crowbar on the inside of the rail. Then the head boy whistled a tune and they tapped their bars up on the rails in time to this. At the fourth tap each man bent his knees and then threw himself back on his bar, lifting the line – sleepers and all – several inches from the ground. They had to work up and down the line for a hundred yards or so to distribute the bend but eventually after about half an hour or so we made the attempt and succeeded in getting past.

I slept peacefully from then until we got in, heralded by a band and officially received, and so on. Bed was the programme as soon as we got on board and it is the programme now. More news to date later on. The last whack has been written from Truxillo. We leave tomorrow for the Mosquito Cays.

Friday night

We are just rounding the corner of the land at the top of the Mosquito Coast and as I have to be up again at two o'clock tomorrow morning I am going to bed at nine o'clock which is in half an hour's time; hence these fevered words.

From Puerto Barrios we went on to a place called Puerto Cortez, staying there a day. A banquet was provided and bands played indifferently well – all by order of the President of Honduras. These places are all wooden-shack-and-unpaved-street type of thing; depending solely on the fruit trade and railway for their existence. I went ashore to take sights to rate my chronometers. You see, what one does is to take the altitude of the sun with a sextant. When it's at its highest, that's noon and you can compare the time with what the chronometer makes it and work out how much the latter gains or loses each day. When you cannot get a horizon you bring the image of the sun down onto a trough of mercury, which is fine except that if the mercury is not steady you cannot do anything. At Puerto Cortez we were alongside the fruit company wharf and every time I was getting along nicely an engine would start shuffling the banana trucks about. In a plain of burning sand and with the sun pouring down and coming off this sand like a blast from h . . .! I got so wild with that engine.

Well, we left that place and went on to a little village called La Ceiba, arriving there about 11.0 p.m. Next morning the usual calls were paid and most of us landed for a banquet which was being held in our honour. It is amusing to see the frantic efforts of some people who come off at 11.30 a.m. and ask to see round the ship. The frantic effort is to stay for lunch of course. When we first came out here we took it all in good part but it seems to happen quite often nowadays and I fear we are becoming a bit hard-hearted.

Next evening we went on to a place called Truxillo, getting there about 9.30. These places are on an absolutely unlighted coast, and we have to more or less blunder along until we see the lights of the houses and then

21

steer for them, anchoring when you imagine you have got close enough. At La Ceiba we hit it off very nicely. Truxillo however rather sold us. We went on and on and it seemed to get no closer till we began to brace ourselves for the bump. At last we said we had gone far enough and anchored. In the morning we were still two weary miles away! We had imagined about a quarter of a mile.

At Truxillo everyone went ashore for a riding picnic and rode some thirty miles up the coast to a Carib village where tea was spread in a sloop which had been beached for the purpose. This was an official function and two hundred men had been employed for three days cleaning up the track along which we came – and the town of Truxillo. The Caribs had been ordered to get their village clean too. The Captain tells me that they have been ill-treating some British subjects, so at La Ceiba he alluded to it in his speech, saying he hoped that nothing of the sort would occur again. You see all the coast is full of Jamaicans, who are always 'British subjects', and then they get into trouble and write to the Consul. The Captain said he had been promised that one of these who had been in jail many months would be released that night. The result of a quiet word or two.

Well, after Truxillo we came round the corner and went down to look at four of the Mosquito Cays. We anchored close to one of them and sent boats round to measure and so on. Mine was a little oval patch of coral 114 feet long, thirty feet wide and three feet high with a dead turtle on top of it. The sun was monstrously hot. Finishing these we steamed on to some more and then set course for Bocas del Toro.

Today is Sunday. We are rolling on our way – all nature sleeps. Two Sundays ago it was Easter and we were at Belize. Several of us landed early at the Church – such a lovely day – nice smells and a rather pretty church with a great deal of mahogany about. I want to hear from you badly – a mail tomorrow I hope.

Wilson wrote me a long letter describing in humorous vein how his ship had gone out one day to lay a line of mines, and then a gale sprang up and he was having a glorious time recovering them. He is in the *Latona* now.

I hope you will forgive the 'guide book' talk. I can't do anything else now, being full of facts and figures and places.

The next letter gives an interesting description of a visit to the site of the

Panama Canal, then under construction. This was followed by a much less satisfactory few days on the Dutch island of Curaçao.

HMS Scylla
Willemstad, Curaçao
Sunday 24 April 1910

The Captain has just rung his bell – what can it mean? We go to sea this evening to St Lucia. A strong gale is blowing and I foresee many hours of sea sick wretchedness hanging on to the fore-bridge rail: 482 miles before the haven of rest is once more reached.

I have knocked off smoking for a while to see what it is like, and find no change. Meanwhile the Doctor is walking the poop outside my cabin with a troubled air. The brooms belonging to the Quarterdeckmen are in a rack overhead and each time he passes he gets his hair brushed. It irks him!

I fancy the last letter went from Colon so we have a bit to make up. Colon leaves a nasty taste in the mouth. To begin with we sighted the light-houses at 1.30 a.m. so I had to be up and about until daylight. Then in the middle of my bath at 8.0 a.m. the pilot arrived to take us alongside the coaling wharf. (It was up in the Canal and we had no chart of the place – usually we never need a pilot.) I had to rush up to the Bridge as I was so to speak. In the middle of coaling four of us had dressed in nice clean whites to go and call on the Governor and there was no gangway so the whites were somewhat sullied after climbing over many coal trucks. Then it started to rain and made us clammy and horrid.

On arrival back after having said 'How-do-you-do' to His Excellency Don José of José, I had to shift into dirty rig and coal. Coaling is so unpleasant that everyone, high and low, takes part. Without exception it was the dustiest and dirtiest coaling I have ever done. It all had to be shovelled out of the trucks and down the shutes, made of two planks nailed together, with two on edge as sides, and then re-shovelled into sacks after a heap had collected on deck. You can imagine how it flew about. This was kept up until 10.0 p.m. Weighed in again at 5.0 a.m. and finished at 8.0. Then again, before I had time to look clean even, we had to move away from the wharf and went alongside the Royal Mail Company's wharf.

Next morning, having spent the rest of the previous day scrubbing coal dust off, up at 4.0 a.m. Down to the Wardroom at 4.45 all ready to grapple with tea and boiled eggs, ordered the night before; but nothing moved. At last the provender appeared and down went two eggs, two cups of tea and much bread in less time than it takes to write this, and then a rush to the station. Just in time to catch the train at 5.15. The Captain, Browne and Orgill (the Assistant Paymaster) coming up at the last moment. It was dark for most of the way and I slept.

At 7.0 we arrived at a place called Empire, and got out, waiting for the train from Panama which was to bring the Vice-Consul. He was going to introduce us to the Engineer of the Canal and generally look after us. When he arrived we climbed a young hill at the top of which were this Engineer's offices etc. It was a remarkable position because it overlooked the Canal – in fact almost tumbled into it – and was just at the watershed. There was a large balcony and we stood out here and had a good look round for about twenty minutes before anyone came. Then he came out – the Engineer – and pointed out various things, bringing out plans and elevations, explaining this and that and giving us no end of information. I do not know if all this will interest or bore you.

The Canal, as I daresay you know, is to be a lock canal; that is, at either end there are systems of locks to raise the ships to the level of the central cutting. In the latter the water will be forty-five feet deep and the surface of the water will be eighty-five feet above sea level. At Panama they are going to have only one lock for the whole lift of forty feet. At the Colon end there will be three locks at a place called Gatun, some ten miles from Colon. These will split up the lift of forty feet into smaller ones. At this place Gatun they are building a huge dam to catch the water from the Chagres River. When this dam is closed the water will rise and an immense lake will be formed, many square miles of land and villages being flooded. The water will also fill the canal and by means of the locks it will be kept at a constant height.

Labour is very expensive out here and what strikes one is the ingenuity of all the labour-saving machines and devices which are used. It is really marvellous in some places what the machines do. In building these locks, concrete alone is used and it is all moulded like metal. To make the walls they have immense iron plates supported on girder structures and running on rails. These are run up into the required position, wedged up tight and the concrete poured in. It sets in a day or two and the iron plate is then rolled away leaving the solid concrete. Again, they want enormous pipes in these walls for the entry and egress of water into and out of the locks, so before pouring the concrete an enormous iron cylinder is placed in the position where they want this pipe to be and then the concrete when setting takes up the form of the cylinder. The iron pipe is not quite complete and has a slit about a foot wide down the side, so to get it out when the concrete is set all one has to do is to screw up on some bottle-screws to contract the iron cylinder and then slide it out.

The steam-shovels seemed to me to be the most human things. You see one standing in a sort of pocket that it has dug for itself, with a long line of trucks with only one side to them, on a line of rails just outside. Two men work the thing and it is a very quick excavator. Down goes the bucket, it pushes into the bank, is hauled up, swings round, the bottom comes out and four tons of earth is in the car. Round again, another dig and up onto the car. In three minutes one car, or truck, is full and a man on the train signals the engine to pull up a bit. And all the time this shovel goes on working. To see it nosing round for a stone it has dropped is too human altogether.

We stood and watched one shovel load a train of about ten trucks in twenty minutes. The men who work these get $200 per month. That is about £500 a year. Each dirt train goes away either to the breakwater being built at Panama or to the dam at Gatun, and there a plough is drawn straight from one end of it to the other, clearing all the dirt off in about four minutes. That is the reason for the one-sided cars. Well, we walked down and into the canal, watching the drills at work, then the dynamite sticks being put in place for blasting, the steam shovels and so on, and eventually the Engineer had to go back. By this time it was 11.30 and I felt like dying on the spot, having been walking in the hot sun since 8.0, and breakfast at 5.0. We had to trail up to a large building and see the models of the locks and after all this I was thankful to see the station once more.

There was no refreshment room so we went straight to the market and drank much cola and ate oranges. Eventually at 12.30 the train came in and we went on to Panama. Three or four others who could not brave the early rising came on in this train and the First Lieutenant, the Paymaster and I went off and had lunch at a hotel. All the others lunched with the Minister at the Legation. In the afternoon, we walked round the town, which was dirty and uninteresting, and came back about five o'clock. The next day on the way back one of the Chief Stokers fell off the end of the train, killing himself. It was an unfortunate thing, casting a gloom over everyone. I drove around Colon with the First Lieutenant trying to

25

find a parson but was unsuccessful. The funeral came off next day. A special train took us to the cemetery and back, and we left for Cartagena as soon as it was over.

At the entrance to Cartagena it is quite a curious thing to see a strip of sandy beach shelving down to the water's edge like it does at Gairloch, very gradually. And yet one passes about eighty yards from the beach in a ship drawing thirty feet or more. Apparently it goes practically straight down after getting to the water.

Cartagena itself was most uninteresting, as all these places are. The Captain, Warner, Browne and I landed next morning and called on the Governor, being taken for a short drive round the town afterwards to see the walks and so on. We left at 11.30 that day and arrived at Curaçao at sunset next day.

The entrance to the harbour is only fifty yards wide with large forts on either hand and then for three-quarters of a mile you steam up between schooners lying alongside the wharves each side, the channel being about a hundred yards wide. Eventually it opens out into a fairly large basin where we anchored, a stiff breeze blowing all the time.

Curaçao is of course Dutch. The British Consul was a nasty little man. On the second day all of us landed at 3.30 p.m. and went for a drive with him in three carriages to see the island. He showed us his fruit farm with hardly any fruit in it, and all the time it was, 'My brother's wife owns that house, that house is my married aunt's cousin's, those pumps were put up by my mother's aunt's nephew,' and so on. Then at the end of it all, when we got back to the Club at 7.30, he, having previously invited four or five people to dine with him, said 'Well, I shall hope to see you about eight o'clock. The Hotel American is the best place to dine at; trams run to my house every half hour,' and left us all.

We did not know whether he was going to put up dinner or no, but in order to be on the safe side we dined at the Hotel, eating rather sparingly. After dinner the Captain, Warner, Hood and I walked round to his house, about a mile and a half, and were ushered into a cold-looking bare room, white walls, polished floor – picture of Wilhemina on one wall, HM King Edward on another and the Consul's wife on another. There we were greeted by three emotionless, flabby-handed females and one male, the Consul's son who turned out to be an imbecile, poor chap. Well, we talked nonsense for an hour and a half and drank some rather good coffee and eventually walked down to the boat.

The Consul showed his perfidy when he sent us off his account. Before we arrived he had sent us – on his own hook – a wireless message, 'Welcome to Curaçao. I shall do all in my power to make your stay pleasant.' Do you know he had the impudence to charge for this in his bill, and to add insult to injury he charged 2 per cent commission for his own pocket. The Captain I am glad to say wrote him a 'stinking' letter:

> Sir,
> The Paymaster has pointed out to me several irregularities in your account, etc. I shall expect your reasons and a true bill by the first possible mail to St Lucia.

Funnily enough we had been expecting high revelry at Curaçao, and as it turned out everything was as dull as ditchwater. Nobody cared a hang whether we came or went. This sounds rather like vanity but it is not really, because the whole time we were on shore the Consul or his brother were dinning into our ears, 'Why don't your ships come here more often? We never see your ships here. Other countries send their ships. Why don't you send yours?' They wanted two dozen each with the Master-at-Arms' cane.

We left at last light and are now in the open on our way to St Lucia. Expect to carry out practice firings tomorrow, get in on Wednesday morning, complete with coal, get clean and wait till Monday.

Halley's comet is on view now. They woke me up at five o'clock this morning to look at it and I just caught a glimpse but it was bright moonlight so I went to bed again. There will be a good chance to see it again on Wednesday when I have to be up for sighting the land. I have got into a fearful habit of sleeping from 1.15 to 3.30 p.m. One can't do any work. Tomorrow morning we arrive.

The next piece is an undated extract from a longer letter and describes a visit to the Cayman Islands.

HMS Scylla,
Kingston, Jamaica

The place is comparable (can one use that expression?) to Gairloch on a wee bit more swell scale. No, that is rather too slashing. It's not so out of the world as that, but there are the soldiers, occasionally a ship, the storekeepers and one or two families. Well, half the girls in our set are storekeepers' daughters and very nice at that. The army people live at the other end (St George's) and have their set. Mr Ingham is a timber merchant, and the nicest family in the island. However, Frank will tell you his news of the question.

We have been having a jolly time. Look at the *Encyclopaedia Britannica* or Harmsworth and under 'Cayman' you will see: 'Three fertile coral islets, 165 miles NW of Jamaica. Discovered by Columbus, etc. Pop. 4000.' Thursday last at 7.0 a.m. we embarked the Governor and his ADC at Kingston and steamed out to try and hit these islands. All went well till 6.0 p.m. when we emerged from the lee of Jamaica and felt the full force of a north-easterly on our beam. I turned in early and had dreams. Suddenly I woke up and heard many feet padding about, ship rolling and engines stopped. I rushed out, my fuddled brain heavy with sleep, imagining we were ashore. However no land was visible and it turned out to be an awning being furled having been split by a wave on top of it. In another dream I could see a low island with houses about a hundred yards ahead and someone had just put the helm over and saved us from going ashore.

However it was all OK. We sighted land when I expected next day, a long low island covered with brush and only thirty feet high at its highest. It was rather a hard thing to pick up in a roughish sea, thirty feet being less than the height of the average house. Well, we anchored. There is only one spot (literally a spot) where one can anchor with safety and we managed to find this. The anchor was let go in sixty feet of water. By our forebridge (thirty feet astern) there was nearly two hundred feet of water and under our stern (300 ft. astern of the anchor) nobody has ever reached the bottom. Rather an abrupt ledge wasn't it? We had to anchor on the corner of the coral, so to speak, on account of swinging round inshore.

The Governor went ashore. The Commissioner's wife gave a party to the officers. She was a jolly, smart lady for such an out-of-the-way place, and gave us tea, with some rather weird cake, in her drawing room. It was nicely arranged but one could sense the isolation – cuttings from *The Sketch*, framed in about 1890, served as pictures. White-painted match boarding, one or two straw mats and cosy corners (home-made) were the chief things.

After tea six of us were taken out to view the Victoria Park. It was a clearing about fifty yards square in which there was a gravel tennis court under construction and several beds in which, with luck, flowers may come in five years' time. At one side was the theatre, of match boarding, with a small stage at one end and room for about thirty people closely packed. She and her husband were the only white people – a three year billet. Mrs Commissioner said she was hard at work teaching the natives to play small pieces. Her Jamaican governess (a coloured lady) played leading lady and the Chief of Police (a coloured gentleman) leading man.

At the entrance was a plaster obelisk about ten feet high 'In memory of Her Gracious Majesty, Queen Victoria etc. etc.' This was 'done by one of the boys of the island,' as she proudly told us. To add to its dignity it had a rather weather-worn stable lamp on the top of it. The inhabitants are descendants of the buccaneers, by now 'café au lait'; no fowls or eggs on the island; no regular mails or steamship communication; no cable. The chief industry is turtle fishing.

Next day, Saturday, we left and on getting out of the lee of the island again got a strong north-easterly which increased to a gale and a nasty sea on the bow. We were all ill. The Captain is a sufferer and we condole with each other, he and I. The Governor, though usually a good sailor, disappeared. His ADC succumbed in the evening. The Doctor, Paymaster, First Lieutenant, Second and Third Lieutenants, Navigator and Captain all went. As a matter of fact on the night before leaving Jamaica half the officers went to dine at Government House and half with Mr J. Astor, multi-millionaire, on his yacht which was lying close to us. The Government House people all complained of upset insides beforehand (poisoning, etc.), so that may have had something to do with it. The 'Astor' brigade were not ill. I turned in at 8.30 and was out again at 6.0 just when getting under the lee of Jamaica.

Weather was then all right until just before we picked up – that is, saw – the first buoy, which marks certain shoals off the harbour, when down came the rain. My word it did pelt. I was soaked in less than a minute, and coming as it did from ahead, it made matters difficult by blurring one's glasses as soon as one put them up to look for a buoy. However we went gaily on at 11 knots, blaring away on the siren (one could only see two or three hundred yards) and eventually found the beacons marking the narrow bit of the channel. The water was the colour of washy tea, the mud from the rivers being in suspension, and this marked the channel rather well, as on each side in the shallower portions the colour was greener, all the discoloured water from inside the harbour keeping to the deep part.

Anchored off Kingston about 5.30 and sent the Governor ashore. This

29

morning I was dressing peacefully at about 8.05 when suddenly 'Both Watches Out Kedge Anchor, etc.' I thought we were going to swing into another ship or something so bucked up. Just then the Quartermaster reported 'American gunboat gone ashore'. Thank goodness it was not ourselves. In going alongside a wharf this gunboat, about 800 tons (like the yacht *Monsoon* at Gairloch) had gone further than intended, and was stuck in the mud. We sent her an anchor and put it some way astern of her with a rope to her stern, and took a wire rope from her stern to our fore capstan. By the way it was still raining fit to bust and had not stopped since last night.

Our skipper went over there and superintended and after twenty minutes steady straining, and she with her engines going astern, she slid off, the Yankees cheering lustily. Our officers who went over there say the American officers did nothing at all. Our skipper directed everything and deserves all the credit. When she came off the Water Police Station was exposed looking in a most drunken condition. She had hit it squarely and brought it low.

It is still raining and threatens to continue for at least six months. They say it started just after we left and has not stopped since. My cabin leaks and being on the Upper Deck gets the full benefit. Everything is damp, the blotting paper and all.

King's Birthday tomorrow. Oh joy! Meanwhile it is dinner time. My hand is quite stiff with writing. I am sorry for your cold. I have one too. Wilson is apparently rather bored with *Surprise* and wants another job. He applied to go with Captain Scott to the South Pole but was rejected.

We had a hockey match one day over at Port Royal – intensely amusing. On the way back the steam-boat went ashore, whereupon six gallant youths, myself leading, jumped out, and, putting shoulders to the stern of the boat, heaved with a will and off she slid. The water teems with sharks. I have two teeth, wicked looking objects, and am wondering how to have them set. Well, must really say, 'Goodnight.' Rain is making such a noise.

The last letter in the collection from *Scylla* describes a revolution in Nicaragua from the point of view of an HM Ship ordered to the area with a watching brief for the safety of British subjects and interests. It seems to have been a small scale, almost comic, affair and the *Scylla's* main preoccupation was to find ways of landing on a primitive coast in order to interpret events.

HMS Scylla, Blewfields,
Mosquito Coast, Nicaragua.
21 November 1910

In my last hurried letter we had just got the telegram to send us off down here. That evening we set out and went to Port Royal to coal, making fast alongside the wharf there. The black people did all the work from 8.0 p.m. to 4.0 a.m. and we slept; I did at any rate. Next morning at 6.0 we cast off and went out of harbour on our way down. On Saturday at daybreak we met the land once more and anchored off Greytown. This is a town commonly known as San Juan de Nicaragua and is at the Atlantic end of the now-abandoned Nicaragua canal. One anchors off the place, in the open sea, and landing is almost impossible. Please now see sketch.

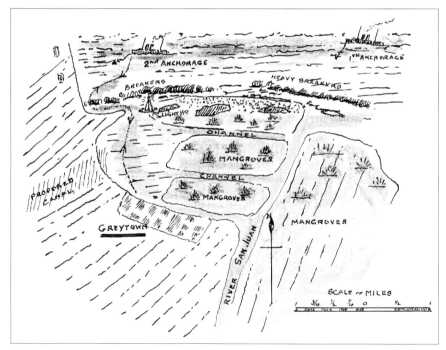

Sketch of the Coast – Greytown, Nicaragua

The 'mangroves' are really a swamp with palms and thick scrub growing. The only firm soil is the shaded part. The heavy shaded part is where the canal was going to be cut through but that scheme has fallen through. The only means of getting ashore is by going through the surf, and that is rather a dangerous proceeding requiring forethought and circumspection. The *Admiralty Sailing Directions* tell one that the only passage is where I have marked 'heavy breakers' on the sketch, so at ten o'clock the Captain set out in a boat to effect an entry at this spot. Luckily just before he got there a small boat was perceived coming from the westward and on getting closer this turned out to be a small dugout canoe paddled by six lusty black people and bearing a letter from the Consul. The Captain transshipped to their canoe and they went back whence they came. Meanwhile the ship shifted from the place marked '1st anchorage' to '2nd anchorage', as that was nearer the entrance that could be used. The whole place was fringed with heavy breakers and the harbour mouth to the left of the lighthouse was silted up with sand and mud from the river.

Having anchored there we on board could do nothing but await the Captain's return. At last, about three o'clock, the canoe was seen coming out again and began to work its way through the entrance along the line shown with arrowheads on the sketch. Several of us, having been snoozing on the poop, had just woken up to watch, and several times we thought he was a 'goner'. The waves broke clean over the canoe, as it seemed to us, and eventually one big one swamped them and they had to paddle back to the shore and bale out. Eventually a quarter of an hour later he was back on board, drenched to the skin. None of our boats could have stood it. This canoe would float even when full of water but not so any of our boats. We sent them back many papers and magazines by the pilot, as they had not had any mail for six weeks. The town was in a state of siege, occupied by the Government troops (1200 men). They had hardly any food and were in rather a miserable condition.

All this excitement was actually about sixty miles up the coast from Blewfields, but Blewfields was busy too. When the revolution started the Governor of the town, one Estrada, turned revolutionary and the whole of the garrison with him. Now these people (whom we will call the Rs for short) and the Government troops (G), captured a tug and mounted a gun on it, and at the battle of Greytown, fought before we arrived, they sank everything that floated near the town, lighters, a small paddle-wheel steamer and all the boats, leaving only this canoe (which the Captain used) as it had been hidden. They then withdrew and are now blockading the

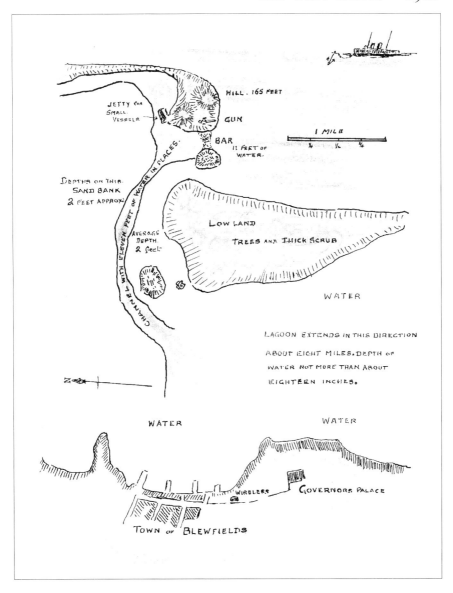

Sketch of the Coast – Blewfields, Nicaragua

port. This steamer, with her gun in the bows (she is like the *Pwrcis* fish steamer at Gairloch) goes up to Blewfields to coal and then runs down to Greytown at odd hours to see that everything is all right. She was

33

rather puzzled when she saw us the first night and came close to have a look.

The Consul here told us that Blewfields was in the hands of the Rs (this was the first we had heard of it) and that at any time the worst might occur; so next morning, being Sunday, at 0730 it was up anchor and away to Blewfields. Church on the poop, with plenty of hymns! At five o'clock anchored off Blewfields Bluff – rolling moderately. (Now another plan, if you will please excuse it).

This morning at 0830 the skipper and I set out in his galley (a long thin boat drawing very little water) with swords, macs and own lunches and so on, and sailed up to the harbour mouth, crossed the bar and started up to the town of Blewfields. As you see by the chart there is just the one channel up to the place, the remainder being an enormous sand or mudbank with one and a half to two feet of water over it. Well, the wind was dead against us and of course that meant tacking across and across and the number of times we grated on to the mud and then slid off again was enormous. Halfway up we met the Vice-Consul in a motorboat coming off to call on the skipper, with his flag flying and all *en règle*. On seeing us he turned towards us and promptly ran on the mud himself. After ten minutes churning the water with his screw and five chaps pushing with oars he slid off and turning round towed us up to Blewfields.

The place was alive with ensigns, American predominating, but no British. The town lookd quite imposing from the water with many fine buildings but the glory rather departed on finding them all to be of wood with tin roofs. The church and school were perhaps the best. The Consul's bungalow had been burned down two months back in a fire and he was now living at the hotel. He himself was a French-Canadian, about twenty-eight, a great humourist when one got to know him, and good at his job I should say.

We got business over, then off swords and had *déjeuner* with him. It was rather weird altogether but above my expectations – fine big airy room but the table furniture of a third-class village inn. Never mind! He brought up a smiling dark personage and introduced Señor Alfonso Diaz. Apparently the cause of all the trouble, he was the chief organiser of the revolution. He sat down and chatted with our skipper, who tried to pump him as much as possible as to future movements.

Diaz said he was confident of success as every day they were getting more and more recruits, deserters from the Government army, and the only thing they were waiting for was a consignment of arms and ammunition which would arrive today or tomorrow. When they got these their first move would be to take Greytown. This necessitates taking it from seaward and landing in the surf so it will be rather a job I fancy. We asked him to be as quick as he could and get things finished so that we could get back to Jamaica and fresh provisions. He promised to do his best!

After lunch a visit to a store to buy stamps for many of the officers on board, arrange about a supply of fresh beef for the morrow and about wireless telegrams; then buckle on swords and away to General Estrada. It was really rather ludicrous. Government House was overrun with all sorts of minor officials or soldiers, one could not tell them apart, and His Excellency lived in a small bungalow alongside. Shown into a bare white room, light yellow carpet all over it, with faint red roses (hideous), a huge over-mantel glass, a clock (not going) and a stuffed jaguar all sharing the mantelpiece. Five or six white wicker chairs and a white-painted wicker table completed the furniture.

The Consul was with us of course to interpret. The General kept us waiting for about five minutes and then appeared in a drill suit, brown boots, panama hat with blue, white, blue ribbon (the Rs' colours) round it. He is a big man, inclined to be fat, very dark of course. They said he is brave, a good general, kind at heart and rather weak in that way, brusque. Nothing very interesting was said. He told us that Zelaya (the next President) was a rogue and feathered his own nest by giving the monopoly of each different product or industry to a certain friend of his who paid him so much royalty on it. Of course that is the whole question. Everyone says so and I am quite in sympathy with the Rs because in that sort of situation trade is simply paralysed. Even the turtle fishermen have to pay so much for a licence to fish, then they have to sell the shell to Señor So-and-So who pays what he chooses for it, and then the meat to another Señor who does likewise. No wonder they revolt. The only wonder is that they have not done so before.

After a short interview we left and wended our way back to the hotel and thence to the boat. As we were shoving off a brass band came down onto the pier to welcome 135 men who had just come in from some gold mines up the coast to join the army. They looked very pleased with themselves and life in general. Tomorrow at 9.30 we are off to Greytown again to watch the fight. I hope we see it well. This show promises to last for another fortnight at least, if not three weeks, at the end of which time I hope we shall be returning to Jamaica to coal and with luck spend

Christmas. The cruise round the Central American ports has been rather upset by this turn-out down here. I daresay we shall do it later on though.

I have been writing this for two and a quarter hours now so will go to bed. I wonder how bored you are with all this. It seems so funny to think of you in the cold while here we are just comfortable in whites. This letter will not go for a fortnght at least. We are at the end of the world.

That is the end of the letters from *Scylla*. My Father evidently did not describe the 'Battle for Greytown'. Perhaps that was just as well. Perhaps it never took place.

There was however a postscript. On one of the occasions when the ship was in Kingston, the three Lieutenants, Warner, Hood and Corson, were ashore one day exploring the countryside and happened on an aqueduct. Walking along its length they met at the end two young American girls, holidaying in Jamaica with their mother. Relationships developed . . . but slowly . . . very slowly. By 1916 however there was a feeling, on whose side I do not know, that the meeting by the aqueduct must either lead on to something closer or must wither away. The two girls took ship to England and married Warner and Hood. Tragically both husbands were lost at sea shortly afterwards. Frances Hood never remarried. Marjorie Warner did remarry – seven years later – the writer of these letters.

Chapter 3

The Persian Gulf – 1913/14

In 1913/14 my Father was Navigating Officer of the ancient cruiser HMS *Fox*. Like *Scylla*, *Fox* was a second class cruiser, built in 1893, two years later than *Scylla*, and slightly larger than the latter though with a largely similar armament, power and speed. She had had a major refit in 1907 but by the time of these letters was in an advanced state of decrepitude and officially reckoned to be of little fighting value. As one of a small number of cruisers and lesser ships on the East Indies Station *Fox* spent most of her time in the Persian Gulf and the letters which follow were written from there.

Now, towards the end of the twentieth century, mention of the Persian Gulf presumably triggers memories of the recent Gulf War and an awareness of the present importance of the area as the source of much of the West's oil. It is not difficult to understand why the Royal Navy along with other western countries maintains a presence there. The reason for British interest in *Fox*'s day may not be so clear.

The Gulf was not obviously a trade route of prime importance to Great Britain. Certainly in the past it had been one of the great waterways of the world. Bahrein had been the site of Dilmun, an important *entrepôt* from the third millenium BC, trading across the Arabian Sea to the cities of the Indus valley on the Indian sub-continent. Ships from Ur of the Chaldees and Babylon would pick up cargoes from Dilmun, bringing back to Mesopotamia gold, precious stones, ivory, frankincense, teak wood, copper and so forth.

By the beginning of the sixteenth century the first Europeans began to trade into the Gulf. The Portuguese led the way, striking out from their already-established trading posts in India. To secure their commercial operations against the pirates who had been endemic in the area since earliest times they established forts along the coast, and notably at Muscat; but they were brutal colonists and by the middle of the century Turkey began to challenge their position. Over the next fifty years Persia sought help from the British to speed the Portuguese departure and some help does seem to have been given despite the new alliance between Britain and Portugal in Europe. By 1660 the Portuguese had lost their foothold in Muscat, their most prestigious post in the Gulf.

Unpopular though the Portuguese had become, the withdrawal of their presence was not entirely beneficial. Piracy once again began to flourish and the Persians asked for British help to contain it. The Shah offered trading privileges in return.

The seventeenth century must have been an interesting time. The Portuguese left, the Turks dipped a toe in the water, the pirates flourished, the Shah of Persia sought British help; and then came the Dutch and the French. The French influence did not take root but the Dutch did, and they greatly impressed the Shah with their strength and wealth. It began to look as though the British would follow the Portuguese out of the Gulf. The Dutch however outlived their welcome too and by the end of the century it was their star which had set rather than that of the British.

The next hundred years saw the rise of Muscat and Oman. Its interior remained mysterious and difficult of access but its coastal people became known as 'the best mariners in all Arabia'. They were also the most prolific pirates! In 1798 the first treaty with Britain was signed whereby the Sultan agreed to deny facilities to the Dutch and the French and to allow the British to open a 'factory' at Bandar Abbas, which had been leased from Persia. Two years later a further treaty was negotiated under which the Sultan agreed that 'an English gentleman of respectability should reside at Muscat as agent of the East India Company in order that the friendship of the two states may remain unshook until the end of time, till the sun and the moon have finished their revolving career.'

By now the British had a secure trading position in the Gulf and thus an active interest in suppressing piracy. However the East India Company in Bombay, who, rather than the Government at home, were primarily concerned with events in the area, were extremely reluctant to become involved in 'security' and their ships were ordered not to interfere with pirates unless they were fired on first. This caution seems to have been due in part at least to their policy of not crossing the path of the Wahabi movement which, consistently involved in the piracy, could offer trading advantages for the Company in other parts of the Arab world. The Wahabis appear as an early version of the present-day Islamic fundamentalists and a militant and destabilising influence across the area. Both Bahrein and Kuwait sought, unsuccessfully, to negotiate treaties with Britain against the Wahabis.

Eventually however the Bombay government could no longer ignore

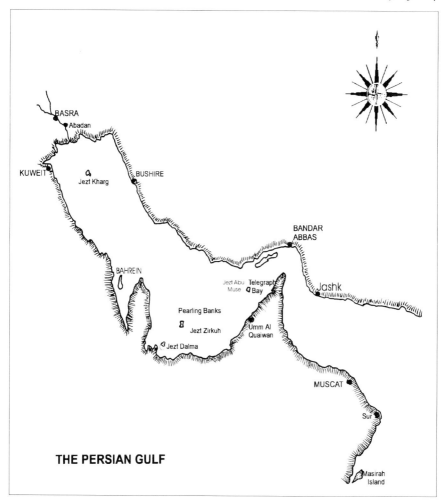

The Persian Gulf

the scale of piracy in the Gulf and at the beginning of the nineteenth century decided to face it down. The home government contributed a frigate and by 1821 the Persian Gulf had been made safe for trade. Britain signed treaties with the sheikdoms along the southern shores of the Gulf promising to ensure that this time the cessation of piracy would be permanent; and the coast became known as the Trucial, or Treaty, coast.

These treaties, a growing trade with the area, an awareness of Russian interest in securing a warm-water port close to the Indian Ocean and the

39

ebb and flow of the tides of Russian activities in Central Asia – the so-called 'Great Game' – all these served to maintain British interest in the area. The discovery of oil near Bahrein in 1932 added a further and important dimension but that of course was long after the old *Fox*'s time.

Many of the letters which follow were written from Bushire, a port approximately mid-way along the Persian shore of the Gulf. In *Fox*'s day it was an important centre of activity and the British maintained a 'Resident' there. His role lay somewhere between that of Ambassador to the Gulf Sheikdoms and, through his 'Agents' in the latter, Political Adviser to the Rulers. In later years the Residency moved to Bahrein, reflecting the growing economic activity on that side of the water.

HMS Fox,
Bushire,
25 October 1913

Many thanks for your voluminous epistles. Masqat is said to be the official way of spelling it. I admit I always feel inclined to put Muscat – that is how it is pronounced.

We've just had a rat hunt in my cabin with two bayonets and a hockey stick. There were so many corners that the quarry escaped through a hole that we had overlooked. The cabin was a fine mess after it all.

Well, we brought Admiral Slade up here at thirteen knots, arriving on Wednesday morning. He went ashore and lived with the Resident, Cox. I went ashore with the Paymaster and Chief Engineer yesterday. We got a ramshackle old carriage with a pair of horses from the Contractor and drove to Bushire. It is about seven miles away from this place along a flat stretch of dusty brick-coloured road. The various consulates stretch out from the town towards Rishahr. First the Turkish, Russian, Dutch, French, German, and then out here opposite the ship, and next door to the Telegraph Office is the British Residency. Each place is in its own bit of ground with walls and towers at the corners, strong gates, etc. for defence in case of raids by the hill tribes. These bandits are only about twelve miles out and hold the road between here and Shiraz, more or less paralysing trade and at present defying the Swedish gendarmerie. They will have to be crushed soon to break the back of this opposition to civilisation.

Well, to return to the present, we had lunch with the Contractor, rather an amusing Armenian who had been doing the job for forty years, he and his father that is to say. An excellent meal was had in a house on the sea shore with the breeze blowing right through. Personally I deprecate the habit of taking gifts or favours from Contractors, but as this was in a sense the Paymaster's party we acquiesced with good grace. After lunch he took us to have a look at the bazaar.

Having walked along a labyrinth of narrow lanes between brick houses for ten minutes we turned a corner and came into a region of shops. Imagine an ordinary lane between houses – twenty feet wide at most – going up and down hill according to the lie of the land. On each side are a succession of holes in the wall, about twenty feet back, ten feet across the front and twelve feet high. Each of these is a shop, crammed with all sorts and kinds of goods – cotton stuffs, quilts, carpets, groceries, china bowls from England, tin mugs, cutlery, hats and shoes packed tight – the owner squatting at the corner serenely watching the passers-by, at intervals a fellow droning out passages from a leather-covered book, groups of beggars at corners.

Above all this, twenty feet up, a sort of ceiling is arranged of grass mats, and one gets shafts of sunlight piercing the shaded light, illuminating some gaudy quilt, flashing on a copper pan. Thanks to this roof and high houses it is cool and there is no glare. More wonderful still, there is comparatively little smell. For these people seem to be fairly clean. They keep their goods cleaner than most out here. One does not see swarms of flies on the dates and melons. There is not much real garbage about. Then a shout from the guide makes you look round and you step sideways quickly to avoid a mule with two sacks on his back hurrying along as if he was catching a train. Then another & another go by – four in all. Some merchant's stock going back to Shiraz or to some place in the interior. To avoid these you've probably been pushed half into one of the shops, so narrow is the way.

We stopped at one of the places where they make hats from the pure wool and I invested in one for one shilling and four pence. They are just the texture and hardness of a bowler when finished but we didn't stay long enough to realise the process. You know the ones I mean. In the nursery at Dunearn there were two pictures of Persians on horses and wearing these. I've always wanted one. By this time we had to rush away to get the carriage and drive back to the ship. On arrival we found a 'Shamal' getting up. That is a north-west wind, strong and gusty. However it has dropped now and we go to Kuwait tomorrow with Cox, the Resident.

This part of the Gulf is studded with little rocks, sticking three to ten feet out of the water. There are about five of these right out in the middle of the Gulf, sixty miles from land, so one has to be careful.

HMS Fox,
Outside the Gulf – Off Jask
10 January 1914

We're a regular sea-bird now – no stopping us. After the mail came last week we were off again to the other side and had a look at the boats to see if there was anything they wanted. These are smaller craft patrolling across the narrow entrance to the Gulf on anti-gun-running patrols. One of the ships, the old *Sphinx*, a paddle-wheel junk built in 1882, caught a dhow with several soldiers and about a dozen rifles on board. They had no pass for the rifles so he towed her into Muscat and searched her. There was nothing to find – and eventually it transpired that the dhow was bringing an outlying Sheikh to pay his respects to the new Sultan – these were his bodyguard on board with the rifles. However as they hadn't a pass we were quite right in stopping her.

We see some most charming effects here at night. About this time of year there is a great deal of spawn floating on the sea, enormous sheets of brick-red gelatinous gubbins in patches here and there. At night this is very phosphorescent, and the other day, or night rather, as we went along, the edge of the bow wave was a continual streak of phosphorescence with occasional brighter patches. The bridge was quite dark of course, as we are on the dhow hunt at the moment, and I am not exaggerating when I say one could read large print by the light of these flashes alone. It would light up the whole of the underside of the awning, much as one sees a fire flare up for a second with a shooting flame.

The night before we left Muscat the whole harbour was ablaze with it – the tip of each little wavelet a glowing mass of fire. I keep a standing (that is, regular) Morning Watch at sea – which means I keep watch from 0400 to 0730 every morning – and out here in this fairly warm climate it's quite enjoyable. The ship, from being asleep and quiet at 0400, gradually wakens up – decks are scrubbed by the watch at half-past four, at six the remainder of the people turn out, and by seven o'clock the sun is up and everything is in full swing, cleaning and polishing for the day. It seems to suit one's own process of awakening to a great extent. Also it's a quiet time, when you can forget everyone around you, and think of things impersonally. At six or a quarter past my faithful servant, a Scottish youth (McMaster), brings up tea and bread and butter, a most welcome diversion, and at half past seven the relief comes up and one goes below to bath and dress with a cheerful sense of having started a lap ahead of everyone else – and also of having done a job of work before the day has really started, so that one can almost claim to be a bit lazy during the rest of the day.

Just now it's full moon and one can see the land at night, but I must say it's not too delightful cutting about as we do at all hours. Last night we patrolled back and forward four times across the narrow part of the entrance to the Gulf on the lookout for smugglers or gun-runners. There is a sluicing tide there which no one knows much about so that one cannot predict what it is going to do. As I say, luckily there was a moon and we could see the land fairly well.

One of my ambitions was realised yesterday when we went up into Tele-graph Bay. Many years ago when they first had telegraph cables, the Com-pany thought they'd run theirs from Gwadar on the Persian coast, across to the Musandam Peninsula jutting up at the entrance to the Gulf, then dip into the water again and so to Bushire. They selected a little islet in a sort of fjord on the peninsula, and built their station there, put up a flagstaff, installed instruments, furnished the place and sent a couple of clerks to take charge. In the summer this place gets like an oven and report says it's the hottest place in the world. I can quite believe it. At any rate, what with the monotony and the heat, one man got fever and died, while the other, the survivor, got melancholia and shot himself. Then they abandoned the place and started a land system of wires. So much for its history.

On our charts the picture of it is tiny, perhaps an inch or so long. You wonder if it is really safe to hazard the ship going in. When one says that it is six miles long you'll realise the scale of the chart one had to work with. However the *Admiralty Sailing Directions* tell you it's perfectly safe and clear of dangers.

One goes in between cliffs, rising on the left hand straight up out of the water to three thousand feet, an enormous precipice of 'basaltic' (is that right?) sort of formation; from a little distance it looks carved into tiers of innumerable small pillars – not like Staffa quite – but having the pillars in separate galleries like so many balconies. On the right hand the hills are about six hundred feet of sandstone and so on. One passes about a hundred and fifty yards from the three thousand foot one, the left. Then one turns round to the left again, and skirts the base of this three thousand foot hill – the channel is eight hundred yards wide here – and after a mile or so one sees the abandoned station, on a wee island not much bigger than the 'Grey Island' at Gairloch. A couple of ruined houses and a dilapidated flagstaff are all that remain.

Past the island and after another couple of miles a straight reach opens out in front of you, half a mile wide, the shore on either side being about two hundred feet high in numerous bays and promontories – and away at the end, three miles away is a wall, absolutely sheer, rising up to three thousand feet again in a cone, and on a minute stretch of sand at the foot, overshadowed by this enormous wall, is a collection of mud houses. If one could only convey the impression of grandeur and desolation. In each or several of the various little bays there were collections of mud huts, but barring at the entrance when there were a few fishermen, we didn't see a living being.

Once one was inside and up at the far end, of course one couldn't see any entrance to the place – completely land-locked, and by land which was in no place less than a couple of hundred feet high, so one had to look sensibly up to see the sky. I think one can imagine (at any rate I felt I could yesterday) the sense of being cut off, not even seeing passing ships, hardly ever seeing a living soul.

One felt – I daresay it was from having heard the yarn, or maybe it was seeing the abandoned station and peeling flagstaff – but one felt as if the place was cursed.

The skipper made the place hideous with the siren, trying for echoes. They were as a matter of fact jolly good, especially at the entrance where they reverberated between the two walls, died away, and then one heard them rumbling in the hills at the back again ten seconds later. I'm glad we've been in, as one had heard a good deal about the place. I'm going to bed now. Two blankets and a rug on the quarterdeck.

Tuesday

En route for Muscat and then straight back again – we've heard that they're pushing through a couple of loads of arms, so everyone is on the hop.

Many apologies for the 'journaliness' of this letter. One can't manage to think of much else but the Gulf at present – I'm glad of it. Goodbye for a season.

44

By the end of January the gun-running activity appears to have died down but my Father had apparently picked up some bug which kept him in his bunk for a few days. In the following letter he has clearly recovered and writes of the beauty of the early Persian spring.

HMS Fox,
Bushire
8 February 1914

Once more about – off the bed of sickness. It's quite ludicrous. The Doctor urges burgundy at one shilling and seven pence the time to increase the blood corpuscles but it doesn't go down to the Sick Bay account!

When we first came here the wind blew strongly, there were low lying clouds over the land, the sea was dirty yellow, the temperature 52° – bitterly cold. This morning we woke to find the wind dropped, and the clouds rolled away. Far off in the distance up to the north, floating in the air almost, was a mountain, its slopes white with snow. Away round from this towards the east one could faintly trace a chain of hills, snow capped, almost invisible against the sky. These were hidden to the east by a fine ridge about five thousand feet high just at the back of Bushire. The low land nearer the sea is all green with young wheat; the sun's warm; the air's clear; everything's lovely. You can't think how uplifting it is when you look at those snow-clad hills – one of them is over a hundred miles away. Most of our fellows are ashore staying with the Intelligence Officer and his wife. We sit and shiver in greatcoats after dinner at night and the glass is only down to 55° or so. I really tremble to think what it'll be like at home when we get back.

This mail will be left at Bushire. We are departing early on Monday morning for some destination unknown. Thank goodness it can't be much colder where we're going. And now to snuggle under two blankets, a rug and a dressing gown.

The 'destination unknown' had however to wait for a while. *Fox*'s departure from Bushire was delayed by a tragic and unforeseen occurrence ashore.

HMS Fox,
At Sea – near Muscat
14 February 1914

We've had a rush of a week. Just as we were going to leave Bushire a signal was made from shore to say that the Resident was dead. It seems he'd shot himself, by accident or otherwise – they couldn't say. At any rate his wife found him with a revolver and a bullet in his heart. This was the fellow who had been the Captain's host for the last two days. It was naturally rather a shock, and of course we waited for the funeral next day. All the men we could spare were landed, being towed three miles to the shore. We all landed, cocked hats, gold-laced belts, frock coats, epaulettes – a weird old-fashioned looking rig. It was a most picturesque sort of ceremony, with all the different nationalities drawn together to offer their last respects.

A storm was brewing and dark masses of clouds massing in the southwest and gradually spreading over the sky made the day quite wintry in general aspect. Gusts of wind blew over the brown foreshore, raising the dust in swirls and blowing the half-masted flag on the Telegraph buildings stiffly out to leeward.

When the party of officers arrived the naval escort of bluejackets was drawn up on the road. A guard of native infantry lined the road to the cemetery, a little walled-in enclosure a few hundred yards down from the Telegraph station. Just after we arrived the gun carriage came up from the Residency, escorted by a guard of native Lancers in khaki uniform and well-mounted. They cantered up to the head of the column, a squad of Persian horsemen in blue jackets and black hats wheeling in to rear of them.

A band of native infantry played mournful squealings on the bagpipes as we all set off at a slow march. Ourselves, the officers, were mixed up in a crowd of foreign Political Officers, a few of our soldiers, secretaries to Consuls and various others, dressed in every variety of gold-lace and silver. Bushire is the head of the political section of the Gulf and there are British, German, French, Turkish, Persian, Russian and several other consulates. All these people attended with their secretaries making a most unique group. There were several women in beautiful fur coats and huge hats. Around all this procession, never trespassing beyond the native troops lining the road, who stood like statues, arms at the present, but swarming and running on to see all there was to be seen, was a crowd of all sorts and descriptions of Turk, Persian, Armenian, riding ponies, donkeys, walking barefoot and sandalled, clothed in thick woollens or some old blanket – all with the universal black or grey felt hat. Carriages there were, with some fine horses in them, belonging no doubt to the various Consulates, the drivers smoking, the horses whinnying at each other and at the bagpipes.

It was a strange mixture. The wind was blowing stronger, the sea breaking in flecks of foam. One noticed our steam boat in a smother of smoke, fussing back to the ship to get their tea. The ship lay away out in the distance, a dirty grey against a dirtier sky. We could hardly all get into the cemetery. Once inside, the high walls shut out everything else. Three volleys, and the 'Last Post' by six buglers sounded well amongst the windy rustlings of the few trees there were. Everything over, we hurried back to the boats. The sea was quite rough and the wind getting up. Most of us got wet and to add to it all a thin spatter of rain was falling. It was an evolution to get away. The boats were hoisted, the anchor weighed and within the hour we were steaming south to meet the Mail.

Next day was beastly – a heavy rain, a strong breeze, a rough sea. The ship, being all closed up on account of this, smelt like an ash heap. However we ran out of it before we met the mail-steamer, and by then it was comparatively calm, so the transhipment took place without any difficulty.

That morning we made our acquaintance with water-spouts. One of these passed about half a mile astern of us. Out of a dark black low-lying cloud came a black tube which curved its way down till it reached the surface of the water. At that point for a space of about thirty yards the water was whipped into spray which was caught up and whirled around furiously, gradually mounting the tube until it reached the cloud. One could see the whirling motion going on and notice the particles of spray moving spirally up. It was just like an elephant's snout or trunk waving to and fro as it blew along with the wind.

The *Dartmouth*, another small cruiser like ourselves but a bit younger, has just arrived to take our mails to Muscat; she's going over to coal tomorrow.

Whilst engaging the water-spout with one eye my attention was caught by something glimpsed by the other eye. On the calm sea curiously enough the water-spout only disturbed a small locality and as I watched the spout there appeared another dark object some distance away as if a ship had broken in half and the two pieces, standing on end, had floated up and were clasped in each other's arms, so to speak. Two dark coloured objects

47

were there, a mile and a half away, without appreciable movement, twenty feet of 'body' showing. I examined them with my binoculars and said to myself, 'They look like the upper ends of two whales standing on their tails, possibly mating.' Their tops were rounded, but slightly square. My experience of whales is NIL! I looked back at the whirling spouting column of water astern and round again at the 'whales' but they were gone.

That last letter has always been one of my favourites in the collection. What it described was something essentially to do with private grief, yet in its own way it gives a picture of another tiny thread in the tapestry that was the British Empire before the First World War, the colour and pageantry of the funeral tending to sharpen and make more vivid the hues of the whole work particularly when viewed against the sombre background of the primitive and harsh surroundings of the Persian coast.

For those of the old *Fox* the experience of the funeral must have been further sharpened by the lowering sky and rising wind of the approaching storm. For the Captain and more senior officers there would have been a measure of concern for the safety of the ship, anchored well offshore in somewhat uncertain waters. For the others the prospect of a long wet boat trip at the end of the day would have acted as something of a damper on emotions stirred by the proceedings.

For myself I have always wondered how all that gold braid fared in the salt spray of the return journey. Perhaps with the start of World War One only six months away it did not matter very much.

HMS Fox,
Bushire
22 March 1914

Breaking all rules and regulations – keeping watch at sea and writing a letter whilst on duty. Heinous crime! It's blowing quite hard and we're going right into it to get up to Bushire in time to catch the mail before she leaves. This week has been quite soul-stirring: we've sort of come out of the shell of routine and played our part as protector of the poor and oppressor of the proud spirit.

I daresay you remember we went to a place with a long name (Umm al Quawain) some months ago in order to induce the Sheikh thereof to pay up a small bill he owed to a neighbour. Well, at any rate we did. The other day the wheels were set going again and, the Indian Government having given permission, we set forth to extract this gentleman's rupees. Taking the new Political Resident with us, resplendent in gold lace and braid, together with several native big bugs, we went down to our friend and asked what he meant to do. To pay the bill or not. The truculent fellow replied that he'd be d . . . d if he'd pay and we could do whatever we liked but we wouldn't get the money. All right.

The day before yesterday we assembled once more in front of this fellow's town – the *Dartmouth*, *Odin* and ourselves – two cruisers and a sloop. *Odin* had been sent to survey the place the previous day, and we crept in as far as we possibly could, about half a mile apart, and then anchored. There was a nice fat brickwork tower about fifteen hundred yards off standing on the beach by itself. Around the bottom of it was a cluster of mat huts in which the poorer people were living. This was selected for the sacrifice and we sent the interpreter ashore to clear the people out of the mud huts.

Some of them departed but most seemed quite apathetic and unconcerned, strolling here and there and watching the naval demonstration with interest. At five minutes to twelve a signal was made, 'Prepare to open fire,' and as the last stroke of the bell sounded the Captain gave the order to shoot. A bang . . . and a cloud of smoke round the base of the tower showed that our 4.7-inch guns had not missed. The people on shore seemed little perturbed; they looked around to see what had happened, and went on with their occupations!

Then *Dartmouth* got going with her 6-inch guns at twenty second intervals. Clouds of dust, a shower of bricks – and at the fifth round the nearside of the tower fell in heaps, while a good-sized hole was knocked in the far side. Meanwhile, on the top of a house with towers to it, about another half mile away, we could see the Sheikh and his staff watching proceedings with interest.

After he saw his tower crumbling, a black flag was frantically hoisted at a flagstaff he had, and the red one was hauled down. This flag seemed to be a pair of what one buys at Marshall and Snelgrove's in black satin, but we couldn't tell for sure at that distance.

So we hoisted 'Cease firing'. In an hour or so the Sheikh's brother, his special ambassador, came off in state, to see the Political Resident and ask him to go ashore to see the Sheikh. Naturally we told him to go back himself. After this I went down to have lunch and heard later that the special envoy had returned with the money required – some thirty thousand rupees. Everybody is most satisfied. The Political Resident is glad it is all over. The other man is glad to get his rupees and we are pleased to have seen a shot fired in earnest and a good cause.

It's a quarter to three in the morning, the wind howling like billy-oh. I hope it won't get up any more. Dined with the skipper the other night, the Political Resident being there. Of course he's been living in the ship for the last week and, low be it spoken, I fancy he's getting very fed up with it. He is one Major-General Knox and has been out here for many years so is steeped in 'Gulf' lore. It's funny to see him wake up and his eyes sparkle if one mentions anything about camels, Arabic, anything eastern; and then someone brings up bridge, Lloyd George – the look of intense boredom.

Usually one can write fairly flowingly during the Middle Watch. It doesn't seem to come tonight. Farewell – time is going on, we'll soon be in the last lap of the commission.

I do tend to find myself agreeing with the Political Resident on the subjects of bridge and Lloyd George!

The next letter is undated but from the text it was plainly written during the summer in the Gulf. It reads as though *Fox* had just got back there after a month or two's change of scene, perhaps for dockyard maintenance in Bombay or Colombo or to give 'Station Leave' to the Ship's Company in the hill country of Ceylon. From its mention of 'vicissitudes' perhaps the former was the more likely, although *Fox's* name was still to be seen picked out on the hillside above Diyatalawa Leave Camp when I had a week's leave there myself in 1946. The sailors would certainly have been 'all right' as mentioned in the letter after a few days in that paradise.

HMS Fox,
Muscat
June 1914

We're here at last after all our vicissitudes, actually beginning the job we came out for. You'll see where it is on the map so you'll understand when I tell you. The monsoon blew freshly from the south-west most of the way across from Bombay until we got close to the north-east corner of Arabia. At about 2.0 a.m. it freshened considerably and blew with tremendous force for an hour or so, then flat calm as we got into the lee of the land. The thermometer jumped up to 82°F in an hour and continued to rise.

Muscat itself is at the head of a cove, of which the sides are rugged cliffs about two hundred feet high, and covered with watch-towers in all stages of decay. Awfully picturesque it is. Two mediaeval castles command the town, looking like gingerbread forts, and exactly the image of those one sees in Grimm's Fairy Tales as the Ogre's stronghold. The houses on the front are ordinary eastern dwellings – brick and plaster, flat roof, loop-holed and so on. The Consulate, Harem, Sultan's palace and one or two others form the front rank.

The native loves flags and on the day we arrived it was the last day of Ramadan. Every fort had at least three enormous red flags (the Sultan of Muscat's colours); the Consulate flagstaff was dressed and everything looked most picturesque.

The air is wonderfully clear and the outlines of the hills are sharp like cardboard, even those thirty miles away. All round Muscat the country is a succession of sharp ridges and peaks and corresponding gullies, so that from the anchorage one sees ridge after ridge, from the hills dominating the town to some ten miles off, every detail like a stereoscopic picture. The water of the harbour is clear as crystal and swarms with little fish like whitebait or sardine. These gather round and swim in streams, weaving patterns in the water, so thick that one could not drop a hat pin to the bottom without touching one.

What makes it more weird is that one sees down about twenty feet, and after watching the evolutions of a brigade of fish down there it comes as a shock to find that the water surface is really only ten feet from your nose. Of course it is as warm as a hot bath – 83° roughly. We bathe a good deal but it doesn't refresh one much. On deck the thermometer goes up to 93° and 94°. It was 94° at 4.0 p.m. two days ago – 92° today.

At nights a wind blows from the north-west and comes across the Persian desert like a blast from a furnace, dry as a chip, hot, baking. I find it hard to sleep and have to get out and do some job about 3.0 a.m. We're just at the end of that though, thank goodness, and with the south-east winds it will be cooler. All one's books curl up in this wind; the charts roll up in their tubes; one can't perspire however much one drinks. It's rather a good show in a way after Colombo as it enables one to get one's clothes and gear properly dry.

Regarding the state of affairs on shore: when we forced the Sultan to institute a bonded warehouse for all arms imported into the Gulf it naturally created bad blood amongst certain tribes who profited by the gun-running game. These fellows, to the tune of anything between 20,000 and 30,000, are marching on Muscat (so rumour says) and will come in about a week's time to overwhelm the place. Of course in the first place you can't trust anything one hears out here. Again, they will never attack while there is a ship here. The skipper wants to issue an ultimatum to them saying, 'Stop where you are. If you advance any closer, I will send and destroy all villages, oases, date palms, etc. within a radius of seventy or eighty miles of Muscat.' I say the Foreign Office won't ever allow this. The old *Fox* must just wait here till things are blown over. Then it'll be time to go home.

The ship's company are all right. At nights we have a guard on shore. One officer, several men and a three pounder gun on the top of one of the castles; so as to command a part of the town said to be of antagonistic tendencies.

Of course the expected attack on Muscat never materialised – if indeed the threat of one ever really existed – and *Fox* was apparently soon released to go north again to Bushire for a spell and thence back south to the Pearling Banks at the bottom end of the Gulf.

The next letter describes a visit to the latter, but does not say just why an HM Ship was required to take an interest in the pearling. One can only assume that it was in line with the general policy of 'keeping the peace' which seemed to be widely accepted throughout the Gulf.

HMS Fox,
Off Zirkuh Island
19 July 1914

I'm sorry you got such a sketchy letter last week. It was this wise. We've been having rather a busy time. Went over to Kuwait from Bushire and stayed there for a day, then back again and picked up some soldiers, taking them for a day's shooting to Kharg Island about thirty miles away. I landed with them and had a look round for gazelle. I saw several but was never near enough for a shot.

Well, we came back to Bushire in a thick sandstorm. It's most curious this sort of storm – just the same appearance as fog, but afterwards you find everything covered with a thin layer of brown dust and the ship looks just like a motor car which has come in from a dusty day's run – yards, masts, shrouds, bridges, awnings – everything looks brick yellow. It's all-pervading, goes into drawers, cups of tea, forms a scum on your bath – and of course you can't see very far in it.

It was in this sort of thing we set out to find the *Sphinx* in order to give her our mails for transhipment to the mail-steamer. Arrived at the spot in the early hours of the morning, blew fog horns, fired rockets, burned searchlights but without success. You see the *Sphinx* had come about 150 miles from the opposite direction in this fog and we had come 100 miles so there wasn't much wonder that we failed to meet. It was a funny sort of situation – we were talking by wireless all the time. 'Can you hear my siren?' 'No.' 'Did you see that rocket?' and so on, and there we were circling about like two blind things. So we, the *Fox*, anchored, and next day by dint of firing guns and so on, the *Sphinx* found us, and it was just as she had been sighted I wrote that letter.

Having sent the mail over to her, we went to Bahrein, and had a certain amount of difficulty in finding the entrance to that place too. We took the Political Agent on board and came out to go round the Pearling Banks with him. Have I told you – or do you know?

The Pearling Banks

This season is the great pearling season. All the southern part of the Gulf round here is shallow, sixty to one hundred feet, and on these shallow parts the oysters grow with the pearls.

Huge fleets of dhows come from all parts, principally Kuwait and Bahrein, and spend the season on the Banks. They are analogous to the

North Sea fishermen only instead of trawling, etc. each boat carries from twenty to thirty divers, usually negroid slaves.

One of the boats I was watching had eight men in the water at once. They each have a rope with a lead about sixteen pounds weight on the end of it, and a loop which the diver puts over his big toe. Another rope is attached to a small basket. Each man has a clip on the principle of the clothes peg slung round his neck, which he puts over his nose to close it. They wear no clothes.

When the 'hauler' in the boat lets go his rope, the diver sinks quickly to the bottom, grabs two or three shells, puts them in the basket, and is hauled up to the surface by his hauler. Each diver has his own hauler or attendant, and there were four divers on each side of the boat; that adds up to sixteen men working. Add to this about ten men spare to relieve these others as occasion arises, and the owner of the dhow, and you come to about thirty souls all told. They work all day, daylight to dusk, and run in to shelter, if they are near land, for the night.

The divers are most of them deaf from working so deep, and their eyes go wrong with so much salt water, but they go back to the same work until they're worn out, I believe. I saw one old man bobbing about on the end of a line, with a white beard down to his waist. He was at least fifty years old, I should think.

The little fleet of dhows on each bank look very picturesque. There is usually a strong tide running and as the dhows get up anchor to shift their ground a little this way or that, the crew man enormous sweeps with big square blades, stuck on diamond-wise, and the craft swings slowly round, the four oars dipping each side, slowly like fingers, the masts moving with the waves, others of the crew sprawling across the enormous yard of the sail, and perched high up on the poop. She picks her way down a lane of other dhows, cuts across a bit and folding her wings settles with a contented splash in a new corner.

Our skipper goes onboard one dhow in each fleet we meet, presumably to hear any complaints – in fact we always said (unfairly) to see if they'll give him any pearls. Anyway, he doesn't seem to have any decent ones!

In addition to there being pearling banks round here, there are four or five small volcanic islands, each of them of much the same sort of formation. None is more than a couple of miles long and a mile or so broad – all except one between two and five hundred feet high – about thirty miles apart. The skipper wanted to see all these and arranged a trip to go round each in turn.

The first one we tried to find gave us a good deal of trouble. It was a bit misty and we ran right past it. Eventually we got there four hours later. I must tell you that this part of the Gulf, again, has been very sketchily surveyed and very incompletely. Ships, or rather the only ship which frequents it during part of the year, are always coming across new shoals and rocks, and inaccuracies in the present chart. The present chart is on a scale of one inch to ten miles approximately – that is, each island is about half a finger-nail long – so you can gather that the chance of finding a new rock by bumping into it was ever with us, but our old man is such an advertiser he wants to go round simply because no other ship of this draught has been before.

As a matter of fact there is a savour of the explorer about it. I felt a distinct elation at sighting dimly on the horizon a bit of hill characterised vaguely on the chart as 'stony desert, shore with small volcanic hills' and about which the *Persian Gulf Pilot* (the nautical guide book) remarks: 'The Arabs say that this is the hottest place in the Gulf'; and again, 'The coast of the mainland is seldom, if ever, visited by Europeans,' and 'It is seldom that even the Arabs land on the coast hereabouts.'

However, we've got so far without bumping, and get clear of the locality tomorrow. At the last island, Dalma, when the Captain landed just after we had anchored, he was greeted by a black man who fell on his neck, entreating to be taken onboard. He'd been a slave for some time in one of the dhows round there and had got fed up, so now he lounges round the upper deck and does nothing.

We go back to Bushire, Kuwait, Bahrein, Henjam and Muscat for coal about the 20th of the month. The last mail has broken down. One of the regular steamers was out of the running for a refit and an older and smaller one had to take her place. This one's rudder head carried away on her way to Karachi and she missed the connection, however it will come up sooner or later.

Wilson gets married in August. He says their respective Ma's met in consultation to arrange affairs; Wilson gained much amusement thereat. I'm sending you a picture of the 'Woman of Samaria' as she is nowadays to be seen. As a matter of fact she is a girl at Muscat, the only one with any passable pretensions to features in the place, either Circassian or Baluchi. I don't quite know which. I'm rather pleased with it as I'd specially landed to see if I could catch the good lady. The pot on her head is made of porous clay and keeps the water cool by evaporation from the outside. Of course it's empty so far. Hope you haven't got bored with all this stuff.

There's nothing more about going home so I'm not thinking anything about it.

My Father had evidently got somewhat carried away by the uniqueness of the pearling fleets' spectacle when he described the divers as 'negroid slaves'. Negroid they probably were but by 1914 they were unlikely to have been slaves. There must undoubtedly have been abuses in the industry and the Sheikh of Bahrein in later years (about 1930 I believe) introduced far-reaching reforms where his writ ran but even in 1914 there seems to have been some attempt at equity between the dhow owners/captains and the divers. The profits of the season would be divided in fixed proportions between the parties involved; and each day's 'catch' would not have been opened until the following morning when all the shell would have been put in a common pile regardless of who contributed what.

There does appear however to have been an element of 'slavery' in that the divers, who were generally held to be something of an irresponsible and improvident lot, would become indebted to their captain or to a merchant ashore and would have to continue working to clear their debts. The 'season' lasted for four to five months each year. It must have been a crippling life even for those divers with the wit to save.

The last letter from the Persian Gulf is dated June and was written some weeks before the visit to the Pearling Banks. I have however kept it to the end because it must surely be the best of the collection.

It describes a visit to a small oasis on the coast of Oman. The occasion seems so extraordinary in that desolate and arid stretch of country that I have sometimes wondered if he and his companion really did stumble upon this wonderful pocket which he describes, or whether the description was something imagined in the brain-twisting heat of a torrid afternoon.

Surely not the latter – though I have never managed to place this tiny paradise.

HMS Fox,
At sea – Muscat to Bushire
16 June 1914

I'm going to bore you with an episode which occurred last week and fascinated me at the time.

We had been up in the Gulf for ten months, ten months of four weeks each. One had become accustomed to the red-coloured, dusty, dry hills; the parched, cindery mountains; the clear, hot, frizzling sun beating down on the rocks from a cloudless sky; the scorching wind shaking the awning at midnight; the sleepy stumbling down the hatchway to find a chatty of more or less cool water; and all the rest of it. The blood was drying up in our veins, it ran stickily, with an effort. One thought of a green lawn with watering mouth.

One of many evenings we left Muscat and went north along the coast. The land here rises straight away from the sea in a sharp slope to a height of four or five thousand feet, and finishes in a table-land which might, for all one can see, go on to eternity. As the ship steams stickily down the shore there is no living thing to be seen. It is a land of mystery and weird enchantment. What is behind? What is beyond?

Great fissures appear from time to time in the worn and dusty sandstone. Deep gorges appear, dark and forbidding, losing themselves a mile or so back from the sea in the general brown waste of rock. Little clusters of brown cubes show where man has settled himself. A solitary dhow appears, wandering like a lost soul in purgatory and looking for shade.

We anchored one morning close to one of these clusters of brown cubes, at the opening to one of the fissures in the cliffs. Like an ant-hill it at once became animated. Small figures ran here and there and congregated opposite us on the beach. Two of us landed – heavy boots, shirt, breeks and a water bottle – prepared for the sickening heat of the growing day.

Donkeys were forthcoming to help carry us and our food, and we set forth, an old man of eighty in a green nightgown, which had once been brown, acting as guide. He made quite a good-looking figure with his pink embroidered turban and a great silver knife stuck in a belt at his waist.

Over the stones, between many squalid huts, past smells one involuntarily respected for their strength of mind, slipping down some rough-cut steps and we were in the gorge. On all sides the sandstone cliffs rose sheer to five hundred feet. One could see them rising higher further along. At the back, a quarter of a mile away, was the sea, but in front, washing the feet of these cliffs as it were, was a lagoon – a sheet of crystal clear water, sweet to taste. Coarse grass and reeds grew thickly round the edges, hiding the bottom of the cliffs. On the other side was a stretch of turf – real green grass turf – on which four or five dun cows were doing their best to imitate a Landseer landscape. We splashed squelchily through the shallows, over pebbles red, grey, brown, envying ourselves and pitying those left on board.

Further up the gorge contracted, then widened out a bit, but was never more than a few hundred yards across. The wonder of it all was this stream – an actual, splashing, running stream of fresh, drinkable water which we noisily and sensually waded through. At times the coarse reeds grew as high as a man so that the people in front were hidden. At times all vegetation stopped for the space of a hundred yards and the water tried to hide itself amongst limestone boulders worn shiny in places by countless footsteps.

And as one went on one sensed the people. A fringe of date palms in little walled-up gardens and terraces ran along each side of the gorge, wherever space could be found. In the shade here, if one happened to glance up, one would see three or four pairs of staring eyes, their owners stock-still, breathless, then chattering excitedly, under their breath lest they make any noise, lying in the shade of the trees and watching the strangers. It was a weird sensation, stumbling over boulders, painfully white and trying to the eyes, nothing but dates and sun all round you, until looking by chance at a fine clump of fruit you'd find yourself the object of a low animated conversation going on amongst a group of almost invisible beings curled up under a tree in the shadows.

Or you'd suddenly realise that the particular bit of cliff with the funny hole in it you were looking at was the wall of a house, the Arab's castle, and there was Rachel at the window. And above you all the walls of the gorge lifted themselves in crags and precipices until they almost touched the blue sky above them.

As one went on the water collected in pools more and the bed of the stream was more and more rocky and difficult to negotiate. My boots with nails in the soles were eminently unsuitable for the job. The donkeys were the most wonderful animals, scrambling over those slippery boulders with a heavy load of human flesh which shifted in the saddle at every move. They found a foothold anywhere whatsoever with the greatest success.

At one place we all stopped to drink at a small pool where the water bubbled up from under a rock, cold, clear but unfortunately tasting rather muddy. Even then, to find a thing like this in dry, dusty, old, scorched Arabia, even this was marvellous. Then, crossing the bed of the stream we charged up the other side under the palms and found ourselves entering a village with a miniature tower and fortified gateway, all on a reduced scale. Just the other side of the houses was a huge tree covered with mangoes – literally covered, one could hardly see leaves for mangoes. It made one think of the orchard at Dunearn and the apple trees in a good year. Here we rested.

The Sheikh and elders of the village were out to meet us almost at once bringing mats and cushions and coffee, and dates and mangoes as presents to the strangers. They are truly hospitable these people. I was really most impressed with the man here. He and all his people, as the custom is, came and squatted round in a ring while we explained who we were and told him news from the outside. A black slave, his leg swollen from some disease, handed round really delightful black coffee in little cups. We drank first and then it went round to others of the circle. The politics of the district and the prospects of trouble from inland were discussed.

The Sheikh then gathered up his people (and this was where his courtesy showed itself) and dispersed the crowd of villagers who had come to look at us all. He gave orders that we were not to be disturbed and said he'd leave us to rest and sleep and would come back later to see if there was anything more he could do for us. And this from a villager who has not been beyond Muscat much – say sixty miles – in his life.

Our steward had put up just the right lunch and we dozed afterwards very peacefully to the sound of running water, rustling leaves, and childish noises from across the ravine. In front and rather below one could see the palms and terraces of the other side with glimpses of water at their feet, whilst above them, rising out of the palm leaves, towered the crags and pinnacles of the sandstone cliffs. Away up against the blue sky a hawk was circling slowly, appearing and disappearing in the spaces between the palm trees. A low murmur came from behind where the donkey-men we had engaged for the trip were swapping lies. Soon the sun had dropped to the side of the mango tree where it found a crack between some leaves and woke me with the beginnings of a bad head.

Shortly the Sheikh came back in a rather more friendly frame of mind. Despite his courtesy he had seemed rather suspicious of our good intentions at first. Now we told him more and at last he smiled.

Presents of dates, chickens, mangoes came pouring in. The dates were made up in the most delightful basket you could think of. They had been brought in a big cloth at first and laid out for our inspection. We said, 'Many thanks, but how can we get them home?' They were a little puzzled at first to get our meaning but once they understood, the solution was quite easy. A young fellow came and sat down alongside the pile on the cloth with several green reeds half an inch or so wide and a couple of feet long and with these he wove two shovel-shaped baskets. These were tied together at their broad end, strand to strand, and when the fruit was packed in, the other two ends were brought up over and tied together. Wonderfully neat! And all made on the spot, ready for carrying.

Later on we made a move and the Sheikh took us down the hill, through little terraces cut up by waterways, across the river and up the other side among the date palms which we'd been looking at. Great prosperous trees they were, each with a necklace of ten or twelve fat bunches of green, yellow or red dates up at the top under the leaves.

Nearly all the stone in the river bed is limestone and this is burnt in primitive limekilns and used for making water channels. These channels, gushing good fresh water, were most cooling to look upon. Maidenhair ferns were growing in bunches where there was a bit of a leak or an overflow. We splashed along with water over our boots in this cool stuff, revelling in it and admiring the wonderfully efficient planning and workmanship which enabled all these thousands and thousands of trees to grow and bear fruit in such an unpromising place. And up above when one looked up were the same grim old cliffs and crags like a skeleton at a feast.

We bathed later on in a deep pool, close by the side of a patch of green turf one might have played tennis on. The sun was getting close to the edge of the cliffs away up above and we waited impatiently for him to hide. At last he dropped out of sight and at once the side of the gorge was in shadow. One felt the relief. The day had been busy and one had a headache.

A triumphal ride back along the way we had come brought us to the Landseer picture once more at the mouth of the gorge. Over the tops of the houses the wireless poles of the ship brought one back to earth again and to the realization of what had been shown during the day.

It is not so much the actual trees and the actual water but the feeling that one has at last seen a minute part of the means by which Arabia and the Arabs make their living; that a corner of the curtain has been lifted and one has been able to catch a glimpse of the real lives of these people, whom one has been accustomed to class with brigands and often scoundrels – pretty shocking really. Yet where could one have received the same courtesy, the same hospitality that had been shown to us in such an out of the way spot. It was quite a revelation of the old, original kindness to strangers, from which have perhaps sprung modern conventions – the tea fight, the lunch party.

But what above all produced the greatest effect was the sight of running water, fresh and sweet, in a country or at least district one had been accustomed to regard as arid, dry and parched. It filled one with wonder to see it sliding along between those desolate red cliffs. It looked almost miraculous that there should be any there at all, for there appeared to be no reason for it.

The dates of course and the village with all its inhabitants would not be there without this stream – they could not live. I wonder if they appreciate their good fortune.

Not long afterwards of course came the outbreak of the First World War, and with it a change in *Fox's* tasks. The ship was soon ordered south to the East African coast to assist in action against the German colonies and at the end of 1914 took part in the bombardment of Dar es Salaam, now in Tanzania and then the main port of German East Africa.

The Acting-Governor of the province was invited onboard *Fox* before the attack and asked to surrender the port. He replied reasonably enough that he must consult his military colleagues first and went ashore to do so. Meanwhile flags of truce were hoisted everywhere. During this lull the senior officer of the British force went into the harbour in *Fox's* steam cutter to inspect a sunken floating dock.

White flags were still flying everywhere but suddenly and without warning fire was opened on the cutter from both sides of the harbour, wounding the coxswain, the stoker and another seaman. My Father quickly took over the stokehold and kept steam up for which he was later awarded a DSC; other members of the crew were also decorated. His family in later years, without in any way wishing to belittle his decoration, did use to point out that the stokehold, despite the stoker having been wounded there in the initial attack, could not have been too bad a place, being to some degree protected by makeshift armour plates.

The German military rejected the idea of a surrender and the port and harbour were bombarded two days later, being by then apparently cleared of inhabitants. It did not surrender until 1916.

As for the old *Fox*, she returned to Bombay at the end of 1914 to refit. The Superintendant of the Dockyard gave it as his opinion that she was not worth the work. *Fox's* captain however had other ideas. Either way my Father came home and was appointed to the new cruiser *Caroline*, again as Navigator.

Chapter 4

The Grand Fleet – 1916

Caroline was a complete contrast to the old *Fox*. Built in 1914, she was an oil-burner with the new Parsons steam turbines giving her a speed of 27 knots. Her construction reflected recent advances in ship design. In particular her armour formed an integral part of the hull structure instead of merely being bolted on afterwards, almost as an afterthought, and this contributed to a sizable saving in weight. In 1916 she was one of four ships in the 4th Light Cruiser Squadron and as such took part in the Battle of Jutland.

The notes which follow were written by my Father while on passage back to Scapa Flow the day after the battle. I have to admit that they may add little to the many other and often more detailed accounts of the battle. And yet . . .

Was Jutland really a missed opportunity for the Grand Fleet? A major naval engagement in the North Sea had been almost inevitable at some time during the War given that Germany had recognised in the early years of the century how quickly and effectively Great Britain could be crippled in any future conflict if she should once lose command of the sea; and in those days it was still the battle-fleet which was decisive in this respect. Mindful of this she had embarked well before 1914 on an ambitious capital ship building programme. Who can doubt the direction of the course which she had set?

With the declaration of war there had been several engagements in the southern half of the North Sea, in particular the battles of Dogger Bank and Heligoland Bight in 1915, in both of which Admiral Beatty's battle-cruiser squadron of the British Grand Fleet gave a good account of itself with its new ships. And in April 1916 a sizable German force including four or five battle-cruisers attempted to bombard Lowestoft and Yarmouth. They had some success. The Grand Fleet put to sea from its bases at Scapa Flow and Rosyth but Admiralty indecision over passing on intelligence warning of the raid had delayed their sailing and a strong southerly gale slowed their dash southwards. Nevertheless the tactics and determination of the British Harwich Force consisting of no more than a squadron of light cruisers and a handful of destroyers limited the extent of the raid. The British did seem to have the edge if battle could once be joined.

The Germans however might be forgiven for believing that a major fleet battle would not necessarily be to their advantage. Despite their best shipbuilding efforts over the past few years their High Seas Fleet was still not sufficiently strong to guarantee breaking the British command of the sea. On the other hand by continuing their previous harassing tactics, perhaps on a larger scale, and by emphasising the threat of 'a fleet in being' they could ensure that the British had to keep some 60,000 men on the opposite side of the North Sea permanently watchful. To the British, who felt that they had the measure of the German fleet, it was intensely irritating. When on 30 May 1916 the Admiralty received intelligence that a sizable proportion of the High Seas Fleet was preparing for sea, it seemed that there might be the best chance yet of tilting the balance of power decisively in our favour.

By midnight that night the Grand Fleet had slipped its moorings at Scapa Flow and Rosyth and was steaming south-east towards the German coast. The fishermen in *Caroline* who had been planning an evening's fishing in the lochs around the Flow had had to change their plans.

Notes written on 1 June 1916 on board HMS Caroline of the 4th Light Cruiser Squadron after the battle of Jutland

Monday 29 May	a.m. we had General Drills. Placed second in most of them. Directly they were over pushed across to the North Shore and anchored. Made Emergency Ship. Great grief as all the fishermen had been counting on a day off and had been preparing flies for Loch Kibister. Firings. Pistol and Jap rifle after Quarters. Too light to have a Night Defence run.
Tuesday 30 May	Dummy loading exercises with torpedoes in the new boxes all forenoon. Phillips on board to lunch. Underway after lunch doing torpedo runs. Four torpedoes fired quite successfully. Then swung for compass deviation. Preparatory signal for leaving harbour. Just our d . . . d luck. Went back and anchored. Signal to us to have steam for 20

knots at 9.30. Rush to get dinner and things ready for sea trip.

Weighed anchor and to sea with fleet passing out at 10.0 p.m. Just outside the boom the telemotor steering gear went adrift and we had a great time.

I was sent below to the Engine Room while we were leaving the Flow and came up to find us in a mist having lost sight of the others ahead.

However Skerries light was in sight still, so we eventually picked up the rest of the Squadron an hour or so later.

Seems we're out for a large combined operation, ourselves to be in the van and to go right up into all the fun.

We (the Owner and I) spent an hour or so marking off positions etc.

A very poor caulk in the charthouse.

Wednesday 31 May — The courses we make good don't seem to tally with the scheme – nor do the times, added to which we went out in a hurry last night so the question is, 'What is in the wind? Is it this Scheme or not?' Spent the afternoon with Malden looking into steering communications.

About 2.30 p.m. an Enemy Report comes in from 1st Light Cruiser Squadron – 'One enemy cruiser' then 'A large amount of smoke etc.'.

Then messages came rolling in from 3rd LCS, Senior Officer, Battle-Cruiser force, and 1st LCS.

We seem to have sighted the German Battle-Cruiser Fleet with attendant light cruisers.

At 4.45 Beatty reports German Battle-Fleet bearing SE.

At 4.51 the 2nd LCS sights the enemy also. What ho!

We kept on our course, increasing speed gradually, a knot at a time. Then, faintly at first but growing stronger, came the sound of guns and firing. Our armoured cruisers are making a devil of a lot of smoke, belching out clouds of thick black rolling stuff.

Smoke appears on the horizon down on the starboard bow, where the noise of firing is coming from. We are at Action Stations now and have been for some time.

Loly had the afternoon. Relieved him for tea, then he came up and I had some. Then up again on Watch.

The smoke down to the southward grew into a squadron of light cruisers steaming hard towards us, firing as they came. The armoured cruisers are dropping back on the Battle-Fleet. Now occasionally one can see a flash right ahead. The armoured cruisers are firing occasional salvos. What at I don't quite know. It is difficult to gather quite what is happening. I haven't realized what is what.

Our Squadron now turns to all points of the compass. The Commodore doesn't seem exactly certain where he wants to get to.

There is a terrible mêlée of the 4th LCS, the armoured cruisers of the Battle-Fleet and the 2nd LCS, which was the squadron we saw coming up just now.

Some more ships are coming up from the southward. By this time one can see bunches of splashes falling short of the ships down to the south. These evidently come from the flashes ahead. Smoke covers everything. I've never seen the armoured cruisers make so much before and some of the coal burners among the light cruisers are making a good deal too. We are very busy on the upper bridge dodging ships and picking up station. Eventually we in the 4th LCS have gone hotfoot to the northern flank of the Battle-Fleet and we are there with several flotillas of destroyers. There is a small German cruiser stopped between the lines with great clouds of white smoke coming from her.

At this time, about 5.50 p.m., I have lost the run of the 2nd LCS and armoured cruisers and, taking a look around, notice that we are a thousand yards or so to the NNW of the battle-cruiser line which is steering easterly and firing. They are being fired at too by an enemy evidently away to the SSE. These must be the flashes I saw before.

Several 'overs' are falling around us and amongst the destroyers. One destroyer (belonging to a division steaming 500 yards or so on the offside of the battle-cruisers) is hit by one of the 'overs' and we can see smoke and steam coming from her amidships.

One battle-cruiser I see has smoke coming from the deck just abaft the foremost turret – a small fire. Loly says it is *Lion* (Beatty's Flagship). I haven't time myself to see which ship it is.

Three battle-cruisers swing down from ahead. I am wondering whether they are enemy or our own. They come and join up ahead of our battle-cruisers so they must be ours.

Suddenly a great cloud of white and then pink smoke goes up from one of these ships (one notices afterwards that it is the leading one), hangs in the air for three-quarters of a minute or less and disperses – there's not much noise. All one can see now are two bits sticking up in the water, red as a lobster. One thinks, 'Good Lord, they've all gone,' and turns back to the helm.

Just now the destroyer which was hit passes across to port with Not Under Control balls hoisted and small clouds of white smoke amidships. Then we do some weird turns, which put us pretty close to *King George V*. Looking at the Battle-Fleet they seem to have half-deployed or to be steering easterly with divisions disposed quarterly to starboard, ships astern. Some of the rear divisions are firing, I believe.

We have turned to the south and are in single line ahead at 25 knots. We just shaved the bows of *King George V* by an acid drop. I was told this afterwards.

I now remember noticing the armoured cruisers away on our port bow. Vague forms ahead of them I was told were the battle-cruisers. We were heading south-westerly now. On our starboard bow was a bright patch of sky and across this, like a brushful of Indian ink, was a screen of thick black smoke. I have a hazy notion of seeing masts over it but imagine it was only a suggestion.

(The Notes now continue at a more measured pace)

It felt just like entering a football field or an arena. There was our Battle-Fleet astern and tailing into the mist on the starboard quarter, the Germans in their smoke screen on the starboard bow, one battle-cruiser or armoured cruiser on the port bow.

About this time our four light cruisers in the 4th LCS were told to repel an attack of destroyers coming up from the south-west through the

German smoke screen and we moved in at high speed. *Caroline* was tail ship.

Again about this time to the south the shape of two large ships emerged from the mists along the horizon. The Captain and I peered at them intently. I thought they were German and he eventually agreed. So we signalled back to the Admiral of the 2nd Battleship Squadron who was astern of us asking permission to detach and investigate them, but he refused and the ships disappeared into the mist. From German records it transpired later that they were the two leading ships of the German Battle-Fleet. Had we been allowed to close, and the Admiral had closed also, they might have been brought to action and the day might have ended differently.

What must be taken into account however was that the German destroyers had discharged their torpedoes and the waters between the Germans and ourselves were alive with them, all hurrying towards us. Meanwhile the German Fleet had disappeared into the mist.

Looking round for a moment I saw a 'copperheaded fish' less than a hundred yards away streaking for our stern. My pre-considered evasive action in such circumstances was to 'comb' the track by turning the ship towards where the torpedo was coming from, which I did with full helm. At the speed at which we were going it worked and the 'fish' missed us. It was about at the end of its run as a matter of fact but it might have got our propellers.

It was of course midsummer and so light until about eight o'clock but now it was starting to get dark. There was no sign of the Germans. Our Battle-Fleet set course to the SSE at moderate speed, our destroyers following at some distance astern. The 4th LCS, with ourselves as tail ship still, was ahead of the Battle-Fleet. And so the night passed away. Everything was dark – no lights of course.

But there was just enough luminosity to see and sometime in the Middle Watch the ghostly black shape of a battleship loomed up a quarter of a mile or less away on our port side, again showing no lights. The Captain looked at her, apparently calmly. I, looking too, had to be calm as well but inside I was terrified. We were supposed to be five miles or so from any battleship. If she was British would she take us for a German and open fire? The seconds dragged away. Silence . . . silence! She drifted by . . . faded away. I do not suppose we shall ever know who she was but those few minutes were the most nerve-wracking of the whole affair.

As Navigator it had been quite difficult to keep a track of our twists and turns during the battle despite someone having kept a dead-reckoning plot for as long as he could. The latter did not help much; it just looked as though an ink-stained fly had wandered across the paper!

However we got a reference position for the Flagship during the night and that saved the situation. And we are now returning to Scapa, traversing the scene of yesterday's action with its many pitiful reminders.

The 'Caroline Notes' give I believe a quite vivid description of the part played by a squadron of light cruisers scouting and reporting ahead of the Battle-Fleet. And I have always been moved by the thought of the close juxtaposition of peace and war – one day the fishermen of Caroline were planning an evening's fly-fishing in the lochs around Scapa Flow and two days later, without crossing any dividing lines as it were, they were involved in the shock of the largest fleet action of modern times.

It may help in understanding the Notes to have some idea of the general pattern of the battle. The Notes describe the wanderings of Caroline's track as akin to the movement of an ink-stained fly, but the battle did have a pattern.

The Grand Fleet had put to sea at 10.0 p.m. on 30 May following intelligence passed on by the Admiralty that ships of the German High Seas Fleet were raising steam. At the time it was not known exctly how many of the latter were preparing to sail. Past experience suggested that it could well be just the German battle-cruiser force but this would still be quarry enough to bring out the whole of the Grand Fleet.

The main body under the Commander-in-Chief, Admiral Jellicoe, sailed from Scapa and Admiral Beatty with his battle-cruisers and a squadron of fast new battleships put to sea from Rosyth. It later became clear that, like the British, the Germans were not at first aware of how many of their adversaries they had triggered into action.

Beatty's ships were faster than the main body and Rosyth is closer to the German coast than Scapa Flow so Beatty had a lead on his Commander-in-Chief and the latter was still forty miles astern of him by the time that he came up with and started to engage the leading ships of the High Seas Fleet. These were the enemy battle-cruisers, a sizable force in themselves, and which Beatty took to be the only Germans at sea. It was just after 4.0 p.m. on 31 May.

The first engagement was costly for the British. Beatty's battle-cruisers were slightly faster than his battleship squadron and were first into action. In this opening round two of his battle-cruisers were sunk and his flagship *Lion* was badly damaged. However his battleships were not too far astern and were soon in action to redress the balance.

Visibility was not good that day but it was not long before Beatty saw emerging from the mist ahead the shape of the main body of the High Seas Fleet. This would have been the 4.45 p.m. sighting mentioned in the Notes.

Beatty, still engaging the enemy battle-cruisers, turned north towards Jellicoe both in order to avoid obliteration by the now much superior German force and in order to draw the latter towards the approaching Grand Fleet. The Germans did not apparently appreciate the situation into which they were being drawn.

The Notes describe the picture as seen from *Caroline* as Beatty approached from the southward, drawing the High Seas Fleet after him and continuing to engage the German battle-cruisers. The action then developed:

6.30 p.m.   Germans within range of the Grand Fleet. Admiral Jellicoe's flagship *Iron Duke* opens fire.

6.35   The German Admiral, Scheer, appreciating that he has come up with a much superior force, turns away and vanishes into the mist.

7.00   Scheer closes again.
Jellicoe has however achieved an excellent tactical position and the High Seas Fleet comes under concentrated fire.
Scheer retires again, ordering his destroyers and battle-cruisers to cover his retirement.
This was presumably when *Caroline* and the 4th LCS were ordered to drive off the German destroyers, which they did.

7.45   Beatty sights the Germans again but the light is now fading. Scheer once more turns away

It must have been about this time that *Caroline*, as mentioned in the Notes, sighted two large German warships and asked permission to close them, but was recalled by the Admiral of the 2nd Battleship Squadron.

As it was, Admiral Jellicoe had by this time achieved a prime objective by placing the Grand Fleet between the Germans and their base and this offered the promise of decisive action, if not that evening then certainly the next day.

However it would soon be quite dark and Jellicoe had always appreciated that a night action between fleets of this size was likely to be counter-productive: very difficult to tell friend from foe, even more difficult to aim accurately, and there was always going to be a real chance of damaging one's own ships as much as those of the enemy. Jellicoe had in any case lost contact with the Germans in the darkening murk and he decided therefore to stay covering their line of retreat, and to wait perforce for daylight.

A spirited action was however fought by the Grand Fleet destroyers in the early hours of the night in an attempt to prevent the Germans reaching safety, but Admiral Scheer managed to filter his ships through the British lines under cover of the darkness. At one time the two fleets were steaming so closely together that they became one huge mass though neither side appreciated this at the time. This was when *Caroline* sensed the darkened shape of the German battle-cruiser *Moltke* passing so close to her.

The Grand Fleet spent the next day patrolling off the German coast but by then the High Seas Fleet was well tucked up in harbour, and claiming a victory. Certainly they had had the fewer casualties, 2900 against 6900, and had sunk three battle-cruisers for the loss of one themselves and an old battleship. But their 'victory' had not altered the strategic position in the slightest, had not given them command of the sea and they had hardly fought an aggressive battle. The British were left disappointed and frustrated. They had started with a convincing majority in capital ships – 37 battleships and battle-cruisers to 27 – and were credited with 120 hits to the Germans 55. Clearly the British shells had been the less effective, a shortcoming that Jellicoe had earlier suspected was likely. But it was the battle-cruiser losses which were particularly worrying. Paradox-ically it was in this area that the Germans had probably profited from their earlier reverses at Dogger Bank and Heligoland, where they had had problems with 'flash' entering the magazines. They had had time before Jutland to correct design faults in this respect. The British on the other hand had been successful in these actions and the problems had been postponed to Jutland.

Apart from this the Jutland experience effectively torpedoed the argu-ment for the battle-cruiser. The design had found favour at the beginning of the century as an answer to the Japanese and Italian concept of more heavily armoured cruisers as commerce raiders. The theory was that the battle-cruiser, with less armour and rather less firepower than the battle-ship but more speed, would be powerful enough to outfight anything able to catch it and would itself be fast enough to outrun anything heavy enough to beat it.

The first two ships of the class had had a resounding success two years earlier. In November 1914 Admiral Craddock's cruiser squadron had been overwhelmed by Admiral Von Spee's ships at the battle of Coronel in the South Atlantic. The British at once dispatched the battle-cruisers *Invincible* and *Inflexible* to restore the situation. Despite being coal-burners they made a very fast passage and reached the Falkland Islands on 7 December. They were coaling in Port Stanley next day when Von Spee appeared off the islands to follow up his victory. Putting to sea at once the two battle-cruisers quickly brought Von Spee's four cruisers to action and sank each one without serious loss to themselves.

The British only ever built two more battle-cruisers after Jutland, *Renown* and *Repulse*. The latter was sunk by Japanese air attack off the east Malayan coast during the Second World War. *Renown* lived on happily into the succeeding chapters of this book.

HMS *Caroline* is still (1997) afloat, as Headquarters Ship to the Belfast division of the RNVR.

Chapter 5

A Return to Wester Ross

My Father was still in *Caroline* by Christmas 1916. The Grand Fleet was continuing to maintain a high degree of readiness from its Scottish bases but after Jutland there was rather more time for recreation for the Ships' Companies.

The letter which follows describes two days leave, which he managed to obtain whilst *Caroline* was at Invergordon, and which he and a messmate used to make an expedition over to the family's former holiday cottage, Carn Dearg, at Gairloch in Wester Ross. It always seems to me to reflect not only the joy at revisiting, in the middle of the uncertainties of war, a place of very happy memories, but also an awareness of his good fortune at surviving Jutland.

Carn Dearg means, I believe, Red Rock in Gaelic. To my father and his two brothers it had been an earthly heaven in the summers before he went to sea and up until his last previous visit in 1907. My grandfather had built the cottage, more a small house really, in the 1870s. Rumour had it that it had been something of a love-nest up until the time of his marriage. Either way he used to reminisce in later years of standing one evening at a window of the Gairloch Hotel looking out across the water to Carn Dearg. A fellow guest was gazing in the same direction, perhaps catching the last of the light towards Skye. After a while he turned to my grandfather and mused, 'I wonder what sort of an idiot built a house out there at the end of the world.'

Grandfather was an architect, practising in Leeds, so it was quite an expedition for the family to reach Carn Dearg. Sometimes they would go by train to Inverness, change there for Achnasheen at the head of Loch Maree and thence by horse-coach to Gairloch. Or they would take the steamer from Liverpool; or the *Claymore* from Greenock, or the paddle-steamer *Gael* from Oban. Normally they would land on the pier at Gairloch but on one memorable summer's evening the Captain of the Liverpool packet allowed himself to be persuaded to stop off at Carn Dearg and put the family ashore, baggage and all, onto the rocks below the house.

My Father's recollection was of a kindly and well-ordered community of fisherfolk and crofters with whom, rose-tinted memories notwithstanding, the family seemed to have established a mutually warm relationship. Most of the holidays there appear to have been taken up with the sea and the beach, simple in the extreme, messing about, fishing, sometimes 'helping' the proper fishermen with their boats. Sundays however were strictly observed.

There were three places of worship, all up at the head of the loch, some three miles away. Many of the church-goers used to come past Carn Dearg, some in carts, some walking in heavy boots, or barefoot and carrying their best shoes to save the leather. Besides the Established Church and the Free Kirk there was an open air meeting place in a grassy dell known as the Cow's Bed. The Corson family attended the Established Church and would be driven down there in the wagonette by Duncan or Sandy or Murdo. These three were staunch Free Kirk men and as the service at the Kirk was very much longer than the one at the Church the Corsons would have a long wait before they could set off home. Most Sundays the Minister being a kindly man would ask them over to the Manse until all were ready to return to Carn Dearg. They would be lucky to be back by tea-time.

Despite the long Sundays Carn Dearg was still a paradise. A chance to revisit it after nine years, in the middle of a long war and after the trauma of Jutland, was indeed a gift from heaven.

HMS Caroline
Invergordon,
15 December 1916

I've just had the most glorious time in all my life. Quite tophole, without a single hitch.

As you see, we're at Invergordon. One day, after a spin in a car ashore, I thought to myself, why not have a shot at Carn Dearg. So with another fellow, he and I wondered if we would get leave – thought we wouldn't – then thought we might as well try; and eventually somewhat fearful, we asked for the leave – and got it!

We figured out all the distances, arranged for the car, wired the hotel at Gairloch, worked out elaborate arrangements for telegrams to call us back if need be.

The anticipation was glorious. An RNVR man, insurance agent in private life, and I were the two going. Picture us landing in the early morning, only just getting light, slithering over frozen puddles, carrying a small suitcase each, and greatcoats. Snow on all the hills around. Quiet and calm with no wind. Clear as crystal.

It was a long wait for the train to Dingwall, a dreary ride and then at last we got to where the car was waiting. I have a leather coat, lined inside with camel fleece, which is for dirty weather on the Bridge at sea. This came in most handy. With this on, a comforter three times round one's neck, another greatcoat and two more rugs to keep the knees warm, well, who could want more.

We couldn't have chosen a more wonderful day. Freezing hard, quite still, a clear sky . . . and you could see for miles. It was a pretty run, going gradually up through fields and hedges, getting wilder and wilder as we went along. The road for the most part ran by the side of the railway and one knew all the names of the places from years back.

Gradually the moors took on a more and more familiar aspect, heather and bracken a lovely brown, all the pools frozen over, the lochs black and still, reflecting in a wonderful way the white hills around them. The snow on all the hills was down to about three hundred feet above us, so the road was quite clear and the country looked much as it does in summer, with sugar-icing on the higher slopes and the hilltops. It was really lovely, whizzing along the frozen road, up and down the little dips by the side of the loch with a vista of white peaks away and away in the distance . . . it was the dream of several years come true.

Then we started to freeze. One's feet became like ice. One began to feel shivery and lost all interest in the scenery as the familiar names went past.

At last, thank goodness, there it was – Achnasheen. We slowed up, turned down to the station and brought up alongside the Gairloch mail coach . . . same old name, McIver Coaching Office. It took one back ages. On the platform was the same old porter, John. I asked him, 'Good day. Do you remember Mr Corson?' 'What did ye say? . . . Mr Corrson was it? Och, yess indeed. Him that built Carn Dearg? Yess, yess. I mind him well. But he's not been here these tenn years,' and so on and so on. You can imagine it was meat and drink to me to see all this and hear it all again.

My pal, who's a most cheery soul, had made friends at once and we got the awful news that we were just at the limit; anywhere to the west

75

of us all whisky was prohibited. So we hastily got hold of a bottle from McIver's and asked them to disguise it as well as they could as though it were for a baby. Motto . . .'Be Prepared.' A hot drink had put new life into us and sent the warmth tingling into our toes . . . and so we proceeded.

Glen Docherty is really a most beautiful spot. I'd never realised what a lovely view it was from the top – right away down to Loch Maree at the end. The road was bad there, being repaired, but we clattered down, swung across a temporary wooden bridge at the bottom – the stone one was being rebuilt – and drew up with a flourish at the Kinlochewe Hotel.

It looked small and less imposing than of old but inside was clean, comfy and cosy. A fellow named Robertson has both it and the Loch Maree Hotel and runs them both. No one was staying there of course but they lit a fire and gave us some excellent broth and stewed venison. A pretty young girl waited on us but primly refused us red currant jelly . . .'No luxuries in wartime!' It was fine to see all the place again. Everything inside was clean and in good order. It may have been old-fashioned but it was very well kept.

While waiting for lunch, to get ourselves warm we went for a brisk run along the road and got into conversation with one of the natives, asking him questions about the place. He told us he worked for Kenneth Mackenzie. And then of course I asked the inevitable question, 'Would you know of Mr Corson of Carn Dearg?' With a ready grin he replied, 'Och, aye. I mind him well. Many's the dram I've had from your father at Carn Dearg.' This tickled my pal immensely. I didn't know who the fellow was. He wasn't one of our well-known people, at least not one that I knew.

After lunch on we went. Ben Slioch on the other side of the loch was grand with its snow-covered cap. A faint curl of smoke, blue smoke, from one of the cottages at Lord Ronaldshay's place, just completed the picture.

We stopped at the Loch Maree Hotel and ordered our lunch for the following day from a red-haired young woman who appeared to be in charge of the whole place. The *Mabel*, that little steamer on the loch, was hauled up on a bank close by the hotel. She hasn't been running for two years they say. The loch was awfully pretty with not a breath of wind to ruffle its surface. The islands and the trees on them were reflected in an unbroken mirror. It was just gently laplapping on the shore as it always used to as we drove along amongst the silver birches about the road.

Then away up and to the foot of the rise which goes over to Gairloch. The postbox on the roadside for the mail to Letterewe amused my pal immensely. 'Letterewe Letterbox' is painted on it! Climbing the hill Bad na Scalloch looked cold and bleak and the smaller loch this side of it was frozen over. A flash down the road, past the Kerry Falls, fairly full and looking very fine, and then before we knew it we were by the Shieldaig road and Kerrysdale House.

So far there had not been a drop of rain or snow but now a light drizzle came on and we put the car's hood up. A few minutes later we reached the Post Office where we asked for any telegrams. Thank goodness there weren't any!! Then it was down past the pier, where the steamer was in, past the Kirk, down the hill and we drew up at the door of the Gairloch Hotel.

And here was Miss Haig. I didn't remember her then – at least only very faintly – but she soon placed us and made us comfortable in a little room along to the left rendered hideous by pictures of Gladstone, Disraeli, Bright and two or three huge religious subjects. It was about three-thirty and getting dark so we ordered dinner and fires in the bedrooms.

Here we are at last after nine years, years of looking forward to seeing the place again. Out on the point you could just see the outline of Carn Dearg. The cottages in Strath were just grey blobs against the black. It was very, very pretty but there was a faint feeling that it should be prettier. I couldn't find the reason at the time but found it later on next morning. Of course the hotel was empty, and the furnishings were atrocious. I remember I always disliked them.

Well, we strolled down to the pier. I called at the Burgesses' house but was told he was down at the pier. So down we went. The *Claymore* was in. She and the pier were very much smaller than one had imagined, but no Mr Burgess. Later on I heard that he was dead. On the pier we met another fellow, the 'Coast Watcher', who claimed to have known me and you . . . he asked after you particularly, but his name I had forgotten.

And so back to the hotel for a cup of tea and a stroll to Strath. Past Auchtercairn, the 'Polis' station, across the wooden bridge that always echoed so nicely as the horses clopped over it with the wagonette behind. And then I tried to find 'Ross the Tailor's' shop. It was quite dark and one couldn't read any signs or see anything. Eventually I knocked at a door and someone came along and wanted to know who or what we were. I think he took us for something to do with the Excise. However from him we learnt that Ross was dead and his shop 'was not'.

So we strolled on in the dark, came to Macintyre's shop, or where we thought it was and knocked at the Post Office enquiring for any telegram. The light inside was at once put out and someone appeared a few doors down the street. We asked our question but getting, 'No. Nothing for ye,' we asked for the Macintyre family . . . how were they getting on. Apparently they were rather decimated. Father and mother dead and a son killed at Jutland. Forgive me if this is all stale news to you. I believe much of it is.

This good girl who was talking to me was almost half-doited (really half of them up here seem half-doited). She was a Ross, sister of the man who came and tutored us at Carn Dearg once upon a time. I didn't remember her but she recalled it that way.

Then we were taken to see the Macintyres. One brother had been out at the Front, had been wounded and is back, looking after the shop. A sister is a school teacher. These two were so lugubrious over their family affairs that we thought we had had enough for one evening and wandered back to the hotel. Miss Haig gave us a very good dinner, and we retired to rest, personally in an enormous four-poster bed with a hot bottle and a fire.

Next day my pal was somewhat lazy and stayed in bed until well after nine. I got up, had a chilly sort of bath, a very good breakfast – porridge made in the inimitable fashion which one only gets at Gairloch . . . fresh whiting, etc. Then, taking the car I went out to Carn Dearg. Passing Duncan's house I went and knocked on the door but someone inside was intoning prayers with great noise and in quite good voice. I thought it tactful to retire and try again later, so I went on.

The March Dyke was open, hung on one hinge only but the wall had been reinforced with a wire fence all up along it. Past the Far Corner, past the Near Corner and there we were, the car and me.

As to the house, they've added to the porch on the sea side and taken away the small bit of verandah at the side of it. They've made a clean sweep of the larder, built a porch to the kitchen door and a small string of wash-houses, sculleries and stores over the ground where the larder used to be. There are several little outhouses at the back, granite-built but to me at any rate they look horrible excrescences.

Up the hill, the high side of the garden has been enclosed by a well-built high wall and the rest has a high and solid wooden fencing all around it. The big reservoir is empty of water but partially filled with grass, stones, heather, etc. The small one seems to be in use with a good cover. The trees are well and strong . . . not very many of them, but coming on. The shrubs round the house and the two patches of grass and heather near the front and back haven't been touched. The wall along the front is just as it used to be. They've put a light wire-and-wood fence on the path to the well, and stones along the path so that you can keep dry feet.

Down at the stables nothing has changed. They've got three boats in the coach-house . . . no carriage and the stable's full of coal, wood and cement. A few slates are falling off at the back giving rather a forlorn look generally. I didn't get inside the house at all but I'm told they've divided up our long room across the centre and laid a system of waterpipes around the house.

As for the prospect, the view is too lovely to describe. I said there was something wanting in the general effect when we first arrived. Now one could see it. I had quite forgotten how perfectly beautiful the loch could be from this end. It had the sort of effect of someone bashful and quiet saying, 'Yes, I know I'm good-looking if you take the right way but it isn't for me to push myself under your notice.' Just to see the colours. If ever it was lovely in summer I think you could hardly beat it in winter. Calm . . . calm . . . not a breath to ruffle the glass-like surface. Everything so wonderfully reflected that you think it must be a picture. The browns of the lower hillsides merging into pure white snow-caps. Buish Benn dominating the whole corner, watching his reflection in the water below. The hotel and Kirk just grey spots against the general dark brown with glimpses of snowy pinnacles, just looking round the corners of the nearer hills. It was too lovely for words.

Then round to the right, far away across Port Henderson, the Applecross hills look like white sugar-loafs, continued the sweep of the Cuchullins, past Rona and its white lighthouse in the foreground and on to the rounded lump of the Quiraing. Between Longa and the Sand shore, where we used to watch the sunset from the hill by the stables, the Shiant Isles showed up dark against the pinnacled masses of the Hebrides.

On this winter's day I felt I'd never seen a view round England or Scotland to equal it. It was magnificent . . . it was more than that . . . much more, but what words can convey it? It was many times more fine than in the summer. It was perhaps the contrast between the dark, sombre brown of the lower hills and loch against the calm white of the hills and the islands far away – not a boat or a sign of life in the loch. One steamer away out at sea and two drifters fishing miles away. (And now having rhapsodised about the view I have just put a match in my waste paper basket and nearly had a big fire. I had to empty waterjugs and flood the cabin.) However, back to Gairloch.

The next call on the way back was to Duncan's house. And there I met quite a gathering. There was Duncan himself and Osgood, an Exciseman, and an old widow, Mrs Someone, and another old fellow. Duncan was quite old and white-haired, probably not as old as he looked though. Everyone was slightly embarrassed and shy to start with. Duncan asked after you and Father and Frederick, Aunt Jean and Douglas. I felt that he was really pleased to see someone of us and Osgood too. He had his wits about him. I'd almost forgotten him. They were all very anxious to know, 'An' how is Mistress Corrson . . . Is she keeping well? That's gude. An' where is she stopping now?' When one mentions the Macintyres, 'Yess. Yess. They've had a lot of bad luck in that family. Mistress Macintyre is . . . gone . . . an' Mister Macintyre . . . an' the son too . . . ye heearrd he was in the Navy no doubt . . . He wass killed in the Arrdent . . . that was hiss boat. He iss gone too.' 'Bonny Sandy? Och, he is in Sand. Alec Bain that was. Ye mind him now?'

Then on the way back on the hill up by the schoolhouse I came across my pal talking to another old fellow who turned out to be the driver of the coach. His name escapes me but he had a special message for you. He wanted to be remembered. Took us out to Auchtercairn, which is his house and farm apparently; gave us milk and cake and made us promise to go and stay with him when we should come up for the fishing 'after the Warr is over'. We also met his wife, a plump good-looking lady, very capable and self-possessed.

All things come to an end and at last we had to go. Had lunch at Loch Maree, stopped to say goodbye to John the Porter at Achnasheen and had a non-stop run home. It was a glorious trip – not a hitch anywhere.

And then in the evening the owner, our Captain, and his Missus gave a very cheery dinner party and as Mr Pepys used to say, 'All was merrie.'

Chapter 6

Between the Wars

My Father's letter of 1916 about his trip to Gairloch was the last in the collection which my grandmother kept. In 1921 however he was appointed Navigator of the battle-cruiser *Renown* for the world tour by the Prince of Wales aimed at bringing the country's thanks to the members of the Empire who had supported the allied cause during the War. He never spoke much about this time in later years except to warn me some forty years on of a rocky patch in the entrance to Hong Kong harbour which the great ship had apparently narrowly missed on its visit there. As Navigator he evidently felt that he bore the responsibility for the near-disaster as for many years after he had recurring nightmares of the moment and to the end of his life there remained in our house a large-scale Admiralty chart of the harbour with the patch circled in red.

The Royal party was evidently unaware of the close shave as he afterwards went as Navigator of the Royal Yacht *Victoria and Albert*. This was a four year stint, no doubt enjoyable at the time but tending to be held against him afterwards when it came to getting a command of his own.

To his family he was sometimes apt to wonder whether an incident in the Yacht might not have contributed to Their Lordships' reluctance on this score. The custom was that when the Sovereign, King George V, came onboard the officers would be fallen in by the gangway as a formal welcoming party. His Majesty would pass slowly down the line, perhaps giving a few words here and there. He would know most of the officers quite well, being averse to too many changes amongst them.

The strict rule was that you did not speak unless you were spoken to. On one such occasion the King stopped in front of my Father, whom he knew better than most because of the time he used to spend on the Bridge at sea whilst my Father was 'navigating'. He seemed to be about to speak, but the seconds passed and no word came. My Father began to feel that although protocol demanded silence on his part, politeness suggested otherwise. He said, 'Good morning, Sir.' The King gave him a withering look and passed on. The Admiral, Royal Yachts, was furious and my Father saw all hope of later joining the Board of Admiralty disappear in an instant.

Another source however, whilst not discounting this vignette, describes His Majesty's influence as more helpful. The King took a considerable interest in the Royal Navy and the twice-yearly lists of those selected for promotion to Commander and Captain were always shown to him before publication. Towards the end of my Father's time in the Yacht His Majesty noted that his Navigator's name was once again absent from the Captain's List. A terse message was quickly on its way to the Second Sea Lord voicing, so I understand, the Sovereign's concern and deep displeasure that Their Lordships should apparently be prepared to appoint as Navigator of his Yacht an officer in whom they did not seem to have sufficient confidence to promote to Captain.

My Father did eventually leave the *Victoria and Albert* as a Captain, but the only command he was allowed was a small sloop, HMS *Heliotrope*, back in the West Indies. That was better than nothing in those days after the Washington Treaty of 1921 which severely limited the size of the navies of the Great Powers; and it appears to have had its lighter moments.

The Station extended in the north up to Canada. On one visit there the ship put in to St John's, New Brunswick, on the Bay of Fundy. The tides there achieve an almost unrivalled difference in height between high and low water, some fifty feet I believe. Presumably the *Heliotrope*rs knew about this but maybe not all of them could at once come to terms with what it meant for a ship berthed alongside a jetty. At all events, on the first evening there the Captain and all of the officers except the Officer of the Day went ashore for some official 'do'. They left the ship with apparently sufficient slack in the warps to allow for the change in tidal levels. On return however they found the wharf empty of any sign of their ship. Greatly concerned they rushed to the jetty's edge and looking over found there the *Heliotrope*, deserted by the tide and hanging almost in mid-air, suspended by her mooring wires.

Returning south after this novel experience *Heliotrope* called at Savannah, or maybe Charleston – I cannot remember which. The American Civil War had been over for sixty years but memories are long in those parts. Southern hospitality remembered that Great Britain had tended to favour the South in that struggle and both sailors and officers were made particularly welcome. One memorable dinner party ended up with everyone round the piano. After the favourite Southern songs were exhausted there was the inevitable 'Well, Captain, how about something from England?' In his bath my Father could be quite tuneful but on this occasion his mind went, predictably, blank; until, that is, he quite suddenly came to and found himself well into that marching song of the Yankees, 'bring the good old bugle, boys . . . we'll play it as we used to from Atlanta to the sea . . .' He also found that the rest of the party had fallen very silent. 'The Battle Hymn of the Republic' might have been worse, but not much.

He had one further command at sea as a Captain, the Fleet Repair Ship *Resource* in the Mediterranean Fleet. With a designation like that it was perhaps not surprising that she was nick-named 'Despair Ship *Resource*'. In fact with all that technical skill on board she often came in extremely handy and seldom more so than in 1934 when an earthquake destroyed the Church and most of the town of Hierissos in Greece. *Resource* was sent there to help and spent a week assisting wherever needed. Eventually the Greek authorities took over responsibility for disaster relief and the ship was just weighing anchor to return to Malta when a boat was seen putting out from shore. A ladder was quickly lowered and a deputation from the town, led by the school-master, climbed up onto the quarterdeck bringing with them the bell from the ruined church. A number of the hands were swiftly mustered and a short religious service was held at which the bell was formally presented to *Resource* as a representative of the Royal Navy and in recognition of the help that had been given. The shipwrights made a small belfry for it and the bell was installed on the quarterdeck for the rest of the ship's time in service. When she evntually ended her life after the Second World War my Father obtained Admiralty permission to take possession of the bell and it was re-hung in a tiny belfry in our home.

After *Resource* another commission in the Mediterranean followed as Captain of the shore base, the splendidly fortified and preserved Fort St Angelo overlooking Grand Harbour, Valetta. St Angelo had a ghost which my mother swore she saw. Even apart from the ghost it was full of memories for us children. Most vividly I recall a hot summer's night when my brother and I were sleeping on the balcony to the house to catch any breeze that was going. There was a full moon and for some reason I woke about midnight to see there below me two aircraft-carriers coming in between the breakwaters into Grand Harbour. They made no sound and apart from their navigation lights seemed to be totally blacked out. They might have been ghosts themselves for all the signs of life onboard. Slowly they came up to mooring buoys in Bighi Bay and made fast. It was the most impressive and beautiful sight I had ever seen.

HMS *Hood*, the 'mighty *Hood*', the largest and fastest warship afloat at the time, was part of the Mediterranean Fleet. Our former Nanny, an

East-ender from London and one of the best women I ever knew, had married into the Navy. Her husband was now a Chief Petty Officer and Captain of the Foc'sle on board *Hood*. As such he would have been one up on the Roman centurion of biblical fame: when he said to one, 'Come', he would not only come but would do so at the double. What more natural than that he, when in harbour, and his wife should lodge in a spare room at St Angelo. What more natural too that my younger brother, who still worshipped our one-time Nanny, as we both did, should see her husband as a rival for his affections. One day he made a plan to remedy the situation.

We shared a tiny dinghy, the *Titmouse*, and one afternoon my brother persuaded Stan to come for a row. Well out into the Grand Harbour he pointed out to his passenger that his weight in the stern was causing a certain amount of water to lap in over the transom. Spying a handy buoy he suggested that Stan might care to perch on the buoy while he himself baled out. With the Captain of the Foc'sle, HMS *Hood*, thus firmly marooned he then rowed smartly home to enjoy, as he thought, the affections of his beloved. He would have been about ten at the time.

A year or two later my Father reached the top of the Captain's list and retired just as the Second World War began. Unable for some time to get back into the Navy he spent the months after Dunkirk at home in Dorset raising the Marshwood Vale platoon of the Home Guard. It was an interesting sidelight on those times, when many of us were borne up by the 'Dunkirk spirit', that this latter enthusiasm appeared to have passed clean over the heads of the good farmers of the Vale. Many an evening my Father would come home spitting blood at the recollection of some neighbour who had given it as his opinion that 'Hitler couldn't be worse than this lot.' I suppose farming really had been at a pretty low ebb throughout the 1930s and the countryside did show it. However, with the sterling support of a Yorkshireman, an ex-soldier settled and farming in the Vale, a platoon was duly raised, and imbued with a martial spirit as well as a measure of efficiency.

By 1941 my Father was back in uniform and in 1943 went out to Bombay where we met briefly as I describe later.

Meanwhile as the Marshwood Vale platoon continued for some time to have a nautical flavour it may perhaps be permissible to remain with them for a few more lines. My Father was in fact succeeded by an ex-Indian Army colonel but he did not stay long with us and we were soon being asked to welcome a full Admiral as our platoon commander.

Admiral Sir Dudley North had been Flag Officer, Gibraltar, at the time when those ships of the French Navy which had not elected to join the British had broken out of the Mediterranean. Mr Churchill was so furious at their escape that he ordered that at least one head should roll; and it was Admiral North's bad luck that it should have been his. We and his other friends thought this grossly unfair. After all he had had no resources with which he could have stopped the French. However, Gibraltar's loss was Marshwood Vale's gain and Admiral North became a well-respected platoon commander.

I treasure particularly the memory of one Sunday morning parade. The Admiral was reading out the orders for a battalion exercise the following weekend. Paragraphs 1 to 8 went smoothly enough; we knew the patter by now – start time, rendezvous, blank ammunition only and so on. The Admiral came to paragraph 9: 'POWs will not be taken.' He stopped and looked at us over the top of his reading glasses. 'POWs will not be taken,' he repeated. 'H'mm, anyone got a POW?' We shifted uneasily from our reveries, consulted our neighbours, drawn up by now in the straightest of disciplined lines. 'Have 'ee got a POW then, George?' 'Naow, oi don't think oi've seen much o' they this year, Will. 'Tis been a bit wet, see.' 'Oh well,' said the Platoon Commander, sensing that further discussion of so vital and interesting a subject could well take up most of the rest of the parade, 'Look, I'm not bringing my POW. I suggest none of you bring yours either.' The Germans would have had a difficult time with us.

PART TWO

Chapter 1

Another Beginning

It was 12 January 1944 and I had been wandering round Euston Station for what seemed like hours before I finally met up with Clover. Collier lived in Scotland, so we would meet him when we reached Glasgow.

All three of us were newly-promoted Midshipmen, directed by the Lords Commissioners of the Admiralty to join the old cruiser HMS *Hawkins* in the Eastern Fleet based on Ceylon. Collier and I were just nineteen, so-called 'Special Entry' Midshipmen, not really as special as it might sound as we had entered the Royal Navy as Cadets only the previous year and had had no more than eight months' training before passing out. Clover on the other hand was a 14-year-old entry and had spent four years at the Royal Naval College, Dartmouth. Most of the four years had been taken up with general education, so, as we were quick to point out to him, it did not guarantee a greater understanding of naval affairs than we had ourselves. It was just that he had been dazzled by gold braid and buttons with anchors on them at an earlier age than we had.

For virtually the whole of Clover's time at Dartmouth the College had been evacuated to Cheshire to avoid the German bombs, though whether it was any safer up there than in Devon was questionable given the damage that Liverpool suffered. The Admiralty had taken over the Duke of Westminster's country seat at Eaton Hall and the 'Special Entry' Cadets were encamped there as well in a shanty town of Nissen huts which, to distinguish it from a mere gypsy gathering, was named HMS *Frobisher*. The inmates such as Collier and I, being presumed to be more worldly than the schoolboys next door, were kept well away from the latter lest we proved a corrupting influence.

We were a relatively happy little community and I found that naval life promised to be little different from what I had imagined as a result of my early contact with it in Malta before the War. At Eaton Hall we were chased around, lectured and advised by a coterie of old sea-dogs. There was Chief Yeoman of Signals Troon. One could imagine him ever at the Admiral's elbow along with the Flag Lieutenant, Admiralty Signal Book always half-open ready to broadcast the Admiral's orders to the Fleet with a mastful of flags or a quick burst of flashes on the signal lantern. Our time with him centred round a wonderful toy called the Tufnell Box. Inside was a beautiful collection of toy flags, all the flags in the Signal Book in fact, and two toy masts on which they could be hoisted. The Chief Yeoman would take the part of the Admiral and we would signal backwards and forwards to each other through the masts. No one ever went so far over the line as to hoist 'England expects . . .'.

Rather noisier was our Gunnery Instructor, Chief Gunner's Mate Bollen. He had I remember some ancient gun mounting on which we could be drilled and generally chased around but our main diet with him was of wall-charts and notes. It would have been tactless and unfeeling in those days to have even wondered why, if our gunnery systems were all so well thought out and efficient as we were told, *Bismarck* had managed so very quickly to sink 'the mighty *Hood*', and Japanese bombers to account for *Repulse* and *Prince of Wales*.

Then we had the hard men, our two Physical Training Instructors. It could have been thought rather excessive to have two; we weren't all that unfit. Chief Petty Officer Savage was a small bouncy man with a gravelly voice. He seemed to be perpetually springing up and down on his toes as though he had just made a good landing over a vaulting horse. As the ex-PTI of the aircraft-carrier *Ark Royal* his account of the poor ship's last moments when she had been sunk shortly beforehand became a *Frobisher* classic. 'The Captain and I were the last to leave the ship. We were on the port side of the flight deck as she settled in the water. I said to the Captain, "After you, Sir." "No, Savage," he replied, "After you." That was right you see. The Captain is always the last to leave.' Sergeant Jenkins, Royal Marines, was our other PTI. A man of steel himself, he looked for the same quality in us too; dare I say in many cases and certainly as far as I was concerned, without too much luck. However, as with all our instructors, those who asked his opinion on naval matters would get a considered answer. It might not be Admiralty pattern but would certainly be based on experience. One day someone wondered whether, if officers and ratings were playing in the same team and were having a drink afterwards with the opposition, it was the done thing for Wardroom and Sailors to use the same bar afterwards. The Sergeant's reply was vivid, memorable and uncomplicated!

We did have some engineering instruction as well, and could have done with a great deal more. The only piece which seemed to stick in the memory of most of us was the difference between a male and female coupling.

Eaton Hall stood on a slight rise above the River Dee, and of course any handy piece of water had to have boats on it. *Frobisher* boasted an assortment of dinghies and whalers, and a motor cutter with a duty crew of cadets would run down the Dee to Chester at weekends for 'Liberty-men'. The service was hardly competitive with the local bus but on a sunny afternoon it had its attractions and of course it was great fun for the crew.

But the point of having boats was not so that we could have fun messing about on the water. At sea in the Fleet boats were an integral part of life. Very often you could not get ashore except by boat. Not quite so often but certainly from time to time there was a call for boatwork out at sea. And who was going to run the boats but the Midshipmen? Us, one step up the ladder. And then of course there was the dreaded subject of 'Power of Command'. What better way of teaching and improving power of command than in a sizable boat in unpleasant conditions? And finally as far as the Seaman, or Executive Branch cadets as they were known in those days, were concerned boatwork was thought to be a sensible bottom rung on the ladder which would lead eventually to command of a proper ship. Quite reasonably we were not encouraged to think of all the Snakes in the game.

Conditions on the dear old dozy Dee were much too comfortable and undemanding to give the training which our tutors sought, but the ocean of the Mersey lay conveniently to hand and there we went every so often for a workout. There the RNC had its thirty-two foot cutters, leviathans of boats, six oars aside when pulling and a single enormous mainsail, and foresail, when under canvas. So to the Mersey we used to go; much too often for me. I could sail and handle the boats, dare I say it, quite adequately and could do my bit with an oar when needed. The wind dropped on one occasion when we were a short distance down-tide from our mooring so it was 'Out oars and pull'. We pulled hard for an hour against a six-knot tide and at the end of the time had not moved an inch nearer our goal. My antipathy to the river was that with wind against tide, which happened not infrequently, it was only too usual for a lively chop to develop in which several of us would turn quite green. Matters improved not at all when we got ashore and sought the shelter of a 'hotel' nearby for our lunch of grisly pasties from the Eaton Hall kitchens. Rock Ferry was where we sailed. It was aptly named.

All that was behind us now and Clover and I caught the 9.30 night train to Glasgow where the three of us were to board some unknown ship which would take us to the Orient. The ship turned out to be a requisitioned passenger liner of I believe the Orient Steamship Company. We did not expect her to sail as soon as the three of us were onboard together with our tin trunks full of uniforms and tin hat boxes full of solar topees which we were never to wear. We did not anticipate either that the ship would be hanging around for a further two days before dropping down the Clyde and away to sea. In the meantime I had a bath, and this left an indelible impression on me. It was not that I was unused to bathing. Rather it was that the bath water which came I supposed from the Clyde was impenetrably brown, so dark in fact that one could not discern a toe at two inches. I got into it very gingerly, thinking that we were probably taking suction from some messy shipyard gutter, and was agreeably surprised to find that it was really quite sweet and soft. Dear old Clyde! It must have been peat water from the hills. It left not a stain on the bath or myself. I've never seen anything like it again.

So we sailed out into the Atlantic, bound first of all for the Mediterranean but making an enormous sweep to the west to confuse goodness knows whom. It was our understanding that the U-boat war had been won some many months previously. Anyway we passed Gibraltar eight days later and in another eight days had reached Suez, sixteen days out. It is perhaps an interesting reflection that during the Crimean War mail from England used to reach the Crimea in ten days.

What was life like onboard a troopship? In general quite unremarkable. I suppose there must have been some two thousand souls embarked. Conditions were a bit cramped but I cannot remember any unpleasantness or upsets. We had drafts from all three Services, women as well as men. The women of all ranks shared accommodation with the officers, or rather their quarters were contiguous. Liaisons developed, dissolved, reformed as on any lengthy sea voyage. It was amusing to see how ex-Dartmouth Midshipmen were in no way less forward than their *Frobisher* companions in chatting up the Wrens.

The time passed. Boat drills in the morning; some sort of lectures until lunch; and for the rest of the day: Bridge, Books, Conversation, Exercise or Sleep. Sixteen days to the Suez Canal. Arrival off Port Said at least provided some diversion but one had read so many descriptions of passage through the Canal that as a passenger it was novel, of great interest and a very welcome change from looking at nothing but water, but little more. Making the passage at night eighteen years later as Captain of a destroyer was a different kettle of fish. My main memory in 1944 was of how bitterly cold it was in Suez on a Monday night and how swelteringly hot in the Red Sea only twenty-four hours later.

It was another three days to Aden and on 13 February we reached Bombay, thirty days out. On the way into harbour we passed another, smaller, troopship coming out. The word soon got around: she was the ship that was supposed to take those of us for Ceylon down to Colombo. We had missed our connection.

From my own selfish point of view, and impatient as the three of us were to reach *Hawkins* particularly after such a long and dull voyage, this missed connection was not entirely intolerable. My Father was by then Deputy Director of Shipbuilding and Repairs (India) having managed at last to get back into the Navy, and was billeted in the Taj Mahal hotel. The hotel squeezed another bed into his room and we persuaded the Naval Movements organisation that it would be for the greater good if I were to stay there rather than in a transit camp. The three of us, Clover, Collier and I, managed to stay in touch and we settled down to wait.

We had to wait for three weeks. We saw a little of Bombay: great wealth alongside great poverty, fine parks and the edges of very undesirable slums. I doubt very much if the general spectrum of the condition of the population was very different then from what it is now. All the same at a distance of fifty years I must admit to being rather appalled at the lack of interest I seem to have taken in my surroundings during those three weeks. I suppose though that we were all impatient to see our journey's end.

As ever the good news came at last and we joined another troopship for the four-day passage down to Colombo. This one used to trade before the war between Aden, Bombay and Singapore and the cockroaches on board were the biggest I have ever seen. The occasional rat also made an appearance, sauntering quietly along the deck beams of our cabin. There were other attractions though. It was only a short voyage, the sea was calm and each evening from the First Class Promenade Deck we could watch and smell the Indian cooks on the foc'sle making and cooking the chippatis for the soldiers' supper. There was a large Indian Army contingent also onboard, bound for Ceylon. I never thought to ask what they would be doing there when the Japanese were a thousand miles to the east in Burma. Had I delved a little I would no doubt have found out that they were for internal security duties, an insurance not only against the possibility of Japanese-inspired subversion but also a bandage to the long-running sore of Tamil-Sinhalese hatred; and come to think of it I suppose they could also have been intended as some sort of calming influence against the heady breeze of nationalism already stirring in some quarters in India. How little one looked below the surface in those days. Again I suppose our thoughts were fixed firmly on *Hawkins* which we would be joining in a day or two.

It was not to be however. When we reached Colombo we found that *Hawkins* had given us the slip and had sailed a day or two earlier, destination of course undisclosed. We did begin to wonder whether we were regarded as quite so essential to the war effort as we ourselves had thought. Instead of joining our vintage cruiser we found ourselves shunted into a transit camp in the paddy fields outside Colombo.

The camp was not unattractive – *attap* huts built in the local style with thatched roofs and open-work sides were grouped around a stretch of levelled and gravelled earth. We spent five lazy weeks there, wondering why there seemed to be no room in the very sizable Eastern Fleet for three Midshipmen. The favourite occupation was swimming and surfing at Mount Lavinia, some three or four miles out on the other side of town. There did not appear to be much of a bus service so it was hitch-hiking both ways. This never seemed to be difficult and one thing I do remember was how pleasant and friendly the vast majority of the Ceylonese proved. We did wonder why all those troops whose evening meals had lightened our own evenings on the passage south from Bombay had also been sent to this charming country. I cannot say that it bothered us all that much though.

In the evenings I often used to explore through the paddy fields along the tiny dykes separating each stretch of cultivation and one full moon got as far as the local Buddhist temple at Kelanniya. It was an enchanting site, the rain and damp-streaked stonework set in the middle of what appeared to be good honest jungle, crowds of earnest worshippers swirling round the outside, stall-holders selling 'snacks' and charms, the whole scene lit by a brilliant moon and hundreds of tiny oil lamps. I kept well in the background and no-one seemed in the least put out at the presence and interest of a non-believer. In fact I found the same acceptance wherever one explored outside the camp. A large walking stick used to make everyone burst into laughter, and in returning their amusement I always felt rather safe.

Outside interest was essential as there was little enough to occupy one within the camp. A rat-snake penetrated my cabin one evening and led to a hunt which ended in a kill, whereupon the Ceylonese stewards gave me a severe lecture on the pointlessness of killing such a harmless creature. A more welcome visitor was an Australian bush-baby, a delightful furry animal rather like a koala, a sort of animated teddy bear. Its name was Oswald and its usual perch was up in the rafters over the Wardroom where it would retire with a banana. Thank goodness it was house-trained.

The Commander in charge of the camp was a character. An enormous man with a huge midriff, he had been in command of a Forward Fleet Repair Base on Addu Atoll, a tiny island at the southern end of the Maldive Islands. Quite why a 'Forward' Base should have been located well to the west of Ceylon when the Japanese were more than twice that distance to the east did take a little working out. A year or two earlier however it had not seemed so strange. Then the Japanese onslaught had appeared to have an unstoppable momentum. Carrier-borne aircraft from a force in the Bay of Bengal had bombed Colombo; and we had lost two 'County' class cruisers, *Dorsetshire* and *Cornwall*. East Africa might well have had to become our main base in the area: hence Addu Atoll's 'forward' status. A repair base was established there and manned by the Navy. Many of the sailors involved would be 'hostilities only' and the skilled artificers required could be expected to hold trade union cards. The legend was that one of the latter objected to working non-union hours and was hauled up before the Commander for refusal of duty. At the Commander's Table for defaulters he still refused duty, adding for good measure and no doubt with a smirk, 'And there's nothing that you or anyone else can do about it in this God-forsaken spot.' 'That's where you're wrong,' replied the Commander who thereupon pulled out a pistol and shot the man through the hand. After which he apparently never stopped working. An unlikely tale? Probably.

At last on 13 April, three months to the day since leaving Glasgow, we were told that we were to join the battleship *Valiant* at the Fleet's base at Trincomalee in the north-east of the island and we took the night train from Colombo complete with our tin trunks, tin hatboxes containing each a solar topee which we were never to wear, our green suitcases and, probably, a canvas hold-all each.

Chapter 2

Eastern Fleet

R ather to our surprise we found that *Valiant* was actually where she was supposed to be, moored in Malay Cove in Trincomalee Harbour. Trincomalee must be one of the great harbours of the world and in 1944 it was the base of the Eastern Fleet. There were three battleships, *Valiant* and *Queen Elizabeth*, both of the same class, and the Free French battleship *Richelieu*, the battle-cruiser *Renown*, which was my Father's old ship some twenty-two years earlier and now the Fleet Flagship, two aircraft carriers, *Illustrious* and the USS *Saratoga*, some six cruisers and enough destroyers to go round.

At the southern end of the harbour on a small promontory stood the naval headquarters. This was where many of the Wrens who had lightened the voyage from Glasgow for some were bound. Opposite, on the other side of the harbour, lay the Naval Air Station at China Bay, and near the harbour entrance below the bluff of Battenberg Hill was the small dockyard. The latter was much too small to be of significant use to so large a fleet but Colombo was round the corner. If they couldn't cope there, it was Durban. We never seemed to use Bombay – I don't know why.

Most of the larger ships had interesting histories but I am ashamed to say that at the time none of us had very much idea of their early stories, the present being more demanding. However we knew that *Valiant* had fought at Jutland and that during the present war she and *Queen Elizabeth* had been damaged by Italian frogmen at Alexandria. My Father had navigated *Renown* round the world on the Prince of Wales' tour as mentioned in Part I. As for *Richelieu* one could only wonder at the steadfastness of those seamen who had left country and families in order to continue the fight. They tended to keep themselves to themselves at the time. Little wonder! And then we had three Dutch destroyers, *Tromp*, *Van Galen* and *Tjerk Hiddes*, a more extrovert and hard-drinking lot.

In later years, in some cases much later, I came to know more of the histories of these ships. After the fall of France for instance, *Valiant* had had to take part in the distressing action off Oran in North Africa in July

HMS *Valiant* 1943: *Queen Elizabeth* similar

that year when the Royal Navy had been forced to fire on French ships who had escaped from Toulon but were refusing to join General de Gaulle.

Subsequent service was more to her taste. In November 1940 she was part of the force attacking Italian ships in Taranto harbour when 21 Swordfish torpedo bombers from *Illustrious* sank or very severely damaged three battleships and a heavy cruiser, a reverse from which Italian morale never fully recovered.

In March 1941 she and two other battleships, *Warspite* and *Barham*, came upon three Italian heavy cruisers at night off Cape Matapan and sank all three in two minutes. Half a century later the ruthlessness of this makes me shiver somewhat. At the time it was of course them or us.

In December 1941 the boot was anyway on the other foot. *Valiant* and *Queen Elizabeth* were mined by a team driving 'human torpedoes' and led by a Lieutenant de la Penne. Two years later Italy changed sides and de la Penne joined us against the Germans. In 1945 he was decorated by King Umberto and allied officers attended the ceremony at Taranto. The King of Italy was about to pin the medal on de la Penne when he realised that Admiral Morgan, Captain of *Valiant* when she was attacked, was present and suggested that he might like to make the award. He did.

Illustrious's pre-eminent action was of course Taranto. One wonders if the Japanese took the success there, along with the experience of their pre-emptive strike against the Russian Pacific Fleet before declaring war in 1904, as their model for Pearl Harbour.

That leaves *Richelieu*. In 1940 she had not completed building but was able to steam. Like many of the French ships which left France she did not at once opt to join de Gaulle but broke out of the Mediterranean to Dakar in French West Africa. She was one of the ships the escape of which so infuriated Mr Churchill that Admiral Sir Dudley North found himself moving from the post of Flag Officer, Gibraltar, to that of Platoon Commander, Marshwood Vale Platoon, Home Guard. Cornered in Dakar *Richelieu* eventually declared for the General and crossed the Atlantic to America where she completed fitting out in 1943.

In April 1944 it did not take long to settle in. Midshipmen did not aspire to anything so grand as even the tiniest cabin and made do with a chest in the Midshipmen's Chest Flat, a 'flat' being the generic name for any sort of space for which no one could think of a better title. Naturally our bathroom was anything but handy: through a watertight door, normally closed at sea; through a watertight hatch, normally closed at sea;

down into the depths on one side of the ship, up again on the other, all through watertight hatches normally closed at sea; through the Royal Marines' messdeck and finally down through another hatch to the *bathroom*. The Marines were traditionally housed between the sailors and the officers to protect the latter in case of mutiny. From the comments one heard as we Midshipmen in our bath towels passed through their messdeck I would have taken my luck with the mutineers.

There were three officers' messes, the Wardroom for the general run of officers, the Warrant Officers' mess, and the Gunroom for ourselves. Of these the Warrant Officers' was the best place for a party and a story. In the Gunroom there were fifteen or sixteen of us: three Canadians, half a dozen RN and the remainder RNVR or RNR. Nationality or background made no difference. The mess was presided over by the Sub-Lieutenant of the Gunroom and he, I seem to remember, had authority to use the cane if required!

After three months of hanging around we found life in the Eastern Fleet refreshingly brisk. We had only been onboard for two days when we were rounded up and allotted Action Stations and the whole Fleet began to prepare for putting to sea. In 1944 there was little or no threat from the Japanese in the Bay of Bengal or the Indian Ocean. All the action was in the Pacific and conducted almost entirely by the Americans. The strategy of the Eastern Fleet was to constitute a threat which the Japanese could not ignore and to force them to maintain forces west of Singapore which they could otherwise have deployed to the Pacific. At the same time the British and Indian Fourteenth Army was beginning to push the Japanese out of India and through Burma. It would have been unthinkable to have left their seaward flank wide open. So there we were, about to make a nuisance of ourselves, not very dangerous against the level of opposition expected, just something of a pot-boiler but exciting enough for three newly-joined Midshipmen.

Once at sea we learnt that we were off to bomb Japanese positions at Sabang on the northern tip of Sumatra. It took us three days steaming to get there, a novel and most satisfactory experience. In harbour we would spread our bedding, basically a hammock and some blankets, on a quiet corner of the quarterdeck out of the way of older officers walking up and down in the relative cool of the evening after dinner. Now, at sea we were either on watch or sleeping in the Gunroom, on the table, under the table, on the settees along the ship's side, anywhere where there was space. It all added to a satisfactory air of excitement and anticipation which was in no way lessened by the thought that there was virtually no danger of being sunk or even damaged.

I had an Action Station in the Air Defence Position above the Bridge where I was instructed to work various loud hailers. As no one ever listened to these as far as I could see when they were working, which did not seem to be very often, I felt that this task was probably going to be within my limited competence.

We took the Japanese by surprise at dawn on the fourth day. Bombers from our two carriers lumbered up off their decks and spotter planes encouraged us by reporting that the consequent explosions ashore seemed to be occurring in more or less the right spots. By breakfast time it was all over. We turned and headed back west at high speed rather like someone retiring from a hornet's nest which he hopes he has exterminated but which it could be tactless to treat as out of action for the moment. There was very little retaliation from Sabang but that night the anti-aircraft batteries of the battleships had a happy hour shooting at something or other. As a tiny cog in the machine and one whose expertise with a loud hailer was very much *de trop* after dark, I had no idea what was going on and so was receptive to rumours that in fact we had been shooting at each other. I was unwise enough to record this as fact in the Journal which as a Midshipman I was required to keep and this earned a very sharp retort from our Gunnery Officer who was 'Snotties' Nurse'. 'Quite untrue,' he wrote, 'We were attacked by Japanese aircraft. Learn to check your facts with very much more care.'

Either way the BBC was kind enough to announce the raid next morning by which time we were well out of range of the Japanese though not of course of each other. That made us all chirp up. Whether it worried Tokyo in the slightest was open to doubt. Most important of all, perhaps it cheered up the Australians and the Americans.

Two weeks later we were at sea again, this time to attack Java from the south. Once clear of the harbour the Captain opened his sealed orders and let us know that the whole Fleet was to steam down to Exmouth Gulf in north-west Australia where it would refuel and then move into position for air strikes against Surabaya. It was nine days steaming down to Australia, exercises and practices for the guns' crews all the way down, and for Midshipmen a tailor-made trip to practise star and sun sights. We had learnt the theory of these at Eaton Hall. I found it, based as it is on spherical trigonometry, difficult to comprehend and was only too pleased when at the end of a bruising session the Instructor Officer had said,

'Well, if you can't understand it, all you've got to do is to take care with the sextant which should not be beyond the wit of most of you, and then fill in your results on this form which the Admiralty provides. Look, it even tells you what to do next. You can't go wrong.' It was very encouraging. Most of our first results were quite the opposite. However, taking 'sights' passed the time most agreeably. For 'morning stars' one would have worked out which four or five heavenly bodies one was likely to see in those latitudes next morning given always a clearish sky which was not guaranteed. Next morning it would be just before twilight when one emerged from one's steel cocoon, chose a position where one might expect least disturbance from other bodies up early and settled down with deck watch and sextant. The sextant measured the altitude of your target body above the horizon. A mirror on a movable arm caught the reflection of the star and one moved the arm to bring the reflection down until it just kissed the horizon. As the arm was hinged about a graduated scale one could then read off the altitude of the star. One needed the exact time at which the altitude was taken, so, as soon as the reflection was satisfactorily mated with the horizon one started counting seconds, read the time from the deck watch, subtracted the seconds you had counted from the deck watch time, tried to remember all the figures and noted them down. Hopefully you would get three or four stars out of the five you had chosen the previous evening. You then sought peace and quiet somewhere to get out the Admiralty form, work down the columns to get a result, and plot this out to see how far away it put the ship from where you thought it was. By then breakfast in the Gunroom would be over and you would have the rest of the day to work out where you had gone wrong; and to prepare for an evening star sight. Never mind. The peace of the morning and the lovely light over the sea at dawn and dusk in the tropics made it all very pleasurable.

For most of the trip down to Exmouth Gulf the weather was not too bad and I managed to sling a hammock on the quarterdeck which was most agreeable. As we got further south the Pole Star at last dipped below the horizon and we began to see the Southern Cross, a romantic enough constellation but not in my view comparable with the spread of the Plough and Polaris. On the ninth morning the Fleet made the Australian coast and there waiting for us was a little gaggle of tankers with fuel. Did Captain Cook sight such a barren shore in Botany Bay? If he did it can surely not have given him much pleasure. It was as though the desert had run out of sand and had to make do with water instead. Much later the

101

son of a friend of mine was shipwrecked on an island not far from Exmouth Gulf. He could hardly have chosen a less alluring spot.

We spent no more than the daylight hours there and then put to sea again to close within striking distance of the Javanese coast.

The air strike from *Illustrious* and *Saratoga* apparently went just as planned. We never heard how it compared with our foray against Sabang the previous month. The Japanese did indeed mount a somewhat half-hearted response but none of their planes got anywhere near the Fleet. This time I followed the official line in my Journal. We were back in Trincomalee by the end of the month and the following week *Valiant* went round to Colombo to give everyone a few days' leave.

Two of us Midshipmen were guests of a rubber planter in the south of the island in the foothills near Galle and were given a bag of potatoes to take as a present to our host. It struck us as an odd gift but it was received more gratefully than several bottles of whisky. In fact the whisky shipments seemed to be getting through quite well as was only too apparent after evening visits to the local club, visits which as often as not ended up with our host calling me 'Mary' on the way home and trying to embrace me as well. His wife, poor woman, was proper embarrassed. As for me, being rather unwordly in those uncomplicated days, I just thought there had been rather too much entertainment that evening.

Next morning anyway was another day and quite early we would be making the rounds of the estate and the factory. I remember being struck by the latter where there seemed to be so much chatter and so little production. The workers all seemed chirpy enough but our host was evidently worried at the undercurrent of animosity between the mainly Tamil community and the few Sinhalese, and the beginnings of moves by the Tamils towards 'industrial action'. It tended to cast something of a sadness over that beautiful spot.

Back in Colombo I found that I had been put in charge of the ship's 45 ft launch and was thrown into the world of boat-running which had been so indelibly burned into our consciences at Eaton Hall. The launch was a huge vessel with a life saving capacity according to the Seamanship Manual Volume II of well over a hundred souls. Alternatively it could land a field gun if required. Its more normal use was for landing and bringing off libertymen and for shifting stores. It was built on the 'double-diagonal' principle. Instead of the planks of the hull running fore and aft and rising above each other like lines of tiles on a roof, much shorter planks were used, nailed and I think glued, diagonally across each other to form a double skin. Between the wooden skins a layer of heavy canvas was laid and the whole hull was built over a jig. Once it was removed from the latter it kept its shape and did not need any ribs. It was immensely strong, fairly light and impressively flexible. In contact wth a solid object such as a jetty or even a quarterdeck ladder the launch's hull would bow inwards slightly as though made of heavy rubber and the 'solid object' would as often as not take the knock. This was all right with jetties but was definitely unpopular with quarterdeck or other ladders.

The other speciality of the launch was that it was controlled by 'Kitchen' rudder gear, invented I always believed by a Mr Kitchen. Two hemispherical plates were mounted one on each side of the propeller. With the plates open to the rear, water from the propeller was forced out straight aft and the launch went ahead. With the cups moved so that their after edges touched the wash was deflected forward and the boat went astern. Thus the gear did away with the need for a reversing gearbox. Another cunning aspect was that the cups could also be angled so that the wash could be thrown out to one side or the other. This meant the stern could be moved from side to side whilst the boat could be held stationary fore and aft, and so the launch was immensely manoeuvrable. There was a price however. There were two control wheels at the steering position, both mounted on the same shaft. One controlled the cups for directional steering and the other for ahead/astern and sideways movement. If one got in a tangle coming alongside, not infrequent in my case, one could easily turn the boat more or less inside out, to the consequent merriment of the passengers and the silent but quite obvious satisfaction of one's Leading Seaman coxswain who was considerably more experienced and deft with the miraculous machine.

Thus running the launch was quite a sport, and that was without the libertymen. Taking them ashore was no problem. Everyone was sober and provided you did not fiddle round too long getting alongside the shore jetty, the Midshipman was in the clear. Bringing them offshore at 2200 was a different kettle of fish. The Shore Patrol would maintain a semblance of order on the jetty but once out in the darkness of the harbour you were on your own. Trincomalee was littered with anti-torpedo booms to foil for instance such torpedo attacks as had crippled *Valiant* and *Queen Elizabeth* not long before, and, whilst avoiding these, one still had to discourage too much falling about in the boat itself. A few songs and ribald laughter were not frowned upon in the black void between shore and ship. On approaching one's home stretch however the rules required that quiet and good order prevail. If not the Midshipman would get it in the neck from the Officer of the Watch and be directed to circle the ship until he had induced his passengers to pipe down. It was all good fun.

A favourite memory of that time was of one of our Canadians. He was running the motor cutter, a slightly smaller version of the launch. One dark night he broke down in the middle of Trincomalee harbour. Nothing served to galvanise the engine. The libertymen were becoming critical. However his signal lamp was still working and he called up the signal station on Battenburg Hill:

HULLO HULLO. FROM *VALIANT'S* MOTOR CUTTER.
I CANNOT GO. PLEASE INFORM *VALIANT*.

Quick as a flash came back the reply:

BAD LUCK. YOUR MESSAGE BEING PASSED TO *VALIANT*.
MEANWHILE SUGGEST YOU TRY *EXLAX*.

They were happy uncomplicated days. Many mornings the gunroom would go pulling before breakfast in the Captain's gig. This was a very light craft, scarcely bigger than a large dinghy. Under sail it carried two lateen sails, each on its own mast. Both masts as I remember stayed up without any rigging. It was a much more satisfactory boat to pull than a heavy old whaler and presumably we were only allowed its use in order to chivy the Gunroom to take morning exercise. Our own motives were not entirely honourable. It was rumoured that the Wrens from NHQ had a bathing spot not all that far from Malay Cove, where they were wont to take an early morning dip in the altogether. Unfortunately this happy spot, if it ever existed, always seemed to be just beyond our range.

I was never quite sure if *Valiant* was a 'happy ship' or not. I did think of her as being content and efficient. Our Captain knew his job and was something of a character which certainly helped. He had a lonely task, messing always more or less by himself as was the custom of the Service; and with a competent Commander such as we had as second-in-command there was little enough for him to do whilst we were in harbour. Fortunately the Captain of *Illustrious* was a chum and he was often over there of an evening. He would return, obviously having done well, and climb the short quarterdeck ladder from his boat, not unsteady but clearly concentrating hard. The Officer of the Watch would wait to hear whether he was pleased or not with what he found on the quarterdeck. On a good evening the order might then come, 'Shake the Chief Cook,' and the

Captain would make his way carefully forward to the Ship's Company galley where he and the Chief Cook, who was an old shipmate, would go over past experiences until the early hours. One might have thought that these sorts of goings-on might upset the Ship's Company but it was quite the reverse. We rather liked the idea of a Captain who was normally God but who from time to time was apparently happy to come down to earth. I doubt one could get away with it today.

The sailors were of course mainly 'hostilities only' men. Living conditions were cramped but I suppose just about adequate. Messdecks had changed very little over the previous seventy years or so. If one goes round *Warrior* in Portsmouth today one can see a reasonable facsimile of *Valiant*'s messdecks in 1944. There are the same broadside mess tables each seating a mess of about twelve men, almost identical cupboards for the mess cutlery and crockery hung on the ship's side, the same hooks for slinging hammocks from the deck above. The arrangement was no substitute for home comforts but a messdeck did have a certain sense of space when cleared up.

We had one more go at Sabang when I was on board. In July the Fleet steamed once again over to the mouth of the Malacca Straits and this time carried out a gunnery bombardment. Our spotter planes reported that the gunfire was a good deal more accurate than our previous air strike: this aspect needed rather careful handling in my Journal. A little later three or four of our 8-inch gun cruisers carried out another bombardment of Sumatra. The plan was to steam in line ahead past the target and once past, to turn and steam back in the opposite direction to give it a second shelling. The rumour got about however that as the ships turned at the end of the first run one of them continued firing on the turn but forgot to alter the bearing on which the guns were trained. Thus as the turn progressed her fire swept across the remainder of the force. I gather it was off-putting but luckily nothing worse. I left the reporting of this to others.

Chapter 3

Durban and Back

Shortly afterwards however the Fleet suffered a good deal more damage than the Japanese were ever to inflict. Trincomalee was a splendid and very secure anchorage. There was however no dry dock in Ceylon which could take a battleship for a bottom scrape and periodical maintenance of underwater fittings. Durban had the nearest facilities but that was nearly two weeks steaming away. As an emergency measure the Admiralty had commissioned the building of an enormous floating dock in Bombay and this was now arriving in sections in Trincomalee. The sections were soon bolted together and the whole gigantic structure was put to the test. A destroyer was docked first and of course that was no problem. Next one of our County class cruisers was put on the blocks and raised clear of the water. She would have been 10,000 tons displacement but all went well with her too. *Valiant* was to be the next step up. At some three times the cruiser's weight this was quite a jump but the dock was supposed to be able to lift much more than us, so in we went. It was quite a windy day when our turn came and the wind was blowing across the dock entrance, nearly at right angles. Not ideal conditions to take a large ship in. However our Captain turned down the offer of tugs and took us straight in at quite some speed, destroyer fashion, and then went full astern to stop us popping out the other end. We ended up in just the right position. Very good!

The dock had been sunk to the depth needed to get us in by flooding its hull. Now its compartments began to be pumped out and both dock and huge battleship started to rise in the water. All went well at first and by teatime there were only a few feet further to go to have us right out of the water. We must have risen some twenty feet and were getting a splendid view out over the harbour but one did need something of a head for heights. Just before tea we seemed to stop going up; and then the dock began to sink again. What had happened? No bother, we heard. They're just taking things steady. After all, it's the first big lift.

As dark fell we were rising again but things were obviously being taken very steadily indeed. I was Midshipman of the Watch of the First Watch, that is from 2000 to midnight. In dry dock there was obviously little enough water-borne activity going on round us and the Midshipmen were having some sort of instruction next day, so the children were being sent to bed early and I was let off at 2200. In dock our own bathrooms were closed and we had to use those inside the dock structure: all the waste went into the same harbour but our own bathrooms would of course discharge into the dock bottom first. Since the whole purpose of our being in dock was to have as many people as possible working under the ship, it was not going to be very pleasant to have a constant shower from above.

So coming off watch I went over the gangway and down inside the hull of the dock. I was just cleaning my teeth when the whole structure began to creak and groan like a sailing ship in a heavy sea. The dock was obviously not happy. At first there were just minor noises of discomfort and I wondered if maybe this was to do with getting *Valiant* finally out of the water. But within seconds it became clear that something much more serious was under way. I gathered up my towel and soap and fled up the ladder and over the gangway to what I sensed was the comparative safety of the ship: at least that was home.

The Officer of the Watch had heard and felt nothing. 'Sir,' I panted, 'the dock is making very odd noises. I think something is happening to it.' I was told not to be silly and to go and turn in. Just then the Lieutenant of Marines shot over the gangway. 'Something bloody odd in that dock,' he said. 'Don't like it at all.' The Lieutenant carried a lot more clout than a mere Midshipman and the OOW had to listen. He sent for the Duty Lieutenant-Commander who sent for the Commander who sent for the Engineer Commander. By this time it was obvious that something was seriously wrong – even that the dock could be collapsing.

On these occasions, a former eminent Admiral had once observed, people do what they have been trained to do. In these rather unusual circumstances Emergency Stations seemed the natural reaction and we were all soon dashing round closing all those watertight hatches below decks normally closed at sea and now very wide open. No one liked being below in what might soon become a sinking ship and the job was done in treble-quick time. By this time the dock really was collapsing in the stern section. Our own quarterdeck was under water and the bow was cocked up towards the sky. We were listing 15° to port and all that was stopping us sliding off the keel blocks into the bottom of the dock and thereby possibly capsizing everything, were the timber shores. There were ten of these, huge 12-inch square timbers which had been hammered into place on each side of the ship to keep us upright when out of the water.

How long before they might collapse? I tried to work out the stresses involved but eventually gave it up as beyond the Eaton Hall syllabus.

Happily my own stresses were reducing by this time. My Action Station at the time was on the Bridge as I was doing my turn as Captain's 'doggy', a supposedly half-way intelligent messenger. I found the Captain up there as well and he was good enough to compliment me on being for once in the right place at the right time. I did not of course mention that I felt that if we were going to capsize the Bridge was probably as good a place to be as any. It did not occur to me either to wonder whether CPO Savage's Eaton Hall classic about the sinking of *Ark Royal* might have any relevance to the present situation.

In the midst of all this to-do HMS *Howe* entered harbour on passage to join the British Pacific Fleet. She was flying the flag of Admiral Sir Bruce Fraser, the newly-appointed C-in-C of our ships in the Pacific. He had previously had a considerable success in the Battle of North Cape, in north Norwegian waters, when his force had sunk the German battleship *Scharnhorst*. I doubt that the sight of *Valiant* in obvious difficulties can have cheered him much.

By morning it was clear that the dock had settled on the bottom of Trincomalee harbour. As for ourselves there was no doubt that we were going to be out of action for a very long time, if not for ever. The most immediate casualty was the Cold Room which had lost all power during the night. It did not take long to warm up and the meat, its main cargo, soon began to smell very powerfully. Who got the job of clearing it out? The Midshipmen of course. I suppose that was only reasonable. Two of our four propellers would not turn properly and a detailed inspection of the hull suggested that the ship had broken her back. Game, set and match!

Disasters often strike in pairs. There was a second one, less catastrophic and in some respects rather amusing, a few weeks later. The Eastern Fleet submarines were berthed near the harbour entrance and astern of them lay some of our fleet tankers. One afternoon a party of Wrens from NHQ were being shown round one of the boats. A member of the party, taking an intelligent interest or more likely flirting with a sailor, asked what a particular button did. 'That fires one of the stern torpedoes,' said her guide, 'Hands off!' 'Go on,' said the girl, delighted to get a reaction to her gambit. 'Tell me another.' You can guess the outcome. The sailor tried to stop her. She led him on. In the ensuing no doubt very satisfactory wrangle the button got involved. It was not long before a torpedo was speeding across the harbour and as is bound to happen on these occasions, it found a target, a tanker. In a very short time the harbour was covered in a film of oil. It was still there when I came back two years later.

With *Valiant* obviously out of the war our ship's company began to be dispersed to more useful occupations. Clover, Collier and I found ourselves drafted to *Queen Elizabeth*. The news that as a result of the dock fiasco she was to sail shortly for Durban to dock and refit went a long way to make up for having to leave billets in *Valiant* which had proved pretty pleasant. We sailed for South Africa on 21 September and reached Durban twelve days later.

We stayed in Durban for almost exactly two months. I am not sure whether this was the span of the refit period that the Commander-in-Chief back in Ceylon allowed us, or whether the timing was fortuitous. Either way it was long enough for us to form alliances there which were hard to break when in December we finally put to sea again to return to Trincomalee. The Gunroom had little enough to do during the refit and we secured generous amounts of leave. Two of us had a week in the back-blocks of Natal in a township so quiet that we did wonder on arrival quite how we were going to pass the time. The journey up there had been something of an experience. First there was the bus from Durban down the coast to where the railway began its delightful and erratic climb into the interior. The track snaked and dodged its way up the valleys, round the shoulder of this hill and that, seeking always a gradient that it could master. Sometimes progress was so sinuous that one light-hearted and predatory fellow traveller would jump off as we slowed on a particularly difficult hairpin, walk across the bend with his gun and rejoin us before we picked up speed again on the other side of the loop bringing a partridge with him.

Arrived in Harding we stayed with the Bowles family on their farm. One evening we were watching the cows come in for their milking, a quiet, transcontinental pastoral if ever there was one. 'Now there's something you boys can't do,' said Mr Bowles jokingly. By chance in fact I had had to do quite a lot of it. My mother was determined at the outbreak of war that her family would not go without milk so she bought a Jersey cow. Unfortunately she had forgotten that a cow only gives milk when in calf and for a time thereafter. To cover the dry period she bought a second animal but could still not get the lactation periods quite right; so we ended up with three cows and enough milk to feed a village. I found that African cows worked more or less the same way as English ones and the black herdsman was greatly amused by my eventually more-or-less successful efforts.

We really were in the back of beyond with no indoor plumbing of course, just a privy not too far from the back door. One evening after dark my companion was struck by a call of nature and dashed outside to the privy. Almost at once we heard a loud cry of pain and terror and he dashed back in again with his trousers still round his knees. 'I've been bitten, I've been bitten,' he yelled. 'It was a big one. Is it fatal?' 'What was it,' we all asked, unspoken visions of puff adders, black mambas and the like. The farmer dashed out to the privy with torch and shotgun. In a moment though he was back holding up a hen's egg and almost incoherent with laughter.

A week or two later we were sent off for a fortnight's Air Course at the Naval Air Station at Wingfield outside Capetown. This I felt was the low point of our South African holiday. It was certainly something to be taken up in a Swordfish, the legendary 'Stringbag' of the Fleet Air Arm. Its great advantage, it was always said, was that it flew more slowly than any enemy gunner could credit and so anti-aircraft fire always missed ahead. All the same it achieved notable successes against the Italians at Taranto and against the German battleship *Bismarck*. I only had one complaint against this particular flight. I was of course in the rear cockpit and for some reason was not strapped in. After we had been airborne for a few minutes the pilot shouted through the speaking tube, 'Going to try a loop.' I shouted back, much louder, 'No, I'm not strapped in.' 'What was that?' as the nose of the aircraft began to rise. 'Not strapped in,' very loudly indeed. 'Oh,' and we dived instead, 'Would I have fallen out?' I asked, when we had got down and I had finished being pulverised for being so stupid. 'Probably!'

The fortnight was in fact made bearable by a weekend when I managed to get leave and had a couple of days out at Somerset West, a tiny village we had seen from the train on the way down, round the bay to the east of Capetown. I believe it is now something of a shanty town. Then it was a completely unspoilt tiny hamlet of a few houses. I did find one problem on arrival: there was no train back to Capetown on the Monday morning. 'Don't worry,' said the inn-keeper. 'I'll fix something with the station-master,' and he did. Meanwhile I had a wonderful day, apart from a near-miss with a puff adder in the heather in the morning, climbing up the mountains behind the village. Back at the inn I asked the manager the origin of the tracks and wheelmarks over the hills. 'That's where the *voortekkers* hauled their wagons up,' he said. I didn't doubt that he was right. It wasn't all that many years before 1944 after all.

Otherwise I found the Air Course something of a sad experience. We learnt that the Fleet Air Arm had started as the Royal Naval Air Service during the First World War. When peace came it was absorbed by the Royal Air Force who won a political battle that all military aircraft should be placed under their control. The Navy regained its air arm in 1937 but considerable damage had by then been done. The more junior officers, those who did the actual flying, were as it were the descendants of broken homes and they lost little time in telling us about it. Everything was wrong: the aircraft were sub-standard, the aircraft-carriers not a patch on those of the US Navy and so on. If things did not improve, we heard, many would like to transfer to the RAF. It all left a bitter taste. The Commander (Air) and his deputy explained things to us more rationally, giving a historical perspective, but it was not difficult to see why non-flying senior officers sometimes had a possibly ambivalent attitude to the FAA.

I was lucky enough the following year to serve in the British Pacific Fleet for a short while and saw those carriers, aircraft and fliers in action. As is so often the case those at the coal-face turned out to be a wholly different proposition from the ones at the pit-head. But then we went and made the same mistake in the 1960s when the Navy had its carrier-building programme axed on the grounds that air defence of surface forces could be provided by missiles and that offensive air operations in any likely trouble spot would be within the range of a new generation of land-based aircraft. Carriers would thus be unnecessary. Subsequent 'little wars' have once again illustrated the fallacy of this argument.

Back in Durban I doubt whether we could have had more hospitality. Most of us seemed to get taken into families. In my own case the liaison lasted through to a second visit to Durban two years after the war, and beyond.

It would no doubt have been well-received on board to have stayed in Durban for Christmas but we were needed back north where we were now really beginning to pile the pressure on the Japanese in Burma. A week before Christmas we once more entered Trincomalee harbour. What a change we found! The harbour which we had left three months earlier had been home to a fleet of four battleships and two aircraft-carriers. Now it was more like a bus station with ships moving through to the Pacific. *Richelieu* had gone, presumably back to France. *Renown* had left. *Valiant* was limping home. Engrossed in the affairs of our own part of the world

111

we saw the flood setting strongly east but did not appreciate the size and speed of the build-up in the Pacific which that betokened.

Queen Elizabeth was the only capital ship left to the Eastern Fleet and so became the Fleet Flagship. The Admiral and his staff moved in, the Wardroom had to overflow into the Gunroom and those of us at the bottom of the heap got rather squashed. However, it was Christmas.

My experiences of later Christmases away from home were never particularly jolly. We always seemed to be treading a rather thin line between making a cheerful go of things for the Ship's Company whilst hoping against hope that things would not get out of hand. Christmas 1944 passed off fairly peacefully. The Wardroom visited the Gunroom for a drink before lunch, there was a sailing race in the afternoon, the Admiral visited the Gunroom in the evening and we then dealt with a huge Christmas dinner. I suspect many of the Ship's Company were spiritually still down in Durban.

The days of pot-boiling air-strikes and bombardments against minor Japanese positions in the Dutch East Indies were now over. We had heard nothing from the Eastern Fleet while we were enjoying ourselves in South Africa but now at the beginning of 1945 there was a new spring in the air and we were definitely on the offensive. There were secret conferences on board at which Midshipmen were detailed off to ensure security. They were a curious choice for guards. We majored in bombardment practice and the Royal Marine contingents of the remaining ships of the Fleet were for ever ashore doing whatever Marines do do before an operation.

The real action started on 18 January. Without warning we found ourselves putting to sea and setting off at high speed to the north-east. A small escort carrier set out with us but she could not keep up and it was devil take the hindmost. Two days later we sighted the coast of Burma and learnt that we were to give support to a landing from the sea at Akyab. Quite soon however we did begin to wonder what all the hurry had been about. We spent a very quiet afternoon at anchor off the mouth of the Arakan River and I had plenty of time to attempt a sketch of the coastline for my Journal. As the land was flat and almost out of sight this was not too taxing: a few palm trees look much the same at Akyab as anywhere else.

After breakfast next day we moved a few miles south to provide a bombardment in support of a landing on Ramree Island by troops of 15 Indian Corps and Royal Marines from the Fleet. In the event this was largely unopposed but the General in charge was kind enough to say that the sound of our 15-inch shells lumbering overhead was greatly appreciated by his soldiers. It was not much more than a walk-on part as far as we were concerned. My main memory was of the delightfully fresh weather off the Burmese coast, a splendid change from Trincomalee. Apparently the Japanese attempted a little aerial retaliation but none penetrated as far as us. It was very quiet even by Sabang or Surabaya standards. The Marines came back after we had returned to Trincomalee, very pleased with themselves.

For us Midshipmen it was now back to school. We were to have our Seamanship and Navigation Board in a couple of weeks time. Success or lack of it could determine seniority in the future so at the time it seemed well worthwhile to make an effort. A more welcome diversion was that the Admiral found time to start having the Gunroom to breakfast, two at a time. The breakfast itself was much the same as we would have had anyway and the company meant that we had to find clean white uniforms but the occasion went better than we had expected and we appreciated the gesture, *fin de siècle* maybe but a nice touch.

Our Seamanship Board came and went. Our own officers had taken quite a bit of trouble to help us prepare for it and no one was too horrified at the result. This family feeling was not untypical in either *Valiant* or *Queen Elizabeth*. To an extent, and although I did not fully comprehend it at the time, there was I think an unspoken feeling that we were all together a long way from England and that we sank or swam together. I remember an occasion when two of our Gunroom were having an argument outside the Charthouse. It was probably pretty puerile but eventually came very near to blows. Before any hits were landed the Chief Quartermaster, one of the most senior ratings on board, who was busy near the Bridge, materialised and was soon lecturing the would-be contestants on the standards that the Ship's Company expected from its officers. It was an avuncular and well-judged interruption.

Chapter 4

To the Pacific

The Seamanship Board signalled the end of our 'Big Ship' time and we were split up amongst the destroyers of the Fleet to see how the other half lived. Twelve or fifteen years earlier Midshipmen were kept clear of destroyers because of the bibulous way of life in some of those uncomfortable craft. A year or two before I went to Eaton Hall I had come across an envelope full of my Father's old 'flimsies'. A flimsy was a very potted version of the Confidential Report made on an officer every time he left a ship, so potted in fact that most were quite bland. Each of my Father's flimsies however included the remark 'Does Not Drink'. I knew this to be untrue. I never felt that he drank to excess but he certainly appreciated a glass or two of wine or a glass of gin. I asked what the flimsies meant. 'Well,' he said, 'there used to be a good deal of pretty heavy drinking, particularly in small ships. It got so bad there that Midshipmen were never sent to them. Eventually Their Lordships decided that enough was enough. Wine bills were restricted and Wine Books had to be inspected by the Captain every month, and Confidential Reports had to confirm that officers did not drink to excess.' It was something of an eye-opener.

By 1945 life in small ships was not quite so rumbustious, though as I was to join an Australian destroyer I thought I might still see some more exciting domestic life than in an RN ship, and first impressions were not unpromising. There was quite an active party for some WRNS girls in progress on board HMAS *Norman* when I joined in Colombo in mid-February, the occasion being the ship's forthcoming return to Australia and, no secret apparently, its subsequent deployment to the Pacific. I could hardly believe my luck. There were four ships in the Squadron, *Napier*, the leader, *Norman*, *Nizam* and *Nepal*. The ships were UK-built destroyers of, not surprisingly, the 'N' class. They were a continuation of the pre-war destroyer design which had by then developed to the point where, from the 'L's onwards, ships had three enclosed 4.7-inch gun mountings instead of the open mountings of their predecessors; and of course there were the usual two multiple torpedo-tube mountings amidships. The only slight

HMAS *Norman*, 1944

The photograph in fact shows a sistership, *Nepal*, no good picture of *Norman* being available

drawback was that the officers' accommodation was in the after end of the ship so it was a potentially wet and wave-swept journey to the Bridge along the Iron Deck in heavy weather, and being above the propellers meant that one had a noisy ride at speed. But they were well-found ships. *Norman* had the added drawback of being somewhat crowded. My collection of tin boxes did not go down too well and there was no chest into which clothes could be unpacked and stowed. I shared the tiny flat outside the Captain's cabin in the stern with an English Sub-Lieutenant RNVR. He had been one of Winston Churchill's private secretaries after the former had become Prime Minister but had managed to slip away to join the Navy. Churchill endured a few months without him but felt the lack of his expertise so keenly that he had him hauled back. Another year in Downing Street was however enough for Ben, who eloped once more; and here he was, safely away from England in an Australian destroyer in the Indian Ocean.

The Australians were certainly welcoming towards us but I soon found that a low-key approach had no place in *Norman*. You were expected to give as good as you got in the way of an argument. A certain degree of politeness was required towards more senior officers but this was seldom taken to mean that you should not say what you thought, whatever the company. There was an added twist for Ben and me in that by early 1945 with the war in Europe moving towards victory, the Australians were convinced that we would soon be leaving them to their own devices in the Pacific. The efforts of our own Eastern Fleet over the past year and a half were continually compared unfavourably with the admittedly far greater successes of the US Navy in the Pacific. Neither Ben nor I were entirely aware at the time of the way in which the Indian-British 14th Army were rolling back the Japanese in Burma and were often hard-put to keep the argument on an even keel. It was noteworthy however in the context of much later (*c.* 1993) allegations that we had let the Australians down over the fall of Singapore, that this subject never came up. In *Norman* at any rate the worry was that with victory in Europe achieved we would sit on our hands as far as the Japanese war was concerned. I was soon put to work drawing a large diagram showing the signal flags used by the US Navy.

Apart from this it was an interesting trip southwards and 'homewards'. We started off escorting two small carriers, *Ruler* and *Fencer*, destined for the Pacific, but as we got nearer to Australia and thus further away from any Japanese submarine threat they pressed on and left us to our own devices.

Fremantle was our first landfall but we stopped there no longer than was needed to refuel, embark huge quantities of fruit and send the Western Australians off on leave. We sailed the same evening for Adelaide. The weather was now turning really cold. I was wearing pyjamas and two sweaters beneath my blue uniform on watch and two pairs of gloves but was still cold. The weather across the Australian Bight off the south coast of Australia was forecast as bad. We were particularly cautioned to take great care rounding Cape Leeuwin at the south-west extremity of the continent. *Nizam*, ahead of us by some days and in a great hurry, had cut the corner too fine, encountered tide-rips and overfalls and nearly capsized. The word was that she had lost ten men overboard. *Napier* had apparently had the same experience rounding Cape Otway at the other end of the Bight: she was rumoured to have gone well over on her side, got water down the funnel and there were even footprints found afterwards on a freshly-painted deckhead (ceiling). She certainly lost two men overboard from 'B' Gundeck which was quite high up in those ships. We stood further out from the land after all these warnings, took it more slowly and had no trouble but we were all in lifejackets, even sleeping in them, for the passage of the Bight.

And so we made Melbourne, rather than Adelaide, sent the Victorians off on leave and on 18 March came to Sydney. Sydney Harbour has been much better described elsewhere than I could possibly attempt after the passage of half a century. I will only say that it was every bit as magnificent as the Wardroom and sailors had told me. The weather was warm again after the Bight and we moored for fuel alongside what appeared to be someone's garden.

We were to be given leave and the Captain asked what I planned to do, if anything. I said that I thought I ought to see something of the country and planned to hitch-hike round as much of the south-east as I could. This met with no approval at all: it was a risky undertaking for anyone and he would not want to have an accident or worse to an English Midshipman on his conscience. He would arrange something through the Australian Red Cross. He did; and a day or so later Seddon, my opposite number in *Nepal*, and I were buying tickets for Quirindi in the 'outback' of New South Wales. We had a wonderful ten days up there with Fred and Joan Moses, thirty-five miles from the nearest town. There were horses to be ridden – and fallen off of – kangaroos and foxes and rabbits to be dealt with as pests, hills to be climbed and a Woolshed Dance to be invited to. It was the rural Australia of which one had read and the characters we met were straight out of history. Fred and Joan are still alive in 1996 but the way of life that we found in 1945 seems from all accounts to have undergone a sea-change. Cecil, the station hand, an 'old' soldier invalided out of the army after the rigours of fighting the Japanese along the Kokoda Trail across New Guinea, was our guide. His picturesque language was a good deal more idiomatic than was usual even in *Norman* but he certainly showed us the country. I may have earned a small mark of approval by skinning a kangaroo. We salted the hide well for passage home to England but I do not remember it being particularly appreciated in *Norman* during the early part of its journey. But of course few if any of our sailors had seen as much of the Outback as Seddon and I.

It was only very much later that I heard from Joan how her husband's family came to Australia. His great grandfather had been transported aged nineteen, for stealing a bale of silk. By the time he died forty-seven years on he had become widely respected in New South Wales both as a pioneer and a successful trader. His son, Fred's grandfather, went on to 'build up' several stations, was active in business and the State Parliament and, perhaps even more memorably, helped found the Hawksbury Race Club. What courage for a family to achieve so much after such a start.

In retrospect the six months from Autumn 1944 to Spring 1945 was more like an expensive world tour than war service: South Africa, Burma and then Australia. Now however *Norman* had to do some work. On 1 April the 7th Destroyer Squadron left Sydney to join the British Pacific Fleet operating off the Philippines. Happily we had a following sea and thus made an easy passage all the way up the Great Barrier Reef and across the Coral Sea. It was an astonishing thought that the Japanese had penetrated this close to Australia two years earlier and were only prevented from reaching the sub-continent by their defeat at the hands of the US Navy in the battle of the Coral Sea. No longer did I find it difficult to see why mentally at least the Australians had now swung away from Europe and towards the United States.

Despite the warlike overtones of the area, and Guadalcanal of the Marines hard-fought landing and victory was not all that far to the east, I could not help associating these waters more with the myths of the South Seas. We steamed on through the Solomon Sea. Soon we were passing between New Guinea to the west and New Britain on the other side. The Admiralty Islands and the US base at Manus lay not far ahead.

Many of the islands that we passed had been fought over but now the coconut plantations were being replanted and some of the trees looked already quite tall. Apparently on those which either had an existing airstrip or where one had been established the strategy was not to worry about any Japanese still lurking in the bush. So long as the airfield was secure they could be mopped up later.

We refuelled at Manus and then set course along the north coast of New Guinea for the Philippines. We could see the New Guinea mountains from fifty miles off – the old hands reckoned that that was the best distance to be though I did think that the much closer glimpses we had caught of the land on our passage north showed an attractively wild part of the world.

We reached Leyte on 13 April, twelve days out from Sydney. The long passage had given me plenty of time to work on my kangaroo skin, scraping it and rubbing in preservatives such as Glaubers salt. I am not clear how I found the latter onboard a destroyer, even an Australian one.

Leyte was a major American defended anchorage in Leyte Gulf between Samar and Mindanao and the British had the use of a corner of it for our fleet train. A fair proportion of the latter would be at sea in the refuelling areas waiting to replenish the strike fleet in between operations but we still found enough of it anchored in the Gulf when we arrived to make an impressive sight. The snow-capped peaks further inland made a picturesque backdrop to the repair ships, supply ships of all sorts, the hospital ship and various tankers lying off-shore.

Apparently there were still quantities of Japanese lurking in the country behind the Gulf, as in the islands that we had passed, but even the Japanese were said to be pretty demoralised by this stage of the war and they never constituted a threat.

On this occasion we only spent one night in Leyte but this was long enough to pick up the news that two of our carriers had already been hit by Kamikaze suicide bombers. *Indefatigable* was the first, struck the day we left Sydney; but she was back in operation within thirty minutes. *Illustrious* was the next, hit while we were on passage north. She was not so lucky. The bomber hit the base of the Bridge but the carrier would have been able to continue operating had the aircraft not then slipped overboard still carrying an unexploded 1000 lb bomb. The latter detonated in the water alongside an unarmoured portion of the hull and blew a hole in the ship's bottom. By the time we reached Leyte she was on her way back to the UK and out of the war.

Although these Kamikaze attacks were hardly good news, the ability of the carriers to continue operating in spite of them certainly was. The secret lay in the ships' armoured flight decks. US carriers except for the Midway class did not have this armour and a Kamikaze hit normally meant at least temporary withdrawal from operations. The four carriers of the British Pacific Fleet, apart from *Illustrious*, received five Kamikaze strikes between them. In each case the wreckage was merely brushed overboard and the ships continued operating. I gathered that the Americans and even the Australians were impressed.

All this we knew at the time. Some fifty years later in the course of researching the background to the development and history of British naval aviation in the period leading up to, and during, the Second World War I came across a detailed 1988 study on the subject by a well-respected American authority. He concluded his work with the words, 'The record, properly read, seems to have been an outstanding one, strategically, operationally, technologically.' So much for the whingers at Wingfield!

That April 1945 we did not have time to mull over all this and after reaching Leyte we sailed again next morning escorting two tankers north to Area Mosquito, one of the designated replenishment areas used by the Fleet. 'Mosquito' was about two hundred miles into the Pacific from the northern tip of the Philippines and nearly five hundred miles from Leyte. It took us three days to get there. I suppose we were all zig-zagging to confuse any Japanese submarines in the vicinity but it was a slow passage.

At dawn on 18 April we came up with the British Pacific Fleet. It was a wonderful and heartening sight. The ships seemed to spread from one horizon to the other. Four aircraft-carriers provided the offensive punch – four armoured carriers, capable of brushing Kamikaze attacks over the side. They may have carried fewer aircraft than their US counterparts but the latter used to park a proportion of their complement on deck whereas RN ships kept all theirs in hangars, a reflection no doubt on the Atlantic weather conditions for which they were designed. The difference was always good for an argument but US Navy observers were on record as to which ships they would prefer to operate from – *Indomitable*, *Indefatigable*, *Formidable*, *Victorious*, all relatively new ships. I suppose they fielded two hundred aircraft between them, both fighters and bombers. Admiral Vian, Flag Officer, Aircraft-Carriers, flew his flag in *Indomitable*. Protecting them were the two new battleships: *King George V*, flagship of Vice-Admiral Rawlings, and *Howe*. The latter had passed through Trincomalee heading east the previous year on the night in August when *Valiant* sank the floating dock. *King George V* had followed her with three carriers and supporting cruisers and destroyers in January so I suppose the Fleet must have been operating for some two or three months by the time we arrived. Two more carriers, much smaller, and a scattering of frigates protected the replenishment group and filled out the picture. They all looked weather-beaten and salt-stained, streaked here and there with rust as we went round delivering mails and passengers which we had brought up from Leyte. Was it my imagination or did I really get a little less ribbing from my Australian friends from then on? Either way, as each of the passengers disappeared across the jackstay to the ships they were to join I saw my chances of getting a chest to myself improve!

We spent about a month thereafter in the Pacific, sometimes escorting tankers or supply ships from Leyte to the replenishment areas and vice versa, sometimes exercising out of Leyte Gulf. During the latter time I managed two trips to the beach but each one involved a three hour trip in both directions and as many changes of boat as one might expect on a cross-country train journey between say Southampton and Dover. My main memory of these trips was of the staple conversational topic of the 'friendly' Philippinos – 'of course if the Japanese had treated us better we would not have let you come back.'

On two of our journeys up to 'Mosquito' we were subsequently grabbed to join the Fleet destroyer screen and continue with them up to the flying-off area for air strikes. The Fleet's task was to neutralise Japanese airfields in Formosa and in the islands of the Sakishima Gunto chain extending south-west from Japan in order to support the American operations against Okinawa further up the chain and nearer to Japan. We would be operating just under one hundred miles from the nearest Japanese airfield on Miyako Jima and warning time of a Kamikaze attack was reckoned as ten seconds; but no opposition materialised.

Our second attachment to the Fleet screen was short but not at all sweet. It was a very foggy morning when the Fleet reached the flying-off area. Before operations began the Captain of 4th Destroyer Squadron in *Quilliam* was apparently ordered to take up anti-Kamikaze positions with his destroyer squadron between the four carriers and was leading his four ships into the middle of the Fleet at 25 knots. Visibility was down to two hundred yards – not far at 25 knots – and what with one thing and another *Quilliam* collided with *Indomitable*, hitting her in the stern. The carrier was not badly damaged but *Quilliam* sliced off a large part of her own bow.

Norman's station was not far astern of *Indomitable* and so we were the first upon the scene of the collision and were ordered to take *Quilliam* in tow. The weather was calm and we soon had a wire over and began trying to tow her stern-first, but those bits of the bow which had not disappeared to the bottom of the Pacific gave our charge a determined sheer to one side and we made infinitesimal progress. Eventually the light cruiser *Black Prince* was detached to take over from us and later still the rescue tug *Weasel* was summoned up to let the cruiser back to her proper place, covering the carriers. So *Weasel* with *Norman* escorting her wended a snail's pace return to Leyte where *Quilliam* was popped into a floating dock for emergency repairs. We ourselves set off at high speed to catch up with the Fleet which had now apparently done a good enough job to allow its withdrawal for a spell of maintenance in Sydney.

With her bow pointed for home the ship was like a horse heading back to stables and there was no holding her. On the passage north one fuelling stop, at Manus in the Admiralty Islands, was enough. Going home at this speed we needed another between Manus and Sydney and called in at the tiny Mortewa oiling jetty in Milne Bay on the eastern extremity of New Guinea. Mortewa bore the same relationship to the facilities we were accustomed to as a village garage with a hand-worked pump might to a 24-hour petrol station. The jetty was hardly the length of the ship. More intriguing was the absence of any visible civilisation other than the pump crew's prefab at the base of the jetty. The foothills and jungle swept down to the beach. It was unclear whether there was human life in 'them thar hills' or whether, if there was, it was headhunters or by now almost forgotten Japanese. I was itching to get ashore for an hour or two but the ship was impatient and we were soon off to sea again, flying south through the China Strait into the Coral Sea.

By the time we reached Sydney at the beginning of June we found the British ships hogging the harbour. Four enormous carriers were pressed into Wollamolloo Dockyard, two on either side of a dock jutting into the yard. There was theoretically room between them for *Norman* to squeeze in as well but our Captain was weary after so long at sea and decided that someone's measurements were wrong. We went back to the garden anchorage of our previous visit. Next morning the gap looked that little bit wider and we just managed to squeeze through. One could reach out and touch an aircraft-carrier on either side without too much difficulty.

Which brought me to the end of my stay in *Norman* and my time as a Midshipman. I had had just over three months on board; and it had seemed the most natural thing in the world to serve in the Royal Australian

Navy. Certainly the Captain and First Lieutenant, and I think the Second Lieutenant also, had been to Dartmouth. For what it is worth they spoke with little trace of an Australian accent. I may be wrong but I seem to remember that the Captain's wife was English. The routine was almost identical with that in an RN ship. Certainly their tropical rig was khaki instead of white and their shorts were rather shorter than the vogue in the RN at the time but these were cosmetic differences. After the war, when the Australian defence staff sat down to consider the future shape of their armed forces, it was obvious to them that in any future conflict in the Pacific that was likely to pose a threat to Australia, assistance would probably come more expeditiously from the United States than from Britain. Thus their thinking and equipment was bound to become strongly US-orientated. This is logical. However, to one who enjoyed his time with them and admired their ships and men it can only be a rather sad development.

Chapter 5

Return to the East Indies

As a Midshipman one had been something of an overgrown schoolboy in uniform, an apprentice to the naval trade. To move up the ladder further formal instruction was needed. We all came home for courses for promotion to Sub-Lieutenant. Ours finished in Spring 1946.

By then the Navy was more or less back on a peacetime footing. Ships were spread among six 'Stations'. The Home, Mediterranean and Far East Fleets were the largest, each based on a fleet 'mix' of an aircraft carrier, one or two cruisers and a number of destroyers. The gaps in world-wide coverage were filled by the much smaller East Indies, South Atlantic and West Indies Squadrons. There were also one or two battleships in commission which could be available on the Home and Mediterranean stations from time to time.

At the end of courses I was still feeling the pull of the East Indies. I had seen little enough of the shore side of it during the war apart from Trincomalee and Colombo but the weather was warm, there was still the romance of Empire and the enormous human interest of so many different races, religions and civilisations. I asked for a frigate or destroyer on that Station and drew a cruiser. It did not seem a bad result at the time and by the beginning of April I was back in Colombo where the ship was in dry dock at the end of a maintenance period.

The East Indies covered a huge area. Aden marked its western boundary, Singapore its eastern. In the north its shores ran up to the foothills of the Himalayas and the Persian mountains. To the south it looked towards the Antarctic. One or two cruisers and perhaps four frigates comprised the squadron which protected British interests. Most of the land mass round these seas was coloured red on the map and if a squadron of that size was judged sufficient for the task it seems hard to justify any claim that it was only an iron fist which kept the Empire together.

The cruiser I joined was one of the Colony class, with a main armament of nine 6-inch guns. I cannot say that she provided a particularly happy home as far as I was concerned. The main problem was that as a Sub-Lieutenant I could normally have expected to be the kingpin of the

Gunroom, the Midshipmen's mess. This would have been a position if not of influence then at least of some interest involving as it would do the charge of bringing on one's younger brethren. As it was, another Sub-Lieutenant, more senior and wiser than I, was already in office and I found it quite difficult not to be at a loose end. I endured this state of affairs for some five months, which I must say encompassed a very enjoyable cruise down the Arabian and African coasts to Simonstown for a proper refit, and there by mutual agreement with the Commander I left the ship and took passage back to Ceylon to find a billet where there might be prospect of more gainful employment.

Compared with my first arrival in Ceylon two years previously, when all of us in our naval draft had to spend five weeks in a camp outside Colombo waiting for our ships, the wheels this time moved at enormous speed. The naval staff in Trincomalee assured me that a fast and desirable frigate in the Persian Gulf needed a Sub-Lieutenant, even a very green one, and that I was to get up there as soon as possible. There was just going to be time to have a nostalgic look round Trincomalee, swim and sunbathe at Sandy Cove, munch a hand of bananas on a climb up Chapel Hill, note that the thorn tree up the hill where I had cut a walking stick some eighteen months before still bore the scars, sniff the horrid smell from the film of oil which still covered the harbour as a result of that wartime Wren loosing a torpedo at a tanker during her visit to a submarine. The harbour itself had the air of a fair ground after the caravans and the roundabouts had packed up and left. There were still ships moving through to Singapore and elsewhere but the moorings for the heavyweights were empty. I was not too reluctant to take the night train to Colombo with Midshipman Bob Williams who had also been appointed to *Loch Glendhu*.

The Trincomalee to Colombo train was hardly one of the great railway journeys of the world but it had its attractions. The distance was not more than 160 miles and the journey took eight or nine hours so the train was no flier. I suppose one could sleep but the jolting and shuddering as we stopped at each tiny station hardly helped. Far better in any case to savour the damp jungly smell through the window, wonder at what lay behind the puny flickering oil lamps on the platforms and rejoice in the relaxed travel as compared with the 2.30 from Waterloo to the West of England.

It was light by the time we rolled slowly up to Colombo. The paddy fields slid gently past, their muddy water breathing a gentle mist. Patches of jungle almost brushed the side of the train. I suppose the temple at Kelaniya and the old camp at Kinnya, no doubt mouldering quietly away by now, lay somewhere not far beyond the fields and paths and trees. We were uncomfortable passengers by the time we pulled into Colombo, sticky with the sweat of the night, only too conscious of the smuts from the low grade coal which was all the old train rated.

But the last and perhaps the greatest attraction of the journey was still to come. Travelling north from Colombo to Trincomalee one arrived in a similarly dishevelled state, but then there was only the prospect of a tedious journey to the jetty, wait for a boat, and then out to one's ship where the bathroom would be filling up, and breakfast afterwards would as likely as not be in a steaming hot Wardroom. It would all hardly compensate for the sights and smells of the night's journey.

Arrived at Colombo however from the southbound Night Mail there would be a rickshaw or a carriage or a taxi to the Grand Oriental Hotel just in front of the Customs House and harbour. There one could spend a wonderful hour in a lukewarm bath before the most civilised breakfast imaginable in a wonderfully airy dining room. And afterwards? Well, there was always the flight onwards to the Persian Gulf to be arranged.

We started early next morning and took two days in very basic and rather uncomfortable Dakotas to reach Karachi. I always liked the story of the Sikh pilot flying Dakotas over the 'Hump', the wartime supply route from Burma into China. To avoid the Japanese the trick was apparently to fly up the Burmese valleys as low as possible, just lift up to clear the mountain crest between the two countries and then dive down into the valleys of China. It was demanding on pilots and aircraft, terrifying I'm told for passengers. The Sikh used to brief his passengers on the joys to come, adding cheerfully, 'I can only advise you if you do not like the view from one window to look out of the other one!' It wasn't like that flying to Karachi but the south-west monsoon had started and much of the low country was under water. We came down at Bangalore for what appeared to be a third breakfast and then flew on over the higher, drier, gaunt uplands of southern India to our night stop at Bombay. Next day was even wetter and we flew low along the coast to Karachi. We had the aircraft to ourselves that day. The cloud was almost down to the water and the Captain amused himself by reminding us every half hour or so of what we must do if, almost when, we ditched. Herds of horses and flocks of sheep grazed down towards the shore-line and stampeded as we passed to seaward of them at a very few feet. As a way of seeing a new side of India it was not without interest but we were quite relieved to reach Karachi without having had to put our newly-acquired knowledge of how to ditch in a Dakota to the test.

At Karachi everything changed. We had joined the BOAC (ex Imperial Airways) flying boat route to India and the Far East and were to start for the Gulf next morning before sunrise. I could never work out why BOAC used to delight in such early starts. I used to think it was something to do with the cooler morning air giving more lift to get the boat off the water, but as they used to come down at Dubai in the Persian Gulf for fuel and then take off again quite easily that explanation cannot have been anything like right.

Anyway to start the day with a delightful boat trip out across the calm water in the cool peace of a north Indian dawn was indescribably pleasing. And how much more exciting to be handed up into the monster's side hatch from a gently rocking boat than to climb an Everest of steps on a probably rain-swept runway. We were the only two Europeans aboard and there were not many locals either. No stewardesses I was sorry to see. However the splendour of the inside of the wonderful machine, the spiral staircase to the upper deck, the feeling of space and order and of course the excitement of the unaccustomed take-off from water, all these were highly satisfactory.

We were away just before the sun came over the horizon, tearing across the water with the bow wave coming higher and higher until the boat began to plane on its stepped hull like a powerboat. Suddenly the wave faded, we lost contact with friction and a moment later the sea was dropping away below us. Through those wonderful big windows we could actually see where we were going. To the north the mountains of Baluchistan ran up towards Afghanistan, grey, rocky, inhospitable at least from the air, grandly impressive, the country of the Great Game that used to be played between the spies and agents of Russia and British India. As we came up to the Persian border the land became even more mountainous. It was a rivetting panorama.

Meanwhile out to port the Muscat coast was coming over the horizon, almost as sharp as the Persian side with the country running up to the near 10,000 ft of the Jebel al Akhdar, the Green Mountain. I knew nothing of it then and only a little more in later years, but there was always the mystery, when we were cruising in crippling heat along the grey, barren, rocky coast, of that high country inland where men said that even grapes grew. And so on over the Musandam Peninsula to Dubai where we came down to refuel.

Dubai was a very modest settlement in those days, lying along both shores of a large creek. As we flew over we could look down almost into the houses, the more prosperous establishments built round courtyards like small forts, the lesser dwellings content with just a yard outside the door. A few plantations of date palms grew on the edges of the town but there was no grass anywhere. It looked as though the desert stretched into the midst of the straggle of houses and crept up to the reed-beds which fringed the creek. We did not see the dhows until we had touched down and were slowing up between them but these represented the main reason for Dubai's existence in those days – trade. Trade between India and the interior, with the desert tribes, perhaps even those of the Empty Quarter, the Rub al Khali. Trade to the ports along the Gulf. A large finger in the smuggling of gold from India. On this first visit I was only dimly aware of the place of Dubai in the economy of the Gulf. But I did know that Dubai was on the Trucial Coast as I have described in the first part of this book.

As the flying boat slowed and settled in the water the door was flung open and all at once we were in a different world from the one we had left in Karachi. It was only ten o'clock in the morning but in August the Gulf was reaching towards the peak of its summer heat and the air from the desert came as though from the proverbial furnace. It was already over 100°F in the shade of the BOAC post where we passengers were taken to be cooled down with lime juice.

The BOAC huts were the only part of Dubai that we saw from the ground and then we were off again for the short hop to Bahrein. Bahrein was our naval base and the largest outpost of civilisation on the Arabian shore of the Gulf. The sheikdom was an island and had no oil of its own but was connected to the Saudi Arabian mainland by a long causeway and pipeline to Ras Tannurah, the refinery for the American-owned Aramco oilfield complex. Much of the oil from there was pumped along the pipeline to a terminal at Bahrein. None of this activity looked very appealing from the air.

An inner anchorage enclosed by a reef stretched from the oil terminal towards the town of Bahrein and we managed a good look at the latter as the boat came down to the water but there was little enough sign of any naval activity and certainly no ships. We had been told in Trincomalee that *Loch Glendhu* was on 'Special Service' but no one could, or would, tell us what this was. It sounded intriguing but did not seem to include much time in Bahrein. We did not seem to be expected either. We waited for an hour at the airport, thinking that in this outpost someone might have heard of our impending arrival but eventually coming to terms with our miniscule role in the scheme of things we took a taxi out to the Naval Base, HMS *Jufair*.

Bahrein was hardly more attractive from the ground than from the air. The town seemed caught architecturally between the early nineteenth and mid-twentieth centuries and not benefitting much from either. The effect was made no better by the developments of the past fifty years or so being built over the much earlier Arab style. It was a shame that the twentieth century showed almost no regard or understanding of previous years. The taxi driver was hardly communicative but we soon gathered that the British were not the most popular of beings, at least in the estimation of the bazaars. I don't think that we were aware at the time of the trickle of pan-Arab propaganda beginning to spring from the loudspeakers of Cairo and which later swelled to a flood, but it was an unpromising welcome. There was no doubt about the heat and the humidity though; quite enough to turn anyone's brain and make them thoroughly distrustful of strangers.

Outside the bazaar limits we came to what can only be described as urbanised desert, flat stretches of sun-burnt coral, white sand and dust. Here and there a few houses had strayed out of the town and surrounded themselves with high lime-washed walls as some protection against the climate, against stray goats and perhaps even against other humans. Did they belong to well-to-do Bahreinis, perhaps hankering after something in the way of a country seat? A few date palms and dusty oleanders gave a little interest to the hardly-attractive landscape, and over it all towered the high wireless masts of HMS *Jufair*.

The masts were the badge of the base, tangible evidence of its main role as the centre of British interests in the Gulf. Communication seemed to be all-important: communication between the Political Resident and his Agents in the other, smaller states and sheikdoms, and of course communication with HM ships in the area. The political set-up appeared to have changed very little from what it was in the old *Fox*'s time before World War One. The Residency had moved to Bahrein from Bushire but that seemed to be all. I say 'seemed to be all'. As Williams and I came up to Jufair it might for all we knew always have been on the shore outside the town of Bahrein. I do not think we had ever heard of Bushire. Anyway, there it was in 1946 and I learnt later that the Arab's name for the Political

Resident was 'Lord of the Liver'. This was no invention of Cairo's propaganda machine. It might even have been held to imply some respect for the British position, 'The Liver' being the Arabic name for the Persian Gulf.

Jufair was almost literally an oasis in the middle of all this heat, architectural sprawl and inclined-to-be unfriendly inhabitants. It stood on the shore of the inner anchorage that we had seen from the air, a modest establishment of barrack blocks built in the local stone for the sailors manning the communications facility, naturally a football field, swimming baths, an open-air cinema and suchlike. The Wardroom was a two-storey building in the colonial style, kitchens and offices on the ground floor and a high-ceilinged upstairs extending almost the whole length and breadth of the building and open to wide verandahs on all sides. This was where we lived and ate. In the summer it was cool and airy. In winter we could see by the well-blackened fire-place at one end of the room that it needed to be cosily snugged down against the cold winds from the Persian mountains. This at least was a welcoming place. Alongside was a date garden set round a swimming pool. The dates were coming up to harvest time but the number one rule in the mess was 'No Date Picking' – the officer in charge of the base was obviously a gardener! We did find later that by gently shaking the appropriate tree we could achieve an early clandestine harvest of one or two fruits falling into the pool, slightly green but still delicious.

The cabins were all in a block, long and thin, set almost down on the beach to catch every breath of wind. And then at a decent distance apart from the hoi-polloi of comparatively junior officers was the Residency from where the Lord of the Liver tried to keep the area more or less friendly to Britain.

The shame was that we learnt almost on arrival that the base was in the process of being closed down. It must have been a slow process though as I stayed there again some twelve years later, in the winter. The fires were certainly needed then.

We had a couple of days in the comparative comfort and ease of *Jufair* and then word came that *Loch Glendhu* had arrived and anchored in the outer anchorage in company with *Norfolk*, a County class cruiser and flagship of the Commander-in-Chief, East Indies Station. The outer anchorage was away by the oil terminal, some three miles off, and might just as well have been on the moon as no one was prepared to send the base's only boat, a motorised dhow, out that far. However the bush telegraph revealed that a fast launch from the cruiser was coming in next day and we resolved to hitch a lift back in that, which we did. Meanwhile there was just time for a last tasting of the windfall dates round the Wardroom pool.

Chapter 6

A Frigate in the Persian Gulf

That period, a year after the end of the Japanese war, was not without interest at sea. The Navy had of course paid off much of the wartime fleets and great numbers of wartime sailors had returned to civilian life. For both political and organisational reasons however there was a limit to the speed at which ships and men could be waved goodbye, and *Loch Glendhu* along with many other ships in 1946 was still manned largely by so-called Hostilities Only sailors. That and the climatic effects of a Persian Gulf summer certainly showed when Midshipman Williams and I finally got on board that August morning.

My heart sank as the launch brought us closer to the ship, sides streaked with rust stains and dirt, paintwork looking decidedly woebegone and off-duty members of the Ship's Company lounging on the upper deck and giving one to wonder if piracy had indeed been finally vanquished in the Gulf.

Onboard it was clear that the delights of the East were no substitute as far as the wartime sailors were concerned for a quick passage home. Most of them indeed bore their last few months in the Service with great stoicism but the atmosphere of impatience to leave which hung over a sizable minority was quite tangible. And of course the climate did not help. Ashore it had been sizzling hot. On board life below decks was almost unbearable. Shorts, sandals and prickly heat were the order of the day. The officers did indeed put on shirts for meals, but the latter consisted only of a quick dash together down to the Wardroom for food and drink and a hasty return to the upper deck dripping in sweat. There was always at least one casualty stretched out somewhere suffering from heat stroke. Air conditioning was not of course on the menu.

The general ambience was not improved by what I can only call a 'happening' which occurred almost as soon as we set foot onboard. It was a crushingly hot afternoon. We were still lying in the outer anchorage, some three miles off shore where there was indeed a little wind, but as it blew directly off the desert it did little enough to moderate the heat. Onboard the cruiser the crew were slightly better off than ourselves. The County class were comfortable ships – 8-inch gun cruisers built for 'Imperial Policing' in the tropics. With high deckheads and wooden decks, there was a general feeling of space on board. Not relevant to the emerging situation but often a source of some amusement to those in humbler vessels were the three funnels of the 'Countys'. Rumour had it that the third one had only been added to the design 'to impress the natives'. Be that as it may they were a pretty and distinctive feature. The cruiser's Ship's Company seemed to have been less flattened by the heat than our own and on this particular day the First Lieutenant, a keen sailing man, had decided that it would add to the gaiety of the afternoon if he were to sail any libertymen mad enough to want to go ashore, into the Base in the ship's cutter; the latter was the same genus of boat as those we had sailed and pulled on the River Mersey during Eaton Hall days. That afternoon, several thousand miles from the Mersey, the cruiser's cutter was spied making over for *Loch Glendhu*. One or two of our sailors had elected for the trip ashore and having been inspected by the Officer of the Day were waiting on the quarterdeck. Also on the quarterdeck was a crowd of off-watch stokers and sailors sheltering from the heat of the day under the awning. They watched with languid interest as the cutter drew alongside, stemming the quite appreciable tide. Unfortunately the helmsman, the First Lieutenant of the flagship, misjudged the latter and the cutter hit our quarterdeck ladder vigorously enough to do it no good. It would be overstating things to say that an ironic cheer went up from our half-naked, sweating sailors who were by now draped over the guardrails to get the better view, a thing which no self-respecting ship should countenance. There was however a very audible rumble of hardly suppressed critical comment amongst which phrases such as 'Wotcher, Nelson' could be heard above the rest. Hardly a mutinous display perhaps but certainly one which went well beyond the bounds of good order. Worse, the Officer of the Day did little to check it. The First Lieutenant of the flagship was hardly amused and our Captain was summoned over later that day in sword and medals, the naval equivalent of sackcloth and ashes, to make an official apology to the Flag Captain. It was hardly surprising that the former was not amused either and he ordered the Officer of the Day to row over next day to apologise to the First Lieutenant. This would have closed the affair had not our wretched fellow passed out from heat stroke half way over. Luckily he was being watched with interest from both ships, was swiftly rescued and soon recovered but I did begin to wonder whether I might

133

have done better to have stayed in that other cruiser now refitting in Simonstown.

Shortly afterwards however I was made Navigator of the ship and life took a distinct turn for the better. What sort of ship was it that I was going to be allowed to navigate round the Persian Gulf, and later the entire East Indies?

The Loch class frigates were built towards the end of the War as 'cheap' and hopefully 'cheerful' long-range convoy escorts. They shared a common hull and machinery design with their sister class, the Bays. By that stage of the War they had to be extremely basic. Shortage of steel allowed nothing else. And what steel there was had a very basic specification. Given the slightest chance it would begin to rust and in the warmth and damp of the tropics that rust if not quickly checked would have a field day. The sound of the chipping hammer was never absent and on several occasions sailors had been known to announce lugubriously to the Chief Boatswain's Mate, 'Me 'ammer's just gone through, Chief. Think I've made an 'ole.' Never mind – we survived. The Lochs were the anti-submarine version, the Bays the anti-aircraft ships. The illustration on p. 227 shows a Loch Bay class frigate, in this case *Largo Bay*. *Loch Glendhu* was similar except as described below. Why not combine both capabilities in the same hull? Principally because by the later stages of the War anti-submarine weapons had become relatively sophisticated, powerful, heavy and large. A single combined A/S and Anti-Aircraft version would have needed a larger hull than the Lochs or Bays leading to fewer ships for the same outlay. We could end up with say four escorts for a convoy instead of six. Gaps in anti-submarine cover would result. On balance it was thought preferable to have more ships and accept that each could not fulfil both roles. It could be argued that was the right decision – or maybe not. Anyway that is what we had, and *Loch Glendhu* was an anti-submarine frigate. Her principal armament was an anti-submarine mortar, the Squid. This replaced the depth charges with which we began the War. Depth charges could only be dropped after the ship had passed over a submarine. The underwater detection beam however could not point directly downwards so depth charge fitted ships could expect to lose contact with their target before dropping their charges – not very efficient. The Squid mortar on the other hand fired a pattern of six charges which dropped in a circular pattern some distance ahead of the ship, thus allowing one to keep contact right up to the moment of firing. The great disadvantage of the weapon in the Lochs in peacetime was that the rails for the bomb loading trolleys took up a lot of deck space which was then not available for more highly-prized pursuits such as parties for the locals. One might almost think that we had returned to the bitter arguments at the turn of the century between ships which actually used their allowance of practice ammunition to improve their gunnery and those which quietly lowered it overboard at dead of night to avoid dirtying their paintwork with nasty cordite marks.

We did have a surface armament, an ancient hand-worked 4-inch gun presumably for confronting a submarine after the latter had been blown to the surface. It had a range of some five miles but the arrangements for aiming were so primitive that the only chance of scoring a hit was to close the range to a few hundred yards, and then you needed a gunlayer and trainer who could compensate for any movement of the ship. Its only use to us was for firing salutes to the various rulers of the Gulf states, but even in this role it had a tendency to misfire which could cause enormous embarrassment – a Ruler and his subjects could be relied upon to make a careful count of the 'guns' he received and any shortfall was instantly put down to lack of respect rather than the more charitable and likely explanation of a misfire. In the end we were sometimes driven to continuing a salute with rifle shots after a bad misfire, until, that is, a year or two later, when we were finally fitted with some proper saluting guns and 'war' was able finally to give way to 'peace'.

We always understood that the long-term plan for the Gulf post-War was to have a squadron of four ships allocated to the area of which two would be up there at any one time. They were to be Bird class frigates, much more upmarket than the humble Lochs and more importantly, air conditioned. Lovely names – *Wren, Wild Goose* and so on. We never saw any of them and continued our solitary and occasional patrols for the two further years that I had on the station, alternating with our opposite number *Loch Quoich*.

A day or two after I joined we sailed for Basra, as ever to cheer up the British service and civilian contingent there and to reassure the pro-western elements in the country of our continued interest and support. The politics of it all tended to pass over the heads of us junior officers but writing now some half a century later it does seem incredible how little any of us onboard from the Captain downwards knew of the history of the Gulf and its surrounding States. In Part One of this book, in introducing my father's letters written from HMS *Fox* in the Gulf before the First World War I have attempted a very brief account of how British interest came to develop in the area up to the beginning of this century. I supppose there might have been some excuse for us in *Loch Glendhu* not to have been too aware of this in 1946 but surely we ought to have had an inkling of events in Iraq after World War One, no more than twenty-five years earlier.

We had never heard for instance of Gertrude Bell, the Englishwoman who arguably was the kingmaker of modern Iraq. Working as an archae-ologist at Ur before the First World War and absorbing there the ancient history of the land she became so convinced of the destiny of those provinces conquered from the Turks during the War as to constitute a vital and influential force in the establishment of modern Iraq. She was actively concerned in choosing the first king, Feisal I, and remained his friend and confidante long after the Iraqis began to run their own affairs. Later she became the first Director of Antiquities and though often ill and by then lonely she remained as such until in 1926 in a bout of depression she took her own life. King Feisal himself led the funeral cortège to the British Cemetery.

I marvel now that we could have been so ignorant of history so recent. I suppose we thought that having just won a long war it was ordained that we should help to maintain a presence in an area where we knew with certainty that we had been actively involved over some two hundred years and where we had agreements freely entered into with rulers all along its shores. You may say now, and Cairo Radio lost no chance of broadcasting the message then, that our only interest was in supporting those who could help us secure our oil. But our relations in the Gulf were in most cases with a still oligarchic society, sometimes as in Muscat, where in some ways our treaty ties were the closest, with a near-feudal regime. It was in the interests of all that we should work with the grain of events and hope that we could influence them where practicable for the greater good.

Anyway at that time of year our most immediate problem was to survive the rest of the summer and keep the body and soul of the Ship's Company together. On this first trip to Basra the climate finally caught up with our Engineer Officer and I still have the clear nightmare memory of helping to chase him round and through the trucks in some sort of railway marshalling yard quite close to the ship in order to persuade him that he be invalided back to England.

I fear that all this talk of hot weather privations in the Gulf risks becoming a bore. Perhaps I may be permitted to let it rest with two tall stories. In a letter in Part One of this book my Father recounts a visit to Telegraph Bay which he describes as reputedly the hottest place on earth. I cannot now find Telegraph Bay on the chart but an Elphinstone Inlet looks as though it might be the same place. It fits my Father's description well. Apparently in the not-too-distant past a frigate decided to repeat *Fox's* visit to the inlet and to spend a day or two there. Trying to mitigate the temperature onboard they let the boilers die. This helped less than anyone expected but when the time came to get under way again there was no steam to run the boiler room fans, so no one could get down below to light the boilers and the ship was immobilised. Help had to be summoned to tow them out.

Another one concerns the British India Steamship Company which used to run services up the Gulf and continued after the War. They had the reputation of fielding a smart and efficiently run organisation and as might be expected the Officer of the Watch in their ships was required to be properly dressed at all times and whatever the weather. In hot weather this would normally have been a white shirt and a pair of white shorts. On this particular occasion the OOW felt that it was too hot for a shirt; the Captain should be having his afternoon nap and there would be no one about to notice if he took his off. The Captain however for once could not sleep and coming onto the Bridge was furious to find the ethos of the BI Company thus impugned. He ordered the OOW, who happened to be his First Mate, to stand his watch the next day in full whites, long duck trousers and white jacket with high collar buttoned at the neck. This incidentally was, and I believe still is, formal tropical rig in the RN. In fact it is not unduly uncomfortable but it is certainly more sweaty than shirt and shorts.

I should mention at this point that the BI colour scheme for their ships included a black-painted funnel with two white rings round it.

The next afternoon the Captain shortened his siesta and came up on the Bridge to see that the First Mate was doing his penance. He was thus distressed to find that his second-in-command was standing his Watch dressed in nothing at all except for a black top hat with two white rings painted roughly round it. The Persian Gulf summer!

The passage up the Shatt al Arab however to Basra on this first trip was a sheer delight. On this occasion we took a pilot. Later we would know the way ourselves. First we had to find him. The meeting place was normally the Light Vessel at the mouth of the river and locating this was not always that easy. We relied on star sights morning and evening to fix our position but in the Gulf the vagaries of the light at dawn and dusk made it quite difficult to be sure of the line of the horizon and the position lines which the three or four stars gave could often work out to be miles apart. One turned then to dead reckoning: estimating from your ship's course and speed since the last sight, and the currents in between, where you thought you were. But here another problem crept in. No one seemed to be quite sure of how the currents in the Gulf worked. My Father mentioned this difficulty in his letters pre-War which form Part One of this book. I believe that things are rather more organised now, though probably less fun. All this uncertainty introduced a delightful measure of art into navigating around the Gulf.

It also meant that our Captain was certainly not leaving the fate of his ship in the hands of a new Navigator and took his own sights as well. Our results that morning off the Shatt al Arab differed by tens of miles but by some mischance and probably with some help for once from our not very efficient radar set we did manage to grope our way to the pilot and to pick him up at more or less the right time.

The Light Vessel marked the entrance to the river but one had to take that on trust. There was no sign otherwise that we were not still out in the middle of the Gulf. True there was a slightly muddy tinge to the water but that was all. However the pilot said, 'Steer this way,' and our chart gave the same course so we set out confidently enough and by and by we did begin to sense that the horizon on each side of us was becoming more and more solid; and after another mile or two it became clear that we were indeed coming into a river.

It was not all that different from what one might have expected. On the Persian side it was mostly marshlands of tall reeds. It was not until we were nearly up to the Anglo-Iranian refinery at Abadan that the banks began to draw in and take solid shape. Apart from the chimneys and 'cracking towers' and warehouses of the refinery as we passed Abadan it was a mainly pastoral and peaceful scene with palm trees necklaced with dates, huts of sun-dried bricks, sailing boats with tall lateen sails, canoes and rowing boats. And of course ocean-going steamers passing up and down. The river was wide and there seemed plenty of room for all though the chart showed that much of the seemingly peaceful water was in fact pretty shallow.

A few miles upstream from Abadan we passed the ruined palace of the erstwhile Sheikh of Korramshahr. Up until the end of World War Two he had ruled over southern Persia and was a man of substance; his palace even had a battery of saluting guns. After the War we helped to depose him in favour of the Shah in Teheran. No doubt we had our reasons but I remember even in 1946 wondering whether they justified the subsequent outcome.

A furnace-hot wind was by now blowing across the Bridge from either the Persian or the Iraqi side depending on which leg of the river we were on but otherwise it was a delightful passage. I suppose it took maybe four or five hours.

We secured in Basra just below the main docks at Ma'qil where the RAF had created a small oasis alongside the river. I do not know what they did when we were not there – it must have been a left-over from the days when they operated flying boats in the area. As far as the British were concerned Iraq was still an Air Force 'area of influence'. Mesopotamia you will remember had been carved out of the Ottoman Empire after the First World War and we had started the concept of 'aerial policing' as a means of maintaining some sort of order throughout that vast country. This would have been in Gertrude Bell's day. I do not know what she thought of this concept. I wonder in retrospect how that sort of policy would fit in with our thoughts today. It must have meant the bombing, and destruction even, of villages of recalcitrant tribes, an unattractive thought. Was this the best we could do? It was certainly used on the North-West Frontier in India as an alternative to troops on the ground. There the justification was that the alternative could be costly in soldiers' lives and the almost impossibly broken country made ground operations difficult in the extreme. Possibly in a turbulent area and as a selective measure it was justified to ensure a widespread peace and the better-being of the majority. Or was it that the threat of it was a sufficient deterrent? From this distance one can only hope so. In 1946 we were just grateful for the hospitality of the RAF at their main base at Habbaniyah out in the desert beyond Basra and at the little river-side post at Ma'qil.

There were still flying boats about but they were the BOAC boats, in one of which Williams and I had flown up to Bahrein. They were like corpuscles moving up and down the arteries of the Empire, and each night one would land on the Shatt al Arab alongside us. Shortly after dark one might be up on deck sniffing the slightly cooler air, and from the south would come the noise of a large machine. Soon over the palm trees one would sight the bright white landing lights in the wings floating down towards the water. The red and green of the wingtip navigation lights coloured the dark line of the wings between them, and then just alongside the ship the huge boat would touch down, great plumes of water spraying up from the bows, the whole blotting out the lights on the other bank and their reflection in the water as the machine, its size magnified by the dark, swooshed past. Our letters would be in England next morning.

Chapter 7

The Persian Dawn

We made several more trips up to Basra whilst I was with the ship. My last one must have been I suppose some two years later, by which time relations with Persia were becoming rather edgy over the question of Abadan, and Persia was becoming Iran. On the last occasion it was decided by 'the powers that be' that we should pay a courtesy visit to Abadan to try to maintain some sort of civilised relationship with the Iranians. Thus on our way down the river we secured alongside the refinery – horribly smelly – and prepared to exchange visits with the Governor. Our Captain made the first call, which apparently was received in friendly enough fashion, and we prepared for the Governor to come back to us. The understanding was that he would arrive by road at 11.30, so we had a Guard of Honour drawn up on the Quarterdeck with the strictest instructions from the Captain of the Quarterdeck that he didn't mind what happened as far as the Governor's reception was concerned but if any of those fixed bayonets so much as touched his awning he'd have the sailor concerned repairing any damage that very afternoon, tropical routine or no. Tropical routine meant starting work in the very early morning and laying off during the heat of the afternoon. Lookouts were posted all over the place to give early warning of the gubernatorial arrival. Special permission had been obtained to use our saluting guns alongside the refinery.

No one came. By 1150 'Clear Up Decks' and 'Cooks to the Galley' had been piped, but pangs of hunger amongst those concerned with the reception were having to be stifled, rivers of sweat wiped off perspiring faces. By 1210 it was decided to post yet another lookout in the very deep field to give even earlier warning of an arrival and the Guard was stood down for a quick dinner. The officers relaxed a bit too.

Nothing happened. Then just as we were starting lunch there was a sound of hurrying feet outside the Wardroom door and the Boatswain's Mate's head appeared. 'Boat coming down the river, Sir. Got a big flag up. Can't see what it is but it's coming this way.'

Pandemonium! Captain to First Lieutenant, 'Hell. Get the quarterdeck ladder out.' First Lieutenant, 'It's being mended, Sir. It'll have to be a jumping ladder.' Captain, 'B . . .'

Just then there was another patter of feet and the Boatswain's Mate reappeared. 'Someone's climbing up the gash chute.'

It was of course His Excellency.

He turned out to be a very decent, civilised character. There were apologies all round and we sent him off with a full Guard, a noisy salute and no bayonets through the awning.

Basra was quite popular with the sailors, principally I think because it was the only place where we could get alongside a jetty and give them a run to the canteen without the complication of a boat trip. Otherwise we would spend our time visiting the sheikdoms lower down the Gulf. I always remember one such visit. It was just after I had joined and the ship had not been long in the Persian Gulf either. We arrived at the 'capital', which in reality was a stretch of sandy coastline indistinguishable from miles of other sandy coastline except for a few woebegone-looking huts and a small fort, the latter probably a relic from the days when the Portuguese dominated the trade in the area. I would not like readers to think from such a condescending description that we were offhand about these minor sheikdoms. In fact we mostly had a rather high regard for the Arabs of the desert and the Gulf waters, a very different breed of people in those days from their cousins in the souks ashore. For one thing it was a wonder how they managed to survive, and to live with a certain degree of dignity, in such a harsh environment, and in general to show such hospitality within their straitened means to strangers. The fact remains however that my description of this particular 'capital' is not wildly inaccurate.

On the visit in question we soon got through the formalities, a salute with the right number of guns and no misfires, visits by our Political Agent and by the Ruler, and then the officers were invited to a feast ashore. This was not vastly popular as the weather was extremely hot but it was a three-line whip and no escape. In fact it was quite a 'do' – a sheep roasted on a spit and stuffed with birds stuffed with other smaller birds and so on like the fleas *ad infinitum*. This was what I meant above about the desert Arab. These poor people had little enough to live on themselves and yet felt it right to put on a feast such as this one to which we were invited.

We all sat outside under a rough black marquee affair – the black tents of the *Bedu*. A few rugs covered the ground, hardly the luxurious deep pile carpets of cinema fiction but at least they kept our white uniform trousers from the worst of the dirt. The roasting sheep did smell delicious and there was indeed a miniscule breeze blowing through the open tent, but the heat was terrific and it looked as though there was not going to be anything to drink. Being new to the Gulf and its ways we had asked the Agent beforehand about local 'table manners'. He had said that it was difficult to explain local customs and so on. The safest thing was to follow the Ruler. So we kept a beady eye on him and were much relieved when halfway through the meal a large black man – in our imagination perhaps the Nubian slave of fiction – came in with a big copper pot and poured out a measure of tea for the Ruler. Somehow we seemed to have cups and saucers that day, slightly unusual for the desert, and the Nubian came round and filled all our cups with this rather uncertain looking brew. How soon could we drink it? All eyes were fixed on the Ruler, willing him to make the first move, which he soon did, pouring his tea into the saucer. Obviously, we thought, he has been well-brought up and we quickly followed his example. Like Tantalus however we were just as quickly denied the life-saving properties of the sickly liquid when the Ruler's scrawny Seluki dog loped into the tent, drank up his master's saucer and then quickly finished off ours also.

Muscat was a different kettle of fish altogether. We made several visits there. At the time we were not particularly curious as to the reason. HM ships had been visiting for ages. But why? It was outside the Gulf, entirely feudal, no oil that we knew of. I often wonder nowadays if someone knew something that we didn't and was not letting on.

Most of the Gulf states in 1946 seemed more feudal than democratic in their political life. It was just the way things were, no more gruesome than many so-called democratic regimes today. Bahrein with its open, vociferous bazaar and proximity to the oil town of Dahran in nearby Saudi Arabia was slipping towards a degree of democracy. Kuwait we had only visited once and we had never penetrated inside the walls of the old town. The Agent did however lay on an evening beach picnic for us complete with fresh fish smoked over a driftwood fire on the sand, which still remains a very, literally, fragrant memory. We were indeed scheduled to make another visit later on our way, yet again, up to Basra but as we arrived one of the sailors reported a bad stomach pain which our young, and delightful, Doctor diagnosed as probably appendicitis.

'Right, Doc,' said the Captain. 'We'll anchor here at Kuwait where it's nice and calm and you can operate. We'll be able to see how the Wardroom doubles as an operating theatre like we've written into our War Orders. The Doctor wasn't so sure. He remained to be convinced that the Wardroom could be made sterile; and anyway he felt he needed a second opinion. From this distance I can well understand his reservations. At the time we did not see it that way but a compromise was arranged: the Doctor could go ashore to find a 'second opinion'. Then our Arabic Interpreter made his contribution. By now, as in all these emergencies, it was dark. He pointed out what we knew, that the tide was out, but added what we did not know, that there would be a long wade ashore after our boat grounded and that the water was full of sting-rays. 'Catch you here,' he said, pointing to the upper thigh, and adding, 'Many fishermen hurt. Some die.'

Of course we couldn't let the Doctor die alone, in the dark, on a foreign beach, so lots were drawn for a companion, and who should be unlucky but myself. We duly waded ashore in the dark – lights being judged unwise as they were likely to attract the obnoxious rays. And then we couldn't contact the shoreside doctor. There was only one option left: we cancelled the visit, weighed anchor and set course for Basra and civilised medicine. Inevitably as we entered the Shatt al Arab the patient announced that the pain had gone.

There would have been no problems like this at Muscat. Openly, brazenly feudal and apparently proud of it, Muscat had the American Mission Hospital just round the bay from the Old Town. They would have coped of course most efficiently.

The Old Town stood at the head of a tiny cove, edged on either side by high cliffs which served in summer as most effective heat reflectors. Old Portuguese forts stood one on each cliff. Both were prisons, one holding the common criminals of the country, the other housing, so it was said, the Sultan's uncle. As proof of the Ruler's clemency it was also said that the uncle was allowed to have his wife in prison with him!

I first visited Muscat in a cruiser, HMS *Jamaica*. How a ship that size managed to fit into the cove was quite a miracle. Even *Loch Glendhu* seemed to take up the greater part of it when swinging at anchor there, but maybe we were further up towards the beach. The tradition was that ships visiting painted their names in white paint on the cliff rocks of the eastern headland. No one seemed to ask the Ruler what he thought about this maritime graffiti. It was just assumed to be part of the scene, which in a way it was for there amidst all the others was HMS *Fox*, immortalised before the First World War.

At the head of the cove there was only room for two main buildings, the Sultan's palace and the British Agency. The former we of course never penetrated but I remember well going to dinner in the Agency. For some reason it was another beach landing to get ashore as it had been in Kuwait, but this time, far from dicing with death by sting-ray, when our motor-boat could get in no further, two sturdy Muscatis, or more probably black slaves, waded out with a sedan chair and carried us ashore one by one and dry-footed. The Agency continued the story-thread of confidently solid primitive existence. It was built of the local dark, lava-like rock round a small open central square. In the middle of the latter stood what attempted to be a fountain though in that dry country the attempt did not come off too well. Facing the gate was a piece of light ordnance that looked like the last of the Gatling guns but was probably something more prosaic. Two very authentic Baluchi guards protected the gateway from the alley outside. The Ruler had a small army of Baluchs, either a contingent on detachment from the Indian Army or a force recruited directly in Baluchistan. I cannot remember which. The story went that the Commander was always a British officer on contract, who without the solace of a wife or anyone else was usually invalided home after a year or two with an unserviceable liver.

'Old Muscat' did not extend far beyond the head of the cove. Then one came to the gate in the town wall and this was a miniature museum in itself. Everyone coming in from the outside had to leave his weapons, firearms or whatever, at the gate. There they were hung on nails all over the inside walls of the gatehouse and made a brilliant trophy display, particularly as most were decorated and trimmed with patterns in silver. What proportion of the rifles worked was another matter.

Outside the gate was the hockey pitch and on the way to the hockey pitch was what appeared to be the Sultan's harem. At any event as our hockey team of relatively young, upstanding and sunburnt sailors passed we would be aware of a chattering above our heads like a troop of monkeys and of eyes peering excitedly out. The team was always cautioned before landing on no account to respond in any way to all this female interest on pain of, if not death, then at least being responsible for grave damage to the British connection. After the excitement of 'passing the harem' the hockey itself was usually fast and friendly. I cannot remember whom we played. It somehow always seemed rather incongruous against that medieval background of a gatehouse full of weapons, imprisoned uncles and the like.

Down the coast and round the corner from Muscat the Sultan's possessions ran southward to Masirah Island and Salalah. Masirah was leased from Muscat and was mostly given over to an RAF airstrip and outpost. Salalah was the Ruler's country residence where he hunted and spent a good deal of the summer. We never landed there but apparently that stretch of the coast received a fairly adequate rainfall from the north-east monsoon and prospered so well that scrawny crops of wheat could be grown. And further inland was the mysterious Jebel al Akhdar, the Green Mountain, 10,000 ft high. We never got up there either.

We did see a good deal of the coast though because on one of our later spells in the Gulf we took a beach survey team with us. They brought a lot of gear with them, including two outboard engines for our heavy old dinghy which they thought they were going to use for their surveys. As ever the outboards were hopelessly unreliable and the dinghy was too heavy for them anyway. The team was forever getting stuck, usually on a lee shore, normally after dark and invariably at a most unpopular time, as when we might be having a film and be near a good bit. An Aldis light would be sighted in the distance SOS-ing and away would have to go the motor-boat, sometimes if conditions were bad with one of the officers in it to help. We never did learn what they were supposed to be doing. Who would want to make an over-beach landing anywhere round Muscat?

Anyway the team of four petty officers had obviously been specially selected, and breathed fresh life into the Ship's Company for a few months. They also brought sheaves of aerial photographs with them and these were of considerable interest. Most of our charts dated from the great days of the Victorian surveys. They gave every indication of being extraordinarily accurate in the areas which they covered and which had been surveyed; and were always being updated by Notices to Mariners, so that we never felt that we might be navigating blind as it were. It was interesting though to compare up-to-date photographs of the coastline with the drawings shown on our charts. I suppose we came across quite a few discrepancies and settled these in favour of the photographs but there was only one major difference.

The chart showed a fairly unbroken coastline to the south-east of Muscat but photographs identified a sizable indentation some ten miles out from the town, hardly a bay, more a small inlet. It was not really of great significance, much too small to afford shelter for instance to anything the size of *Loch Glendhu*, but, as it was obviously there, it ought to go on the chart.

That could have been the end of it. We could have reported it to the Hydrographer, who is responsible for all the charts issued, and we might have looked at it from the sea, added a few sketches from seaward to adorn the chart and called it a day. As however we happened one day to be passing this new feature on our way up to Muscat after a visit to the rather grumpy fishing village of Sur, I managed to persuade the Captain to leave me ashore a mile or so east of the inlet so that I could walk along the coast, see the inlet and rejoin the ship in Muscat.

This worked very well. The coast line consisted of low rocky cliffs. Most importantly it was clear of scrubby growth which could have made progress difficult. I didn't expect any paths and indeed there were none. The 'new' inlet held no surprises, but I do have to admit that I got something of a thrill at the thought that just possibly I might have been the first European to walk round it. What did surprise me greatly and pleasantly was to come over the top of a low fold in the cliffs and find below me in a small valley a perfect little oasis. I suppose it extended to perhaps an acre. A low wall made a square enclosure of this little area of green. Inside were a few date palms and many vegetables and fruits, all laid out with neat paths between them. The contrast with the rocky aridity of the desert outside could hardly have been more arresting. Even more surprising was the sight of the owner of this luscious plot hard at work, cultivating and watering. He showed no surprise at my appearance over the hill so I complimented him on his garden and passed on. I had not at the time read my Father's account of finding a similar tiny speck of fertility further down the coast – his description is in his letter of 16 June 1914 in Chapter 3 of Part One of this book. Perhaps these little patches of cultivation wherever there was a supply of water were more common that I had supposed, and I had merely come across a market garden close to Muscat. At any rate this present 'discovery' was a most pleasing happening.

I hesitantly suggested to the Captain when I got back on board that the inlet might be named Khor Corson. It was hardly a surprise that the impertinent idea was promptly vetoed and he forwarded for Their Lordship's consideration that the inlet be named after the nearest Muscati settlement. Quite right too!

A last vignette on that lovely, backward, romantic Persian Gulf of the 1940s. An airliner crashed into the *khor* at Bahrein one day whilst we were anchored there, and sank. Some of the passengers escaped; quite a few did not and were drowned. There had been one or two similar fatalities at Bahrein but this was the first when an aircraft had crashed into the sea. Being on the spot we at once sent a boat over to see if we could be of any help and were just slightly embarrassed when the answer was 'Yes. You could send some divers over to help get the bodies out.' The embarrassment arose because the only divers of any sort on board were another Lieutenant and myself. We had thought, while the ship had been undergoing a previous maintenance period in Singapore, that we could spend a few mornings up in the Base swimming bath experimenting with the ship's Shallow Water Diving Gear and this would be so much more pleasant than sitting out the time in a hot and grubby ship in dry dock. This worked very well until our bluff was called that day in Bahrein.

We could hardly back out then. The Shallow Water Diving Gear was like a very primitive scuba set. There was nothing for it but to try to remember how the wretched things worked, put them on and get down inside the aircraft. I cannot remember what the shark situation was; at least there were no sea-snakes. We found a lot of these when we revisited the Gulf later. The main problem in this particular operation was the amount of buoyant rubbish floating around inside the fuselage. It was slightly eerie to say the least to be ferreting around inside a water-borne blanket trying to find a way out and all of a sudden to come upon a pair of legs or worse. The story went that the poor people thus drowned were taken eventually to the local morgue. One in fact was not drowned at all, came to in the middle of the night and sat up on his slab to ask where he was. The caretaker, a devout Mohammedan, was so startled that he began to wonder whether his creed covered such eventualities and later became a Christian.

We were nearly marooned in the Gulf that summer. On the day before we were due to sail for Colombo one of the electric fans in the boiler room went 'on the blink'. Our Electrical Artificer, allegedly a skilled craftsman, seemed unable to mend the thing and in the course of his surgery dropped it, not once but several times. Difficult to blame him, as it was blindingly hot below in the boiler room, but of course without that fan we could not raise steam. Gloom all round. In those simple days however 'heavy electrics' was still in some ships, though not in *Loch Glendhu*, the province of the seaman Torpedo Branch. Luckily one of our most ancient Petty Officers had been a torpedoman. He took over and saved the day. I only recount the incident as an illustration of how wonderfully simple life could be some fifty years ago!

I have only talked about the Persian Gulf in summer. It had a winter too, cold and savage in many instances but in the spring and autumn there could be spells of really wonderful weather, cold crisp mornings, warm days when the air was clear and it was a joy to be alive. I particularly remember one Morning Watch when we were on passage at the south end of the Gulf and making up for Bahrein. As the light strengthened we began to pick out the Persian mountains, snow-topped over a hundred miles to the north-east and the words of Flecker's translation of 'Hassan' came to mind:

> Thy dawn, O Master of the World, thy dawn;
> The hour the lilies open on the lawn,
> The hour the grey wings pass beyond the mountains,
> The hour of silence when we hear the fountains,
> The hour that dreams are brighter and winds colder,
> The hour that young love wakes on a white shoulder.
> O Master of the World, the Persian Dawn.

Chapter 8

Tales from
the Hills and the Islands

After our first tour in the Gulf in 1946 we were thought to be due for some 'Station Leave' and each Watch was to have ten days. On this occasion the ship had come into Colombo and a day or two after we arrived our particular party caught the 0645 train and climbed up through the hills to reach the rest camp at Diyatalawa some ten hours later. Our train driver saw no reason to hurry and we had a delightful journey. We soon left the palm and paddy country of the coast and started to wind up through the rubber plantations towards the yet higher tea-growing areas. One might have expected the air to get fresher as we moved up but we found there were advantages in staying imprisoned behind closed windows to keep out the smuts and smoke from the railway's low-quality coal. Gradually the tea gave way to jungle or where that had been pushed back, to grassy hills. The clouds came down and brief showers of rain swept across the country giving way in turn to more summery piles of meringue-like cumulus. We began to think of the Scottish Highlands on a fine day. The contrast with the grey rocks of the Musandam Peninsula which was all we had had to look at no more than a week before could hardly have been more complete.

By mid-afternoon we had reached Haputale, the highest point on the line and then, coming out of a tunnel, we saw Diyatalawa in the distance. On one side of the line we could still look down for thousands of feet over what seemed as many miles to the country we had climbed through over the past eight hours. From that distance one could only sense what seemed an endless stretch of jungly vegetation. A river glinted here and there in the distance. Occasionally there was a glimpse of a loop of the railway line far below us. The engine had indeed done well to get us thus far up. Quite soon this splendid panorama was eclipsed as we came below the rim of the Diyatalawa bowl and looked down on the camp beneath. The bowl was huge, like the shallow crater of an extinct volcano and seemingly some fifty miles across. In the hollow lay the Rest Camps, three of them left over from the War. Two we were to find out had closed down and our relatively small party did tend to rattle round a bit in the third.

The most welcome aspect of course was the cool. At night there were log fires, blankets on beds, and one began to be reassured that the torpor of the coast was a purely local effect. Even up here, as in the Gulf, one could not escape the imprint of one's forebears: there on the map was Fox Hill and on the hill so honoured was the ship's name and badge, all picked out in white stones. From my Father's letters the old *Fox* had seemed to have been in an even worse state of preservation than *Loch Glendhu* and to have had a somewhat unhappy Ship's Company into the bargain. Diyatalawa had evidently cheered them in 1913 sufficiently to complete that memento of a visit as it cheered us up thirty-three years later. It did not occur to us, regrettably, to be similarly artistic.

We had another spell in the hills the following year. That time two of us elected to make our own arrangements and lodged at Haputale with an ex-Colombo Harbour Pilot and his wife. The idea was to hunt leopards, which were apparently unreasonably predatory in those parts. The Pilot's wife met us at the station, a mere halt on that lovely, lonely line, no more than a stopping-place in the middle of a pine forest. She was a little, spherical-shaped woman, with wide-brimmed hat, weather-beaten face, jodhpurs and riding boots and with an enormous revolver strapped round her globe-sized waist. 'It's not really dangerous here,' she assured us, 'but better safe than sorry.' 'People?' we asked, 'or' – more eagerly – 'leopards?' 'Well, you never know, do you.'

We slept in a grass hut, little enough protection against predators, and early each morning were out trekking through the jungle. Perhaps it was lucky that we came upon no animals on any of our expeditions – except for one. We had taken the day off from the jungle and hired two contraptions which the owner assured us were bicycles and had pushed up above Haputale to the Horton Plains. This was a huge flat grassy stretch literally on top of the world and a track led from Haputale to the Government Rest House on the further edge of the plain. The place was aptly named World's End. I suppose one could see virtually the whole of the south of the island thousands of feet below, laid out like a sand table at one's feet. We borrowed fishing rods from the Rest House keeper who was delighted to have company, and spent an hour or so round the start of a small river not far off. There were certainly fish there and plenty of rises but the banks were badly overgrown and casting was impossible. We

151

were forever getting hooked up on something or other. When we took his rods back the Rest House keeper asked us politely whether we had had any luck. 'Ah,' he said, when we told him of our frustrations. 'Long time ago other gentleman fishing there. He hooked up too but one time he look round, he find he hooked baby leopard. He catch him in ear. Just then great big fish he rise in pool almost out of water. Gentleman, he put down rod and seize his gun and next time that fish rise he shoot him.' And of course the Rest House keeper demonstrated the size of the fish with outstretched arms. He could not actually show us the fish, which in the circumstances you might have thought would have been preserved. At the World's End, with that view 2000 feet below one, it was possible to believe anything.

By now the afternoon light was beginning to fade and with the short twilight of those latitudes we knew we had best get a move on to make Haputale before dark. We had reached the 'home' side of the Plains and started down the steep narrow track between banks of bamboo by which we had come up that morning before we realised that our 'bicycles' had virtually no brakes. By then it was too late to do much about this and we could only pray that we would not meet anyone coming up. Our prayers were not answered. Rounding a bend I came across a fair-sized leopard lying stretched out across the path. I could not stop. There was hardly time to wonder why such an animal should take forty winks in such a spot. I could only swerve to miss most of him and managed just to clip the end of his tail. Brakes or no, I accelerated sharply and had no time to look round to gauge the leopard's reaction to a bicycle wheeling over his tail. Round the next corner however I had no option but to run into the bamboo to check my flight for right in the middle of the path was a local and he showed no sign of moving. As I picked myself out of the thicket I could see that he was excited but not noticeably unfriendly. 'You seen a leopard?' he shouted. 'I just shot one but him get away. I think him wounded. If I no find him, him one very dangerous animal for humans.' We took a happy leave of each other when he heard that his quarry had not got away but was anchored securely across the path round the next corner.

Unfortunately we never saw Diyatalawa again, but that first visit in 1946 had been a lifesaver. The ship that I had joined in the Persian Gulf some two months earlier had been in a pretty run-down state with a Ship's Company to match. The ten days up-country worked a sea-change in the sailors, and, while we were in Colombo, the dockyard there tried to fit some air conditioning, one unit in the Sick Bay and another in the Wardroom. If the latter smacks of soft living for some the argument was that air conditioning all the messdecks was simply not on the cards. The Wardroom machine in fact never worked. Rumour had it that the skilled workmen connected the cooling gas circuit to the water supply! Maybe it was for the best – we were all destined to sweat together.

As to the sailors, we managed to get most of the 'Hostilities Only' men, who had been impatient for relief when I first joined, off home, and a draft of new young post-War volunteer spirits brought a breath of fresh air. So we set off from Ceylon with a Mine Disposal team for the Andaman Islands in relatively good spirits, which two or three weeks of sailing, picnicking and hunting round those lovely islands improved still further. I cannot recall that we blew up any mines.

The Andaman Islands lie in the Bay of Bengal. Before the War they were a penal settlement for hard cases from the gaols of India. During the War they were of course occupied by the Japanese who mined the surrounding waters quite heavily and maintained a significant garrison ashore. Much more interesting from our point of view at that time however was the reported continued presence in the jungles of small settlements of Jarawa pygmies, hostile to strangers and marksmen with the blowpipe.

Port Blair, the chief town, lay at the head of a fine, sheltered bay. It could hardly justify being called a capital but it was a focus of considerable naval activity when we arrived with a whole squadron of ocean-going minesweepers anchored in the harbour. These were pretty little vessels, well able to look after themselves in open waters, their neat and tidy design at once conveying a sense of relevance to their job. One got the impression that they had been crafted together unlike our ugly selves who had plainly been launched directly off the shelf. We did not see much of them as they sailed, their sweep presumably completed, almost as soon as we arrived. It was pleasant enough though to meet again two Royal Indian Navy officers who had been through Eaton Hall with the rest of us.

We ourselves were soon off too to the remote hinterland of the islands, Macpherson Strait, Port Anson and Port Stewart. We assumed that our Bomb Disposal team had business there and they were certainly very active searching stretches of the shores where presumably 'suspicious objects' had been reported, but we never heard much in the way of explosions.

The rest of us had a wonderful time. I as the Navigator was able to spend days out in the whaler under sail allegedly sounding out reefs to

confirm their positions on our charts; as though our Victorian hydro-
graphers could have missed anything! We were the merest amateurs by
comparison. Others spent their afternoons combing the jungle after deer
or traces of the Jarawa. For the deer's sake I am happy to record that
the animals won hands down. As for the humans we did see a few old
primitive huts which were at once pronounced to be of Jarawa origin,
but no darts flew from the undergrowth and it was the hornets which
were the enemy. Port Anson from its description in the *Bay of Bengal
Pilot* sounded as though it might have been a tropical Tobermory but it
turned out to be just a beautiful, deserted and land-locked bay. We spent
several days there while the bomb disposers consulted their records and
the rest of us got lost in the jungle. A companion and I spent twenty
minutes in something of a panic one afternoon enmeshed in an acre or
so of bamboo and wandering round in ever more desperate circles. My
fellow-hunter was more dedicated than I and was forever snaking his way
through the stems on his belly while I tailed on behind, desperately trying
not to catalogue all the real serpents which I imagined we must meet.
Eventually we got a grip on ourselves and stopped to think things out.
We had come up a little hill from the beach and must now be lost
somewhere near the top of it. The hillock was north of the beach. If we
calmed down and went downhill in a southerly direction more or less
towards the sun we were bound to strike the sea, and so it worked out.
A hundred yards and we were on the sand, as relieved as maybe at escaping
from that awful maze.

A couple of sailors, also on the trail of, I suppose, a deer, needed a little
more help to extricate themselves. It had been mid-afternoon by the time
we ourselves found the water again. An hour or so after one could sense
that the light was not as strong as it had been. Not too much later it
would be starting to get dark. We began to count up the hunting party
most of whom were by now beginning to straggle back along the beach
to our boat. We seemed to be two short and began calling into the tangle
of trees and undergrowth to locate them. At last we got a reply, seemingly
not too far off.

'Come on. It's time we got back to the ship.'

'We're coming as fast as we can.'

Then silence for ten minutes. More calling. More replies but seemingly
from a slightly different direction. The light continued to fade. Calls
and replies became increasingly concerned until it began to be clear that
our two sailors were not at all jungle-friendly and were by now too

disorientated to move anywhere, let alone in the right direction. In the end we told them to stay where they were and we, by now jungle-hardened veterans, chopped a way in to get them out. It was only fifty yards or so but it might have been fifty miles as far as that somewhat shaken pair were concerned. It was something of a lesson for all of us.

Quite different from the jungle were the oysters. These seemed to grow, and to be found, in great profusion on the rocks on the opposite side of the bay from Port Blair. The first crop which an intrepid explorer brought back were treated with some caution to assess the after-effects of consumption. No one being the worse next day, an open season was declared and we lived very well on them for the rest of the time that we were back at Port Blair. Our stock of sherry ran out before the oysters.

We ended our stay in the Andamans with some sort of a 'do' on board for a group of Burmese from the Karen hill-tribes of Burma. Apparently they had been caught in the islands by the Japanese occupation and despite all pressures from the invaders had declined to co-operate with them. We were all struck by the oddity of coming across such a civilised, though not necessarily sophisticated in the western sense, group in these surroundings and a fireworks display was arranged to amuse them and give some indication of our admiration for their stand. Of course half the rockets did not go off!

Our cruise through the attractively off-track parts of what was still the Empire continued with a visit to Car Nicobar on our way to Singapore for our annual maintenance period and bottom-scrape. Car Nicobar was just as attractive as the Andamans though in a different sense. The joys of the latter, for us anyway, lay in its wild primeval jungle, its empty bays and coves, its navigational amusements and hazards. By contrast the Nicobars, or at any rate Car Nicobar which was the northern islet of the group and not one of the largest, were redolent of the South Sea Island paradises of Robert Louis Stevenson. A British Commissioner and his wife and daughter exercised dominion over the island and acted, or at least he did, as Chief Engineer, Magistrate, Chief of Police, the lot. Unfortunately Sawi Bay, which was our allotted anchorage, was very open to the weather, and the weather during our short stop was unsettled by a cyclone further north towards Calcutta. Also our motor-boat was having one of its fits of the sulks so anyone wanting to make contact with the shore had to sail in by our whaler. These distractions however in no way dampened the spirits of the islanders who one afternoon, when we ourselves were keeping Anchor Watch to see that we did not drag our anchor and drift ashore, diverted us with a most splendid canoe race past the ship. Two canoes, forty paddlers a side, all going hell for leather through the weather. It put us thoroughly in our place as we in the Wardroom returned to our Monopoly, which was our staple diet when storm-bound.

Chapter 9

Singapore for Christmas

Singapore a couple of days later was not an entirely welcome change. The Japanese War had ended some fifteen months earlier but the Dockyard had not yet come to terms with the aftermath. Most dockyards tend towards a degree of untidiness at the best of times. Singapore had not been fought over or badly devastated but piles of rubbish, or rather heaps of sad-looking ironwork, lay everywhere. The 'workers' seemed sullen and hardly active. The only group which gave much impression of order or action were the Japanese prisoners. Without them very little would have been accomplished. By then they were hardly prisoners in the sense of living behind barbed wire and did not in fact appear to be subject to restraints of any kind. One could see in them one of the pillars of the Japanese post-war economic success, a docile and energetic work-force. At the time with memories of wartime horrors so raw we did not feel sorry for them. They were not badly treated and were certainly not slave labour; and over the months they were slowly being repatriated. In Indonesia in fact they were still serving as formed units under our control to keep the peace in the absence of sufficient British troops and in the face of quite wild Indonesian determination to avoid being recolonised by the Dutch.

Relations with the Malay and Chinese dockyard workforce did improve over the years that we knew Singapore. Indeed it was rumoured that the RN Commodore in charge of the Yard and the chief Convenor of the Unions used to have fairly regular clandestine meetings to discuss whether and when it might inconvenience the Yard least for a section of the workforce to take 'industrial action' over some claim or other.

For the sailors Singapore had certain obvious attractions, but a regular part of each of our visits was the Naval Provost Marshal's tour for groups of visiting Ship's Companies of the haunts that they might well have been patronising the night before. The Chinese girls so attractive by moonlight turned out to be as often as not transvestites. The streets which had seemed quaint by the light of the street lamps were revealed as in many cases not much better than rubbish dumps. The tours certainly had an impact until the next run ashore, but, after months of celibacy in the likes of the Persian Gulf, the Andamans, the Nicobars, the bright lights continued not unnaturally to beckon.

Living conditions in the Base however were attractive. With a ship in dock the Ship's Company would move out *en bloc* to HMS *Terror*, the Fleet Shore Accommodation. This was a bright and airy place, a barracks if you like, but nicely set on a slight rise above the dockyard. Playing fields and swimming baths were everywhere and after a while there hardly seemed much point in making the long trek into Singapore city.

The Wardroom used to go 'ashore' for the occasional Chinese meal in Bugis Street. It did not impinge on my limited conscience until my next visit to Singapore some fifteen years later that this was just as infamous an area as other nether regions of the city more patronised by the sailors.

Anyway our visits to Singapore were not primarily about visits to Bugis Street or anywhere else. It was rather a matter of having the bottom of the ship scraped of weed and repainted with anti-fouling paint; and in our case of trying to discover why we never seemed to be able to reach our full design speed. The engines were not in themselves all that old, but being reciprocating steam engines they were mostly an entirely new field to our engineers. Almost all RN ships had been powered for years by steam turbines, dating from the time when Sir Charles Parsons had electrified the world with his dash through the Fleet in his turbine-engined yacht *Turbinia* at the 1897 Spithead Review where the Navy was assembled for Queen Victoria's Jubilee. One associated reciprocating engines with the venerable paddle-steamers such as those which used to run along the south coast between Bournemouth and Brighton. The little bits of oil-soaked wick which brushed and lubricated the bearings on the crank shafts at the top of each stroke of the pistons were probably little different from the arrangements in HMS *Warrior* built in the 1860s and now preserved at Portsmouth as a fascinating link in the development from sail to steam.

Our trouble was that whenever we did a full power trial or otherwise tried to reach our full speed of 19 knots we never seemed able to achieve much more than three quarters of this figure without the ship starting to vibrate in a thoroughly alarming manner. As the speed built up the mast would develop a wriggling motion like a snake in full flight. The engine room crew would be seen abandoning the engine room and hanging rather shame-facedly round the top of the ladder down to the compartment, and eventually on the Bridge our collective nerve would break and the Captain would order a return to the more placid life at cruising speed.

Even when far from home the men of the Royal Navy always manage to have a jolly time. On this Christmas Day their guests were offered not only singing and dancing but a "variety of viands" not to mention champagne, various wines, "four water grog and colonial ale".

CHRISTMAS-DAY ON BOARD THE GALATEA.——Christmas-day in port on board a frigate like the Galatea, where there is a complement of well-nigh 500 men, thousands of miles away from home, was by no means to be lightly observed. The whole of the mess tables on the lower deck had been marvellously decorated with flowers, fruit, evergreens, and paper of many tints, each side of the deck showing a series of bowers of luxuriant foliage, prettily interspersed with oranges. The religious services over, the tables were lighted up with a lavish display of wax lights arranged in pretty little chandeliers, and the leafy avenues were rendered brilliant by many lamps. The ordinary fare of the mess table had given place to such a variety of viands that caterers for entertainments to Royalty might envy the tact and genius displayed. During dinner visitors, and especially the ladies, were besought, in the most winning and persuasive manner, to partake of the good things provided, and were enjoined to eat, drink, and be merry, and make themselves thoroughly at home. Compliance with the earnest and pressing invitations could scarcely be avoided, and great was the delight for "Jack" to see his guests enjoy themselves. There was a plentiful supply of diluents, ranging from champagne and various wines to "four water" grog and colonial ale. Dinner and dessert were followed by dancing on the gun-deck, and fiddles, flutes, concertinas, and accordions were kept going at a rapid rate. Then came the chairing of the officers. One after another, from the commander down to the tiniest "middy," was seized, placed on a chair lashed with two handspikes, and duly hoisted and carried round the decks in triumph. The ludicrous procession was accompanied with vocal and instrumental music, the chief burthen of which was a repeated and prolonged outburst of "He's a jolly good fellow," sung to the usual popular tune, and followed, as the delighted occupant of the chair was shot out at his cabin, with three times three rattling British cheers. When the list of officers had been exhausted, the petty officers were also treated to a taste of the triumphal entertainment, but with much less delicacy of handling; and when the spree had well-nigh run its course, the dogs belonging to various parties on board were decorated with ribands, and underwent the chairing process in a state of blank bewilderment, and with countenances on which the most comic consternation was expressed. After tea singing and dancing were resumed, and set-dances, circle-dances, and step-dances were carried on simultaneously with unflagging zest and vigour. One great feature of the day's amusement is that the boys on board are for the day promoted to the rank of men and petty officers, and these in turn take the place of the boys. Great scope is thus afforded to the youngsters to have some playful retaliation. The proceedings were full of good humour, and the visitors will not soon forget Christmas-day on board the Galatea.

——*Melbourne Argus.*

Christmas 1868 – A cutting from *The Times*

What was wrong? Each year our bottom-scrape and maintenance period overran its planned completion date as the Dockyard tried to work out what sort of gremlin we harboured. Some said we needed different propellers. Another theory centred round a bent propeller shaft. There were several others. Nothing worked however, certainly during my time on board. I heard a year or two later though that a new Engineer Officer joined shortly after I left. He was an 'old and bold' from the Clyde, no less. He took the ship over whilst she was refitting and at the end of the refit there was once more the obligatory full power trial. As the revs built up the ship began to quiver in time-honoured fashion. The mast started to 'snake'. The Chief Engine Room Artificer made to abandon the throttles as was his wont. The new Engineer Officer however, so we were told, leapt to the foot-plate and spun the wheels wide open. By now the engine room was totally empty of any crew other than himself. The vibration increased, reached a crescendo – and then quite suddenly died away. A wonderful calm crept over the ship. She sped through the water faster than ever before. The mast stood like a sentry; and the Captain reached for the engine room phone to ask what had happened. 'Aye, weel, it was ever this way on the auld steamers,' replied Chief at the other end. 'Ye have to get them through the shakes and then they're awa'.' 'Of course! Everything shakes at its critical speed. Why on earth hadn't we thought of it before? Unbelievable.

In 1946 though we had not mastered this particular trick. After our bucolic swing through the Andamans and Nicobars we stayed over in Singapore for Christmas. We did our best to make up for being eight thousand miles from England but it was hardly a patch on Christmas 1868 on board the frigate *Galatea* in Melbourne, Victoria, Australia. The cutting (p. 159) from an old copy of *The Times* describes the day. It sounds a much more jolly time than we in our bachelor existence were able to arrange! After World War Two we seemed to be rather more inhibited. Christmas was a season with certainly plenty of goodwill all round but also hopefully a time that would not end in too many tears from the demon alcohol. Living ashore in *Terror* gave us a flying start in both respects and plenty of struggles on the playing fields after Christmas lunch carried us well through to the evening.

The fire party left on board the ship however, which was by now sitting with another frigate lost in the bottom of the biggest dry dock east of Suez, were not quite so lucky. It was an unpleasant existence at the best of times down in the bottom of that great hole, sited as we were so that when it rained, which was regularly once a day, we got the run-off from all the gutters in the vicinity. One of the fire party decided at some point on Christmas Day that it was all too much and that he must get up to ground level. Rather than brave the gangway which was guarded by the Quartermaster he hit on a 'do-it-yourself' route along one of the shores which kept the ship upright on the keel blocks now that there was no water round her. These shores were massive 12-inch square timbers but there was a thirty foot drop below to the bottom of the dock – no problem for a tightrope artist, but for a slightly worse for wear sailor?

As the Officer of the Day onboard I became aware of a slight indefinable feeling that something was going on when our would-be circus artist was half-way across. There was then the question of what was to be done. There was not much that anyone could do by then other than to persuade his messmates to keep quiet until he reached the other side. Something similar occurred some ten years later when the new Forth Road Bridge was being built. One night after the pubs closed a sailor attempted the first crossing of the Firth along one of the cables just then hauled over to support the bridge roadway. He reached the other side intact where he was met by the police, and eventually ended up before Flag Officer, Scotland, who felt that the maintenance of good order required a fairly severe punishment. In fairness however it had to be recognised that the sailor had achieved a remarkable feat and he received the Admiral's hearty congratulations as soon as sentence had been passed.

The following year we were in Bombay for Christmas, in company with the East Indies flagship with the Commander-in-Chief embarked. That year we went to particular pains to ensure that no untoward happenings should upset the Christmas spirit. The Captain, accompanied by the rest of us, made the rounds of the messdecks before lunch and managed to admire the cheerful decorations whilst limiting the intake of rum which the ever-hospitable sailors pressed on one. We ended up in the Wardroom feeling that the ship was in pretty good shape and its company in good spirits. The Wardroom in those *Loch* and *Bay* class ships was somewhere near the middle of the ship and alongside the main fore-and-aft gangway, a somewhat noisy location but one which kept us right down in the heart of things. Lunch went cheerfully enough though by the time we got to the Christmas pudding it did seem that the rest of the ship was rather quiet. Ah well, perhaps everyone had taken to heart this business of being in company with the flagship, etc., etc.

Lunch was just over when there was an urgent knocking on the door and there was the Quartermaster asking for the Officer of the Day in rather agitated tones. 'You'd better come down to the Quarterdeck, Sir.' 'What's happening?'

Anything might have been happening but I certainly was not prepared for what had actually come to pass. Every single one of the flagship's boats was now made fast astern of *Loch Glendhu* and the Commander-in-Chief's barge was just being tenderly brought alongside, not by its own crew but by a team of our sailors. I am afraid we pirates thought it was rather a clever operation to have secured such a fleet from under the noses of the cruiser's people who were supposed to be on watch. Not unnaturally perhaps the losers did not share our view and our Captain was soon under way in full ceremonial uniform, sword and medals, to apologise.

The Flag Captain was a neighbour of ours at home and I was injudicious enough to remind him of the incident some thirty years later. It still rankled then. However he was a kindly man and not at all without a sense of humour. His house and garden overlooked the narrow road through the hamlet in which he and his family lived. One day he was gardening near the wall which flanked the road when a car drove slowly past, stopped and a woman got out. 'Could you tell me where so-and-so lives?' she asked in a rather affected voice. The Captain sensed a game and putting on his broadest country dialect gave her directions. In a few minutes she was back again. 'I couldn't find the house, my good man.' She hesitated, and then, 'I'm actually coming to live here and I'm looking for a gardener. I suppose you couldn't come and work for me?' 'Oi'm afraid not, Ma'am. See, Oi've got plenty o' work yerabouts.' 'I'd pay you very well; more than you get here.' The Captain scratched his head. ''T'is very temptin', Ma'am, Oi'll say thaat. But o'course Oi get plenty o' perks yere.' 'Well, I'm sure I could manage that too.' 'Well-l, Oi doan't know 'bout thaat Ma'am; see Oi sleeps wi' Mistress yere.'

The woman never did settle in that village.

Chapter 10

Station Safari

By the end of 1947 we were beginning to fall into a routine of annual visits round the East Indies Station. Starting from Singapore, rather quiet for a day or two at leaving friends made there during those overlong refits, but glad to be at sea again, we would make for our base at Trincomalee. Our pay and stores accounts were kept there and needed a yearly stock-taking. Then we would head west for the Seychelles and the East African coast.

In those days the Seychelles had no contact with the outside world except by wireless and the monthly steamer from Mombasa. We only ever visited the capital, Mahé, but that was enough to cheer us up. In the late 1940s before the twentieth century curse of Tourism had devalued the island scene they were as near paradise as surely as it must be possible to get. Left so much by itself the population could not help being to an extent inbred. It showed most amongst the white islanders, many of whom were of French stock. Sometimes one came across a French family who had fled France during the War, and they were often something else again. For the sailors the white Seychellois girls were particularly welcoming. I remember a dance for the Ship's Company on one visit. It was at the Sports Club and for one dance I was partnering a handsome matron with the build of a hockey goal-keeper. Happily conversational opportunities and requirements were limited by the noise but naturally I managed to squeeze in how much we enjoyed our visits. 'We love them too,' volleyed my partner. 'The sailors do so much to improve the islands' white stock.' For the Wardroom, Government House, halfway up the mountain and overlooking the bay, was equally welcoming. It was sometimes difficult to escape the unworthy thought that just once in a while His Excellency was not too displeased also to have extra-island company though of course for him and his wife the attraction was entirely intellectual.

From the Seychelles we would make the passage over to Zanzibar with its almost overpowering smell of cloves, its narrow alleyways in the old town, the elaborately carved doorways opening off the alleys into the private courts of the more important houses; and then west again to the African coast, Kilwa Kisiwani, Lindi, Tanga and Mombasa.

In fact we only visited Kilwa once, which was a pity. It was not until years later that I learnt that it was thought to have been the seat of an ancient African civilisation, though one afternoon pottering through the bush after some sort of game or other I chanced upon what looked like the dilapidated remains of some primitive stone buildings and I did wonder what they could have been. Kilwa however, or at least the part we saw of it, was a very out-of-the-way place. Our only contact with the shore was the District Officer and he had never seen the 'ruins', so it was difficult to find out more. The local wild life was, at the time, more relevant anyway. We were anchored up some tiny creek which seemed to be a playground for the local hippos. Still more important, the DO had arranged a small safari for anyone interested to watch a herd of elephants who were rumoured to be on passage through the neighbourhood. Four of us signed up immediately, two sailors, the ship's Butcher who often went shooting with us, the Leading Seaman Captain of the Foc'sle, and another watchkeeper and myself. We were to be away for two days and would be guided by a small posse of game wardens.

I suspect we thought the game wardens were also going to act as our porters and the expedition was slightly surprised when it found that the 'white man' was going to carry his own kit. Luckily we had planned on minimum scales anyway but these were quickly further reduced when we got the message. Our little caravan was still quite an impressive sight however as we moved off through the thick scrub around the coast.

We did not walk very far that first day but it was quite enough for us. The elephants unfortunately must have heard of our coming and as we passed each tiny collection of huts the message was always, 'A little further.' The day wore on and it began to dawn on us that we were not going to see any elephants at all. Eventually arriving at what appeared to be an old camp site the Chief Game Warden said, 'Stop.' He was dead right.

The other three had hauled camp beds along with them and soon made themselves more or less at home in the huts on the edge of the clearing. I had an idea that huts were for snakes as well as humans and that camp beds, being not far above ground level, might well prove attractive to roving serpents. I had therefore settled on a hammock, which I now slung between two trees. Either way that night in the African bush not far from Kilwa Kisiwani was sensational. The moon was full. Although there was a small village not far off, almost as soon as it got dark not a sound was to be heard and by the time we turned in the silence was so complete as to be quite deafening. In my hammock the only sound was the buzz of a mosquito which had inevitably got into the net along with me. I swatted him eventually and then the silvered moonlit countryside was completely still. The silence however kept me awake. It is remarkable how disturbing the really complete absence of any noise at all can be. And then I thought I began to hear indistinct rustlings from beneath my hammock. It sounded as though it might be an impala or some similarly sharp-horned animal browsing. It occured to me that if I made a noise it could well lift its head sharply, driving the needle-ended horns which I was by now convinced that it possessed, painfully into my backside. So I lay very still and continued thus for what seemed like half the night until I came to realise that the noise came from within my hammock and was in fact no more than my tummy rumbling.

Next morning after a wash and a swim in the allegedly crocodile-infested river we set off in search of smaller game. We did not find much but I will always remember that morning as one of those times when one is brought face to face with the truth about one's self. Towards midday it was of course very hot. We had drunk our way through our water-bottle ration when we came upon a small hamlet where for some reason a woman was selling mangoes. One penny each and I had a penny on me. No one else had any money; you don't expect to need it in the bush. I hung back as the others passed thirstily through the huts and when alone bought one mango. Did I share this with my comrades? I did not, and to this day have always recognised that I would be a hopeless companion on a desert island.

From Kilwa we steamed north up the coast to Tanga. This had been laid out by German colonists before the First World War and as one might expect was to a very tidy plan. The settlement stood on a bluff above a well-sheltered bay and the spacious ordered layout and snug anchorage was always reflected in the welcome we got ashore. They did field a fearsome hockey team which we never managed to match. We would not spend long in Tanga. It was a tiny spot, but when not playing hockey I found the cemetery of absorbing interest. The gravestones vied with each other in describing the exploits of the owner during his life on earth and I could not but feel that a very readable novel could be crafted round their stories.

North again lay Lindi, much in the news in those days as the coastal base of the grandiose Ground Nuts scheme. Some may remember this as the great project intended to bring prosperity to this part of Kenya after World War Two. The plan was a spectacular failure because either the climate or the soil was unsuitable; maybe it was both. When we knew Lindi the scheme was still being driven forward and the settlement was littered with tanks from the war now converted as bull-dozers or ploughs. All was by no means gloom there at that time though. The club's dance floor was a source of great pride, sprung on two tiers of old motor tyres which the devotees claimed made it one of the most sophisticated in Africa. I felt they had rather overdone the suspension! We counted thirty-five Europeans in Lindi.

And so back to civilisation when we reached Mombasa. This was much more a sailor's town than the little settlements down the coast. For the Wardroom the continuous absorption of hospitality over the past few weeks and its return on behalf of the whole Ship's Company would by now be becoming something of a burden. Two days visiting followed by a day's steaming and then another two-day visit could prove rather taxing for us unsophisticated lot. And of course it was worse for the sailors, which made it worse for us all.

But the country, the navigational amusements, the different histories, all these were the plus side of the coin, though again most of it was a side which the sailors glimpsed only too dimly. From their point of view Singapore, the Seychelles and perhaps Mombasa were not at all bad. Otherwise it was up to us all to amuse ourselves.

I am not sure we ever thought very seriously about what a frigate was supposed to be doing in the East Indies. The short answer I suppose was showing the Flag. And after all we had maintained a naval presence to keep the peace in the area for some one hundred and fifty years. Don't ask a silly question! We cheered people up, did not oppress the poor and were a visible sign of a paternalistic Empire most of which at that time was not ready for and did not seek its independence. For anyone who thought more widely, either ashore in the places we visited or onboard *Loch Glendhu* itself, we were also a visible reminder of the way naval forces deployed around the world as they then were could be concentrated quite quickly in a particular spot should the need arise. This unique ability was demonstrated more than once until a Labour government decided to withdraw forces from 'east of Suez' in the mid-1960s.

None of this I am sure was in our minds as we made the short passage from Mombasa to Lamu. It was harder to leave Mombasa than it had been the anchorages further south simply because we had spent a few days longer there and dug ourselves in further. A visit to Lamu though was a sovereign salve for battered hearts. For one thing the navigational exercise of getting into the tiny creek, tiny at any rate for a ship of even our size, was an intriguing one. Both the Harbour Master and the Resident Naval Officer at Mombasa had been generous with their local knowledge and we had no real difficulty but here and there a few yards off the 'deep-water' channel would have put us aground.

Once in the anchorage, and even more so perhaps when at last ashore, it was very evident that Lamu was a real pearl of a place. Situated on an island just off the coast it was one of the prime trading posts, 'port' might be too grand a word, for dhows from the Persian Gulf. Big ocean-going *baggalas* lay at anchor, seemingly not too busy but with their captains or *nakhodas* involved in trade of some sort. In those days they were all sailing ships, a huge mast stepped about a third of the ship's length from the stern and then raked heavily forward carried an enormous yard to which was laced the main and only sail. At the stern was a raised poop with a ladder leading up to it from the main deck. The *nakhoda* could usually be seen, in harbour at least, sitting cross-legged on a carpet on his poop, haggling and bartering with merchants from shore. We asked what they brought down from the Gulf. No one ever seemed too sure but I suppose there were dates from Iraq, perhaps spices and carpets from Persia, maybe pearls from the lower end of the Gulf. From Lamu they would sail on to Zanzibar, another Arab outpost, and then the river mouths of the African coast to load cargoes of mangrove wood. This was used for house-building in the Gulf, there being no ready supply of indigenous timber there.

Ashore the Arab influence was particularly strong, houses straight from the bazaars of the Gulf, beautifully carved doors as in Zanzibar. It was an attractive and unique place in those days.

Mogadishu, our next stop up the coast, was entirely different. There the Italian influence had transported a Mediterranean seaport to the Indian Ocean. Before the War it had been the capital of Italian Somaliland. Now, with the latter being a British protectorate, it was still the capital and the Italian influence remained strong. I don't know that the Somalis noticed much difference between the two administrations.

And so we steamed north to Berbera, rounding Cape Guardafui on one occasion during my Middle Watch and on the most unimaginably beautiful night. The moon was full, the sky completely clear, the sea like a pond. The light reflected back from the water was enough to bathe the ship in an attractive glow, not enough to throw into relief the sharp edges, the

167

CONFIDENTIAL.
Secret & Private.

Aden 9th. January 1949.

The Captain,

THROUGH: THE 1ST. Lieutenant, Aden.

Dear Sirs,   RE: FAREH DEERIA, Seaman.

       I beg to state that I have already reported against the conduct and character of the abovenamed Seaman Fareh Deeria to the 1st. Lieutenant, who investigated the matter and the evidence Abdo Kassem sweeper deposed that the Accused told the crews to run away from the ship as the steamer is bad.

       I now preferred to bring the matter to your kind notice as the ship now in the harbour, and it is easy now to turn and discharge him away before any more abetting results from him when the ship is abroad the sea, and for the interest and benefit of the staff, I find it my humble duty to discover to you the real and true facts.

       This Accused entices and encourages the crews by saying to them that it is better to run out from the ship. The matter was raised by me to the Division Officer & Cockson, and the Division Officer enquired and ascertained the fact from the evidence Abdo Kassem Sweeper. Really speaking this Accused is a dangerous person, and I have a right to enlighten the matter secretly, before any trouble is caused by this Accused in future when the ship is abroad the sea.

       This Accused also alleges to the crews that "Do not listen to the Tandil and that the Tandil has no power or influence whatsoever". I have several times explained this fact to the Division Officer & Cockson.

       My advice is that this Accused should be discharged from this ship and given a chance in other ship, as he is a troublesome person in this steamer. This is my views, I have enlightened it.

       Further I advise that to book up two sweepers one sweeper will act for the English people Bathroom, and the other for the Somalie Bathroom. One sweeper shall have to write our Arabic letters which is necessary and important. In fact one sweeper is now leaving the ship, and to replace the Accused Somalie we require 2 sweepers.

       I have done my duty to explain to you the matter, and the proverb says to remove your tooth is better than to bear the pain.

       And for which I shall ever pray, I remain,

       Yours Obediently

i.e.   Sherey Abdillah
          1st. Tandil
          Aden.

The Tindal's letter

nooks and crannies of its wartime build. To port the low hills of the Horn of Africa were sharp and black along the horizon. To starboard and nearly a hundred miles off lay Socotra, administered I believe from Aden but too wild to be visited much by HM ships. What peace, detached from the distractions and perhaps worries of the shore! If only all life could be like that. What a good thing it isn't!

It was good to visit Berbera because it gave us an insight into the background of the Somali seamen whom we were to pick up in Aden. British Somaliland as it then was, and of which Berbera was the 'capital', was a desperately poor part of the Empire. Berbera reflected that. Outside the rather scrubby town most of the people were herdsmen, tending goats and camels, always foraging for grazing for their animals and following the latter over the border into the Ogaden region of Abyssinia from time to time in the process. It was incredible how they survived at all. But there they were, tall, thin people, some of the women really quite handsome, most of the men looking as wild as they come. Their forays over the border were a constant source of diplomatic friction, though the migrations backwards and forwards must have been going on for so long that inter-governmental protest and apology, claim and counter-claim had become as ritualised as August Bank Holiday.

On reaching Aden we duly embarked our eight Somalis. Six I recall were seamen and the other two engine room ratings in a manner of speaking. The idea was that being much better adjusted to the climate than our own sailors they would be able to work at painting and cleaning in conditions which normally flattened Europeans. Living conditions for them were far from ideal. During the hot weather they seemed to live mostly on the upper deck, their pathetically meagre gear packed away in cardboard suitcases and stowed wherever the Chief Boatswain's Mate would not disturb them. In the colder weather of the Persian Gulf winter we did manage to move them down below and eventually we persuaded them to stay there for good. Their senior rate, the Tindal, was little Sherri Abdullah. I was their Divisional Officer and I acquired an Arabic primer the better to understand them but they were a clannish crew and we never really achieved much in the way of conversation. If there was a serious matter to unravel the Tindal would have to translate. Life was not always a bed of roses for him as the letter opposite explains. It would have been written for him by a letter-writer ashore to his dictation. I seem to have a vague memory of the Farah Derriah mentioned in the letter, a short stocky man unlike the general run of the tall, lean tribesmen. He was probably a townie from Berbera. At this distance in time one suspects that the root of the Tindal's trouble was a disagreement over the terms of trade which the Somalis carried on between our different ports. The return on their investment in goods was probably pathetically small by western standards but then their pay was not tied to our scales either.

Dear Somalis. In those bad old days of Empire race prejudice, at least from our side, was not a problem. I think most of us felt a little sad about their meagre lifestyle and were certainly appreciative of their efforts at ship maintenance in that tropical heat. After I left the ship I heard on the grapevine that poor Sherri Abdullah had been done to death with a chipping hammer. The general supposition was that disagreement over the share-out of 'trade profit' was at the bottom of it. I do not suppose that any of the Somalis anyway would have fingered the murderer.

Aden was the Somali's 'home port'. Aden, that Gibraltar of the Indian Ocean, guarding for the British and for others the sea trade route through the Red Sea from Europe to the Far East. Each year between 1944 and 1949 I passed through it, east to west, west to east, south to north and north to south; and each time I found its blasted lava rock spell-bindingly irresistible. What could be the attraction of a place which was once a punishment station for battalions which behaved badly in India? In my own case I suppose it was its unique barrenness. If you wanted to survive there you were thrown back on your own resources. You either made your own amusements or fell prey to enervating depression. The sheer rocky peak of Shamsān either crushed you with its sun-scarred cliffs and gullies or elated you with the way it reached to the sky. Perhaps in the end it was the feeling that for Europeans at any rate you had either to co-operate with each other against the nothingness or become nothing yourself.

In later years when we handed Aden over to the new state of South Yemen I could not help feeling that a keystone had been knocked out of the arch which made sailoring East of Suez such an attractive way of life. Of course the general revision of HMG's defence policies, as well as the instability in the Interior and the Hadhramhaut, probably made its retention insupportable. And yet . . .

Chapter 11

By Whaler to Kiltan

The Laccadive Islands lie about one hundred and fifty miles off the west coast of India. There are perhaps half a dozen small islets in the group. We visited Chetlat, Kiltan and Androth on our way back to Ceylon from one of our periodic swings around the Persian Gulf. The islands are tiny, a mile or two long and not quite as wide. They stand on pinnacles of coral which rise almost sheer from the ocean floor, and are home to miniscule fishing communities. It was almost incredible in the late 1940s to think of people existing in such isolation. I would find it yet harder to believe that they could still be there today.

As with our beach surveys in the Gulf no one told us why we were sent there. With the benefit of hindsight I can only think that we were to reconnoitre the group as a possible site for an airfield, as a refuelling stop *en route* to Singapore should facilities be refused on the Indian sub-continent after Independence. In the event of course Gan in the Maldives, further south, was chosen.

We visited each of the three. I do not remember much about Androth. At Chetlat however the village arranged a feast to which we were invited. As so often in the Gulf, it was humbling to come across a community which must have been living not all that far from the edge of starvation and yet felt it right to offer such hospitality. I hope that we made a trade of provisions in return. In the event we could have done without the meal. It was, naturally, based on coconut meat and dried fish. In large quantities both tend to be indigestible. But there was also a sort of junkety, milk-based concoction for afters; and since there were no cows, or even goats, on the island, where did the milk come from? The junket was not helped down by the observation of one island-watcher who swore that he had seen a large number of women vanishing into the bushes that morning before we had landed. Ugh!

The beach survey team could not achieve much in the group. Outside the reef which circled each islet you were straightaway in a thousand fathoms. Inside it was mostly shallow enough to walk ashore. However they had brought with them photographs of the lagoons and these provided the catalyst for a sailing expedition in our whaler from Chetlat to Kiltan. Another watch-keeper and I set off with four or five sailors in good time before the ship was due to leave Chetlat and aimed to beat her to Kiltan. I suppose the distance between islands was some twenty-five miles, so in the middle we had the Indian Ocean completely to ourselves. It was, I remember, a beautiful day, wind perhaps force 3, one or two white horses to give us a reasonable turn of speed. Never enough wind to make it other than a bit of a picnic.

The odd thing was that we actually found Kiltan pretty well where we thought it was. I suppose that in a sail over that short distance we should have been shot if we had not. It was still quite a thrill, not to say something of a relief though, when a tiny speck began to appear over the horizon and to grow into something recognisably solid. As we approached land however we began to appreciate that the journey so far had been nothing. The testing part lay ahead. Out in the ocean we had not noticed much of a swell. Approaching the land it became clear that there must have been something moving on the deep because the sea was breaking all along the reef which enclosed the lagoon wth a far-from-friendly frenzy. From a small boat it looked unpleasant. The island was tiny enough for us to sail round to the other side to see if things looked more settled there. They didn't. We came back to where the aerial photograph which we had with us showed a break in the surf, but the photograph must have been taken on an even calmer day because today we could detect no chink in the encircling breakers.

By now the ship was beginning to heave up over the horizon. In half an hour or so she would be up with us. Honour dictated that we should have reached the shore by then. We looked even harder at the photograph, this time searching for some evidence of a mark ashore to lead us into the passage which the camera showed. Eventually we thought we had one and determined to give it a try. I went up into the bows, relieving our seaman lookout. If we were going to hit a rock I would rather see it myself first. We edged in towards the surf. People appeared on the beach, clearly waving us away. Too late now; we were committed. It was our photograph against their local knowledge and for the moment we had no access to the latter. A coral head loomed up to starboard and we shaved past it. We were getting into the surf now. Another head moved towards us on the port bow, throwing the ocean aside as a trough in the waves let it drain, sinking out of sight again into the succeeding wave. We missed that too. Something appeared ahead. Coral, or what? I shouted to the helmsman to put the tiller over but he couldn't hear. I shut my eyes waiting for the now-inevitable crunch, the inrush of water through a shattered bow. No one used life-jackets in those days, not in this weather anyway. What monsters or poisonous fish waited for us in the lagoon? But nothing happened. A friendly surf lifted us roughly over whatever was on the bottom and thrust us smartly forward into the calm, limpid, waters of the lagoon. A large punctured balloon deflating was as nothing to our collective sigh of relief. We sailed smartly over to the beach, jumped ashore and raised a Union Jack on an oar. The islanders took it in good part and sent out a canoe through an entirely different entrance to meet the ship, which had just arrived.

From Kiltan we were due to make for Colombo. I was still Navigator then, and, with our unreliable radar set, best navigational practice dictated that if you were making a landfall on a coast without good landmarks you should aim well to one side of your intended arrival point and then turn down the coast until you reached it. Common sense really. We did just this when making the coast of Ceylon some two days later. I had in fact got a good star sight that morning and felt confident enough of our position to adjust our speed to make Colombo at 0800. After which I went down for breakfast feeling pretty content with the world. At half past seven I was cleaning my teeth in the bathroom before going up to take a look at Colombo as I thought about five miles ahead, when through the scuttle I caught sight of the lighthouse on the end of Colombo harbour breakwater. Help!

On the Bridge, seconds later, I found the Officer of the Watch dozing over the pelorus and the ship about to enter Colombo harbour as though on autopilot. A more confident Navigator would have blamed an erratically strong current down the coast. Either way there was just time to turn the ship round and make a good pretence of marking time until 0800 and all before the 'High Command' realised that anything was wrong. Luckily the Captain's scuttle was on the opposite side from the lighthouse!

From Colombo we were due to continue easterly to Singapore for our annual bottom-scrape, refit and agony session of a full power trial. Crossing the Bay of Bengal we began to become aware that all was not well in Malaya. We had no doubt picked up the latest Station Intelligence Report in the mail at Colombo. Normally these seldom or never contained any news horrific enough to disturb our annual peregrinations around the limits of the Station so the Report would circulate onboard with a stately progress to match. This one however did make us sit up. It warned in urgent paragraphs of a disturbing increase in the activity of Chinese Communist groups throughout the country, forecasting that the latter were now certainly embarking on a campaign aimed at subverting Malaya into a Communist Chinese state. For once the forecast was eerily accurate. It was to be ten years on before the communist threat was finally contained and then overcome.

In some ways all this was no doubt an inevitable development from the War. In Malaya it was only the Chinese who seemed to offer any meaningful behind-the-lines resistance to the Japanese and so of course they attracted the bulk of what support in the way of weapons supply, etc., that we were able to give. Whether we thought that they were more Chiang Kai-Shek orientated as opposed to supporting the communist view I do not know. Maybe we did not at the time recognise the difference. Any enemy of the Japanese was our friend. Either way, after the War's end they came out in their true colours and the resultant 'emergency' was only ended many years later by a political settlement which paved the way for Malaysian independence. It seemed a hard way to achieve what was inevitable anyway.

In 1948 the spreading terrorism had to be contained on the ground, mostly in the jungle, before any worthwhile or lasting settlement could be contemplated. *Loch Glendhu* reached Singapore a few days before a State of Emergency was declared and was soon invited to man two small patrol boats to help prevent landings of saboteurs and supplies along the three hundred and fifty odd miles of the east coast of Malaya. This was not immediately popular with our Captain or Heads of Department – the First Lieutenant and the Engineer Officer – as it would inevitably mean a depletion of the forces available for repair work on board. Those of us who might expect to go off up the coast took a more positive view.

A day or two later the rumours began to gather substance. We were to man two Harbour Defence Motor Launches and these were to be made ready to sail almost at once. Each was to have a crew of ten men. Ted Sebborn and I as the Lieutenants with the fewest responsibilities onboard during a refit were to be in command. I pointed out to Ted that I was three weeks senior to him and that settled that one quite amicably.

How long were we to be away? No one knew. Where were we to go? Up the coast of course. What was the weather going to be like: at just over seventy feet long the launches were quite tiny for the open sea. At least we had the answer to that one. It was the end of the south-west monsoon and the north-east weather was not expected to pick up for some months so the east coast should be quite sheltered. The only other fixed point seemed to be that a dockyard tug was to go with us as our supply ship; and, 'For goodness sake get a move on. You're to be ready to leave tomorrow.'

Another dockyard tug delivered the two launches alongside us in the afternoon, HDMLs 1030 and 1031. Certainly the 1031 boat, and I think both, had sunk during the early part of the War in one of the east coast rivers as a result of the monsoon and had lain there during the Japanese occupation. Subsequently they had been raised and refitted and were alleged to be ready for service. I must admit though that the news of their previous exerience did not at once fill us with joy or confidence. Still, they looked all right and the bits that we could get at immediately seemed to work. Anyway, there were apparently no other boats available.

Each boat had an armament of two 20-mm Oerlikon guns, one forward and one aft; and a machine gun mounting on either side of the Bridge, each carrying two Lewis machine guns. There was a large wheelhouse amidships just below the Bridge and small messdecks in each end of the boat; and that was all. No washing places of course. A bucket on the deck and plenty of seawater was however provided.

My own crew was to be led by Petty Officer Hedges, a venerable old Long Service and Good Conduct medal man with some twenty-two years at sea. In *Loch Glendhu* he was known universally as 'Daddy' Hedges and must have been the oldest man in the Ship's Company. I suppose he would have been forty. Not quite the sort one might expect to go dashing round in motor launches as far as the Navy was concerned but he was a very steadying influence in the boat and I was always glad of his support. Petty Officer Engineering Mechanic Oxtoby looked after the engines, two big Gardiner diesels which despite their years on a river bottom purred away like sewing machines and were a constant reassurance to us all. I think Oxtoby came from Birmingham or somewhere in the Midlands. I had really hoped for an Artificer rating. Someone with that skill could have rebuilt the engines if necessary while we were away but in fact Oxtoby looked after us very well and was forever poking his head up through the engine room hatch to announce that he had got something else working. He had Leading Engine Room Mechanic Dixon to support him, not quite as experienced mechanically but a hefty cheerful soul whom it was good to have around.

Then there was Telegraphist Taylor from Glasgow. It was handy that we could only communicate with the outside world through the morse key as it needed a trained ear to interpret his delightful broad Glaswegian. He nearly did for us all one day up the coast. We were exercising Action Stations. Taylor's post was the starboard Lewis gun mounting on the Bridge. We had thrown a couple of old boxes overboard and were shooting at them, Lewis guns included, when the inboard gun on Taylor's mounting jammed. In the best traditions of the Service he kept firing with the other gun but was not prepared, nor were any of us, for the way in which using this one gun only would swing the whole mounting round. Quick as a flash the one gun still in action swept across the Bridge. Those of us in the way were just that bit quicker and managed to disentangle Taylor from the mounting before worse befell.

To my shame I can only remember two of the Able Seamen. Both were Seven and Five men; that is their engagement term was for seven years with the Fleet and five on the Reserve List. Both had joined since the War and had been with us for a year or so. Price was tall, gangling, and had always seemed somewhat awkward, but in the launch he quickly proved a most splendid cook, not an easy task at which to persevere especially in the tropics and with only the tiniest of galleys. Able Seaman Sharp had come out from England in the same draft as Price and had been my Navigator's Yeoman when I had been, supposedly, navigating *Loch Glendhu* round the East Indies. That meant that he kept the Navigation Department in order, corrected the charts and so on – one of the more cerebral jobs onboard. It was a great snip to have him with us and with his carefully trimmed beard he always despite his youth looked like the old salt on the Players cigarette packet. These were the main players on board the 1031 boat. No one let us down and we got through our two months up the coast with few if any cross words.

Meanwhile we had rather less than a day to provision and ammunition the boats and have them swung for compass adjustment. The latter meant measuring how much the magnetic material in the launch's structure affected the magnetic compass on different headings throughout 360°. We didn't of course have the luxury of a gyrocompass.

At last it was all done. We had collided with the jetty at the ammunition depot, which was unpopular with the crew. If they were expected to do their own jobs properly they didn't see why the Captain shouldn't do his. But by noon on the day after the boats were delivered alongside us we were ready enough for me to climb up the hill to the Naval Headquarters and ask formal permission of the Admiral to proceed. Up until then no one had seemed in the least worried at what we were to do up the coast and I thought it worth-while just to mention the point to the Admiral. 'Don't be damned silly, boy,' was the sharp reply. 'Just get up there and do whatever is needed.'

Chapter 12

Malayan Emergency

Sped on our way by this expression of trust from on high we set off from Singapore dockyard, dropped down Singapore Straits and out into the China Sea. In fairness to the Admiral, one of the wettest sins at sea was to ask for instructions. In any particular situation you must use your own judgement. If those on high don't like your decision you will be roasted. It happened to us a few days later. That time it was very unfair of course!

For the present I thought that propriety would best be served if the launches were to lead the flotilla down the Straits but, once outside, the Captain of our tug – and supply ship – suggested that as his navigational equipment was a good deal more comprehensive than ours we might all be safer if he were to take the lead. And so the evening came of the first day and we had the first of Able Seaman Price's suppers. Not bad at all, for a beginner!

The sea was flat calm. The twin Gardiners purred away below like a couple of kittens and even Petty Officer Oxtoby seemed pleased with his machinery. The sun set over the mainland of Malaya in a rosy glow which fitted well with our expectations of the next few weeks. I did have something of a shock during the night though. The arrangement was that I would stand the Middle Watch each night at sea from midnight to 0400 whilst PO Hedges would do the First and Morning. When I finally heaved myself up from the wheelhouse, which was my cabin, for this, my first Middle, I found a beautiful moonlit night, calm and almost as clear as day; but looming almost over us, and in my imagination much closer, was Pulo Tioman, a large island on our route. 'Help,' I thought, 'What on earth is the tug doing? We're almost ashore.' Hedges showed me the course on the chart which we appeared to be making good and it did seem that we would clear the island handsomely, but had he got it right? The black bulk of Tioman looked much too close in the moonlight. Rather desperately I called up the tug with the Aldis hand signalling lamp. 'A-r-e y-o-u s-u-r-e w-e a-r-e c-l-e-a-r-i-n-g T-i-o-m-a-n?' 'H-o-p-e s-o,' came back the reply almost at once. So someone was awake and on the ball up

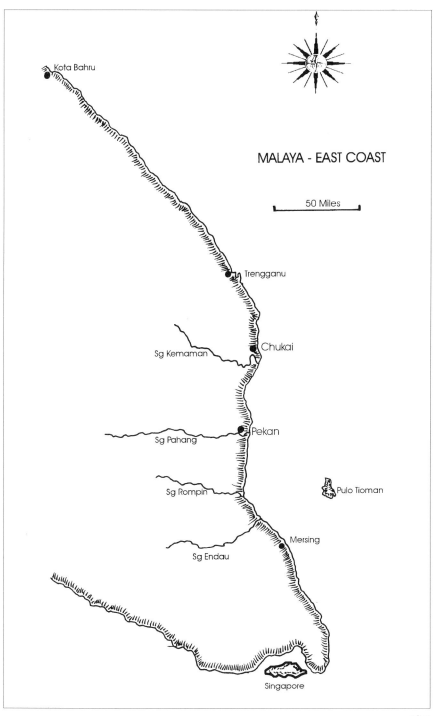

MALAYA - EAST COAST

50 Miles

Kota Bahru

Trengganu

Chukai

Sg Kemaman

Pekan

Sg Pahang

Sg Rompin

Pulo Tioman

Mersing

Sg Endau

Singapore

179

there. Obviously they knew better than I what they were doing. I had better relax. Quite soon Pulo Tioman was fading astern.

Next day we passed Trengganu and dropped off Ted Sebborn and the 1030 boat to base themselves there; and the tug as well since it was about the only place on the coast where it could get into some sort of a port. Ted Sebborn would look after the coast south from Trengganu whilst we would take on the northern half, basing ourselves at Kota Bahru at the northern extremity of Malaya and on the border with Thailand. If anyone was going to do any smuggling from the north that would be their nearest point of entry.

But when we eventually reached the place I began to have second thoughts. For a start there did not seem to be anything there. Trengganu may not have been a port in the accepted sense of the word but it did at least boast some houses and there were a few signs of activity. Kota Bahru seemed to be just a name on the chart; there was precious little on the ground. And as we closed the coast it became obvious that the water was so shallow that we would have to anchor way off-shore all the time – unpopular with all of us.

On this first visit however the District Officer who administered the area had arranged a canoe to get me ashore. He had been a prisoner of the Japanese and was it my imagination or did the misery of this experience still show in the poor man's face? Anyway he did not seem unduly concerned about the possibility of terrorist activity in his part of the world and was much more worried that our small ship's presence would upset his people. A few years later we got the same reaction from civilian authorities in Borneo when we arrived with very little notice having been sent from Singapore at high speed to bolster the area at the beginning of the Indonesian 'confrontation' campaign in 1962. At Kota Bahru the DO was chiefly concerned that the windscreen of his new car leaked in the monsoon, and what did I think of this new stuff Bostik as a leak-stopper. I'd never heard of it.

So what with one thing and another, and bearing in mind the Admiral's words, I decided that there must be other more pressing tasks than at Kota Bahru and that we had better find somewhere between Trengganu and Singapore that would appreciate us more. The 1030 boat could stay based on Trengganu and cover to the north. The DO thought that was a much better idea; and of course it would leave his community in peace! I located a place called Chukai on the chart and next evening we felt our way up the river leading to the town. It seemed to be just what we wanted.

Chukai was somewhere between a large village and a very small town. A useful sized jetty lay in a bend of the river, there was a small bazaar and it turned out to be the administrative centre of a District so we had landed on the doorstep of a District Officer as well. It might have been over-egging things to call the guardian of the jetty the Harbour Master but as we needed to stay on good terms with him for such essentials as water and the use of his jetty when not required by the various coasting craft, that's what he remained to us. It was just possible also that he might turn out to be a useful source of local gossip if not actually of usable intelligence.

The morning after we arrived I had another minor brainstorm *à la* Pulo Tioman. I had agreed with our two Petty Officers before we left Singapore that we were going to maintain as reasonable a standard of good order on board as circumstances would allow, so when I turned out next morning and saw no signs of activity about the decks other than our sentry I put it to PO Hedges that we seemed to have omitted Both Watches of the Hands from our routine. Both Watches was an article of faith throughout the Navy, the moment when the greater part of the seaman complement would fall in at the beginning of the day and be detailed off for work. As most of the seamen knew their jobs already it could be said to be a superfluous time-waster, but at least it got everyone off the messdecks after breakfast. When I raised the subject with Hedges that bright morning in Kemaman he looked at me for a few moments in a rather pitying fashion and then said gently, 'Sir, when you take out the Cook of the Mess and the hands who have been sentry overnight, there's only one man left to be at Both Watches. Do you really want to go on with it?' How could I have been so daft?

I found the District Officer in a bungalow on the other side of the town, apologised for not having called the previous evening when we arrived, and solicited his opinion on the security situation and how we could contribute to the peace of his District. As at Kota Bahru he replied that the District was perfectly peaceful as it was and short of a grave and, in his view, unforeseeable deterioration in the situation, he envisaged keeping it that way. So what were my plans? An embarrassing question, so I came clean and said that I had been told to do whatever was necessary. He agreed that that seemed to sum up the situation quite nicely and added that I should not go pottering round the bazaar on my own and should on no account let the sailors do so as it might 'upset the natives'. One was quite quickly becoming aware of how delicate was the political balance.

Obviously we could not hang around Chukai all the time. It was equally clear that the chance of two slow old HDMLs intercepting gun-runners or infiltrators was mathematically insignificant over such a long coastline. There was really only one option and that was to 'do something'. That came down to steaming around in an outwardly determined fashion and it seemed that this might be made to appear more purposeful if we were to turn up unexpectedly and randomly in odd places along the coast. Carrying the line of thought further it seemed that as far as possible we ought to try to make landfalls and departures under cover of darkness. It took me some time to work this out. A quicker brain wouuld have seized the point at once.

Working in and out of Chukai in the dark was an interesting navigational exercise but hardly a problem. There were no conventional navigational aids such as lights and buoys but the only potentially difficult spot was the sand bar at the river mouth and it was not too difficult to find features ashore, a conspicuous tree or rock, a dip in the hills inland, to lead us safely into and out of the river even at night. Once over the bar one held to the middle of the river on the straight stretches, moved over to the outside curve on the bends.

So we started our campaign of stealth by night. For several nights we met absolutely no one, no ships, no boats, no fast canoes, nothing. I began to get rather bored with my regular Middle Watch. Hedges must have had more than enough of his endless round of Firsts and Mornings. I can only think that the rest of our crew were kept going by Price's 'pot messes'.

Then on the fifth night of this somewhat pointless cruising our lookout reported something ahead. We could just make out a dark shape perhaps a couple of miles away. It had to be a ship; and it wasn't showing any navigation lights. Could we possibly have stumbled on the vanguard of the Communist invasion of Malaya from the north? That was highly unlikely but we altered course to intercept. As the two of us approached each other we called the dark shape on our Aldis light. What ship? Where bound? No reply. We were at the time outside the three mile limit and in international waters so we could not do much more. There was certainly no chance of our following her; she must have been doing eighteen knots to our eleven knots maximum and if we maintained that for more than a few hours we would soon be out of fuel. So the most I could do was to send off a signal to Singapore reporting a suspicious vessel proceding at high speed down the coast without lights. We thought we had done a good night's work despite not having been able to get her to talk to us.

Singapore's reply came in a coded signal a couple of days later. It was extremely uncomplimentary. Apparently the ship had been the regular Bangkok-Singapore passenger ferry. It reported to Naval Headquarters that it had been harassed in the vicinity of Pulo Tioman by a strange vessel which identified itself as an HM ship and which had fired across its bows when it had refused to stop. What, the signal went on, did we think we were doing? The ship was steaming without lights to avoid harassment or attack by pirates further north. Unless I behaved more reasonably I would be replaced.

It did seem to me that NHQ had gone overboard, to put it mildly. How were we expected to know about pirates off the Thai coast? No one would, or could, give me much information before we sailed. Just get on with the job; and when we actually do something, look what happens. And NHQ appeared to have accepted the ferry's highly imaginative version of events without question or even asking for our comments. I was extremely angry. However, coding and decoding these signals was by hand and very slow. By the time I had coded up what I really felt, calmer reflections had taken over. I tore up my reply and just acknowledged the signal, adding that we had certainly not fired across anyone's bows and – oh dear – promised to be more careful in the future.

A letter came up a few days later from our own Captain in Singapore, pouring oil on these rather troubled waters and saying that despite their unfriendly signal everyone wished us well. No doubt the Admiral had sent for him and asked why on earth he had let two idiots loose up the coast, didn't he have any responsible officers who could have been spared, etc., etc. Anyway I was more than grateful to him for writing. It did occur to me to wonder at the time how a letter got up to us at Chukai, the country between us and Singapore being supposed to be aflame with banditry. Things were quite confusing. But at least we had 'done something'.

A funny thing happened whilst we were operating out of Chukai. I used to call on the District Officer when we were 'in harbour' for any length of time and we would swap news. To get to his office I had despite his warnings to walk through the bazaar. I had a large and rather handsome walking stick at the time which used regularly to attract interest and comment and thus seemed to act as a sort of passport across the area. On one occasion I noticed down a side street a white European face. It seemed to belong to a child, probably a girl, of perhaps five or six years of age. This seemed to me to be fairly remarkable. There were supposed to be no Europeans in the area at all but the child was unmistakably white and not a halfbreed either. I mentioned the sighting to the DO but he confirmed that without a shadow of doubt his own family was the only European one anywhere near Chukai. I never saw the child again and soon forgot about it all.

A year or two later however, and after I had left the East Indies Station, the English papers carried reports about riots in Singapore which were said to have been caused by accounts of a Dutch family who had fled from Singapore when the Japanese invaded. Apparently they left behind a baby-in-arms because they could not find any way to take her with them. The child was to stay with her Malay amah in whom the couple had great faith, and they would return as soon as the situation permitted. There was confidence if you like! After the War they did come back but the amah had of course vanished and so had the baby. The couple spent years searching for the pair and, according to the news reports, eventually tracked them down to 'a village in Pahang'. Surely this must have been Chukai. The timing seemed most possible and anything else would have been too much of a coincidence. The riots came into the story because when the latter came to light it caused strong resentment amongst Malay opinion, whipped on by troublemakers no doubt for their own reasons, that this child, callously (as they claimed) abandoned by parents years before and cared for by Malays, should be seized back from the latter and from the Muslim faith into which it was claimed she had been introduced. Worst of all was the rumour that she was now being prepared for confirmation as a Christian. I sometimes wondered if the DO in Kemaman knew of the child's presence in the village all the time, had an inkling of the background and realised the nature of the time-bomb not far from his door. Politics can be very demanding.

We had been 'up the coast' for about four weeks when a signal came down in that miserable code from 1030 to say that Ted and his crew had experienced all that Trengganu had to offer and would not object to a change of scene. What about swopping beats? Also, the tug had disbursed all her supplies and wanted to return to Singapore. Why couldn't 1030 move down to Mersing and cover the southern half of the coast from there and as we seemed to be so well dug in at Chukai it could be quite simple for us to patrol northwards to the border. Good friends as we were to the 1030 lot it did cross a few minds that they might just be inching their way back to Singapore! Still, it was no skin off our nose and operationally it made little difference.

Patrolling the north coast was hardly different from looking after the south. We still didn't come across any subversives, didn't even meet the Bangkok-Singapore ferry again. We did however spend one night anchored off what the Malaysian travel industry now calls I believe 'The Beach of Passionate Love'. We would not ourselves have called it that. The sea was alive with sea-snakes which would surely remove much of the attraction of midnight bathing, so essential after all to passionate love, particularly if the water is warm. We had hardly nosed in towards the shore when one of the wretched creatures got sucked into an engine water intake and caused us quite a bother.

Anyway, the sea was calm that night, the palm trees waved serenely in the gentle evening breeze and we looked forward to a night at anchor and a change from pottering along the coast. And who knows, what better place for an infiltrator to land?

Able Seaman Sharp was the Quartermaster on watch that evening and shortly after we had all turned in he came down into the wheelhouse, shook me and said, 'Someone shouting from ashore.' He sounded as though it were urgent. An urgent call from the beach just before midnight? Could this be the signal we had all been waiting for? A landing down the coast? Or maybe a bandit, wounded and desperate, had swum out to a waiting boat and it was up to us to 'do something'. The problem of the moment was that we were just too far offshore to hear what the message was. By the time we got our people roused, engines started, anchor up to move closer inshore the quarry might have escaped. Someone must go ashore. At the back of my mind I knew it had to be myself. But the sea-snakes. Before it had got dark we had seen the wretched things wriggling alongside and I wasn't at all sure how the conscience was going to persuade the body to respond. A thought flashed through my mind, 'A Carley float. I'll paddle ashore on a float.' Sharp however was also thinking and evidently faster than I was. 'I'm going, Sir. You're needed here,' and before I could stop him he dived overboard and was swimming. All I could do then was to throw him a float and shout, 'Push that in front of you.' You may gather why I thought so highly of him.

He was back within five minutes. 'Well, where's the fire?' 'There's no emergency. They just wanted to ask us to a party!' I was very, very cross but in the morning I could see that it was not the stuff to make a fuss about against the background of what we were all trying to do.

A few days later Telegraphist Taylor came bursting up from his tiny W/T office with another coded signal. I groaned. 'It's a'right,' he said. 'It's no from Singapore. It's yon 1030. Op Immediate.' Operational Immediate meant the signal had the highest priority for handling, to be dealt with before any other except for 'Flash'. A 'Flash' goes through at the speed of light. This one looked as though it might cheer us up. 'District Officer Mersing reports a thousand bandits massing to attack Mersing. Request your assistance.' I shouted down to Taylor, by now back combing the wave bands again. 'The signal decodes as "1000". Are you sure you've got the number right?' 'Aye Sir, there's no doot at a'.' How could there be with Taylor on one key and his chum at the other end in 1030.

A quick calculation showed that we had just enough fuel and a little to spare if we set off at our full speed of eleven knots. It was almost derisory but even Petty Officer Oxtoby and his team couldn't squeeze any more. On the way down we had a refresher Action Stations drill, which was when Taylor nearly stopped the whole thing with his inadvertent attempt to slaughter the Bridge team. And we dug out a satisfying array of sub-machine guns and other regalia that we had heard landing parties were wont to carry. Quite what ten sailors from us and another ten from 1030 were going to do against a thousand bandits I don't know. Naval landing parties are anyway more dangerous to themselves than to the enemy. On the other hand they have been known to defuse a sticky situation by offering the opposition a game of football.

Chapter 13

A Visit to Pekan

By midday next day we were in sight of Mersing. The town was not noticeably on fire so maybe we had arrived in time. The landing party – in other words the lot of us – went below to get rigged up. It was then that a certain feeling that everything was not quite as it should be began to settle on all of us. For a start I found that I could not stand up when fully accoutred. I shed a couple of magazines and half-emptied the water bottle and I was then just about able to heave myself off my bunk but with all the remaining equipment I was still too bulky to get through the wheelhouse door. From noises all over the boat I surmised that others must be having the same difficulty.

We were almost into the little harbour at Mersing by now. A quick change of plan was needed if we were to contribute anything to the defence of the town against the hordes from the interior. Plainly we were not cut out to play soldiers. It seemed that our best contribution would be to steam in looking suitably aggressive and then see how the situation developed. So we grouped ourselves round our two Oerlikon cannons and stripped Lewis gun mountings and entered harbour at full speed. By special and universal request Telegraphist Taylor was asked not to touch his guns unless the rest of us had already fallen in battle.

As we motored smartly up to the jetty I began to get the impression that something was missing from the scene which I had expected. It was, I soon realised, that 1030 was not there; and there was no welcoming committee either. But of course we had to expect the unexpected. Maybe a seaborne landing was taking place along the coast and no one had bothered to tell us. I set off up the jetty to investigate, inviting the guns' crews to keep me covered in case it was an ambush.

At the head of the jetty I found the Malay harbour master having what must have been his lunch. I asked where I might find the District Officer. Yes, he had certainly been down that morning but was probably home by now – lunch-time and then siesta. It began to be frustrating to see how faithfully the pattern of events was repeating itself: the urgent call for assistance, the air of surprise at our arrival, then the 'Wish you weren't here. You're upsetting people' syndrome.

I managed eventually to run the DO to earth. He was not having a siesta and was in fact quite concerned about the situation, but, 'A thousand bandits? Did Sebborn say that? A bit on the high side I'd think. Maybe a hundred or so but I'm sure you realise how difficult it is to get anything like an accurate picture.' Difficult indeed when all he had to go on was village gossip. Where was 1030? 'He's gone up the Endau to see if anything is moving up there.'

So that was that. We all bought large bunches of delicious Mersing bananas and settled down to catch our breath. In due course the Army moved into the jungle behind Mersing and the town was saved, but not before the versatility of sea power had been convincingly demonstrated. There were in fact quite a number of bandits in 'them thar hills'.

One morning shortly after we arrived Hedges came into the wheelhouse and said, 'One of the lads has got a dose,' meaning that he had VD. It didn't help to speculate whether this was from Singapore or Chukai, though if it was the latter someone had been kicking over the traces despite the DO's warning that we should keep out of the town. I said, 'We're sure to be relieved in a couple of weeks. Can it wait that long?' 'No, Sir. They don't like it at all up for'ard.' And of course he was quite right, so I had to confess again to Singapore that we were going to be a nuisance. This time I took the precaution of sending the signal, in code of course, to *Loch Glendhu* who responded quickly and sympathetically. A replacement arrived within a day or two, grinning from ear to ear. 'It's taken a f . . . armoured brigade to get me through to here,' he said. I pictured our diseased sailor going back in a tank.

The 1030 boat came back from the Endau pleased as punch. The Endau was one of the great rivers of the east coast, running well back into the interior. 1030 had apparently penetrated up to the point where the branches of the jungle trees were meeting over the water and to prove it they brought back a monkey which they claimed had decided that a launch's mast would make a better perch than a jungle twig. We made the trip ourselves on a couple of occasions but found no monkeys and certainly no bandits.

We had been away 'up the coast' for nearly six weeks now, plodding along more or less happily but beginning to look forward to the prospect of a proper bath rather than a bucket of salt water on deck each morning. The 1030 boat was in a bit of a state however with one engine overheating.

Relief crews would have to take over sometime as *Loch Glendhu's* refit was coming to an end, and it would make good sense to stagger the change-overs so that at least one launch was left on the coast all the time. As 1030 had this engine problem it was clearly sensible that she should be the first to return to Singapore, so off she went.

I was not particularly keen to moulder away round Mersing for our last two or three weeks, especially now that the Army was on the ground and would obviously make a much better job of the security situation than we ever could. So I asked the DO whether there was not something useful that we could contribute. 'Well,' he said, 'I know X up at Pekan would be glad of a visit. He does feel a bit out on a limb. You could go up the Sungei Pahang.'

Pekan was the capital of Pahang State and lay three or four miles up the river of the same name. Pahang was a particularly jungly place and bad bandit country. The Army had not yet managed to penetrate far into it and it was not surprising that the DO there should feel a bit lonely.

The entrance to the Sungei Pahang was apparently rather shallow and tricky. After our experience at Chukai and on the Endau I told the DO at Mersing in an over-confident moment that we would like nothing better than to go over to Pekan and would be off that evening. 'Hold on,' he said, 'You'll need a pilot,' and thank goodness I came to my senses and took his word for it. The harbour master apparently knew just the man and it was arranged that we should pick up Chick just before dark some few miles south of the river mouth two days later. Arrival in the dark had become almost an article of faith by now with the idea that as the locals anywhere rose at cock-crow next morning they would see a large White Ensign bellying gently in the morning breeze over their creek.

The concept of time and place can be elastic in the East but we met Chick on the nose. He was a huge man, a Malay, and could only just squeeze onto our tiny Bridge, but he had a cheerful open face which I decided, rightly for once, inspired confidence and he proved a most impressive pilot. A slight drawback was that he spoke no English at all but I had a Malay phrase book and we didn't need to talk much anyway. I had no idea at all in the dark whether he was hazarding the ship and had to leave it all to him.

So we set off towards the river mouth some three miles away. For fifteen minutes we motored quietly along and then through the medium of the phrase book and gesture he said that the water was getting shallow and we should take soundings. We had a sailor ready in the bows with a long pole and he started work. It was soon clear that the pole need not have been anywhere near so long; the water was shallow indeed. Chick of course could not see the pole in the dark so the leadsman would sing out the depths and I would translate, again through the invaluable phrase book, for our pilot. No problem. We were showing no lights of course, just creeping along to make a nicely unadvertised arrival. In fact I expect that every village within miles knew exactly where we were planning to go within minutes of the DO and myself taking the decision. Never mind!

We began to see the lights of a small village somewhere ahead of us and then the smell of fires, presumably cooking the evening meal, came wafting over the water. Soon Chick said, again through the book, 'No more sounding. Water too shallow.' And indeed it was. There might have been six inches under the keel if we were lucky.

The lights came closer and closer. Chick moved the wheel gently this way and that. Gradually we began to get the impression that the land was all round us; but it was only an impression. It was too dark to see anything. Eventually he gestured that we should stop engines and anchor. Chick and I then exchanged messages through the phrase book, dimly read by the light of a shaded torch:

'Is this Pekan?'

'No. Pekan up the river.'

'When do we go on?'

'No go on. No water. Stop here.'

'But I must go on. I have come to see the Tuan District Officer.'

'No water this ship. Canoe coming.'

'Are you coming too?' I couldn't discount the rather ridiculous idea of an ambush somewhere, in which case I would have felt safer with Chick's enormous bulk in the way.

'No.'

Just then there was a sound alongside and a canoe with an outboard motor took shape out of the dark. There did not appear to be much choice.

I would not have missed the next twelve hours or so if I had been offered instead the chance of catching every bandit in Pahang. There was no moon and it was quite dark but the stars were twice as brilliant as in Europe. The Southern Cross was obscured by the tall forest trees on either side of the river up which we were now travelling at respectable speed, but a reassuring band of stars was up there twinkling down along the path between the trees which the river kept open. Nobody spoke much but I managed to find out from one of our piratical crew that the pairs of little ruby red lights winking like tiny red cats' eyes along each bank had alligators behind them.

I suppose we motored three or four miles up the river. Then in the distance we began to see rather more substantial lights, white this time. Pekan! The jungle on either side began to draw back. We were almost up to the lights ahead by now and I was starting to get an impression of a river bank of trimmed grass, topped here and there with trees that bore the hand of man. We were heading for a small white-painted pontoon moored to the bank and connected to the shore by a gangway, painted white as well. Even in the dark with only the occasional light to point up the details I got the impression of a place well-ordered, in good taste, where nasty things were not supposed to happen. A European was on the pontoon, the District Officer. We climbed the gangway to the bank and the brutish present began to seem even more unreal with every step. We came up onto the short, mown grass of the *padang*, the village green. In the dark I could not make out more than the general appearance but it was plain that on two sides at least and leading down to the river stood graceful houses, built in the Indonesian/Malayan style with high curved roofs of thatch reaching up into the darkness. One house, even in the dark, was clearly more important than the others: the Ruler's Palace. The District Officer's bungalow was opposite across the *padang*.

I had arrived just in time for supper; or maybe in this well-ordered world it was dinner! I gathered that the DO and a District Nurse were the only Europeans in Pekan, and for a good distance around. Wasn't that rather lonely? Well, yes. It could have been but there was a lot to do. The Sungei Pahang, a large though shallow river, stretched a long way back into the State. The Ruler had a houseboat on which he used to make journeys up-river to visit the water-side villages (a houseboat that moved?) and he liked the DO to go with him. It all sounded very chummy.

What about the security situation? Well . . . and just then there was a distinctly nasty bump from the back quarters. The DO was up in a flash with a large revolver and prowling round the house. I had a rather nice Luger pistol which, strictly against the rules, I had bought from an Able Seaman who had bought it from an Indonesian who had probably retrieved it from a Jap who would almost certainly have pinched it from an unfortunate Dutchman. Despite this peripatetic past it worked very well for quite a few years. I joined in the hunt, not feeling too happy by now and almost willing to have swopped the DO's very good supper/dinner for a bowl of Able Seaman Price's appetising pot mess.

We didn't find anything. I asked the District Officer how he, and even more the District Nurse, could continue in such a situation. 'Well,' he said, 'the Ruler is very well liked. I seem to have made friends. If strangers were about the place I'm pretty sure I would know.' 'What then?' 'We'll have to wait and see.'

For myself, I was quite on edge by now, and when he mentioned casually after dinner that he was very sorry that he had no spare room to give me a bed for the night but that he had fixed me up in the Government Rest House across the *padang*, I didn't think I would get much sleep.

However, I did; and morning dispersed the anxieties of the night. How could this lovely place ever be soiled by communist bandits? The sun shone, dew glistened on the *padang*, gardeners swished the grass with scythes to give a finish as neat as any lawn-mower's and we had paw-paw with lemon juice for breakfast. I could have stayed for ever.

Back onboard I felt quite restless after such a wonderful, almost unreal, visit and for once we did a daylight flit from the shallow, alligator-infested and totally enchanting Sungei Pahang. Mersing was quite suburban by comparison when we got back. We did try one more river, the Sungei Rompin between the Pahang and Endau rivers but this was too shallow for us and we ran impressively aground on the bar. I doubt whether even Chick could have got us in. In full view of the village too.

Soon another signal in code arrived from NHQ. 'HDML 1030 arriving Mersing 18th. 1031 return to Singapore after turn-over.' So we stocked up with bananas and other goodies which were cheap up the coast and washed sets of white shirts and shorts for a reasonably clean return to civilisation.

For some reason quite unknown to me the old boat took it into her head to run aground on a mudbank off Changi and just short of the dockyard. By then we were more or less spruced up for entering harbour so poling off wasn't particularly popular but we had a few minutes in hand and reached the dockyard berth on the dot.

The Captain of the Fleet was there to welcome us. He was the senior staff officer responsible for morale and personnel and of course he would have been considerably and properly interested to see the state of 1031's crew after two month's camping in a launch up the coast. I have to admit I was pretty proud of them, properly fallen in on deck for his inspection. I doubt it had been possible to iron uniforms but at least they were well scrubbed. The only break in the ranks was LME Dixon who had lost his cap. How could he have done that when his job was mostly in the Engine Room? Anyway it gave the Captain of the Fleet scope for a suitably caustic comment. I did think that someone might have said, 'Well done,' but that was never the way of the Service.

By the time we returned from the Coast I had been away from England for nearly three years and much as I enjoyed the East Indies I was beginning to wonder whether those who had survived there for more than say two and a half years were regarded as 'over the hill'. Eventually of course, but only after considerable prodding from our end, a draft note did arrive and I went home to do a Destroyer Gunnery Officer's course. Counting the War I had been east of Suez for five years with a six months' break at home for Sub-Lieutenant's courses in the middle. Our Captain let me have a day off to wander round and say goodbye to Colombo before the troopship sailed. The four-week passage home was not particularly easy. I found long-haired friends from Singapore, Colombo and Mombasa all on board.

Chapter 14

Home Fleet Destroyer

I enjoyed the course at the Gunnery School, Whale Island. If one could put up with the rather brisker atmosphere there than in some of the other schools, which I could, it was a comfortable enough place to live. There was just one snag. When we all got our next sea-going billets I found that mine was to HMS *Broadsword*, an almost brand-new destroyer with a brand-new gunnery system, the Flyplane Predictor System Mark I. The trouble was that this system was so new that we hadn't covered it in the course! I mentioned this to our Course Officer. He did not seem too concerned. 'Never mind,' he said, 'I know some of the team there quite well and I'm sure they'll be able to tell you all you need to know. It's mostly electrics anyway and that's not your department.'

I got nowhere when I pointed out that surely the object of the course which I had just finished was to give me a workable knowledge of the system from which I was going to be expected to get results at sea. For a start, what was a Flyplane anyway? 'Don't worry. You've got a very good Gunner's Mate and the Weapons people will see you right. Look, we can let you have some pamphlets on the theory if you like.' So I joined the troopship for Malta, which was where *Broadsword* was finishing the trials of the new system, with a heap of pamphlets which were so much double-Dutch as far as I was concerned, and still with almost no comprehension of the system for which I was going to be responsible.

After two years with it in *Broadsword* I did finally begin to understand what it was all about. As it marked quite a milestone in the development of naval anti-aircraft gunnery I pass on an outline of my learning to the reader.

We fought most of the Second World War with a naval anti-aircraft fire control system which assumed that the aircraft which you wished to shoot down was flying not too fast and at a more or less constant speed on a more or less constant course and at a more or less constant height. The system was happiest if the target was aiming himself directly at your own ship. In practice firings you shot at a sleeve, a target towed on the end of half a mile of wire by an aircraft tug. The latter could hardly manoeuvre very ferociously with all that wire and sleeve behind him so the conditions for which the Fire Control system was designed were quite often attained. From time to time a sleeve would be shot down. War conditions were of course totally different. An attacking aircraft would evade as much as he could. It was a stroke of good luck if you hit him.

The US Navy had a considerably more successful system, the Mark 37, but by the end of the War both the Americans and ourselves were working on something that would be a substantial improvement on even that. Ours was the FPS I. Basically it was an early form of computer. An attacking aircraft still had to be tracked by two aimers in an enormous contraption called a Director, one aimer keeping the aircraft in his sights for elevation and the other for direction. The resulting movement of the Director was fed down to the 'black boxes' of the FPS, combined with range data obtained by radar and the information fed into some high speed sums which calculated what the aircraft was actually doing at any given moment as opposed to what it ought to be doing, as with the old system. The FPS then predicted where it would be by the time the shells from the guns worked their way up to him. It all worked surprisingly well.

Part of the reason that I did not find the Gunnery School pamphlets as helpful as I might have done was that we had the usual miserably rough passage through the Bay of Biscay. Even this had one bright spot. Turning inboard again one afternoon after being seasick over the lee rail I came face to face with an acquaintance from home in Dorset. He was in the Army and going further on than I to join some regiment in Singapore. Subsequently and after his National Service he took up the Law and later became a judge. I did sometimes wonder, were I ever to appear before him, whether this shared experience in the Bay of Biscay would affect any sentence passed.

The probability had to be against it. There was for instance the story, not necessarily apocryphal, of the Sub-Lieutenant who was hauled up before the Bench in Portsmouth for speeding. The Chairman of the Magistrates was a Mr Gieve who naturally, this being a naval story, was Chairman of the firm of outfitters of that name. 'Fined two pounds,' sentenced Mr Gieve. 'Thank you, Mr Gieve,' replied the tactless Sub-Lieutenant. 'Put it on the bill if you would, please.' 'Four pounds,' came the retort from the Bench.

Arrived in Malta we disembarked in Grand Harbour which I had known so well fourteen or fifteen years before. St Angelo dominated the dockyard side of the water, facing Valetta and the Barraca bastions. I ought to have felt very much at home but somehow even in the sun and colour and warmth of the late Maltese summer I was slightly apprehensive – a new boy going to school, or worse, a teacher going to look after a subject which he did not himself understand.

Broadsword was round at Marsa Xlokk, a sheltered bay on the south-west corner of the island, much used as an overnight anchorage by ships exercising in that area. I was too much on edge to contrast my arrival there with the time three years before when I joined *Loch Glendhu* in Bahrein. Had I done so I would have remarked a difference indeed. Instead of the scruffy and desperately heat-marked ship and crew of 1946 here was a bright new ocean racer, a state-of-the-art machine to the extent of having the forward of her two funnels concealed within the foremast. Instead of a single gun forward that looked as though it might have been a relic of the Siege of Ladysmith there were two twin 4-inch gun mountings and on the after end of the ship more guns, two twin 40-mm Bofors mounts. The latter had the cheerful name of STAAGs – stabilised ta-chometric anti-aircraft guns. Each had its own little radar set and was credited with being able to 'lock on' to the fastest manoeuvring target and then to shoot it down. That was the theory. I was to find later in *Broadsword* that the ravages of salt water and the vibration in that part of the ship at speed meant that in practice two highly-skilled artificers had a full-time job keeping the mountings working. I cannot remember them having much consistent success even so.

Amidships were two quadruple 21-inch torpedo-tube mountings on the 'iron deck', the long low length of the hull stretching from the stern to the 'break of the foc'sle', the point just over half the distance from the stern at which the foc'sle rose as a shelter against the weather and provided most of the accommodation for the crew as well as the deck level on which stood the Bridge structure and the forward armament mountings. In fact despite the funnel up the foremast *Broadsword* was basically the same shape as her predecessors. The iron deck was still swept with waves in heavy weather as in *Norman* and it was not until a few years later that the move began towards ships with a relatively high free-board amidships designed to keep this area usable even in heavy weather. Change comes slowly at sea.

The ship had just finished a series of firing trials with the new Fly-plane system. As well as the normal Wardroom complement there was a trials team onboard, boffins and experimental officers from Whale Is-land. The air was thick with conversations about 'Ipots'- induction

HMS *Broadsword*

potentiometers – and stabilisers and other gadgets which might have come straight from science fiction as far as I was concerned. Apparently the trials had gone very well and the pressure was now on to carry out a further series in the United States next summer. The US Navy had apparently an almost limitless supply of 'pilotless target aircraft' for us to shoot at. These could be manoeuvred from a controlling aircraft in the same way as a model aeroplane and were thus the most realistic targets available. And who knows, the USN might just be so impressed with the FPS I as to want it themselves.

Even without the interest of the trials *Broadsword* was obviously a good ship, a very good ship. There are two sides to this equation and the sum is more than just the addition of the two halves. The ship needs to be sea-kindly, strong and handy; the Ship's Company needs its share of human assets and to have as many as possible of the run of human vices well under control. A sound result is a pretty good place to live.

We were one of the four ships which made up the Sixth Destroyer Squadron, all new Weapons class destroyers, *Battleaxe* – the leader – *Crossbow* and *Scorpion*. We never saw much of *Scorpion*, I don't know why, and *Battleaxe* being the Leader tended to be slightly above the salt, professionally. That left *Crossbow* and ourselves as 'chummy ships'. We normally berthed alongside each other and were both Chatham-manned; and both were commanded by almost the last of the Lieutenant Commanders still, in the post-War years, thought to be capable of command of a destroyer.

Chatham-manned meant that we were manned from the Chatham Port Division with, as you might expect, sailors recruited mainly from around London, East Anglia and the eastern side of the country generally. The other Divisions were Portsmouth and Devonport. This Manning Port system had been set up after the Invergordon Mutiny of 1931 which I mention a little further on. Previously ships had been manned from wherever the sailors were the most available. The Manning Port idea was an attempt to give the sailor some sort of family identity on a par with the County Regimental system in the Army, but of course the numbers involved – some 50,000 men in each Port Division at that time – meant that the 'families' were too large to have much worthwhile identity. All the same each Port Division certainly had its own characteristics. Chatham ships were effervescent, quick to react to either success or disaster, up or down – 'Chatty Chats'. Portsmouth ships were more 'Home County', a bit steadier either way. Those from Devonport were the real 'Oggies', the sailors often in sea-boots even in the hottest weather and, despite orders to the contrary, calling each other 'M'dear', descendants in their imagination of Drake's crews. They were the men for the long haul. I never served in a Devonport ship. I always wished that I had.

Chatham was fine though, particularly *Crossbow* and *Broadsword*. We knew that we had the best Captains in the Home Fleet, both thoroughly professional, both terrorists on the Bridge when circumstances required – which was most of the time – but both approachable, modest beings in more normal circumstances; tough on their Ship's Companies but defending them absolutely against depredations from without by either Squadron or Fleet staffs. Neither ship would have swapped. Lieutenant-Commander Jack Bitmead was *Broadsword*. He was a bit kinder to his ship in heavy weather than *Crossbow* which often returned to harbour with bits of wreckage on the iron deck, stanchions bent and so on.

We left Malta shortly after I joined and made our way solo back to England. The Mediterranean Fleet was about its own business and the Home Fleet on the last leg of its summer cruise in northern waters.

The passage was something of an eye-opener for me. In the East Indies, working 'tropical' routine, a hush would come over the ship shortly after midday and apart from those on watch it would be siesta time for all until teatime. Thereafter there might be more activity but nothing too strenuous. In the Home Fleet it was quite different. No tropical routine of course, and some time after tea instead of settling down to letters and books there would be Evening Quarters. The whole Ship's Company would muster on deck by Divisions – Foc'slemen, Quarterdeckmen, Engine Room, Cooks and Stewards, etc. – and some sort of drills would be programmed. These would vary with whatever the Captain, First Lieutenant or the officer deputed as 'master of ceremonies' had the imagination to dream up. In later years Evening Quarters came to be considered something of an unwarranted interference with what might be thought the leisure hours and I cannot recall coming across it after leaving *Broadsword*, possibly because, as the years passed and peacetime economies became more and more pressing, ships were increasingly required to make the most of time at sea for weapon training and other exercises which had a tendency to continue round the clock. Life was perhaps duller thereby but the taxpayer had a right to demand value for his money.

'Away Seaboat's Crew' used to be a hoary old chestnut for Evening Quarters, and was still on the menu in later years whenever there was a quiet moment. The seaboat was the twenty-seven foot long Montague

Whaler, pointed at both ends and propelled when under oars by five strong men and true. Under sail, as when a year or two earlier we had sailed from Chetlat to Kiltan in the Laccadive Islands, the boat would be ketch-rigged: two masts with a main and foresail on the mainmast and a tiny mizzen sail aft. As a seaboat it was always under oars. It would be housed on davits just aft of the break of the foc'sle where it would be protected to an extent from the weather. A long 'boat rope' would be led from its bows to some convenient point well up on the foc'sle. The theory was that the boat would be lowered and slipped whilst the ship had a knot or two of headway on and towed thus momentarily on the boat rope it could be steered quickly out from the ship's side without any messing about with oars. Most of the art lay in judging the right moment to slip the boat from its falls. On the cry 'Aawaay Seaboat's Crew' it would be lowered to within a foot or so of the water and when the sea was calm, dropped quickly in. With a bit of a lop on, or worse, judgement was needed to give the order to slip as a likely-looking wave approached the boat's bow so that the whaler would drop onto something of a cushion. A wave misjudged or a dopey crew could result in an unpopular drop into a trough – not good for anyone. A good launch was a pretty sight indeed, the whaler slipping into the water with a cheerful splash, sheering quickly away from the ship, the crew then pulling strongly to pick up the lifebuoy, box or whatever had been dropped for their benefit.

To get the boat back there was no nonsense with mechanical winches. These were judged, rightly, not to be fast or responsive enough to pluck a boat quickly out of an unco-operative sea. 'Clear Lower Deck' would bring all the junior rates not otherwise gainfully employed on watch out onto the iron deck where they would find the long rope 'falls' from the whaler's davits laid out for them as for a tug-of-war. 'Pick up the falls,' as the whaler's crew hooks the boat on to the lower blocks. Then, quickly, 'Hoist away,' and anything up to fifty or sixty manpower whips the boat out of the water and up to the davit head. Primitive and effective!

And so on an early autumn evening we rounded the North Foreland and came up through the traffic, the shoals and the lights of the Downs, through the Barrow Deep and anchored for the night off Sheerness. Chatham lay further up the Medway but the dockyard consisted of closed basins which could only be entered at the right state of the tide via a lock from the river. We would continue up there next morning.

We stayed in Chatham to refit until after Christmas and by the time we sailed again early in the New Year for the Home Fleet Spring Cruise to Gibraltar I had more or less come to terms with the Flyplane Predictor System Mark I, at least in theory.

The Spring Cruise was always my favourite. 'Cruise' was not in fact quite the right word. The Commander-in-Chief's staff would endeavour to co-ordinate ship's programmes so that as much of the Home Fleet as possible would join forces in the western Channel and then proceed in company to Gibraltar, exercising on the way. Typically the exercises might consist of anti-submarine games with a couple of submarines previously positioned somewhere in the Bay of Biscay, exercises with aircraft from the Home Fleet aircraft-carrier which would carry out dummy air attacks that we tried to repel in equally dummy fashion, detecting them on radar, or by lookout if they were coming in low, and getting the armament aimed at them before they could in theory fire their rockets. Usually of course they would come in so fast and so low that the guns were left waving around and pointing at the wrong bit of sky, whilst there would be a good deal of terrorising on the Bridge because yet another attack had got in undetected. Dating from wartime days when it was fairly unusual to shoot down an attacking aircraft with a gun, we used to be quite cock-a-hoop if the gunnery team could ever report 'Target' meaning they were ready to open fire, before the attacker had screeched overhead.

At Gibraltar we would as often as not meet the Mediterranean Fleet which might include another aircraft-carrier, maybe two more cruisers, and more destroyers. It would be quite a gathering, but certainly the first part was hardly a cruise in the accepted sense of the word.

Chapter 15

A Magic Cruise

The charm of that Cruise would lie in the weather. It would be early January when we left Chatham. As Foc'sle Officer one would be standing, not surprisingly, on the foc'sle as we locked out of the basin. High up there one would have a fine view down the river and back up to Rochester on the other bank but the wind as likely as not had originated in the Baltic and picked up speed as it crossed the North Sea so that now it penetrated even the most windproof of winter clothes. The dockyard mateys lower down on the dockside would be muffled to their ears in their working jackets, flat caps jammed down securely so they could hardly see. Never the fastest of movers at the best of times, they were almost immobilised under the weight of woollies, wellingtons and gloves. Sometimes it would be snowing; always it was bitterly cold. A few hours later we would be rounding the South Foreland. A lumpy sea would be running up the Channel and personally I would be beginning to feel miserably sea-sick.

By the time we were off Portsmouth we would be searching round for *Battleaxe*, Portsmouth-manned and coming out of her home port. Our Captain would be on the Bridge, capless in the gale, leaning on the forward bridge screen, peering happily into the murk of the tail-end of a winter afternoon, clearly glad to be at sea again whatever the weather. Dockyard was not the most active of places from his point of view. Yeoman of Signals Thomas would be wedged somewhere on the starboard side of the Bridge with the Signalman of the Watch and a couple of signal code books handy. He would have known the contents of both books by heart, backwards, but good practice dictated that he confirm with the book the meaning of any flag signal received before interpreting it. He and the Captain were a splendid team when at sea, Thomas always up there when the Captain was on the Bridge – which of course was an open one in those days – in weather like this wearing an old long navy-blue watch coat stretching almost to his ankles. His nose always seemed to have a dribble on the end but beneath this charmingly ragged disguise was an unequalled professional competence. The Captain might argue with him;

the First Lieutenant might question his interpretation of a signal; we junior officers would do no more than ask his advice.

The Channel was far less crowded then than it is now but a radar screen would still have shown more than enough echoes for the Operations Room team to have to plot the most likely ones to sort out which might be our Leader coming out from the land. Eventually we would be getting a good idea as to which of the fat little blurs of light on the tube was going to be her and just then through the gathering January dusk would come the first faint stab of light from a 20-inch signal lantern.

Who saw it first? Maybe a lookout if he was not wiping spray from his binoculars. Maybe the Officer of the Watch if he was not trying to put a fix on the chart gleaned from an indistinct glimpse of some part of the Isle of Wight and the Nab Tower. Probably it was the Yeoman just as the Ops Room reported, 'We have possible *Battleaxe* 300°. Six miles, Course 250°. Speed twelve . . .' – Twelve knots, Economical Passage speed. Meanwhile the Yeoman is in business.

'From *Battleaxe*, Sir. Join me. My course 255°. Speed 12.' The Captain kicks the Officer of the Watch. 'Come on, Officer of the Watch. What the hell are you waiting for?' A mumble from the Officer of the Watch who has his head into the chart table trying with a damp pencil to get his fix on to a soggy chart. 'Yessir. Eighteen knots?' 'Twenty. Come on, get on with it.'

Down below crockery starts sliding around as we increase speed from 12 knots, which was not particularly comfortable plugging into a south-westerly, to 20 where we begin to take off from every third wave. After one particularly vicious and noisy landing the Captain relents slightly. 'Hmm. All right. Come down to 18.' Thank goodness for small mercies, but the errant, wandering crockery still continues to slide off the odd table down below, given a chance.

Soon we are getting within range of flag signalling. A hoist of two or three flags goes up on *Battleaxe*'s yard-arm. There is too much spray about for the average human on our Bridge to make out the colours, added to which it will soon be almost dark. Never mind, we are quite close to *Battleaxe* by now. Both Yeoman Thomas and the Captain have anyway a shrewd idea of what the signal will be. Meanwhile a shout over the intercom to the Flag Deck, just behind and below the Bridge, 'Flag Deck – what the hell are you doing? Get that Answer pennant up.' The Answering pennant is in fact slowly rising at our yard-arm but after three months in dockyard everyone can do with some freshening up. The pennant means that *Battleaxe's* signal has been seen and is being digested. The Yeoman really does not need the book for this one and in any case it is too wet on our Bridge to open it. 'From "D", Sir. Take station astern. Close order.' Close order is two cables, 400 yards. It sounds a long way but doesn't look it, particularly in heavy weather. We're all being freshened up!

And so we plug on down towards Gibraltar and in a couple of days the English winter fades away. Four or five miles to port is the north coast of Spain, Cape Finisterre, a green land at this time of year, little white houses, peace and calm after the gales of the Channel and Biscay.

I remember a shipping Weather Forecast from the BBC about that time. It went out in verse, which I believe was subsequently frowned upon by the 'powers that were'. It began -

'The weather off Finisterre is very sinisterre . . .'

We were somewhere off Finisterre at the time and the forecast was dead right, but having it in verse seemed to make the outlook less gloomy. We thought it a pity that the BBC management should object.

Anyway we mostly found that the weather off Finisterre was anything but sinister. Oilskins were thrown off, upper deck lashings which had secured gear otherwise likely to go overboard were cast off and the cold wet anti-submarine exercises of the Bay of Biscay gave place to the more exciting, for me anyway, gunnery practices I mentioned before. We had outrun the submarines; they would come on more slowly and rejoin at Gibraltar.

The Yeoman would be giving his Flag Deck crew flag-hoisting exercises – brightly coloured flags and pennants whipping up and down to urgent cries such as, 'Alpha Juliet Romeo, Stand by – HOIST.' At the other yard-arm might come an answering shout of, 'Answer pennant HOIST,' and then a triumphant, 'Down 'em all.' I suppose it was all pretty primitive and flag signalling was almost a thing of the past for manoeuvring. As formations became more and more spread out it became less and less used. What a shame! The Tufnell Box must be a collector's item these days.

On a passage such as this ships of each destroyer squadron would steam together but the squadrons and individual heavier ships, cruisers and above, would be spread out across the ocean, exercising separately and only planned to join up near Gibraltar. There was thus scope for pleasing gunnery benefits such as the Throw-Off Surface Shoot. This was the other half of the Battle Practice Target firing. In the latter we would be shooting at a huge target some five miles away and towed by a tug on a very long wire. Sometimes the wire seemed hardly long enough as it had been known for the tug to receive a salvo in place of the target. Properly done this exercise provided a good test of accuracy as the fall of shot was filmed from the tug, but the latter had no freedom of manoeuvre with that great target behind it and the Battle Practice Target shoot was as unreal a test of the effectiveness of a ship's surface armament as the AA Sleeve firing mentioned earlier was of the anti-aircraft system.

Whale Island, the Gunnery School, had however worked out another amusement to take care of this deficiency, the Throw-Off shoot. A vital screw was turned in the Admiralty Fire Control Table down below to make the guns point say 5° off the direction in which the aimer was aiming them. Meanwhile two ships would spread out to perhaps five miles apart. The 'ship with the screw' would be the firing ship and the other the target. The target would have freedom of manoeuvre whilst the firing ship would also be expected to twist and turn as it might in action in order to give the fire control team a run for their money. Every so often it would let off a round at the target. According to the book a 5° throw-off at five miles should mean the shell splashing down half a mile ahead or astern of the target according to which way the throw off was applied. The target would have the range of the firing ship on radar and with a little trigonometry could tell whether the shell would have hit or not. The Throw-Off shoot taken in conjunction with a BPT firing gave a reasonable indication of how on-the-ball a ship's gunnery team might be. A disadvantage was that should the target be your Squadron Leader, Captain 'D' had an instantaneous demonstration of your accuracy. With the BPT exercise it was usually a day or two before you got the fall of shot photos from the tug so there was a little time to present possibly passable reasons for all the misses.

Back to the Cruise. During the Dog Watches such noisy exercises would normally be put to rest and Officer of the Watch manoeuvres or ship handling exercises would be on the menu. The rest of the Ship's Company not on watch would in the words of the travel agents' brochures be 'at leisure', that is of course if they escaped the excitements of Evening Quarters or Away Seaboats Crew.

By the time we reached Cape St Vincent at the southern tip of Portugal the Fleet would have joined up and be steaming in close company to reach Gibraltar next day.

Gibraltar was basically a time for getting together again, for showing us that we were all part of a reasonable-sized Fleet and for continuing and building on the weapon training whose threads we had been picking up again on the voyage south after the Christmas leave period. There was a social side too, epitomised if you like by the Royal Marine bands and detachments from the three 'heavy' units of the Fleet Beating Retreat one evening during our time at Gib. As the weather always seemed to be good at that time of the year it could be staged quite confidently on the hockey pitch with the sun going down in a clear sky over Gibraltar Bay. It would have been something of a workaday setting but the old bastions and other fortifications around the ground provided just that element of a 'strange land' to give it a touch more piquancy than the civilised surroundings of Horse Guard's Parade ever could. And anyway these were 'our' Marines from 'our' Fleet, a private show for us if you like, sailors in those days still in uniform when ashore on leave, officers in presentable plain clothes. The Gibraltarians were of course very welcome as well. They were there because we were there and vice versa. In short it was for real and not for the tourists.

Turn the coin over and there are the bars, restaurants and honky-tonks along Main Street and other less virtuous establishments no doubt tucked away in one or two side streets. We used to frequent a restaurant at the far end of the street, chiefly because the lead singer there used to appear with two small plates over her bosom, suspended by delicate chains from her neck. She could make them go round in opposite directions, contra-rotating as it were, and she was singing all the time. It was quite clever.

The days at sea were equally delectable, in a different way of course. I could always have done with more firings – there never seemed to be one that was perfect. One would have thought that, with all the modern gadgetry that we had, it would be simple to hit the target with the first salvo, but it hardly ever worked that way. Maybe it was the fault of the 'Spotting Rules'. These Laws of Moses from the Gunnery School were based on 'bracketing' the target before you sank it. Your first salvo would be aimed a little short. For the second you ordered, 'Up 400 yards.' If that fell over, you came down 200 yards, and bingo, you had him. That was the theory. It may just be worth recalling here that the rules did work: the 'mighty *Hood*' had bracketed *Bismarck* with her first three salvos and the Germans had no doubt that the fourth salvo, due to reach them any second, would be a hit. In the event of course the Germans fired their fatal broadside in the interval.

Having mentioned *Hood* perhaps it may not be too much of a diversion to take that last encounter a little further. She vanished after being hit by one of *Bismarck's* broadsides in apparently the same way as the disastrous magazine explosions obliterated three of our battle-cruisers at Jutland. Launched in 1918 her construction was too far advanced by the time of Jutland for it to reflect fully all the lessons of the battle but she was due to be rebuilt in 1937. In the event she was never taken in hand, presumably because by then aircraft-carrier construction was being given higher priority. Had the projected work been done it is at least possible that it would have included strengthening of deck armour near and *over* magazines to reflect the much longer ranges at which, more than twenty years after Jutland, surface actions could be fought. At the battle of Calabria for instance in 1940 *Warspite*, a battleship of the same class as *Valiant*, scored a hit on a moving target at 26,400 yards. At this range the 15-inch shells would have had a plunging trajectory, piercing decks rather than sides. The unreconstructed *Hood* would have been vulnerable in this respect.

Back to *Broadsword's* little 4-inch guns – even we had a range of some nine miles. The analysis of a shoot though was the thing, the time when you worked out what had gone wrong, did your best to think up exonerating reasons to deflect wrath from above and just sometimes to swill a good result round and round the mouth like a sound port. You never got much credit for these good ones though – that was how they were all supposed to be.

The analysis started with a camera fitted over the Fire Control Table which filmed all the settings used for each salvo: target bearing, range, speed and so on, and the same data for oneself. After the shoot the Gunnery Officer would disappear at the speed of light to the Wardroom bathroom where he would develop the film and see whether the dials supported his view that the shoot just completed was pretty top-class. On one occasion when everything seemed to have gone exceptionally well I dashed down to the bathroom with some sense of anticipation. This time the accuracy of the fall of shot and the completeness of the analysis records was going to establish *Broadsword* as the gunnery ship of the Squadron. As the film began gradually to reveal its secrets in the developer it became clear however that three of the dials were not showing anything of value. Hell! I could see parts of the rims and a few numbers but the pointers, which were of course the whole object of the exercise, were completely obscured. Then as the developer did its work I began to detect a foreign body emerging on one of the dials. It looked as though it might be perhaps a signet ring. Could there be some psychic force in our gunnery system which was now making itself felt? A more rational explanation soon became apparent. Our Chief Ordnance Artificer had his Action Station in the Fire Control compartment. He wore just such a signet ring. It was his hand which robbed us of a full analysis of almost our best shoot!

Despite this the Chief OA was a most amiable and competent man. As the weapon training period progressed and the Flyplane and its team of technicians continued its Malta success in AA shoots, the Chief OA and I began to wonder whether with a few minor adjustments we could not make the surface fire control table produce more effective results as well. One wet Saturday afternoon we locked ourselves inside the Fire Control compartment and went to work. Off came the top of the table, a large box some five feet long by three feet wide and another three feet high. This was all well-charted territory for the Chief OA. We started delving round inside, seeking to see whether a couple of the functions which the table worked on could not be linked up to get the improvement we envisaged. Quite soon there was a useful little pile of gear wheels, widgers, cranks and whatnots arranged carefully on the deck and I began to sense that we were straying off the map. I asked a little hesitantly, 'Can we put all this lot back?' 'We're OK so far but . . .' We both sat back and looked at the table. It was still recognisable for what it was, but for how much longer? We put everything back. Now if we had had access to a spare table we could really have got things moving.

The Flyplane Predictor continued to do well. It went on doing well even after we managed to persuade one of the electrical maintainers to stop fiddling with it during a shoot. This enthusiast had got into the habit during the Malta trials of standing at the break of the foc'sle, about five seconds dash from the computer room, and watching the shell bursts at the beginning of a 'run'. If they were slightly off target he would sprint to the computer and tickle up the relevant Ipot to improve matters. It took those of us watching from the Bridge quite some time to work out why every so often there was a sudden improvement in accuracy halfway through a 'run'. Apparently during the previous year's trials this sort of procedure came under the heading of 'improving the system', and was allowed for. It was a relief to be reassured on this point!

Chapter 16

"Are we seamen or aren't we?"

By no means all our evenings at Gibraltar would be spent with the 'contra-rotating' singer at the end of Main Street. Two or three nights a week we were usually at sea on nocturnal exercises of some sort. A favourite for the gunnery and torpedo teams would be a 'Night Encounter Exercise'. One of our supply ships would be roped in as a target and invited to steam through a predetermined area of ocean. A squadron of destroyers would have the task of locating her and then carrying out a gun and torpedo attack: Cowboys and Indians at sea. We would just have time for a quick early supper after the preceding exercises of the day and then the players would muster at their various stations, a gun's crew – we only needed one for this benefit – the Action Stations Ops Room crew, Torpedo Control team and so on.

The exercise would take place just outside the Straits of Gibraltar in an area which we hoped and believed to be little used by commercial shipping. The squadron would start off steaming in close order, ships four hundred yards apart, line ahead, behind our leader, *Battleaxe*; no voice communication in order to deny the enemy any clue as to our presence and radar sets switched off for the same reason. On the Bridge the Yeoman is watching *Battleaxe*. At this distance all communication for the exercise is by Heather Lamp, a small torch-like signalling lamp which gives a light only visible to Yeomen of Signals. Then it all begins. 'From "D", Sir. Spread on a line of bearing 180°. Distance apart 1 mile. Speed 15. Course 270°.' After all these Dog Watch OOW manoeuvres the Officer of the Watch has an inkling of what is expected of him and without more ado orders, 'Port 20. Revolutions 140,' and shouts down to the Ops Room for a course and speed to get him a mile away on *Battleaxe*'s port beam as quickly as possible. One of the advantages of a night exercise is that it is too dark on the Bridge to use the Battenberg Calculator to solve these 'change of station' problems and they can be tipped into the Ops Room's lap without loss of face. The Battenberg is an instrument like a small round metal tray with two movable arms on its top. Each arm has a movable widger which slides up and down on it.

The instrument aims to solve relative velocity problems – otherwise known as Stationing Conundrums – but with a little practice it is much easier in daylight to choose the course needed by eye. If you have a Midshipman on watch with you he, being fresh from school, may remember the mathematics involved and be able to check your course, but by then you ought to be in your new station anyway.

Meanwhile below in the wheelhouse the Quartermaster winds on 20° of port helm and his mate churns a handle which moves a dial in the engine room to show the revolutions needed. Believe it or not the Artificer on Watch then opens the throttles to what from previous experience he knows ought to give the right revs and then settles down to count the number of times the shafts turn in a minute to check his hunch. Has no one heard of a tachometer?

We are now spread out in line abreast, *Battleaxe*, *Crossbow* and *Broadsword*. As an eminent French general ordered during the First World War, '*Ils ne passeront pas.*' After 15 minutes or so a faint smudge of light appears on one of our radar sweeps; despite radio and radar silence ships are allowed one radar sweep each minute. The risk of being detected has to be balanced against the reality that without these occasional and random searches we should never ourselves find anything at all. The blob is reported to the Bridge whence it passes on via the Heather Lamp. It's probably nothing but if we don't report it someone else will so it might as well be us. After another couple of sweeps the plotters in the Ops Room deduce that whatever it is, the blob is steering west at ten knots. That's not what we're looking for. Try again.

A few minutes later we get something a good deal more likely. Anyway by this time the exercise has been going on for half an hour and if this isn't our quarry someone has got his starting position wrong. Yeoman Thomas however senses the Heather Lamp again: at this distance he must be reading it by intuition. 'From "D", Sir. Target bearing 310°. 9 miles. Prepare to attack with torpedoes. Course 280°. Speed 21.' Down in the engine room the Artificer winds the throttles further open and starts counting again.

On goes the gunnery ranging radar. In the Gun Direction Room I press a button which is supposed magically to line the Director above the Bridge, which in turn points the guns, with the Warning Radar which has now got the target firmly on its screen. By day, with Visual Control, a Layer and Trainer sit in the Director to aim the system. By night, in Blind, the aiming is done solely by radar. Magic! All this electronic activity has obviously been picked up by the target but it won't be very long before a shoal of torpedoes will be chasing towards it at thirty knots and we need all the gadgetry available to get them properly aimed. On the iron deck the tubes are being trained outboard; nothing will be fired on this exercise but it does no harm to go through the motions in the dark.

By now the Gunnery radar has locked onto the target and the cry goes up, 'Radar target.' It doesn't always go like this. Someone must have cheered the circuits up tonight. The range comes down to 10,000 yards, close enough for effective shooting. That will cheer us up even if it only tickles the target and we hope and believe it will do more than that: 'Bridge GDR. Range 10,000. For exercise for exercise, permission to open fire?' This will be followed at once by GDR to the guns: ' "A" gun with SAP (semi armour piercing shell) *for exercise for exercise* Load Load Load.' It does occur to me to hope that the magazines are well-locked and the firing mechanism is still hidden away from the guns as it was before we started this exercise. It has happened before that a shell has been fired by mistake. For the same reason there is no mention on anyone's part of anything that might sound like the stirring word, 'Shoot!'

This really completes the gunnery contribution. Not very demanding? It can be if the drill doesn't go right. It was a bit tougher for the gun's crew on another occasion. That time we were actually to fire Starshell as we would in a real action at night for positive identification of the target. It never seemed to me that Starshell was the best way of going about things; but what better? Anyway as an exercise it gave the gun's crew something positive to do and that was a bonus especially in the dark. That night we had quite a choppy sea. 'A' gun right down on the foc'sle was Starshell Gun. She was continually covered in spray and every so often something a good deal more solid would thud into the gunshield and flood round the back of it. We had just turned into our torpedo attack and were about to loose off a spread of Starshells when the foc'sle telephone buzzed. The First Lieutenant took the message, paused a moment in consideration and then shouted over to the Captain, ' "A" gun asks if we could slow down a bit, Sir. Loading numbers getting knocked off their feet by the sea coming over on this new course.' 'bloody hell, First Lieutenant. Are we seamen or aren't we?' However he did slow down, slightly. Men were men in those days.

Back to the present exercise. We are into the torpedo attack by now, bucking along nicely and with the range coming down quickly. The target hasn't a chance. Spray is whisping over the Bridge. The three of us are in voice contact at last. Three miles. The Yeoman is in the act again.

'From "D", Sir. Standby to turn to port and fire torpedoes. Standby Standby. Turn and fire torpedoes.' The range is down to 3000 yards. Over goes the wheel and with 25° of helm at 21 knots the ship heels outward like a racing car on the wrong camber.

Meanwhile in the Ops Room the Torpedo Control cell is in action. With the gunnery part of the exercise well over I used to stand at the door of our little Gun Direction annexe and try to make head or tail of the Torpedo script. I never did except for the stirring last lines '. . . Fire P . . . Fire Q . . . Fire R . . . Fire S . . . all torpedoes fired, Sir.' That left us with four fish in the other mounting. I should explain that the tubes were fired in sequence as the ship turned so that the torpedoes spread out in a fan on their run to the target. That was the theory. It did not happen like that on one occasion.

The last scene was 'Make Smoke'. This was usually good for a deal of vigorous and urgent cross-talk on the bridge. The Weapons' machinery was so up-to-the-minute that the boilers could do nothing so primitive as to make smoke on demand. In older ships I gather the trick was to open the fuel valve to the boilers wide and, provided the latter were hot, smoke appeared almost at once. We however had a special smoke-making machine and this had to be thoroughly warmed in order to coax smoke from the heavy fuel oil. The principle was doubtless not all that different from the trick with a boiler but whereas the boilers would be hot when steaming our machine was normally dormant and had to be roused. The engine room needed ten minutes' notice. One night we on the Bridge forgot to give the obligatory warning. The Chief Stoker must have known perfectly well that we were doing a night exercise which was going to need smoke at some stage but he was either out of sorts or had decided to stand on his dignity that evening. Anyway when the order to make smoke was passed nothing happened. We were just retiring after an inspiring torpedo attack and there was a certain air of excitement on the Bridge; but no smoke. Phone to the engine room, 'Why no smoke?' 'Machine's not warm yet.' Meanwhile from 'D', 'Why are you not making smoke?' Captain to First Lieutenant, 'For God's sake get the engine room to make smoke.' First Lieutenant to engine room by phone, 'Is the Engineer Officer there? Chief, for God's sake give us some smoke.' Suddenly the blackest smoke I have ever seen came pouring out of the forward funnel, the one that went up inside the mast, and raced away aft as we continued our 21 knots out of the attack. Hardly had the cloud begun than of course the signal came from 'D', 'Stop making smoke.

Exercise completed. Join me. Etc., etc.' The new course to rejoin put the wind astern. Meanwhile the monster below once liberated refused to be caged and its oily noxious breath drifted slowly over the Bridge on a relatively gentle breeze. During the night the Captain had to be called, change of station, fishing boats or something, and was quickly on the Bridge in his bare feet. Soon he was hopping about the place in a very uncertain temper; and as day broke the Watch on deck found the entire Bridge covered with a spotty decoration of tar. The Chief Stoker had made his point.

The Gibraltar weapon training period was the high spot of that 1950 Spring Cruise in *Broadsword* as far as I was concerned. After some four weeks based on Gibraltar the Home Fleet set off eastward to meet the Mediterranean Fleet for joint exercises. I have absolutely no recollection of these except for a visit by our Squadron on the way when we put into Algiers. We were warned that the locals there were experts with rod and line which they used to poke through any scuttles left open and were quite often able to make a catch of belongings left sculling inside. A certain 'exalted person' in another Squadron was reputed to be quite accurate with a catapult should he come upon these fishermen.

From North Africa the combined fleets exercised over to a large bay at the southern end of Sardinia where we all anchored. The Korean war had been not long under way. Were we demonstrating how effectively naval units can be moved around the world if a situation requires it? There was of course no trouble in Sardinia – it just offered a safe and friendly anchorage. From there the two fleets split up and went their separate ways. The Home Fleet was due to make flag-showing and social visits to ports in the south of France. *Broadsword* as the most junior ship in the Fleet was detailed to stay behind until the last ship of either Fleet had left Sardinia and then take both Fleets' mail up to Toulon where our Squadron was bound. We were to ensure that we caught them up before arrival and this involved a hectic dash up the Golfe du Lion into the teeth of a strong mistral screaming out of the Rhone valley. On this occasion the Morning Watchmen when it got light found the entire ship almost white from the salt spray. The First Lieutenant was indeed having a hard time trying to keep a respectable-looking ship.

And so via another visit, this time to Portugal, we made our way home to an English Spring. In a way it was a rather sad homecoming. Our Captain, Lieutenant-Commander Bitmead, had finished his time in command, and a successor had been appointed. His *Broadsword* had been in many ways an outstanding ship. We all knew that second-rate performance just was not on the cards but beneath this very taut regime there was always a sense of humour and perhaps most importantly we also knew that provided we did indeed perform the Captain would stand up for us against all outsiders, including, dare it be said, the Squadron staff! We all felt the same. It is only fair to add that his successor, a more senior officer, also ran a good ship but that first Spring Cruise always held a special magic as far as I was concerned.

Life had to continue however and that summer 1950 the ship was sent over to the US Naval Base at Norfolk, Virginia, to continue the trials of the Flyplane system, this time using the pilotless target aircraft of the US Navy. I have to record, without complacency because it was no doing of mine, that we managed this time to avoid the gaffe which occurred before the previous year's firings off Malta.

On that occasion the ship, although Chatham-manned, was 'working up' for the firings in Portsmouth where they were handy to the Gunnery School at Whale Island. There was a lot of gundrill for the crews of the two twin 4-inch mountings. These guns were hand-loaded and good drill was essential to achieve a high rate of fire. Normally the drill would have been done with wooden dummy ammunition but it was so intensive in this case that the wooden dummies were splintering and the splinters were jamming the breeches of the guns. Permission was therefore given to drill with live Practice ammunition: the live bit was the propellant charge. The actual shells were sand-filled and inert.

Obviously particular care had to be taken that nothing got fired. There were two methods of firing. The primary one was by electric circuits from the Flyplane system and these were of course immobilised for drill sessions. The guns still had a back-up system for firing by hand should the electrics be out of action, for instance through battle damage. This hand-worked gear was fitted at the breech of each gun and for drill purposes had to be removed as well.

On one occasion it wasn't. Apparently the ship's Gunner's Mate was away for some reason and a replacement was deputising. The drill session was going swimmingly when the relief Gunner's Mate decided to introduce a hiccup – a perfectly sensible thing to do – and shouted, 'Misfire.' The Captain of the gun reacted quickly and correctly and hit the hand-firing lever. With the breech firing mechanism still, through an oversight, in place the 'misfire' went off and the shell landed in the back garden of a surprised cottager at West Wittering.

214

Chapter 17

Norfolk, Virginia; Nelson's Shirt and a Lost Anchor Cable

Happily nothing like that happened when we were working up for the Norfolk, Virginia, trials. How could it when we had Leading Seaman Doubtfire as Captain of the Mounting on 'A' gun with Ordinary Seaman Shotbolt as the mounting Trainer and Able Seaman Guntrip as the Layer?

After an interval of nearly half a century the images of those summer months in 1950 spent shooting at remotely-controlled aircraft 'drone' targets are rather dim. I am looking at the pictures as it were through the wrong end of a telescope. One or two elements I can still make out. I know that we hit Norfolk on the nose after a five day passage of the Atlantic when our Navigator got no sight of the sun or the stars, had no electronic aids and was seeking a landfall at the mouth of the James River which was as featureless as I had found the mouth of the Shatt al Arab some four years before. Not bad, we all thought.

The Naval Base was of course huge, laid out to a pattern almost Germanic in its logic and neatness; and quite foreign to our own cosy ports which, like flower beds in autumn, needed a good old sort out before the pearls of eighteenth and nineteenth-century architecture lying amongst the tangle of cranes, shanties and new industrial complexes could be appreciated.

The US Navy was as cordial as ever. A most tangible earnest of this was the loan to the ship of a huge black Buick saloon car. The model in question was apparently something of a cult object in gangster-land myth-ology. At first we didn't quite get the drift of the urchins' wide-eyed enquiries wherever we stopped, 'Gee Mister, where you done the job?' Later, sometimes, we thought we might as well play up to the image.

The weekdays we spent at sea in the practice areas off the coast. What a change from the Channel or even, I was told, from Malta. I do not remember a day's bad weather. There never seemed to be any shipping in the area to interfere with the shoots and in the evenings by steaming a few miles in towards the coast we could find water shallow and sheltered enough to let us anchor for the night with never a worry and with a minimum waste of time.

We had I recall two American naval officers on board to talk to the aircraft who flew alongside and controlled the targets for our shoots. Why two? I do not know. Maybe the Limeys were thought to be a little over-powering for one on his own. As they were soon calling themselves the 'Colonials' they need hardly have worried.

The trials soon took on a regular pattern. This was no bad thing as an important object was to build up a volume of performance data sufficient to give statistical authority. On a shooting day we would weigh anchor early and steam out to the firing area to be ready for the first onslaught at the beginning of the forenoon. The firing mounting for the day would have been checked through, Ops Room and Fire Control teams closed up. My seat was in the Director, above the Bridge, from which the guns were aimed. For company I had on my left the Chief Boatswain's Mate: he had a First Class Gunnery rate of Gunlayer and 'laid' the Director, that is, kept it pointed at the target for elevation. Opposite him on my right was the Trainer, another First class rate who, unsurprisingly, aimed at the target in the horizontal sense. They were pleasant company. The Director was in effect a master gunsight: where we aimed, the guns followed. It also carried two enormous radar 'headlights' which comprised the rangefinding capability. As I explained in the previous chapter they also allowed the Director to track a target blind. The most important part of my own job was to see that by the time we were told to open fire we were actually pointing at the target and not at the aircraft controlling it. Not too demanding and given that our Director was like a conservatory on a turntable, all windows which could be opened, it was the best place to be in that splendid weather.

It was also an intriguing place in that being sited quite close to the guns we could actually watch the shells arching up towards the target, not in a straight line but seeming to the observer to gain height above the target and then drop down onto it. This was something of an optical illusion. Their track was like a cricket ball's thrown from miles out in the deep field to hit the wicket but one was never quite sure until the shell was nearly up with the target whether we were to see a good shot or not. In fact the idea was to get close enough to the drone to trigger the proximity fuse in the shell's head. A direct hit meant of course the end of the drone, and even in the United States the supply of these was not unlimited. On the other hand a direct hit or two was not unpopular with the guns. It took a little while to rustle up another drone so that meant a break, particularly for the loading numbers.

With the day's shooting over and anchored for the night shark fishing was the sport. The devils were all round us, none quite up to the size of 'Jaws' but big enough. There was a slight difficulty in finding enough blood with which to seed the sea. The butcher did not realise until now how many friends he had but even he could not keep up with the needs of desperate shark catchers; anyway, frozen meat does not bleed much. Then some clever dicky remembered that the fire-fighting foam mixture which we carried for fighting oil fires was rumoured to consist largely of old blood from the slaughter houses, but the sharks didn't seem to take to that too much and anyway, as soon as the Engineer Officer got wind of what was happening to his fire-fighting supplies, the mixture was suddenly taken off the market. No one caught a shark.

I recall that His Majesty celebrated his Official Birthday whilst we were out shooting. This was one of the occasions when the Mainbrace could and should be spliced: that is, the sailors got a double tot of rum and the officers, less lucky, a single tot each. Navy rum was fiery stuff. It was kept under lock and key in the Spirit Room and the keys of the latter had equal precedence with those of the magazines on the ship's Important Keyboard. The atmosphere in the Spirit Room, particularly in hot weather, was probably more combustible than that in a cordite magazine. Not a few in the Wardroom found the stuff rather too much. After all, when one could buy Spanish sherry at bargain basement prices in Gibraltar and good French brandy free of duty, why not stick to that. I had rather a taste for rum and on this particular Birthday did a bit too well. The Captain had a dinner party in the evening to which I was invited. The weather was as good as ever but we were lying beam on to a slight swell and the vision of the horizon glimpsed through the scuttle rising and falling albeit gently proved too much. This minor mishap is still only too distinct at the other end of the telescope.

Our time in harbour was limited and not too remarkable. Mostly the memories are cheerful. I recall one dockyard gentleman who, leaning on the steering wheel of his fork-lift truck and watching our sweating sailors embarking ammunition, remarked that he wasn't surprised that England was in such straits if that was the fastest we could work. But then I remember the daughter of one top US commander in the War lately over who reckoned that she was not getting enough attention at a cocktail party which we felt the need to give; and dropped her handbag over the side.

This evened the score a bit and otherwise we were made very much at home.

There were two delightful girls who kept several members of the Wardroom well amused. We named one Body and of course the other had to be Soul. They were a powerful combination. One weekend three of us took the Buick up along the bank of the James River to the small settlement of Rescue to deliver a commission someone in England had sent to an acquaintance there. The lucky recipient in Rescue made us very welcome indeed and his wife even more so. She in fact was so much to the fore that the place was renamed on the spot 'Help, Rescue, Virginia'. One weekend the ship went up to New York for a few days 'rest and recreation'. I don't remember that at all.

I suppose we spent about three months in and out of Norfolk and the FPS I certainly came of age. We all felt that the visit had been very well worthwhile. Goodness knows how many drones we had shot down: a figure somewhere over twenty seems to lurk in the back of my mind. And then there were the ones that got away, which wouldn't have been so lucky in a real struggle when our shells would have carried a potentially lethal load of high explosive instead of, as it was, sand. It would have been mid-summer when we sailed for England. The weather was fine the whole way home and the long light evenings made keeping the First Watch from eight o'clock to midnight a pleasure. We brought a passenger with us, an old Admiral who we gathered had been visiting friends in the States after, apparently, having recently been widowed. I did not myself see a great deal of him but somewhere in mid-ocean the Wardroom arranged a formal mess dinner for him. I had the First Watch that evening and I shall always remember the aura of peace, contentment and gratitude which the old man brought up to the Bridge with him afterwards. He stayed up there until after it had grown dark, no doubt counting over his memories like beads on a rosary. He did not speak much but I could not avoid the impression that that last voyage had perhaps put his memories to rest. For me that evening rounded off a good three months better than some wild celebration.

Not all our Summer Cruises were as diverting as our 1950 detachment to Norfolk. Normally they were spent in European waters. First there would be a gathering of the Home Fleet at some convenient anchorage, probably on the South Coast, and then a passage in company up the west coast and round Cape Wrath to Invergordon on the Moray Firth for a few weeks weapon training. The latter would be balanced over the rest of the summer with visits to UK ports on, frankly, recruiting business. The final lap before summer leave would, if we were lucky, be a trip across the North Sea to Scandinavia or France; recreation certainly but not much rest for those already recruited. *Broadsword* in 1951 had to do without the latter. The Korean War was at its height and I can only think that the Commander-in-Chief, Home Fleet and, who knows, also the Board of Admiralty felt that too much 'R & R' would be inappropriate. In early summer we were in Belfast for a visit by the Queen. Nostalgia can be a bad historian but those were certainly the days in Belfast. The weather was fine, almost too hot. Crowds filled the streets for the Royal visit. *Broadsword* lined a section of the route to keep the loyal, lovely people clear of the road. It was so warm that when the time came to move I found that my boots had bonded into the melting tar. It was extraordinary the way in which the personality of the Queen came over to us, rooted as we were to our various spots. She rode in an open horse-drawn carriage with Princess Margaret. It was quite a wide road so the carriage must have passed a reasonable distance away but I certainly wasn't the only one to feel in some way a sense of acknowledgement from her even over that distance.

From Belfast we steamed alone up the west coast of Scotland, through the Western Isles, surely one of the most enchanted stretches of water anywhere. We tried to prevail on the Captain to take the ship through the Corryvrechan but this did not seem to be on the bill. The Corryvrechan is a notorious few hundred yards of water between the islands of Scarba and Jura just south of Oban. At slack water it is no more than an innocent passage between two islands but at other times with the tide running strongly one way or the other it can turn into a huge and vicious whirlpool. We wondered what the effect would be on a destroyer at say half-tide when the whirlpool might be only up to half speed. The Captain did not see it quite that way.

Otherwise it was a magical trip. We spent a couple of days in Tobermory. During the War this used to be the base where convoy escorts 'worked up' after commissioning until each ship was passed as fit to take on the U-boats in the Atlantic. The Base was run by the legendary Commodore 'Monkey' Stephenson. The story goes that sometimes during an efficiency inspection of an aspiring corvette he would fling his cap on the deck shouting, 'Incendiary Bomb. Do something.' One enterprising sailor was held to have hesitated not a moment and to have at once kicked the cap overboard.

All this was gone when we visited but the bay must still have been one of the prettiest anchorages you could imagine, protected from the Atlantic by a semicircle of low rocky cliffs, themselves overgrown with rhododendron. The bushes were in bloom when we were there, only the common-or-garden purple ponticum but what a sight.

From there we steamed on north through the Kyle of Lochalsh, past Skye through waters the Young Pretender knew well, north to Cape Wrath on the edge of the land, east along the top of Scotland to the Pentland Firth, that notorious passage between Atlantic and North Sea where even battleships had been known to get into trouble if attempting it with a westerly gale blowing against a strong opposing tide.

We joined the Fleet briefly for weapon training at Invergordon and then with the fine hot weather from Belfast still holding steamed on down to Rosyth, the naval base on the Firth of Forth. I came to know it well in my next ship but closer acquaintance made it no more of a friend. Built before the First World War against the threat of increasing German naval power in the North Sea it was Admiral Beatty's base for his battle-cruiser squadron and from where he had set out at best speed to engage the Germans off Jutland. Rosyth had no pretensions to be anything more than a strictly utilitarian facility. Leave the dockyard gates and it was some miles to the nearest civilisation in Dunfermline, and Dunfermline despite its place in Scottish history was nothing to write home about in the twentieth century. Beyond lay the Fife coalfields. Edinburgh was a boat trip across the Firth and then some miles on. I can only think that the reason for our call was to act as host ship to a Swedish patrol craft which had arranged a visit, presumably to show the Swedish flag in Edinburgh. I wonder why they didn't choose Leith, the port of Edinburgh. It would not have been much worse than Rosyth.

The least we could do to give the impression of a welcome in the desert-like sterility of the dockyard was to ask the Swedes over for dinner. In my experience it was quite rare for seafarers of different nationalities, unless engaged in outright warfare, not to be able to establish some sort of *modus vivendi*: maybe having a common struggle with the sea helps sometimes. Anyway we had a good evening with the Swedes and they kindly asked us back next day. From breakfast onwards we were looking forward to a good taste of Scandinavian Aquavit but when the time came to change before dinner we came across a hiccup. *Broadsword* had no laundry and Rosyth was the nearest we had come to a shore-based establishment since leaving Belfast. Some of us were out of a clean shirt. A quick whip round the cabin flat got most of us kitted out but the last in line ended up with a garment which had only one arm. 'Never mind. Come on. No one will know under a mess-jacket.' The evening went very well and the previous night's good international relations looked set to become even firmer. The Swedish Wardroom was however very small, not surprising for a patrol craft. As dinner progressed it did start to warm up. By the end of the first course the Swedish First Lieutenant was saying, 'It is perhaps not proper but we are amongst friends, I think we may remove our jackets.' Mindful of the predicament of our one-armed shirt member we demurred somewhat. The Swedes evidently took this as evidence of British determination to remain correctly dressed despite everything and politely did not pursue the subject. By the end of the second course however, with sweat now streaming down his face and the rest of us wilting similarly, the Swedish Mess President burst out, 'It is now bloody hot. I order the rig of the day is No Jackets,' and he took his off. The rest of us decided that for once politeness went hand in hand with the avoidance of heat stroke and disrobed also. There were murmurs of Swedish sympathy as one of us was revealed to be half-naked. 'Ah, we knew that things were bad in England, but to be forced to wear such an old shirt . . .' The owner of the one-armed shirt waited for the murmurs, most sympathetic but one or two rather hard-edged, to run round the table and then played his ace. 'Actually,' he said, 'this shirt is rather historic. It once belonged to Lord Nelson who as you know lost an arm at Copenhagen. He left it to my great-grandfather who served with him as a Midshipman. It only comes out on very extra-special occasions.' We thought at the time that our hosts believed him. Why not?

And so we steamed on down the east coast, back towards Chatham but stopping here and there wherever the Naval Staff ordained was a 'good place for recruiting'. Blyth on the Northumberland coast was one such. We landed a guard of honour there for something or other and it was quickly spotted by the owner of a travelling circus who decided it was just what he needed to welcome the Mayor to his 'big top'. Our First Lieutenant thought this might be a good recruiting wheeze and was about to agree. Those of us likely to be more actively involved felt we would be encroaching on Sea Cadet territory and whilst in no position to refuse duty, succeeded in arguing the idea out of court.

Further south at, I think, Newcastle we had an interesting demonstration of human psychology. As ever we were giving a cocktail party for local 'believers'. This one was proving very sticky. In an important shipbuilding area our guests ought to have been 'naval-minded' but we did not seem to be making much contact. There were a number of local Councillors, led by a Lady Mayoress, amongst the guests, and maybe, as I found on a later visit to the North-East, they had memories of the General Strike only twenty-five years before when warships were sailed up the Tyne and the Tees to keep the peace. Anyway in 1951 it was proving hard work for the hosts. On our side we had an RNVR officer called up in the context of the Korean War but getting no further east than *Broadsword*. He had already proved rather less inhibited than the rest of us and our First Lieutenant, a man with a not-unkindly sense of humour, had once been driven to liken him to a spaniel which had been hit over the head with a cricket bat. On this occasion all the past was forgiven. At one point during the party he found himself behind the very ample rear of the Lady Mayoress, carrying on a dull and inconsequential conversation with a local. All of a sudden he was overcome by an irresistible impulse to pinch that broad posterior. The volcano erupted. 'You naughty man,' she bellowed in a voice that silenced the whole Wardroom much more effectively than she could ever have achieved in the Council Chamber. 'Oh Lord,' we thought, 'he's done it again.' But no; the Mayoress was obviously something of a deprived person. The pinch punctured her repressions and she became a centre of gaiety. The party sloughed off boredom and went from strength to strength.

That was 1951. The gunnery situation seemed to be under control by then but I was beginning to have the first stirrings of a social conscience. In particular I was coming to feel more and more that we were not giving our senior ratings enough scope to use their undoubted abilities and were not expecting enough from them in return. The problem was that ships and weapons required a considerable number of skilled technicians to maintain them. To attract and keep these craftsmen adequate rates of pay and conditions of service had to be offered and this meant that a high proportion of the technicians had to have the pay and status of senior ratings. It was an article of faith that those who wore the uniform of Petty Officer and above should take their share of the leadership responsibilities involved in running a ship even though on many occasions these would fall outside the bounds of their specialist work. But with so many senior specialist rates the opportunities to develop and exercise qualities of 'man-management' were bound to be thinly spread so when the need really arose performance was sometimes rather less than that required. 'No Opportunities' could result in 'No Inclination'.

In the less technological branches, Seamen particularly, the problem was less marked but still present. The cause however was different. Ships had to be manned in peacetime so that in an emergency they could maintain something approaching a wartime state of readiness even if only for short periods. This required more officers than strictly needed for day-to-day normal peacetime activities. The more junior of these required opportunities to extend and improve their professional abilities in the same areas as did senior ratings. If junior officers were for ever being given tasks that ought to have been within the competence of the latter, where was the job satisfaction for senior rates? The final twist was that it was always difficult to set time aside for training of this sort. Life went on, but it was more rare than it should have been to find Chief Petty Officers and Petty Officers of the calibre of say a Sergeant-Major in a good regiment to whom one could confidently say, 'Carry on.' Equally it was perhaps unusual to find officers brave enough to delegate responsibility and then defend their action to higher authority if something went wrong. We all knew the theory. Practice was difficult.

What to do? I resolved to stake my pennyworth one wintry morning in Campbeltown down at the mouth of the Firth of Clyde. *Broadsword* had just finished two or three weeks at the Joint Anti-Submarine School at Londonderry. I was very fond of Northern Ireland, but anti-submarine exercises . . . definitely not. I could not help feeling that we were fighting the last War. Could one really visualise another round of North Atlantic convoys? And the exercises at sea invariably attracted the most miserable weather. This particular course finished with an exercise which took us over to the Scottish coast and we were awarded the chance of a 'jolly' in Glasgow before returning to Chatham for Christmas leave. The previous winter had seen us in La Rochelle, not devastatingly exciting at that time of year but better than Glasgow. Meanwhile Campbeltown was a night stop before going up the Clyde next morning.

It was blowing hard. We were to secure to a buoy in the harbour and the Captain ordered two chain bridles to be used. Here perhaps you can excuse a description of securing to a buoy; in this case it is part of the cautionary tale. *Broadsword* enters harbour and makes over towards the buoy as smartly as reasonable given the weather conditions. Just before reaching it the whaler is slipped with the 'buoy jumper' embarked. The latter is usually in a destroyer the Painter or some similar shellback who despite his years is still reasonably agile. A boat-rope from the whaler's bow has been taken through a block on the foc'sle. On the word the foc'slemen grab the boat-rope and run away with it: this means not that they abscond with it for other purposes but that they haul it smartly through the block thus propelling the whaler forward at a very satisfactory clip. With good judgement the coxswain will be able to steer it up to the buoy with sufficient accuracy for the buoy jumper to get onto the buoy without falling in. With poor judgement all sorts of excitements are possible. On its passage at whirlwind speed past the foc'sle the whaler will have had the end of the picking-up rope dropped down to it. The rope is fitted so that it can be hooked onto the buoy, and this is the buoy jumper's first task. The Chief Stoker who for some reason always presides over the capstan at these festivities, though normally with a demeanour showing clearly that he feels it rather beneath his dignity, now sets his machinery to heave and the buoy is hauled close underfoot. Meanwhile one of the anchors has been unshackled from its cable after being itself held on a slip so that it does not drop into the harbour. The cable from which it was parted has a ship-to-buoy shackle – whose purpose is just that – hammered on and is then lowered to the buoy and shackled on. If all goes well it takes about the same time to get the ship secured to the buoy as it does to read this rather convoluted description. In Campbeltown because it was blowing hard we had decided to put a second cable out to the buoy as well. Describing how this is done reminds me of those explanations of cricket to the uninitiated. I will leave it out. The important point was that by the time we had two bridles secured that evening it was time for tea and we retired from a windswept foc'sle, as far as I was concerned to make toast on the Wardroom fire.

By next morning the gale had blown itself out and we were due to steam up to Glasgow. I thought it would be a splendid opportunity for the Captain of the Foc'sle, a young and sensible Petty Officer, to get on with all the preliminaries for unshackling from the buoy without me breathing down his neck. He thought so too and feeling rather virtuous at this training initiative I went below to clean my teeth.

I had hardly squeezed some tooth paste from the tube when there was an almighty roar from the foc'sle. It sounded like cable running out. I was up there in a moment and found that I had guessed right. A de-pressed-looking foc'sle party were looking sadly into the depths of Camp-beltown Harbour where one of the bridles of cable had disappeared without trace. Both ends had been unshackled at once and with nothing thus to attach it to either the buoy or the ship it had made its bid for freedom.

No one was very pleased. I put it to my elders and betters that it was all in a good cause and my plea was eventually accepted but it took an Admiralty Mooring Vessel from Greenock to recover the cable. Clearly it's a tricky subject but I still felt one had to try. Difficult!

Chapter 18

A Voyage to Dundee

I had no reason to think that it was the fall-out from the Campbeltown Cable Chase the previous December which led to my exile to the Boys Training Squadron in Rosyth the next month. It was however an unwelcome move from *Broadsword* as far as I was concerned. It would have been much preferable to have got another destroyer gunnery billet, preferably in the Far East; but someone was needed in Rosyth. I was available. It was no use pleading.

In January 1952 the Dockyard looked even worse than it had done the previous summer when we met the Swedes there. A light coating of snow lay over the countryside, not enough to give that fairy-tale Christmas card effect, just enough to make the Dockyard anyway look miserable. A biting easterly wind blew up the Firth of Forth. To cap it all *Largo Bay* was in a floating dock in the main basin, lifted out of the water into the full force of the gale. The only bright spot was provided by the Boys themselves.

There were only two ships in the squadron, *Widemouth Bay* and ourselves. *Widemouth Bay* was Captain 'D'. The Bay class was of basically the same design as the old *Loch Glendhu* but fitted out as the anti-aircraft version. By chance I drew the same cabin as in the latter and our First Lieutenant had been Navigator of *Broadsword* on our 1950 trip to Norfolk, Virginia, so apart from the climate and surroundings it ought to have been something of a homecoming.

The purpose of the Squadron was to give sea experience to Advanced Class Boy seamen before they joined the Fleet. They would have entered the Navy more or less straight from school having signed an agreement to serve for twelve years 'man's time' from the age of 18. After that they could extend for a further ten years if they felt so inclined. This was a Long Service engagement aimed at those who it was hoped wanted to make more of a career in the Navy as opposed to the Short Service men such as Price and Sharp in *Loch Glendhu*. They would already have had a year's training at HMS *St Vincent* in Gosport for those of the Portsmouth Port Division and HMS *Ganges* at Shotley near Harwich for Chatham and Devonport Boys. Why two separate Establishments? I do not know

HMS *Largo Bay* Boys Training Squadron entering the Solent for the 1953 Coronation Review

– it had always been like that. Advanced Class Boys were the cream of the cream of the Long Service entrants, almost certain from their educational background and general outlook to become Senior Rates. Hopefully a proportion would also eventually make what used to be called Warrant Rank: by 1952 the latter had been renamed Special Duties Officers, experts within the specialisations which they had entered as ratings. A few would achieve further promotion still. Obviously the pyramid narrowed quite sharply as it thrust upward but there was no particular bar to advancement for those qualified and committed. The Advanced Class Boys were high quality recruits. We were lucky to have them.

That is not to say that there were no villains among them. A month after I joined the class then under training with us completed their course and left by train for the south under the care of our Senior Instructor, a Gunner's Mate for whom on short acquaintance I had formed a high regard. I was extremely upset to have a telephone call next morning from the Naval Provost Marshal in London to say that a draft of Boy seamen had just tumbled out of the overnight train in Euston very much the worse for wear. Their Petty Officer in charge was incoherent. What was I going to do? None of us could believe it. At that distance, and by then, the only thing we could do was to make sure that that Instructor never came back.

That was a bad start. Thereafter we managed to get things running more smoothly. The Boys would spend three months with us. They would arrive from the Shore Training Establishments keen as mustard, smart as paint and in outstanding order. Our task was to help them make the transition from the very disciplined but basically simple life of the previous year to the much more demanding environment at sea. On the face of it one might have thought that it would be an easier existence. One couldn't in a ship the size of a Bay class frigate always be moving at the double as they had been taught to do ashore, always saluting this, that and the other. They had to move on to accept that self-discipline was the order of the day, to accept that the ship's rules were kept as simple as possible but this did not provide a licence to sit back. The more practical side involved getting them used to slinging a hammock, to feeding themselves under the Canteen Messing system then in force in many ships of the Fleet. Most difficult of all was getting them into the way of keeping clean and tidy – comparatively easy ashore, much more difficult under the cramped conditions at sea. The Messing placed a considerable strain on the Instructors. Canteen Messing dated back at least to Trafalgar and almost certainly earlier. Each Mess of twelve men, or boys, had a daily Victualling

Allowance. Within this they could draw what they wanted from the stores and then had to make up their own meals, which the galley would later cook for them. I always felt that it was not such a bad system as the nutritionists of the fifties claimed. The sailors ate what they wanted and many of them became very adept at dishing up tasty meals, as evidenced by Able Seaman Price's efforts on the east Malayan coast a few years earlier. In later years this do-it-yourself system was 'improved' into Centralised Messing. The Supply Officer or Petty Officer made out the menu which was then cooked centrally for everyone. It may have been a nutritional improvement and the meals were certainly not bad but it still wasn't a patch on Mum's cooking. There were many more grumbles. Eventually towards the end of my time at sea the Admiralty saw the light, increased the Victualling Allowance quite substantially, dramatically improved the training of cooks and somehow lifted the imagination of the Supply staff. The improvement paid off a thousandfold. For the time being however those hungry boys had to cater for themselves. They did not starve and undoubtedly the experience helped to produce the rounded man, spiritually if not physically. But what if the Cook of the Mess for the day was seasick?

Our sea passages were never in fact very long. One could arrange more worthwhile training in the comparatively sheltered and almost unbelievably beautiful waters of the Minches on the north-west coast of Scotland than one could punching about in the normally miserable North Sea. On a rough evening the Instructors used to have a busy time of it getting the seasick fraternity into their hammocks and coaxing the rest of the Boys' messdeck into some sort of order for the night.

This was not to say that there was a complete collapse of Boy morale whenever the wind rose above force 4. King George VI it will be recalled died in early 1952, and King Haakon of Norway elected to attend the State Funeral. He was to arrive at Leith, the port of Edinburgh. As the nearest ships available, *Widemouth Bay* and *Largo Bay* were detailed to meet him at sea with appropriate ceremony and escort him into port. The weather for the preceding few days was foul. I remember painting the ship's side in intervals between squalls and showers. Ships tended to look pretty woebegone in the Scottish winter and we certainly needed freshening up.

It was still blowing hard by the time both ships sailed to meet the King. The sea was rough and visibility very low with driving rain and a north-easterly gale. We managed to find the Yacht as arranged and the plan was to fire a salute of twenty-one guns as we steamed towards each other, after which our two ships would do a smart turn and fall in either ahead or astern of the King. Meanwhile our sailors despite the gale would be manning the ship's rail. Before the salute was fired the drill dictated that the Ship's Company be called to Attention by a ringing blast on the bugle, so we had our best Boy bugler on the Bridge, bugle at the ready. He was looking a bit green but assured me he could get through it all. The Norwegians appeared through the murk no more than half a mile ahead of us. 'A' gun's crew on the foc'sle slunk out from behind the gunshield into the water washing over the deck. The moment arrived. The Captain ordered, 'Sound the Alert.' Nothing happened. I looked round at Eden. 'Come on, Eden. Sound the Alert.' He certainly had the bugle to his lips but there was no sound. Consternation! The bugle call would have set our gun salute going. The noise would have been blown back to Scotland on the wind but there would have been satisfactory puffs of smoke for the Norwegians to count had they been like the Arabs. Somehow we got the gun salute going without the bugle but it was hardly the smooth welcome that had been planned and practised. After the last gun had shaken the ship there were hasty words on the Bridge. Eventually Eden was allowed his say. 'Please, Sir, I'm afraid I was sick into my bugle.' It was impossible to quarrel with such devotion to duty.

As Spring approached our fingers became a little less frozen and I got our Captain to agree to a slight widening of the training syllabus. We were due for a change of scene from Rosyth and a weekend visit to Dundee was planned. Dundee is on the River Tay, the next firth up from the Forth and only a short distance away. What better, we thought, than a sailing expedition from Rosyth to Dundee for any boys who might be interested. Happily the idea appealed to quite a number and we ended up with enough to crew three whalers. *Largo Bay* had two whalers and we planned to borrow a third from the dockyard. The Ship's Gunner's Mate was a keen sailor and volunteered to captain one boat. The Doctor came out of his surgery and agreed that he could well do with a brisk day's sail. With extraordinary foresight as it happened he was appointed to the dockyard whaler. I was to take the second ship's boat.

The weather was settled at the time. We would not have gone otherwise. April is quite early to take on the northern part of the North Sea. It did mean however that with light winds forecast we were going to have to take every advantage of the tides. They can run quite strongly up and down the Firth of Forth. Thus we set off at midnight from Rosyth to catch as much of the ebb as we could all the way down the Firth.

We might have been a raiding party about to land on an enemy coast. The boats were well supplied with stores even though we anticipated beating the ship round there by an hour or two. The crews were so heavily muffled against the cold that they could hardly move. However in the best interests of training we were all still just recognisable as naval crews. There was a brave send-off from the ship and then we were away. The only trouble was that there was no wind.

We rowed quite energetically out of the dockyard both in order to get warm and to catch the tide and quite soon were swirling underneath the Forth railway bridge. Out there we still had no wind and as sixteen-year-old boys, even Advanced Class ones, cannot go on pulling for ever we were fairly soon reduced to keeping the boats heading seaward and praying for a breeze. None came.

As the light strengthened I fell to reassuring the still very chirpy crew that we could well expect a dawn breeze. By breakfast time I had to resort to explaining why this phenomenon, so well-known in tropical waters, was not always evident in Scotland. Soon after breakfast someone sighted a signal lamp flashing from the Doctor's boat, by now half a mile away from us towards the northern side of the Firth. 'Boat leaking. May have to beach.' Grins all round. The Doctor was very popular on board. We all felt for him but with three boats at sea the expedition had become slightly competitive. Nevertheless we tried to encourage him to fight the leak, but it was no good. His signals became more urgent and finally he had to break off and make for Inverkeithing. Inverkeithing was the yard where old ships were broken up. We did not foresee this fate overtaking the dockyard whaler, but the fact that it lies only a few miles down the Firth from Rosyth was a measure of our snail's pace progress.

Meanwhile the Gunner's Mate had cleverly discovered a somewhat more friendly run of current than ourselves and was edging ahead. As the morning progressed a slight breeze did eventually roughen the previous glossy calm of the Firth and thankfully we began to make some progress over the flood tide which would otherwise have pushed us back to our start. By the time we sighted *Largo Bay* coming up from astern we were not much further on than Inchkeith Island at the mouth of the Forth. We weren't offered a tow. We wouldn't have taken one anyway.

The breeze strengthened during the afternoon and pushed us along quite briskly in what passed for April sunshine. The Gunner's Mate was still increasing his lead which made us rather envious if not actually cross. I now began to be aware of a major error in planning the expedition. On the chart the distance between the Firths of Tay and Forth had looked to be no more than a very few miles. The Navigator had been chary of lending charts out to an open boat from which they would almost certainly have been returned in a rather soggy state. I had agreed that we would probably cover the few miles of open sea in a couple of hours and would in any case reach Dundee before dark, but now with no chart we were sailing into waters unmarked as far as we were concerned – a criminal error! However the breeze held. The Gunner's Mate disappeared into the late afternoon haze and we sailed along contentedly alone thinking of what we would do when we reached Dundee. My recollection after two previous visits to Dundee was that navigation of the Tay was quite straightforward.

The afternoon light began to fade. We seemed to be making a reasonable speed through the water but not so much progress when we looked at the land, which was not all that far away to port. Obviously the tide had turned against us but as we were making a coastal passage in good weather I was not particularly worried. We were all getting just a little hungry as we had been at sea rather longer than we expected. Soon it was going to be dark. No matter. We could see the Tay Light Vessel, apparently not too far ahead. The problem remained that we never seemed to get any closer to it. The crew was becoming if not dispirited then certainly a little quiet. We had found previously with sixteen-year-olds that there was a definite limit to their tolerance of fatigue and cold. It was not that they gave up. It was rather that the flame inside began to flicker where before there had been a steady fire. Rest and warmth were essential. We had neither.

All was by no means disaster though. We began to hear a dull rumbling ahead. Maybe I was becoming slightly disorientated by the cold but I was pretty clear in my own mind that we had by now turned into the Tay and I persuaded myself and my crew that the noise we could hear was from a train crossing the Tay railway bridge just above Dundee. The rumbling continued. It is a very long train we told ourselves, or a very busy line and we began looking for the lights of *Largo Bay* and ordering in our minds the supper which would be waiting for us. To make sure that we were not a menace to other traffic on the river or to ourselves I posted a lookout in the bows with orders to keep well awake.

The noise ahead grew louder. I wondered if there was a shunting yard or some similar busy railway activity near the bridge. I never for a moment doubted where we were until the lookout suddenly electrified us all with a shout, 'Breakers ahead.' The noise I had been convinced was a train was actually surf on the shore. We put the helm hard up to bring the boat round and stood out to sea. Just then there was another hail from the bows, 'Looks like a breakwater ahead.' In the act of going about we were in fact being wafted into a tiny harbour. And on a slipway only a few yards ahead was a boat, drawn up clear of the water. A naval whaler – the Gunner's Mate's boat. It must be! We downed sails, extricated ourselves from the damp canvas and pulled over to the slipway, to be met there by a huge policeman. It was all so surreal that I felt he might quite well start talking French. But no. 'Ah,' he said. 'We were half expecting you. The rest of your lot is up at the Station.'

In these days of 1996 when the police and public seem so often to be at opposite ends of the street I like to think back to that evening, after that is we had arrived at St Andrews. The police had of course telephoned *Largo Bay*, long since in Dundee, to tell them our whereabouts; but they then persuaded the local fish-and-chip shop to open and give us all supper despite the fact that it was then nearly midnight. After which we were snugged down in the police station for the night, and I, being the senior officer, had the great comfort of a cell to myself! Crime may not pay but it apparently need not be uncomfortable. Next morning the fish-and-chip shop switched to eggs, and as far as I could see the police account paid. We had no gold onboard. Any time I remember that evening I wonder if castaways would get the same help today. I wonder again.

Next morning the sun was bright, there was a light offshore breeze and both boats were soon away. The locals might have described the weather as bracing. I thought it was colder than that. The Gunner's Mate continued to outsail us and we began to think it must be something to do with his boat. To steal a march I decided to sail across the shallows to the south of the Tay mouth. We must have been back on a chart by then. I wonder how our Navigator let that one slip out. Our rival, more properly, stood out to sea to round the Light Vessel and make the deep water channel of the river. To increase our own chances of being first home we dug out a spare sail from somewhere and set it as a spinnaker on an oar for bowsprit. It seemed to give us a little extra speed but it was that 'spinnaker' which did for us in the end.

We crossed the shallows quite happily; it was only just after high water. Once in the river however we quickly had the ebb tide running strongly against us. And the breeze being offshore was contrary too. It was an unhelpful combination. We soon had to tack to avoid the north bank of the river. Almost as soon as I put the tiller over I realised that our unorthodox rig was going to stop the boat coming round smartly and paying off on the other tack. Sure enough it did just that. We lost way, stopped 'in irons', unable to come right round and under the malign influence of that strong ebb tide were soon cast ashore. It was the drop keel which touched first and it was the drop keel which we could in no fashion raise later. Luckily I suppose we had taken the ground not too far from a bus stop so most of the crew finished their epic journey by public transport. That at least had its comic side! One sterling volunteer stayed behind with me and when the tide rose again we were plucked off the beach by an RAF Air/Sea Rescue Launch. What ignominy! By then we were both so cold that we got the full rescue and revival treatment when once onboard the launch, minus unfortunately the brandy. Back alongside *Largo Bay* and with the whaler hoisted the drop keel came up quite easily. That anyway was a useful lesson for both the boys and myself: things ain't usually so bad as they appears. The Gunner's Mate had to be towed home too – contrary wind and tide! Most unkindly we did find that something of a consolation prize.

Chapter 19

West Coast

I have to hand it to our Captain that he did not at once put a stopper on further hare-brained sailing schemes. In fact there was no doubt that they did have a training value, though some of us were hard put to quantify it, and the following summer I prevailed on him to let us try again. This time there was only one boat involved; obviously the word had got around. The ship was making another foray from Rosyth, on this occasion to visit Alnwick on the Northumberland coast, a nice rural little spot just south of the Border. We were dropped one fine summer evening just south of the Farne Islands and spent a beautifully peaceful night on the beach there with the seals for company. Idyllic! By next morning however the weather had done one of those quick changes and we found ourselves faced with enough wind to cause quite a lop against a contrary tide but not enough to drive us over the current. We tried pulling but Boy-power was obviously failing so we ran into a little fishing village to find shelter for the second night. Our welcome was not nearly as helpful as at St Andrews in the spring and the best that we could raise for a billet was a very smelly but empty fishing boat. Next day however came in far better and with a nice breeze we made the ship by lunch-time. No tow!

My stock rose and towards the end of that summer we made our last and most successful voyage. The ship was visiting Portree in Skye, next stop Gairloch. I got permission to sail on ahead and with confidence more or less restored, set off with both whalers. We spent the first night on Raasay Island, then uninhabited except by sheep and midges. We found a delightful little cove, real *Swallows and Amazons* stuff. At the edge of the water stood a ruined crofter's hut and the Boys with their Chief Instructor, who had the second whaler, decided this was just the place for them. I say with I hope no conceit that I was wiser. Perhaps I knew the Scottish midge better than they did. Anyway after our camp-fire supper I rowed the second whaler a little way offshore and anchored. The bottom boards were perhaps not as comfortable a bed for the night as a bundle of heather but I did have relief from the midges. The shore party did not and it was a very flea-bitten fleet which sailed next morning. We had a wonderful sail across to Gairloch though, a fresh breeze, sparkling blue water, unbelievable views of islands, purple hills and bright beaches. Provisions were good and ample, and we beat the ship to the anchorage. Looking back, the only thing that could have made it better would have been if I had known beforehand of my Father's letter describing that 'return' to Gairloch in 1916. In this book it forms part of Chapter 5 in Part One.

We used to visit the West Coast as often as we could. The anchorages were better and more sheltered than on the other side of Scotland, and they offered more scope for practice in cable work – a subject particularly close to my heart of course. Also it was easier for the Boys to get ashore and out of the ship for exercise. A favourite spot was Loch Ewe a few miles north of Gairloch. This had been a Fleet anchorage during the Second World War and a Boom Defence Depot was still maintained there – incredible thought. Running the Depot was a much-prized job for any about-to-be-retired Lieutenant-Commander who liked fishing. There was thus a delightful relaxed air about the place and a certain generosity with naval transport, which was useful in mounting shorebased training expeditions.

On one Autumn Cruise down the west coast we had just passed Loch Torridon and were steaming south towards the Sound of Sleat between Skye and the mainland when somehow we got a wireless message from shore to say that the good people of Plockton on Loch Carron just south of us were having a Ceilidh that evening. Would we like to stop off and join them? We said to ourselves, 'Why not?'; and we did. The Ceilidh was in a ruined squash court close to the shore and a party of us, Wardroom and sailors, landed over the beach. I am not much given to dancing and the like but that was a magical evening.

The following summer we were programmed to visit Oban when our Captain discovered that a distant cousin, who was in line to succeed as chief of the Maclean clan, owned Duart Castle on Mull just opposite Oban. A party of us were invited over there for dinner and that was another evening out of this world. Duart was some eight miles across the water. The castle stood on a small promontory of rock with the sea almost lapping the bottom of its walls. It was a calm, clear and sunny evening and for once we put our faith in our not-very-trustworthy motorboat to get us there and back. It did, but the experience was such that I doubt we would have worried if it hadn't.

Writing about all this over forty years later makes me realise so clearly what a different world we have now. The State demands more for its money and is no doubt right to do so. Perhaps all one can reasonably reflect in 1996 is how lucky we in the Navy were just after the end of the War. But then that is why I thought it might perhaps be permissible to set down one or two accounts of how Ships' Companies lived and what they did about that time.

On the east coast back in 1952–3 we relied on Invergordon which we would normally have to ourselves. Invergordon was more heavily populated than Loch Ewe, something of a relative term no doubt for those latitudes of Scotland. The locals were very friendly. We, not being given to too much modesty, did not find this particularly surprising, until we realised that most of them were angling for invitations to come onboard for the Coronation Review which was to be held at Spithead that summer of 1953.

We nearly missed the Review ourselves. On the way south from Rosyth we ran into very dense fog. We did of course have a radar set but it was not particularly effective in the context of navigating safely through busy shipping lanes. After a day or so of not being able to see the foc'sle head and one or two near misses we anchored for a breather and told the Commander-in-Chief, Home Fleet, who was organising the Review that *Largo Bay* was going to be a few hours late. It was I suppose no surprise to get a sharp rejoinder, 'Get here or else.'

We must have had about five days at Spithead. There can never be another review like it; never because there simply will not be enough ships. In 1953 we mustered six Royal Navy aircraft-carriers and a further two from Commonwealth Navies; five cruisers from the home team and three from the Commonwealth. Over it all brooded the huge bulk of *Vanguard*, the largest and arguably the best battleship we ever built. And then there were shoals of destroyers, frigates and smaller craft. We took up all the water between the mainland and the Isle of Wight from Portsmouth in the east to Cowes in the west. The picture on the jacket of this book is reproduced from a plan of the anchorage. For us, supposedly a Portsmouth ship, it was in fact a slightly frustrating five days. Like the other frigates we were anchored miles away from Portsmouth, somewhere down towards Cowes. The weather was typical for June, not too brilliant, and the only way our married 'natives' could get ashore was by dockyard tug. It was a long journey. I thought of that anchorage in Leyte Gulf in the Philippines at the end of the Pacific war. However with the Boys' help we managed to get the ship looking reasonably smart, and when the day came the Wardroom's guests did manage to get off to us. There might have been four from Invergordon. After the review we never saw any of them again.

We nearly never saw Her Majesty either. It was not that the lunch party in the Wardroom was anything more than quietly decorous. The general idea was that the Ships' Companies would man the rail as the Royal Yacht approached, and cheer as she passed. Nothing could be simpler. I cannot believe that our lookout confused *Britannia* approaching in the distance with a dockyard tug. It happened however that the lunch party only became aware of her when she was a few hundred yards off. From onboard it looked as though the mad scramble to get the Ship's Company fallen-in and spread along the side according to the drill book approached the worst chaos. In the Wardroom the scene must have resembled the turmoil following an order to Abandon Ship. Possibly however the activity was not too noticeable from *Britannia*, by now acknowledging the cheers from the ship ahead of us; or if it was it was ascribed charitably to a rather smart 'evolution' on the part of *Largo Bay* to get the side manned just in time without needless hanging about. 'Evolutions' were very popular at sea, dating no doubt from Trafalgar and before. One reads that the French Admiral Villeneuve was astonished at the speed and efficiency with which the British seamen were aloft and getting their ships in order after the battle when, to quote his own words, his officers could hardly get their men to move.

Be that as it may, we made it in time and the sea being calm our bugler had no problem with the Alert.

Largo Bay paid off into Reserve at Portsmouth at the end of the year. The winter was even colder than in Rosyth. It was before the days when salt was used to clear roads of ice and snow and the streets of Portsmouth round the dockyard remained slippery pistes of hard-packed snow for over a fortnight until someone suggested spraying them with salt water, which was of course readily available.

Having a little time on my hands and as a change from the dreary task of moth-balling something that had been a living, lively ship, I gave the bee in my bonnet about Senior Rates another chance to buzz and posted a letter to the Flag Officer, Reserve Fleet, on the subject. He replied sympathetically enough, agreeing that we must each keep practising what we all preach. I suppose I thought an Admiral could wave a magic wand.

238

I was not particularly sorry to leave the ship when the time came. I was very sorry though not to meet any of our Boys in later years. I have no doubt that their descendants are just as good. All the same they were likely lads.

Chapter 20

A Family Affair

From the delights of expedition training with the Boy seamen in *Largo Bay* it was back in 1954 to the rather more rigorous life in the Home Fleet as First Lieutenant of HMS *Virago*, a new-design anti-submarine frigate. She had been modernised out of the bones of a 'traditional' destroyer. The latter had had four open-gun mountings, two forward and two aft; and two multiple torpedo-tube mountings on the iron deck amidships. All these were removed. The newest A/S detecting gear and weapons were fitted and the ships emerged as state-of-the-art fast fleet escorts. There were a dozen or so of these major conversions. Apart from the work below decks the most striking change was an entirely new superstructure, all in aluminium, which was bolted onto the original steel hull. This addition covered in the old destroyer's iron deck so that all the way through from the foc's'le to the quarterdeck the deck level was some twelve feet above the water, nearly twice what it had been before. One could work about it in almost any weather without fear of being washed overboard. Other innovations featured an enclosed Bridge with a view to improving working conditions in that area, and thus efficiency in the winter weather of the North Atlantic and Arctic; and there was a bigger and better-equipped Operations Room just behind the Bridge and on the same level. The Captain could hop from one to the other without having to chase up and down a ladder as in the original design. They were well thought out and comfortable ships.

Virago's 1954 summer cruise started off much the same as *Broadsword*'s had done three years earlier. The Home Fleet assembled in Torbay under the wing of the Commander-in-Chief in his flagship *Vanguard*. After a day or two there, which gave time for rude signals to all and sundry to buck their ideas up, to remember that Easter leave was over and one was no longer in a comfortable home port, the Fleet put to sea. The Home Fleet cruiser took the destroyers with her and we all ended up in Invergordon for the inevitable weapon training period. Happily the C-in-C had other business elsewhere. I was very pleased to be back in Invergordon: in *Largo Bay* it had been something of a country hide-out for us from

HMS *Virago*, 6th Frigate Squadron, Home Fleet 1955

241

Rosyth. We had even found peach blossom out there in February one year. After Invergordon we were to exercise up to Scapa Flow and thence across the North Sea to Scandinavia for our summer flag-showing visits.

Scapa gave *Virago* quite a turn that summer. One destroyer was detailed off each day as Duty Ship. The day on which our turn came round had been very quiet, the weather unusually fine. At ten o'clock in the evening it was still light enough to read. The forecast for next day was more of the same. I turned in feeling that this was indeed the life. Two or three hours later I dreamt I heard a vague rumbling sound. My dream offered no explanation, likely or unlikely. All at once it came to me that I wasn't dreaming and that we were weighing anchor. Why had no one called me? I looked quickly out of the scuttle to see if that gave any clue as to what was happening. An incredible change had taken place in the three hours since I had turned in. The calm of the evening before had gone. The previously glassy water of the Flow was now completely white, the water blown into spindrift by a gale which looked to be approaching hurricane force. I shot up to the Bridge thinking that we must have dragged our anchor.

We were already doing some ten or twelve knots and heading for one of the leads out of the Flow. The telephone from the foc'sle began to ring. 'We haven't got the anchors secured for sea yet and the foc'sle is washing down. Can we reduce speed for a minute or two?' The Captain was in a bad temper. Where the hell had I been. Were they all farmers on the foc'sle? I was in a bad temper. Who the devil was supposed to have shaken me? But we all remembered that two men had been lost off the foc'sle of a destroyer leaving Malta in a hurry recently and we did slow down, slightly.

I found out what was happening. A coaster had radioed that it had got into trouble in this sudden storm and thought that it was being driven ashore. What we were going to do about it was not at all clear. It was pitch dark, blowing ferociously and we were now doing thirty knots, we hoped out of the Flow and in the reported direction of the coaster. Our navigational radar was up-to-date and effective but to be sure of making the open sea one would normally have done some pre-planning over courses to steer and so on. With that under one's belt there would not have been too much bother. Our Navigator thought he knew where he was. The Captain wasn't so sure and I well remember shouts of 'Navigator, you're running me ashore,' echoing round the Bridge.

The Chief Boatswain's Mate and I wedged ourselves into a corner on the periphery of all this navigational extravaganza and tried to work out what best to do when we found the wretched coaster. Had the weather been at all reasonable we would by now have been preparing wires and cables ready to tow her out of danger if, when we found her, that appeared the best thing to do. As it was however it was a certain bet that if we started laying out wires and cables all over the deck someone or something would go overboard, and we would probably end up with a wire round one of our propellers. Happily, before we had got very far there was a shout up the voicepipe from the wireless office to say that the coaster had made it into the Flow and we were to return. On the way back in with the wind still touching force 12, hurricane force, we sighted a small vessel coming out – the lifeboat! 'Do you want a tow?' they signalled cheerfully. A different breed, those people. We got the impression that they were quite put out when we told them that the coaster was now inside the Flow.

From Scapa the destroyers exercised their way across the North Sea and four or five days later split up for 'flag-showing' visits to Scandinavia. We had drawn Molde in north Norway, the so-called Town of Roses, where we were to arrive in time for midsummer's day. The exercise ended well south of there and we had a delightful few hours steaming north through the Leads. The passage is not unlike the Minches off the north-west coast of Scotland, islands to seaward giving a relatively sheltered waterway, fjords and mountains on the landward side. The only problem was that our timing did not allow for a stop anywhere to clean up the ship's side which was obviously going to be pretty stained and dirty after the passage from Chatham and across the North Sea. I mentioned before that *Virago's* original steel hull was a wartime build. These were renowned for rusting more or less as you looked at them and needed constant prettifying to pass muster in the peacetime fleet.

We reached Molde on time and as soon as the exchange of official visits was over the Chief Boatswain's Mate and I commandeered the motor boat and circled the ship deciding which stretches of the side needed attention. We quickly came to the conclusion that there were none which did not. The ship did not look much of an advertisement. We would never get it cleaned up even by the time we left. Eventually I said, 'Look. The whole damn thing needs painting. We can't do that on a visit like this, but maybe we could if we did it overnight. It never gets dark here.' The Buffer obviously thought it was a hare-brained scheme but as he had no other suggestions we decided to get on with it. The seamen had by now changed out of their relatively smart No 2 serge suits worn for entering harbour and were falling in for work. We put the outrageous plan to them. It was taken stolidly enough.

Just before dinner however the Chief Boatswain's Mate knocked on the door of my cabin. Some knocks can sound as though they herald bad news. This was one of them. It was indeed the Chief Boatswain's Mate. 'We've trouble,' he said. I knew at once what it was but had to ask. 'It's 12 Mess. They won't have it.' 'What about the others?' 'All right so far,' but we both knew that that could change when they'd had their tot of rum with dinner. If 12 Mess refused duty that was mutiny, and no doubt about it. If all the seamen followed that was disaster, and on a goodwill visit too – nasty thought. What to do?

Whatever it was, it had to be done at once. The only thing one could in fact do was to make it a voluntary evolution, ensure that the terms for volunteering were attractive enough to get the numbers we needed; and the alternative for the miseries who wanted to opt out must be unpleasant enough to hurt without being in any way vindictive.

The hands were just going to dinner by now but there could be no waiting. 'Clear Lower Deck of Seamen' were piped to muster on the quarterdeck. Meanwhile I told the Captain. 'You'd better win this one,' was all the support I got.

On the quarterdeck the seamen of course knew exactly what it was about. There was much shuffling of feet, eyes cast down towards the deck. Wardroom and sailors had normally been on pretty good terms. No one wanted a shoot-out but 12 Mess were looking furtively determined. All I could do was to explain the situation, as I had done after we arrived: no one's fault that the ship's side looks a mess, got to clean it up. Norwegian girls much more likely to be impressed by a smart ship, can quite see the point of those who jib at the idea of night-work, hardly a usual way of doing things, and then such carrots and sticks as it seemed possible to offer.

I was reaching the end of this far from stirring exhortation when it occurred to me that most people are reluctant to step forward out of line. It just could be sensible therefore instead of asking for volunteers to step forward, to put the boot on the other foot and ask anyone who did not want to volunteer to step out. It worked. For a moment it looked as though even 12 Mess were going to stay still but eventually they all shuffled a step forward. No one else did. That afternoon the ranks of the volunteers were swelled by the cooks and stewards and the Engineer Officer twisted some arms in his department. We started after the Ship's Company's supper, Wardroom included, and by two o'clock next morning with the sun still above the horizon the job was finished. The side looked pretty as paint. Goodness knows what the Norwegians thought. One or two did come out in their motorboats to view this strange British midsummer rite. We all slept in next morning and had a relaxed weekend; all except 12 Mess. I never pushed that far again though.

Much later on I gathered that we were not the only ship to experience a little friction in those years though I never heard of any that led to tears. I always liked the account of a fast minelayer in the Home Fleet which had fallen into a bit of a tangle, largely I understood because the First Lieutenant was somewhat out of touch with the situation. A replacement was appointed and on joining he asked to be taken on a tour of the ship. Some of this was fairly depressing but on coming to the Mining Deck he gazed for a moment at the maze of rails from which the mines on their trolleys were pushed overboard. 'But this is fantastic,' he said, 'I've always loved playing trains. We'll have Waterloo up here. There's Charing Cross in that corner. Now where do we change for the Central Line?' Childish maybe, but the Ship's Company realised very quickly that they now had a card for First Lieutenant and a new spirit was born. It did help of course that he was, incidentally, very good at his job.

Looking back fifty years, and before we leave the subject, it never now fails to amaze me that in nearly twenty-five years' service I never heard anyone mention the Invergordon Mutiny of 1931. As early as 1925 *The Times* was reporting attempts by the Communist Party to infiltrate the Royal Navy, at that time still perhaps one of the most obvious outward signs of Great Britain's standing as a world power. The seeds they sowed bore poisoned fruit six years later when the Ship's Companies of six ships of the Atlantic Fleet, assembled at Invergordon for the Summer Cruise, refused duty. The trigger was an unbelievably incompetent attempt by the powers that be to explain to the Fleet a system of pay cuts in the public services required by a Socialist administration caught in the financial crisis of 1929–31. The cuts were announced on the BBC news before any official explanation had been circulated throughout the Fleet. Britain left the gold standard a few weeks later. Whether this was coincidence or not the Communists must have been well-pleased with their work.

The situation was resolved quite quickly. When I joined the Navy twelve years later many officers and ratings would have been serving at the time of the Mutiny and not a few could well have been at Invergordon; but never a word on the subject did I ever hear at any time or from anyone. It was buried in more than a thousand fathoms.

For sure, every time we joined a new ship we had to read and sign that we had read a Top Secret pamphlet on the prevention of mutiny but after that initiation the subject was cast aside and like everyone else we looked to more positive measures to ensure sound and efficient ships.

Virago did not serve all that long with the Fleet and at the end of the summer of 1955 we paid her off into reserve like *Largo Bay*. This time the immolation took place at Immingham on the Humber, a place I cannot really recommend. Hers was a short life after modernisation – only two commissions. By the end of 1955 a new breed of anti-submarine ships was joining the Fleet and I can only suppose that *Virago* and her sisters were seen as a necessary step in their evolution. A number of the class continued to serve on for some years but maintaining a modern Fleet is not cheap.

Chapter 21

Cyprus Wedding

The following year I was sent out to Cyprus as the naval member of the Joint Planning Staff, Middle East. It was certainly a sea-change from the rather hectic life in the Home Fleet. My principal duty was not to be rude to the other Services. As I soon formed quite a high regard for the ability of their representatives in our little cell this was not too difficult despite one rather stirring moment with the Air Force member. For some reason the airmen always had to keep their hand in at flying. Every week or so our confederate would take the morning off and disappear up to the Nicosia airfield for a session. Thus practised he would fly our team round the Middle East when planning needs dictated. One afternoon we were due to return from Beirut but for some reason were late taking off. It was dark by the time we were over Nicosia. The first two or three circuits round the airfield gave my Army companion and myself a good chance to admire the lights. On the fourth circuit we ventured to tell our pilot that we thought that we had a pretty good idea of the view by now. 'Sorry,' he said, 'Fact is I'm out of practice with night flying and it takes a little while to get my bearings before I try to land.'

There was little naval input into the plans. A glimpse at one of the latter may give part of the reason. I think it can now be revealed that in the 1950s one of the roles of the Middle East Command in the event of war with the USSR was to seize four important passes in the Zagros Mountains in Persia to prevent enemy troops spilling into the Iraq oilfields. This was to be achieved by troops from the Canal Zone moving quickly into Israel, commandeering all the buses they could find and then racing across the desert in them and up onto the passes. The Air Force member and I found it difficult to get too worked up about this.

The relatively gentle pace of life in Cyprus despite EOKA's frequent murderous attempts to brighten it up allowed me time to get married. This was a necessary move. Unmarried officers often had to live in tents and this practice threatened to become total after the headquarters moved from Nicosia to Episkopi in the south of the island in 1957. It is a happy thought that a forced marriage of this sort has proved lastingly pleasant to at least one partner. My wife thinks she should appear much more often in this account despite my protestations that I am trying my humble best to give some sort of picture, blurred no doubt, of life at sea; and happily women did not get mixed up in this in those days. To placate her I hope the reader will forgive the following description of a Greek-Cypriot wedding which I was required to write a few years later, and that it may give some idea of the pleasant existence which we enjoyed.

A Greek-Cypriot Wedding

In 1957 our landlord's gardener, Eftymee, invited my wife and me to his sister's wedding and we felt that the chance of seeing a Greek-Cypriot marriage was too good to miss. I had an unworthy suspicion that he asked us mainly in order to secure a lift for the two maids from next door but he was a pleasant and good-hearted character and we were glad to go on any basis.

The wedding was to be in the afternoon in Tembria, a small village on the north-eastern slopes of the Troodos Mountains and some fifty miles from Limassol where we were then living. We planned to have a picnic lunch in the hills on the way. It was early October and the grass was beginning to grow again, freshening the dusty countryside after the last few weeks of the baking summer.

In fact the journey up was not quite as pleasant as we had hoped. The road is hardly straight anywhere and the poor maids, Poppy and Dora, were sick at almost every corner. Fortunately lunch in a pine grove by the side of a stream restored us all and we reached Tembria ready for anything.

It was an enchanting little village, just off the main road and straggling over a rocky hillock which thrust up from the floor of one of the small valleys which ran down the mountainside. To the north one looked out over patches of pine and vineyards to the lower slopes of Troodos, across the stubble of the Mesaoria to the grey Kyrenia hills, the perfect sweep of Morphou Bay and the Mediterranean. In the distance a hazy line of blue showed the mass of the Anatolian mountains. Behind and on either side was the hill, and at one's feet a small stream ran cool and clear beneath the plane trees along the edge of the main street.

Eftymee had come up earlier and we all went down to the house at the bottom of the village where bride and groom were to live. They were already there, being helped by all their friends in the ceremony of dressing for the wedding and encouraged by a three-piece band of fiddle, drum and cymbals. The noise was deafening. I did wonder how many of the cheerful guests were EOKA supporters. Whether the multitude were any help to the couple seemed questionable but at last both were ready and we set off for the church. The ceremony itself was perhaps nothing to write home about. Two genial priests officiated, standing with the man and the woman in the middle of the dusty church while the relations and closest friends of the couple formed a circle round them. Lesser acquaintances shuffled about outside the circle, whispering and giggling to each other while further back mosaic and plaster saints stared stone-faced over us from the shadow of their walls. Huge fat and greasy candles burned near the altar in candlesticks which had obviously not been polished since the wedding before last.

The ceremony over we all processed back to the house for what was plainly to be the main business of the day, the singing, dancing and eating. The dance-floor was in the farmyard at the back of the house, a few square yards of dried mud in front of the goat shed, with shade for the band under the trees at one side and a grandstand on the bank opposite for anyone who could not get room to dance.

The band started off in fine style with some traditional Greek and Greek-Cypriot dances and the local clown pranced around the floor with a glass of water balanced upside down on his head. The only touch lacking to complete the picture was any trace of the old Cyprus dresses or *bracka*, the baggy Cypriot country trousers.

Soon it was time to 'bless the mattress'. The rite wishes the couple a comfortable and productive marriage but at the end of the ceremony it also serves as a salver onto which guests throw contributions to cover the cost of the wedding. Finally a baby is bounced across the mattress, a piece of symbolism on which all were agreed.

During all this frivolity the only people not joining in the celebrations were the bride and groom. They sat in a downstairs room of their house looking out over the farmyard. Their guests came up and talked to them but obviously as a mature married couple of at least an hour's standing they themselves were expected to be rather above such gambols.

By now the afternoon was well on and the shadows were creeping up the side of the valley opposite. It was cooler and damper and in the new freshness of the air one began to be aware again of the different smells of the village, wood smoke and goats, dancers and garbage heaps and, just behind us, an encouraging smell of meat roasting in a mud oven. We had

249

a delightful supper before we left and to crown it all the moon came up over the hill whilst we were eating.

It had been a wonderful day, a chance to see an ordinary Greek-Cypriot wedding in a mountain village. The friendliness of everyone there made us feel as though we really belonged amongst the guests and echoes of the terrorism of the 'Emergency' seemed far away indeed. I think we must have left early. Eftymee did not appear again for another four days. Poor Poppy and Dora of course were sick all the way home.

Chapter 22

Cod War

Appointment in 1958 in command of HMS *Russell*, a small frigate in the Fishery Protection Squadron, should have been an occasion for some excitement, mixed it must be said with some incredulity that I should be trusted with so much of the nation's money and with the well-being of some 120 sailors. Coming as it did however after those two very comfortable and easy-going years in Cyprus there was something of a culture shock, not least because it was a question of back to Rosyth. There was also the point that the First Cod War was in the offing and this was bound to mean our spending most of our time off Iceland.

Most wars seem to be about territory. Some are about principles. Many involve both issues. This one, and subsequent Cod disputes, certainly did. Briefly, from sailing ship days it had been international practice that the territorial waters of sovereign states extended three miles from their shores. Within these waters states reserved the right, amongst many others, for their own nationals only to fish. Outside three miles, on the High Seas, anyone could of course shoot their nets. For hundreds of years the British had fished for cod off Iceland and in other northern waters, for instance off Norway and Russia.

> How odd of cod to choose the cold
> Up there they sport until they're caught
> By only fishers bold.

In the mid-1950s the Icelandic government was under pressure from its fishing industry to extend their territorial waters to twelve miles in order to give their own nationals a greater share of the catch around their shores. To be fair, they could also have been concerned about dwindling stocks through over-fishing. Iceland had already extended the limit unilaterally to four miles in 1952. In retaliation Britain had banned Icelandic landings of fish in this country. A Law of the Sea conference was held in Geneva in 1958 to continue earlier efforts to solve the dispute but this had no success. Iceland pointed out that we had already conceded a twelve mile limit to the USSR. We countered that this formed part of a fisheries

HMS *Russell*, Fishery Protection Squadron 1958

agreement with Russia, and added that an International Law Commission had pointed out in 1956 that '. . . international practice is not uniform as regards the delimitation of the territorial sea . . .'

Perhaps the most important factor on the Icelandic side was that at that time it had a communist government which would shortly be seeking re-election. For Britain we knew that the introduction of a twelve mile limit would be bound to have a serious effect on our distant water fleet. As well, though, HMG saw it as a unilateral repudiation of an international agreement. While not of the same order of contempt as that shown by Germany in the 1930s which had led eventually to the Second World War, the habit could be catching. The Icelanders were, and remain, tough men of the frozen north. We did not fancy repeating the mistakes of previous years and at the end of August 1958 the Fishery Protection Squadron of three Captain class frigates sailed for Iceland.

I had joined *Russell* in June. Some ships one takes to at once. Others take a little getting used to. Some one never really feels a regard for. I did get used to *Russell* but she was never a dear companion. Joining at the end of a refit one walks round the ship with one's predecessor. The operational aspect is of course of absorbing interest and importance. Here the Captain class did score. Unlike most HM ships there was only one machinery set: the boiler, one engine and one huge propeller. For various reasons this was supposed to make for more mechanical efficiency than the more usual two or four propeller configurations. We were never officially told so but I have the idea that the 'one propeller' design came out cheaper than the others. I was never completely convinced by the efficiency theory.

It took a little getting used to from the ship-handling point of view. Our dockyard tugs were mostly single-screw and they were as handy as anything. The main difference was that with twin-screws a ship can very easily be turned at rest by putting one engine ahead and the other astern. With a single-screw ship the large propeller acts as a paddle wheel until you have enough way on to steer by the rudder. Thus to turn short you aim to start at rest and paddle the stern one way or the other with a quick burst of power until the ship starts to pick up speed. Done properly it's very effective. It does need forethought though, a slightly different way of thinking. *Russell* had a dent on each quarter and each bow before I got it right. One dent in the stern was large enough to be classed as a hole. It happened during final ammunitioning before we sailed for Iceland and I thought it merited reporting to our Commodore. 'Plug it with hammocks,' was his typically piratical reply. 'You're not staying behind.' I did feel a little hurt at his idea that I might even have been toying with the thought but we managed to get the dockyard to pull out all the stops and weld on a patch before we sailed.

The Captain class were not ideal for Iceland. More basic than the single-screw aspect were the compromises which had had to be made in the hull design to get our 24 knots speed. The ships were very lightly built and this was to cause problems in the coming winter. They had also been given a flat surface under the stern with the idea of minimising 'squat' at speed. In the latter condition the stern tends to sink slightly. Trim is altered and drag increases. A bit of planing area beneath the stern helps to reduce the problem. We thought the designers had overdone it. In the miserable conditions off Iceland we found it impossible to heave to, that is to reduce speed to the point where the ship is just dodging into the seas with only sufficient progress to give steerage way. In this condition one can ride out most storms, though there is a cautionary tale later on. In *Russell* we could not slow to less than seven knots without that 'flat' beneath the stern thumping down onto a huge wave and shaking the ship like a dog after a wet walk. After one or two such bumps one began to wonder what was going to break first. Increase speed and you got a pounding from seas from ahead. For one member of the squadron it was almost a disastrous design defect.

I did think too on that first walk round the ship after joining in mid-summer that the sailor's accommodation was disappointing. These were new-design ships but the messdecks were the darkest and pokiest that I had ever come across. The Captain's cabin was fine – a nice French window arrangement looked out on to the upper deck and aft to the stern so that I could see whether the upper deck was washing down in heavy weather; and the officers, though cramped, were not too badly off. The sailors' side I thought quite depressing but short of re-designing the ship there was little that could be changed.

Now in the last few days of August we were heading up the east Scottish coast. At least in the two months since I had joined I had managed to achieve one ambition: on a visit to the west coast a few weeks earlier we had made the passage of the Corryvrechan – but only at half-tide. Had we been ashore that August we would have been drinking in perhaps the best time of year in Scotland. The countryside we had left would be beginning to turn to its autumn tint of gold and would continue thus with deepening beauty into perhaps the early part of October. We would have completed our first patrol by then and be back in Rosyth for two weeks' maintenance. Each patrol was to last twenty-six days, two days up, two days back and the rest on station. It seemed a long time as we passed Inchkeith bound north, but even this timing meant that to keep three ships off Iceland for as long as the dispute lasted was going to absorb the resources of the whole of the Home Station destroyer and frigate force. The Home Fleet ships used to quite enjoy a month away from the Commander-in-Chief from time to time. *Russell*, a 'professional' of the Fishery Protection Squadron, did six patrols over the next nine months, more than anyone else we were proud to point out and tending to be more than enough as far as we ourselves were concerned.

The weather on this first patrol was not too bad. We passed through the Pentland Firth, sometimes an unpleasant and even dangerous stretch, and set course for haven 'Butterscotch' on the north-west corner of Iceland. Three havens had been agreed between the then Department of Agriculture and Fisheries – 'Ag & Fish' – and the fishing industry. Each was to be forty miles long by eight miles broad, fitting in between the existing four mile limit and the claimed extension to twelve miles. Inside each haven the British trawlers would fish, protected by an HM ship from interference by Icelandic gunboats. The havens would be moved up and down the coast to follow the cod as it migrated. Besides 'Butterscotch' we had 'Toffeeapple' on the north coast and 'Marzipan' down off the south-east corner of Iceland. Nothing like having a few homely names to cheer everyone up!

An absolutely key player in this game beside Commodore 'Fish' himself was the Trawler Liaison Officer allotted to each ship. How else would we have established a rapport with all those tough, self-reliant, individualistic trawler skippers from Grimsby, Hull and Fleetwood, whom we were there to protect and assist? Most of them cared not a fig for the idea of a twelve mile limit. They earned their, quite sizable, money by their catches. They had always fished up to the four, previously three mile limit and would not be frozen out by anyone. Why could they not go on doing so and blow the politics? Without our Trawler Liaison Officers the Navy, let alone the Icelanders, would have been sunk.

In *Russell* we were particularly lucky in having for this first trip, Jack Mawer. He had been, and still was maybe, trawler-manager of Consolidated Fisheries Limited of Grimsby. Their trawlers were all named after football teams, not only north-country ones I was glad to note! *Arsenal* and *Derby County* stick in the memory. There were several others. They all seemed to be in the last stages of disrepair, streaked with rust, grimed with salt and smoke. After I had known Jack Mawer for a couple of weeks I ventured to suggest that his fleet could well be renamed Consolidated Rust Boats Ltd. He did not disagree. He was of course on Christian name terms with most of the skippers, could tell you more about their backgrounds than they would ever admit themselves, knew the fishing grounds backwards and had a nose for the weather. If anyone reads Kipling's *Captains Courageous* these days, which they ought to, here was a latter-day north-country version of Captain Disko Troup of the schooner *We're Here* of Gloucester, Massachusetts.

Jack Mawer had his meals with me. We had three other passengers who thought they ought to do the same, journalists from the popular dailies. I pointed out that my cabin did not run to such a large gathering and for a while I thought we were going to have difficulties in that direction. What was even more upsetting for them was the realisation once on board that our communications set-up was not going to be able to cope with lengthy reports from all three at the drop of a hat. The public relations people in London had evidently told them that there would be no difficulty in filing whatever they wanted to send but had forgotten to add that it would all have to be transmitted by Morse key. The first night out we had on the one hand a rather depressed Petty Officer Telegraphist and on the other three militant journalists. By good fortune I managed to interpose the ample bulk of Jack Mawer in front of the journalists while I calmed down the Wireless Department. In the end of course things worked out most amicably and our professional pressmen started a ship's newspaper for us.

Passed through the Pentland Firth, the North Atlantic stretched before us like the American prairies. I suppose it was imagination but I came to feel that each stretch of ocean had something of a personality of its own. The Channel was a busy main street with eating places along each side where one could stop off. The North Sea was somewhat suburban. My favourite Indian Ocean was a vast but friendly park. The north end of the North Atlantic did not strike me as friendly. The weather was good when we reached 'Butterscotch' but there was a long low swell running which seemed to come out of eternity. I was glad when a few trawlers turned up and shot their gear. I was even quite pleased when an Icelandic gunboat appeared. As we had a few hours in hand before confrontation officially started I thought I might as well go over and shake hands before the match as it were.

My predecessor in *Russell* had made several trips to Iceland in happier days and assured me that their Fishery Protection people did not have horns. 'Just pretty tough negotiators,' he had said. I was not negotiating and there were no angry words that afternoon so long as we kept off the Dispute. Sometimes at my lowly level one would find that those involved in a 'situation' could agree that it was really only for the politicians; but clearly in this case the Limit was a national obsession.

We had some windy weather on that first patrol; we had some fog; and we had some trawlers. It was the last of these that caused the most headaches. Being individualists there were always one or two who wanted to fish by themselves outside the haven. I was strictly precluded from saying, 'OK. Fish where you like but don't expect help from us if you're jumped by a gunboat.' The Admiralty, 'Ag & Fish', the Owners and our Commodore all expected the trawlers to be kept in line. Thank goodness for Jack Mawer. The trawlers soon found out that we had a doctor on board and he quickly came to be in quite regular demand. I often wondered what they did in the palmy days before the Dispute when they needed medical help; kept on fishing I suspect. It did not take the trawlermen long to divine also that we had a very competent radar department, who were rather better at mending their badly-maintained sets than the maker's contracted technicians back in Hull or Grimsby. If a set went wrong it always seemed to be imperative to get it repaired at once. 'You know how it is, Jack. Got to have that damned set so's we can keep in the haven, see.' Getting an artificer over to a trawler was not always easy given the normally unpleasant weather and one had to make a judgement every time as to whether the risk was acceptable. It could become rather wearing.

If help really was required and the weather was not too atrocious the trawler would be invited to stop and lie beam to the seas. We would then approach her lee side and lie stationary there as close as we dared, perhaps fifty feet off. It sounds quite a distance but the two ships could easily get thrown together by the seas if we were much closer. A line would be fired from a 'line throwing' rifle. This would be used to haul over a heavier line which would in turn be used to haul over our inflatable dinghy with its artificer/doctor passenger. The point of approaching the trawler on the downwind side was that *Russell* with her relatively high superstructure to catch the wind drifted to leeward faster than a trawler with her deep draft. Ideally I would have preferred to lie to windward of the trawler to give our dinghy better shelter for the crossing, but then the two ships would have tended to drift together.

I seem to remember some friction with the Icelanders on this first patrol but mostly we were like boxers circling round each other at the beginning of a fight. Their three gunboats developed distinct personalities according to who was in command. *Odin*, the boat that I had visited on our first arrival, was a small modern vessel. When I went over to her the Captain seemed perfectly reasonable: perhaps as a result he was relieved shortly thereafter. Either way by the time that we met her again *Odin* had become nasty, aggressive and spiteful. *Aegir*, a larger and much older boat, would normally behave in a more civilised fashion. Her Captain was plainly as keen as *Odin*'s to see the twelve mile line enforced but appeared to take a more considered view. Last and largest was *Thor*, the real hammer of the fleet. New, sizable and aggressive, when *Thor* was about we had to retaliate in kind. All of them would try to make life difficult for the trawlers by steaming close across the latter's stern towing grapnels to cut their nets. Our reply had to be to keep between the gunboats and the trawlers, so that the former could not get close enough to cause damage. Looking back on that first Cod War I cannot help feeling that the gunboats must have had orders to shadow-box. Had they been told to go for real damage a lot of collisions would have been inevitable.

As winter approached the weather became more of a problem. Before the 'War' trawlers would run for the shelter of the fjords when the weather became really bad, say above gale force 8. Up to that state trawlers would go on fishing more or less happily if they were on the cod. You had to take care in winter conditions that your ship did not begin to ice up. A few years earlier two brand new ships from Hull had come up to Iceland. They were reputed to be able to take whatever the weather could throw at them. It was winter and they were fishing off the north-west corner of Iceland, not far in fact from where 'Butterscotch' had been established. One day the weather deteriorated, which was no surprise. Then the temperature began to fall and the ships started to ice up. The new Hull ships were fishing well and decided to see it out. Other trawlers in the vicinity were less sanguine and sought shelter inshore. The wind and sea steadily increased and eventually one of the two new Hull ships decided that survival was more important than fish and either hauled or cut away his nets. He just made it to shelter. Meanwhile his companion carried on fishing. After a while he too began to get worried at the extent of icing on his superstructure and rigging, which was making the ship top-heavy. He too decided to run for shelter and tried to turn onto a course for the land. By then the sea was so bad that he could not get round. Trapped in the trough of huge waves and unstable from the accumulation of ice, the trawler capsized. Meanwhile its companion, by now safely within the shelter of a fjord, had been having a running commentary over the wireless as this horrific situation developed. Eventually neither Captain nor crew could stand it any longer. They weighed anchor and steamed out to the rescue; and suffered instead the same fate. We kept the weather very much in mind.

It was certainly turning by the end of our first patrol but we returned to Rosyth in reasonable shape, passing on the way a Russian fishing fleet working close east of the Orkneys. It was an almost unbelievable sight, ships stretching from one horizon to the other. If they were indeed fishing they must have scooped up every fish in the North Sea in the course of a couple of days or so. Thank goodness they were well outside our territorial waters, so if there was to be any argument with them it would have to be at Governmental level. I did not fancy my chances had it been our job to board their Commodore and ask to measure their nets.

The second patrol did not start too well. Not to put too fine a point on it, someone sabotaged our steering gear just before we were due to sail. It was not a very serious attempt and the damage was soon repaired but it was a disturbing thought that after a comparatively bother-free first patrol someone should feel so apprehensive of the future as to try to delay our return. I suppose it might have been some love-sick sailor desperate for another night ashore with his inamorata. We never knew, and mess-deck gossip, sometimes quite reliable in such cases, never gave a clue. If such an irritating occurrence can be said to have a lighter side I suppose this one did. Another sailor had plainly decided to jump ship. He rolled down to the dockyard gate some three hours after we were supposed to have sailed, simulating great distress at, as he thought, missing the ship. All the usual excuses: 'train was late; alarm clock never worked; mother-in-law ill', and so on. He was, we heard, greatly put out to be told, 'You're in luck, Mate. *Russell's* still there.'

It sounds as though the ship was in a bad state. Maybe, but we never had any more trouble; and wily old Commodore 'Fish' had plainly bribed the Captain of our oil tanker to be nice to us after our next refuelling off Iceland. 'Congratulations on the smoothest refuelling I've seen.' I never had that sort of signal before or after.

Refuelling could in fact be something of an experience. It had to be done whatever the weather, gale or fog, day or night. It was essential to stay reasonably topped up so we fuelled every five or six days. Our worst experience was in December. We were relieving *Hardy* from the Portland Training Squadron off north-west Iceland and both were to refuel the next morning, he to return to Portland and we on arrival off Iceland from Rosyth. At that time of year it was not light in the morning until about ten o'clock and by two o'clock in the afternoon the light had gone again. I found in fact it was not too difficult to get used to the very short days. However this particular morning it was blowing a real 'hooli', Storm force 10, just short of a hurricane. We were to fuel first, starting in the pitch dark at 0800. The seas were quite something. Miserably I asked our tanker if he could stream gear for astern fuelling which I thought would be easier for us and entail less danger of collision. No, he replied, it was blowing too hard for that. He was expecting us alongside in thirty minutes. I wished I was anywhere but off Iceland. Just then the cheerful voice of *Hardy* came on the air. 'Do you mind if I fuel first? I've rather a tight programme and need to get away smartish.' Had he not heard that the wind and sea were pretty vicious? Yes, but he had to have the fuel and would manage. He did. By the time our turn came the wind had eased to a mere force 8 and we managed too, but how I blessed and admired him.

The weather worsened as the weeks drew on towards Christmas. Ice began to form in the straits between Iceland and Greenland and it was becoming clear that 'Butterscotch' was soon going to have to move to the marginally more civilised waters on the south coast. Before that however Commodore 'Fish' came on our voice-net one quiet afternoon to ask how things were in our haven. Everything's under control I told him. 'Good,' he replied. 'No gunboats, no trawlers? You can close the haven then and steam up to the edge of the ice. Have you seen it before? No? Well, then it'll make a good break. Off you go.' And I had been looking forward to a nice quiet afternoon, calm sea for once and no trawlers.

I must admit to thinking that the Commodore's plan verged on the irresponsible. It was good to have a break in routine, to give the sailors a new experience, but he knew as well as I did how thin our plating was. I set off towards the North Pole with the greatest trepidation.

We set someone to measuring the water temperature every few minutes, which we thought should give early warning of our approach to the ice. In fact we began to notice a peculiar oily effect on the water surface before the temperature began to drop much. Conversely the temperature on the Bridge began to rise as everyone remembered how easy it was for a lurking lump to pierce the hull, and began making mental calculations of how far it was back to Rosyth dockyard. I reported to the Commodore that we were now close to the ice edge, that ice was beginning to form and that, although we could not see any solid bergs yet, I considered it was my duty to report that I felt I was hazarding one third of his fleet for no very good reason. His reply left me in little doubt that he thought we were being chicken and pompous. 'Continue north until you sight the ice edge.' It was no coincidence that we sighted something seconds later which looked sufficiently like the fabled edge for us to turn south again with a moderately clear conscience. The remainder of the quiet afternoon became all the more welcome.

He was a tough old pirate, our Commodore Barry Anderson. He needed to be. I cannot remember how long he stayed up off Iceland without any break such as we had. He did confide once that what he found particularly tiring was getting the routine for his early morning cup of tea satisfactorily worked out as he changed ships in order to stay permanently in those waters himself.

Chapter 23

A Near Thing

It was about this time that *Palliser*, the other Captain class frigate in the
Fishery Protection Squadron, and we ourselves began to find cracks
across the deck in the midships section of our ships. They were not very
large at first but they could not be ignored. After each patrol it was part
of naval practice to call on Flag Officer, Scotland, back at Rosyth. It was
more of a courtesy than anything else: the operational chain of command
ran through Commodore 'Fish'. The first time we found these cracks in
Russell I raised the subject with the Admiral, courtesy call or no, and said
merely that I was having them welded up. 'Very interesting,' he replied.
'Of course as you know these ships were designed as North Atlantic convoy
escorts. We certainly need to see how they stand up to this winter.' The
art of leadership is said to lie in persuading people to do what they don't
want to do! Admiral Luce became First Sea Lord later and like one or
two others in that post, killed himself through overwork. He had to
encourage us as he did.

When *Palliser* met up with us in port, which was not very often, we
used to compare cracks like two old women discussing aches and pains.
His were worse than ours. When they first started to develop he was
allowed to go down to London 'to bring the matter to the notice of the
Naval Construction branch.' 'You'd never credit,' he said after this foray,
'how difficult it is when you're sitting in a comfortable Whitehall chair
to persuade people what things are like when you're riding out a gale up
north in a ship which you can't heave to.' I took his point.

Palliser's situation continued to worsen and finally she had to be docked
for examination and quite extensive repairs. By then the message had
finally got through down south and the Director of Naval Construction
came up himself to have a look. He was a man small in stature but known
in the Department as something of a driver. He, Flag Officer, Scotland,
and Geoff Hammond, Captain of *Palliser*, all went tut-tutting round the
poor old ship, now exposed in dry dock. At the end of the tour Sir Alfred
turned to Geoff and said, 'Well, Hammond, I do see your point but the
brief I was given in designing this class was to build two ships for the

price of one.' 'I quite take your point, Sir Alfred,' replied Geoff, on his best behaviour before plunging in the dagger, 'the only trouble here is that you've got four ships for the price of one.' The Admiral sent for Geoff next day, 'Sir Alfred was very hurt by your remark, Hammond.'

In January the weather worsened further. 'Butterscotch' was by now off the south-eastern corner of Iceland. For a stretch of eight days we had a full gale from the north-west and on two of those days it was at hurricane force. Thank goodness we were in the lee of the land even though four miles off it. *Palliser* was not so lucky. His haven was well north of us and had no such shelter. When the gale blew up, as usual without much warning, it was several hours before the trawlers in his area could get their gear in and all could move south. He had a pretty nasty time. A force 12 wind just turns the surface of the sea into a white soufflé; the ocean disappears and all you can see is spray. It may look beautiful but it is not really all that endearing.

On a more cheerful note, after eight days of this storm I had grown bored with the wind which had howled around us for so long like the demons of an Icelandic saga. In the lee of the land however the ship was not being unduly hazarded. There was a little icing but nothing serious. I thought an early night would come in handy. I was just turning in when there was a knock on the cabin door and there was our Petty Officer Telegraphist with a telegram giving news of the birth of our daughter. I had just finished reading it for the third time when the wind quite suddenly died. It was I might say reborn some years later in the female spirit.

Dealing with a really sick sailor or fisherman was always something of a problem. Before the 'War' a trawler could put into an Icelandic port and the patient would have the best of care. Now there was no question of that for anyone. A serious case had to be landed at Thorshavn in the Faroes. The islands were then, and I believe still are, Danish though with a large measure of independence. Like other European countries, Denmark, whilst not supporting the Icelandic case, was quite happy to let the UK carry the can, but at least the Faroes did offer a refuge and we twice had to close our haven to land a hospital case. All we could do would be to get the trawlers to move outside 12 miles and wait until we came back. Our first visit on such an errand was in the winter, and we might easily have stayed in Thorshavn ourselves. We had landed the patient and were steaming out again through a narrow channel between two islands when a sudden and very thick snowstorm obliterated everything, including our radar. We were just in the narrowest part of the channel. The water was too deep to anchor. We could only steam ahead at dead slow and hope that the squall would pass before we reached a turn. Happily it did. The snow cleared to give a perfect evening and one or two of us were left feeling rather silly at having worried. But then at the time you never know.

Our second visit was later in the year and almost a repeat of the experience ten years or so earlier with a sick seaman off Kuwait. The man had a bad and persistent stomach pain. Our Doctor diagnosed a probable case of acute appendicitis. I suggested strongly to him that as for once the sea was calm this was the time for a shipboard operation. Medical opinion was however equally strongly opposed, and for all the same reasons as on the previous occasion in the Persian Gulf. We made for Thorshavn, arriving on a bright summer's morning, and put the man ashore. It was only months later that I heard that we had landed a perfectly fit sailor. The Doctor had overslept on the morning of our arrival. By the time he got around to giving the patient a final examination before landing, the boat from the shore was already alongside. By then he had just found to his surprise, and no doubt relief, that the patient's pain had gone and that to all intents and purposes he was quite fit. Rather than lose face the Doctor allowed him to be taken ashore, and on a stretcher too. We never heard what the Faroese thought of our medicine.

It is possible that one or two of the nurses might not have objected too much at the introduction of a fit young seaman into their lives, especially as by then the Faroese fishing season had started and many of the men were away on the fishing grounds. History had it that one of our predecessors had visited Thorshavn during the summer in happier times. A football match had been arranged but it never ran its full course because at half-time a posse of young wives. deprived of the company of their husbands then with the fishing fleet, had invaded the pitch and borne the visiting team off to better things.

As Spring made a hesitant appearance in Scotland the weather off Iceland did begin to give promise of change though not always of improvement. In April-May we in *Russell* were still in 'Butterscotch'; and for a continous twenty-one days were steaming round in fog so thick that we could not see the foc'sle head from the Bridge. I found the first day or two rather trying. We had to be pretty well on the alert for Icelanders bent on making trouble, but when none were around the fog and the consequent need for extra navigational vigilance meant that one could still not relax to any extent. Eventually I came to terms with the situation by parking the ship with engines stopped exactly on the four mile limit for three or four hours at a time and this allowed a little sleep. A radar watch could be kept on the trawlers and anyone who came too close to the limit could be warned off by the Trawler Liaison Officer. Any movement outside the haven but within the twelve miles claimed by Iceland could be assumed to be hostile and I would be shaken. The system worked a treat for just under three weeks.

Later during that patrol things did rather boil up. The fog had cleared at last and we had patrolled up to the north end of the haven leaving perhaps a dozen trawlers fishing busily down the other end. There did not appear to be any gunboats about. We were perhaps half way up the haven when we got word that *Thor* had appeared amongst the trawlers in the south, and was threatening to open fire on any who did not at once move outside the twelve mile line. Where, demanded the angry trawlers, was their guardship? The guardship quickly got the message and at full speed was back in sight of the fracas pretty smartly. As we came up there was *Thor* with a gun's crew closed up round his gun on the foc'sle. Over the R/T the trawlers were deciding who was going to ram *Thor*, who would trail warps to try to foul his propeller, who would do this and that. A common thread through all the angry words was, 'Where the hell is *Russell*?' It seemed to me that for once *Thor* and ourselves might be in the same boat. From a distance I asked him what his intentions were and, getting the usual aggressive reply, pointed out to him that were he to open fire we would be bound to retaliate and that he would probably be sunk. In fact his gun looked rather bigger than our Bofors 40-mm guns, so perhaps we should sink together! We made sure the trawlers heard this exchange and it did seem to calm them for a moment: at least they appeared to be a little less anti-*Russell*. More however was needed and I told *Thor* that I would come over to him to talk. This bought slightly more time but no solution and after a quarter of an hour on board *Thor* I began to find the ship's motion a good deal more lively than *Russell*'s and concluded that diplomacy would have to continue over the R/T. By the time I got back to *Russell*, *Thor* had regained his nerve and threats and counter-threats filled the air. It was all quite ridiculous, rather like a school-ground bickering, but once shots were exchanged, and we would not be shooting over each other's heads, the whole affair could get out of hand. I thought it was time to let Flag Officer, Scotland, into the picture.

A signal was drafted. 'What priority?' asked the Wireless Office. 'Flash!'

shouted the Bridge, 'Has it gone yet?' Flash was the highest priority. Anyone getting anywhere near a Flash signal was bound to drop absolutely anything else and deal with it at once. A Flash priority signal goes through at the speed of light.

But this one didn't. I reckoned I would have a reply from Rosyth in minutes, even if it was only, 'Calm down. Don't panic.' But at least *Russell* would not go down in history as having caused an international incident off its own bat.

It did not appear however to be as easy as the book said. After maybe half-a-minute there was a shout up the voicepipe from the Wireless Office,

'We're having difficulty clearing that signal. We can't raise Pitreavie.'

Pitreavie was the headquarters at Rosyth.

'What the hell's wrong?'

'Time of day, Sir. We're all changing frequencies. It's the Heaviside layer.'

'Bugger the Heaviside layer. For goodness sake . . .'

Silence for a few seconds while we all thought this out, and tried not to hear one trawler telling another that he was going in now, while another was saying that he had a rifle trained on *Thor*'s bridge. Suddenly an excited shout again from the Wireless Office:

'Bridge. Hong Kong's reading us. Hong Kong's reading us. They're giving us a Roger . . .'

'Wireless Office. For God's sake we're not trying to get Hong Kong involved. Where's Pitreavie?'

'Hong Kong's putting it on their tape. It's going out world-wide.'

'It's nothing to do with the world. Have you got Pitreavie? Have you got rid of the signal?'

'Signal's still being cleared, Sir. Hong Kong's putting it on their tape and retransmitting.' Pause. Then a triumphant bellow: 'Pitreavie's reading Hong Kong. Pitreavie's reading Hong Kong. Pitreavie's giving Hong Kong a Roger. We've cleared the signal. Pitreavie's got it.'

Goodness knows what we thought Rosyth was going to do, but at least the burden of starting a real war had been shared.

On the ground the situation was getting no better. Fishermen had no regard for admirals and the like. They had had a trying winter and twelve trawlers to one gunboat was good odds. *Russell* was clearly a pretty pansy outfit.

Rosyth however reacted with uncanny speed. Another shout from the Wireless Office. 'Reply from Flag Officer, Scotland, Do not repeat *not* open fire. Your message being phoned to Admiralty and NATO meeting now in Paris. Essential you delay developments for at least 15 minutes.'

With trawlers now closing in on *Thor* from all sides this was not going to be entirely easy. The TLO however was already renewing his plea for calmer councils and suddenly there was a shout from one of our lookouts, 'Thor is covering his gun.' We heard later that the NATO meeting, on hearing of the imbroglio, had at once and unanimously urged the Icelandic member to get his government to call *Thor* off. A series of quick telephone calls saved the situation. The trawlers naturally claimed the credit. I always thought that it really went to the naval worldwide communication network which had shown that it could outsmart even the Heaviside layer, and that pretty quickly too.

That patrol was not quite our last but it had more than its fair share of incidents. After the run-in with *Thor* we had little more trouble with the Icelanders and Commodore 'Fish' decided that it would be a nice change for us to spend our fortnight's harbour time on the Edinburgh side of the Firth of Forth rather than in Rosyth over the water. A berth was available in the Mine-Sweeping base at Port Edgar, but as ever it was not going to be plain sailing. The entrance to the base was narrow for a ship of *Russell*'s size and because of the strong current across it at anything more than an hour or two either side of slack water we were limited as to our time of arrival. Our relief on patrol for once arrived a few hours late and so we were really pushed for time if we were to catch the tide. All this led to our nearly capsizing on the way home. Here is how it happened.

Because of our late start from 'Butterscotch' we had got permission to exceed our usual economical cruising speed of 12 knots and went off creaming along at 21 knots. This would have been fine had it not been for a brisk breeze from the starboard quarter which was kicking up something like a ten foot sea astern of us. Running too fast in these conditions had its dangers, certainly in the Captain class, of broaching to. The ship would charge up to the top of a ten foot wave and in surfing down the other side would all too often try to sheer one way or the other. If the helmsman did not correct the sheer the influence of the wave astern would tend to push the stern round and this coupled with the ship's habit of heeling outwards from a turn at any speed would roll her over quite alarmingly. This was probably, indeed almost certainly, what happened with *Nizam* off Cape Leeuwin and *Napier* off Cape Otway at the other end of the Great Australian Bight in 1945. The same thing had occurred with a ship of our own squadron with very nearly disastrous results the previous December.

On this trip back from Iceland therefore the helmsmen and Officers of the Watch were well briefed about the situation. I spent hours at the 'French window' in my cabin, looking aft at how the ship was steering, knowing that we were running faster than was prudent, balancing the danger against the carrot to morale of a fortnight on the Edinburgh side of the Firth. To have slowed down, missed the tide at Port Edgar, and berthed at Rosyth until the following slack water was not an option. It was Thursday now. We would arrive tomorrow, Friday. If we berthed at Rosyth first we would be stuck there over the weekend with no dockyard working. We needed to let the boiler die as soon as possible after arrival to allow maintenance to start. To flash up again for a move on Monday would seriously affect the programme. It was Friday noon arrival at Port Edgar or another rest period in Rosyth. The sailors would not be amused with that.

So we ploughed on, chasing up over each wave, sliding down the far side, the bow trying to pay off to starboard, the ship tending to roll outwards, down the slope of the wave. Each time the helmsman caught her, brought her back. Each time it was another potential crisis overcome. Each time it seemed irresponsible to maintain that speed. Each time the carrot just seemed worth it. Early next morning we would anyway make the north coast of Scotland, slip through the Pentland Firth and then chasing down the east coast we would have a lee from this north-westerly weather. So we went on. It didn't get any worse. It didn't get any better.

We raised the Scottish coast at just after 0325 next morning, pretty well on time, and I was on the Bridge shortly afterwards. At that time of year it was broad daylight. There was still the nasty sea astern that we had brought with us from Iceland but we would soon be round the corner and we were quite used to the motion by now. The ship creamed up over another wave, began to surf down the forward slope, edged to starboard and then quite suddenly instead of regaining her course continued faster and faster to starboard and finally broached to, rolling right over on her side.

The Bridge deck was normally some thirty feet above the water but in an instant as we went over it was down level with the sea. Green water was racing along the rail at 21 knots. The Officer of the Watch who had been standing by the compass bowl and the intercom to the wheelhouse lost his footing and slid quickly down into the lower wing of the Bridge.

I lost mine too but being more desperate than he – 'you, the Captain, are always last to leave the ship as she sinks' – I clawed my way quickly up to the intercom and shouted down to Stop Engines. Someone must have had the same idea down below as we slowed and stopped almost immediately and the ship came up, shaking herself like a wet dog. She sat there heaving quietly in the slight swell asking what all the trouble was about.

Happily there was no one about at the time except for the Watch on Deck. They would have been huddled round the foc'sle door and certainly got a shock and a wetting but nothing worse. I remember looking over the after end of the Bridge as we got our breath back to see what damage had been done. All I saw was a rather depressed group of sailors looking up at the Bridge with a collective expression which said all too clearly, 'What on earth do they think they're doing up there?'

We never did discover what went wrong. The helmsman always swore that the grating on which he had been standing slipped. More likely I felt was that he could have put the wheel the wrong way in an unguarded moment at the end of an arduous watch; or maybe his mate was taking over for a spell. Either way it was an unnerving experience and I never felt happy again in similar conditions. We did however make Port Edgar on time. Perhaps the oddest part of the whole affair for me was driving back to our flat in Edinburgh that afternoon with my wife and three month old daughter and reflecting that twelve hours previously our ship had been within measurable distance of capsizing.

A last thought remains. By the time I joined *Russell* my old Captain in *Broadsword*, Lieutenant-Commander Jack Bitmead, had been promoted to Commander and was serving in the Admiralty where he had responsibility for junior officer appointments. It was thus he who sent me to Iceland. He asked me a few years later whether I had enjoyed the experience. I had never been other than strictly truthful with him and saw no reason to break the habit then.

'Yes. I thought you wouldn't like it much,' he said.

Chapter 24

Barrosa –
Devonport to Kuwait

Barrosa was commissioned at Devonport in the Spring of 1962. She was a Battle class destroyer modernised as a Radar Picket ship. The battle after which she was named had been a well-fought victory on 5 March 1811 during the Peninsula War when an allied force of Spanish and British troops defeated a larger formation of the French. Included in the British force was the 87th Regiment, later to become the Royal Irish Fusiliers, and it was largely due to their example and courage in routing twice their numbers of the enemy that the victory was secured. Inter-service attachments are usually, and I think rightly, deemed to have a certain value and thus it was natural for *Barrosa* to be affiliated to the Fusiliers. So to kick off on the right foot we asked them to our Commissioning ceremony.

The latter was partly religious, partly secular. The ship was entrusted to the care of the Almighty and the crew urged to fear nothing; and the Captain was enjoined by the Admiralty Board to put the ship into service, and I suppose also to fear nothing. The Colonel of the Fusiliers came over from Ireland, a very genial character but mightily concerned that the Piper whom he brought with him should stay sober long enough to play at the Service. He did, but not for long afterwards.

The ship had been more or less rebuilt in Devonport dockyard after a collision with a sister ship, *Corunna*, a year or two earlier. Both were reborn as Radar Pickets. Their role was to increase the range at which radar warning of air attack on a Task Group could be obtained. To do this they would be stationed in the outfield a hundred miles or so from the Group and in the direction from which attack was most likely to come. Thus themselves exposed to enemy air attack the intention was that they should have their own close air support. A nice idea but it didn't always seem to work like that.

In their rebuild the ships had been fitted with enormous radar aerials the size of an old-fashioned iron bedstead. Sitting down at Devonport we would test ours on aircraft 'stacked' over Heathrow some 250 miles away.

HMS *Barrosa*

They were very effective pieces of equipment. Down aft we had the first of the guided weapons to be fitted on a regular basis, the tiny Seacat. This was an optically guided missile, in those days at any rate, but most satisfactory to operate and very lethal to targets. To make the best use of all this radar an up-to-date Operations Room, much larger than the usual destroyer outfit, was built in below the Bridge and this allowed us to take on the function of directing the fighter cover of a Task Force. A source of much quiet amusement to myself was the Radio Warfare Room, newly fitted amidships. The equipment and its operation were so secret that only the Leading Telegraphist in charge and myself were allowed to know what went on. He had a smattering of Russian, enough to give an opinion as to whether what he had picked up was Russian or double-Dutch. Each morning when we were at sea he would knock on my cabin door, look round furtively to see that no one could overhear our cryptic conversation, and we would then go over what he had managed to cull from the air waves over the previous twenty-four hours. What never struck me until nearly the end of the commission was that an empty compartment next door to all this secretive activity had been given over to our resident Chinese tailor. It was by no means beyond the bounds of possibility that he had been planted by our friends. The trouble with that murky world, on whose fringe it was certainly titillating to dabble at the time, was that even the most ridiculous thoughts were apt sometimes not to seem all that far out.

I was glad to see that the refashioning of the ship had left the gunnery system almost intact. A single 4.5-inch mounting had gone amidships but we still had two twin 4.5-inch mountings forward of the bridge. No Flyplane system even twelve years after its success in *Broadsword*; only the now ancient American Mark 37 system of World War Two. The original torpedo-tubes had had to go in the interests of compensating for the masthead weight of our 'bedstead' radar aerial – but joy of joys, we had been allowed to keep the open Bridge. After all these changes the sleek looks of the original Battle design had been lost and seen from outside *Barrosa* rebuilt did look something of a hotch-potch. We, the Ship's Company, saw more of the view from inside and we were very happy with that.

The Commissioning ceremony seemed to leave a good taste all round and with that over we sailed a week or two later for our 'work up' at Portland.

Portland was where all ships were programmed to spend some six weeks after commissioning to be lectured, advised and sometimes harried into as high a state of efficiency as possible. The accent was on training at sea and to this end there was a much greater availability of targets to shoot at, submarines to hunt, tankers to refuel from and so on than we would probably ever find again. The Base staff acted as observers and monitors of each ship's progress, comparing the latter against an attainable norm and letting ships know in quite forthright terms if and where they were falling behind. The theory behind the Work Up Base was very good. It had served us well during the War. We had visited Tobermory in *Broadsword* some ten years before, which was where the North Atlantic Convoy escorts used to work up. The practice depended on the staff. I think that one or two of us felt that we might have been treated a little less like raw recruits, particularly as some of us had had more experience than the staff. I did try to point this out politely before we left but the momentum of the programme and the enthusiasm of the staff was such that I doubt the point was taken.

Either way Portland did us all good and in September we sailed for the Far East. Despite the wrench of leaving wives, families and girl friends for upwards of a year – we were not to return before the following October – it was a stirring prospect. For myself I was delighted at the thought of seeing something other than the North Sea or North Atlantic again. Fresh from Portland, and with the Portland spirit still running strongly, we exercised as much as we could all the way, but in reality it was something of a world cruise. We were mostly by ourselves and off the leash.

There was a short stop in Malta where as ever we had to make a sternboard down Sliema Creek to reach our moorings. The idea was that you were then pointing in the right direction to leave harbour if required to sail in a hurry. It was an old destroyer manoeuvre and not difficult, just slightly testing the first time. Surprisingly we ended up in more or less the right place.

Malta stops one dead with memories, childhood days living in Guardamangia just round the harbour from Sliema and sailing toy boats in the Creek. Later childhood days based in Fort St Angelo on Grand Harbour, rowing round to swim at Bighi. Post-war visits on passage with never enough time to explore old haunts. Joining *Broadsword* thirteen years earlier. And here we were again, and only for an instant. We sailed on eastwards again after only a day or two of honey-coloured fortress walls, of smells and sights and cries that hardly seemed to have changed in nearly thirty years. We were required to reach Kuwait in thirteen days' time to join *Bulwark*, the Far East Fleet Commando Carrier, and another destroyer for a flag-showing visit; and this time, unlike our visit in *Virago* to Molde in Norway some seven years earlier, we were determined to work in a couple of days at anchor somewhere in the southern part of the Persian Gulf to clean up the ship after the long passage and to give the sailors a chance to stretch their legs and work off their repressions before a best-behaviour visit.

So on to Suez. A couple of days later and shortly after sunrise the Navigator said he thought it was time we altered course to close the coast. None of us could see anything and we queried if he was sure he was right. He countered that it was very low-lying, and that he personally did not expect to see much before we found ourselves almost in the entrance to the Suez Canal. He was right; and we just missed the daytime south-bound convoy by a matter of minutes. It did not matter all that much. More interesting was the thought that a difference this time from earlier passages of the Canal would be that we would have an Egyptian for pilot. We had been warned that for us he was almost certain to be an Egyptian naval officer, and that we must keep that deadly Seacat launcher well-covered. No one said anything about the Radio Warfare Office. It was doubtless so secret that not many people knew we had one. The Leading Telegraphist did not pick up much to discuss next day, which I suppose was hardly surprising as Arabic was not one of his languages. We were impatient to get on but the thought of the night convoy was some consolation. First we had to have a searchlight fitted in the bows. This was no problem: a self-contained unit was simply lowered on to the foc'sle – and it worked. The 'fishermen' in Suez were as active with rod and line to poke through any open scuttle in a search for something that could be hooked as they had been in Algiers several years earlier. In wartime, after a long grey passage from Glasgow, Suez had seemed a riot of colour and delights so near and yet so far. This time it looked just as colourful but more tawdry. Maybe the hours of waiting dulled the impact.

The night convoy was due to start at 0400 – hardly a night-time movement really but that's how it was. Those of us about to be involved turned in quite early but I, certainly, found it impossible to sleep. It was hot. The night life of Suez alongside was just as noisy as the day's; and even though we were to take a pilot who would be responsible for the safe navigation of the ship, the prospect of watery travel through the desert can never be unexciting. Soon after midnight I was hopping up and down to the Bridge to catch a first sight of the north-bound ships sailing through the sand. Soon after two in the morning we began to sense the faint glimmer of lights far off down the waterway. Or could it be a lorry much nearer? Too much glare we decided for a lorry and soon we could make out the leading ship of the convoy gliding towards us out of the dark, passing us without a sound, somehow jettisoning its searchlight, presumably into a waiting boat, and then slipping out into the Mediterranean. The procession kept coming and coming. Suez thus illuminated looked much better by night.

Our own passage was completely uneventful. A destroyer was no more than a minnow to pass through the waterway. Our Egyptian Navy pilot was competent and friendly. We had breakfast together during passage through the Great Lakes and I think he left us shortly afterwards. I hope and believe that the only 'intelligence' he could have gained during his time on board was that we harboured no hard feelings towards his country. Those who maintained at the time of Suez six years earlier that the Egyptians would never be able to run the Canal were clearly whistling in the wind. We reached Port Tewfik at the southern end of the Canal in the afternoon and set course for Aden.

What magic it was to see those sun-blasted rocks again a couple of days later. I had been based ashore in Aden for two or three weeks some four years earlier as part of a joint planning team sent down from Cyprus to help with something or other, and had taken the precaution to climb Shamsān, the Aden Matterhorn. Like Gibraltar the peak had a legend. In Gibraltar it is that when the monkeys leave the Rock the British will follow soon after. To the annoyance of the Spaniards I believe the Governor regards it as one of his duties to see that the monkeys are well fed. In Aden a traveller is guaranteed a safe and timely return if he will but scale the heights.

This time we stayed only long enough to fuel and then we turned north up the coast for the Persian Gulf and Kuwait. I was, and remain, never sure what it was about the bleakness of Aden and the Hadhramaut coast to the north-east of it that I, amongst I believe many others, found so attractive. In Aden the desolation was so complete that it had to attract if one was to survive at all. Up the coast there was a sharp beauty in the restrained colours, the emptiness of the land, just the lines of natural forces in the shapes of the hills, the mountains and the shore. Every so often we would make out a tiny outbreak of huts close to the beach and once, passing Makalla, what we took for the Manhattan of the Hadhramaut, a town of mud and mango-pole skyscrapers seemingly six

275

stories or more tall. But mostly there was just the bare coast, rock and earth and sand.

For the visit to Kuwait we were to meet *Bulwark* and *Carysfort* in the northern part of the Gulf the day before we arrived. *Bulwark* was a wartime-built aircraft-carrier now converted to carry a Commando of some 650 Royal Marines complete with their helicopters. Shortly they were to find plenty of employment ashore in Borneo during the 'confrontation' with Indonesia. For the present they were embarked in the carrier – not an ideal existence in the tropics. *Carysfort* was another destroyer, this time recognisable as such and lacking our own splendid trademark of that enormous 'bedstead' aerial.

By the time we were due to reach Kuwait our sailors would have been cooped up onboard for nearly three weeks. It would have been flying in the face of experience to expect that no one would let their hair down, and thus the ship too during the visit, so we got *Bulwark*'s permission to act independently for a couple of days and anchor off one of the small islands at the southern end of the Gulf, where we could smarten up the side after the long passage from Devonport and in the evenings land 'banyan' parties for what I suppose would now be called 'beach barbies'. These were always popular, an empty beach, a warm sea, an empty hinterland, it does not matter which. As the pirates careened and scraped the hulls of their ships we sloughed off the barnacles of weeks on passage. It proved as successful as ever at Sir Abu Musa. The only trouble was that the sea seemed to have become infested with sea-snakes since I was last in those waters some fourteen years earlier. Then we quite often bathed from the quarterdeck ladder. It was best at night when movement in the water energises whatever it is that causes phosphorescence. This time we began getting signals from shore about the snakes just as the time came for the partying to break up. We thought at first that the serpents might owe more to the beer than to nature but then we looked over the side and ourselves saw the revolting creatures as well. Some, they told us later in Kuwait, were harmless but the larger 'ocean-going' species could be lethal. Luckily no one was bitten.

I found revisiting Kuwait a sad experience. Of course the oil had made schools, hospitals and 'civilisation' possible. Mine was a selfish sadness but the memory of evening picnics on the shore, now covered with oil jetties and terminals, would keep intruding as we were shown round the new prosperity and were expected to make the right admiring noises. Was this where the Doctor and I had waded ashore in the dark, scared stiff on account of the sting rays but anxious to find a 'second opinion' for our aching sailor? Could that be something like the spot where the District Officer had given us a meal of fresh-caught fish smoked over a drift-wood fire one evening? I was unwise enough to murmur to one Kuwaiti that we in England were sometimes nostalgic over bits of the past which we thought might be better than the present. Did his people ever see things like that? 'Certainly not,' he replied rather sharply. 'We like only the new things.' My wife and I got a similar though more friendly reaction when we were showing a black Ugandan student something of our part of Dorset. The view as ever was breath-taking, spoilt just slightly by the line of tall electricity pylons carrying their vital load across the valley. 'It's a pity about the pylons,' I said to our Ugandan. 'Oh,' was the reply. 'I don't see it that way. Pylons are progress. I wish we had more in Uganda.' Yet further confirmation of the difficulties of using the future to enhance rather than vitiate our inheritance!

The Kuwait visit did not last long. You can only do so much in what even then was just a giant oil refinery. Each of the three ships gave a dinner party for those in Kuwaiti society who had been or might be in the future sympathetic to HMG's view of the world. Ours turned out to have only one guest. Three apiece had been thought reasonable for *Carysfort* and ourselves. Our first guest arrived more or less on time and we settled down under an awning on 'B' gundeck to wait for the other two. Unlike *Loch Glendhu*, we had no maze of mortar-loading rails there to interrupt the social scene and it was a pleasant enough place from which to contemplate the glare of the shore. To cut the story short, the other two guests never turned up. Not overjoyed at the prospect of a solitary meal with just one who, however friendly, spoke little English, I coaxed the Officer of the Day into joining us. He, poor chap, was not at all attracted at the prospect of a second dinner, particularly when it had to be dry. At a suitable moment I asked our guest what he thought had happened to the other two. 'Well,' he replied, 'in our country it is good manners not to refuse an invitation. Having accepted it is up to you whether you turn up or not.' It seemed that diplomatic entertaining in Kuwait might have its own particular pitfalls.

From Kuwait our little group turned back south again and headed for our next assignment, the Seychelles. *Barrosa* had been getting stick on leaving Kuwait for not keeping station sufficiently accurately on the Senior Officer but was let off the lead to make its own way through the Fakh al Asad off the north end of the Musandam Peninsula which encloses the

277

southern end of the Gulf. Interpreted, we used to be told, the name means The Hole in the Wall, and passing through it was always something of a show-off by old Persian Gulf hands. Two rocks stood as Scylla and Charybdis to guard a deep water channel through the Wall. We used to use it from time to time in *Loch Glendhu* to rouse the Ship's Company from their tropical torpor. It was harmless but something to look at. This time we did it blind on radar for practice. Did most of it, that is. No sooner had our bows started to emerge from the Hole than our Navigator, who was conning the ship blind from his navigational radar in the Ops Room, came bursting onto the Bridge to see what real life scenery he was missing.

Chapter 25

Seychelles and Aden to Singapore

A visit by a Commando Carrier and two destroyers to somewhere as small as Mahé, capital of the Seychelles Group, does in retrospect seem to have been overdoing things. Perhaps the islanders had let it be known that they would not say no to an injection of fresh blood: you may recall that on my previous visit in *Loch Glendhu* a dancing partner at a Sports Club dance had volunteered how they appreciated naval visits as they did so much for the population. Our present complement of a thousand Marines and Sailors might be anticipated to change it for many years ahead, though I think we only had two or three days there.

By the time we arrived *Carysfort* had left our litle group and *Brighton* had joined. She was an up-to-date anti-submarine frigate and we were to see more of her here and there across the Station. The plan was that from Mahé she and *Bulwark* would steam over to Mombasa for more flag-showing, while we had the good fortune to win a trip with the Governor and his family to visit some of the outlying islands in the Group. I say 'good fortune' because our commission in the Far East was to last thirteen months, not long by pre-war standards when anything up to three years could be the norm. All the same it was quite long enough for married men to miss badly the company of wives and children. The sailors welcomed the Governor's children with open arms. The Governor's wife was, well, Caesar's wife, but even so her presence was a lightening influence.

The overtones behind this trip were not so happy. The Governor's predecessor had been I understood a bluff and hearty character who related well to the Seychelles bourgeoisie. He had died in a tragic bathing accident off Mahé. No one seemed to be happy with the exact details but apparently he got into difficulties in the water after a beach picnic. He was still alive when brought ashore but in a bad way. Because no one knew much about resuscitation, strange for a sea-girt people, attempts to revive him failed and he died. The present Governor, then at sea with us, was a very different character, well-lettered, studious and quiet, an admirable man who one might have thought would have made an outstanding success of the post. It seemed however that the rougher elements amongst the white

Seychellois had some difficulty in relating to a family so different from themselves. The Governor felt that he had to prove that they did have a meeting point and this voyage, starting with us but continuing in the tiny Government yacht, was his chosen instrument. I could well see his intention and it was possible to have every sympathy with it but I had the gravest reservations about the second leg of his tour when he and his family were to take to the yacht. The south-west monsoon was blowing, the weather was by no means settled, and the yacht itself, when we met up with it, did not sound too reliable. The four hundred mile trip was not to be taken lightly. Flag Officer, Middle East, told me flatly when we got back to Aden that I should have stopped the Governor. Perhaps I was brought up with too much respect for authority but to have tried to do so seemed at the time to be outside my competence.

An indelible memory of the trip was of a magic lantern show we had in the Wardroom the night before they left in the yacht. I suppose we saw the usual not very high standard film. The Governor's wife fell asleep in the chair next to mine and we had a lovely family evening. I am glad to report that the Governor did get back to base without too many mishaps.

For ourselves we set off to catch up the other two in Mombasa, but only to fuel. There had been a cry from Aden for our radar and radio intercept capability so it was back north again at somewhere near best speed. It was a pity to miss Mombasa. A party of our sailors had gone on ahead in *Bulwark* all set to make an attempt on Kilimanjaro which should have been more fruitful than the *Loch Glendhu* elephant hunt from Kilwa Kisiwani; but it was nice to know that we already seemed to have fallen into an operational role on the Station.

The background to our recall was that for some years the Yemenis to the north had been stirring up trouble in the Protectorates on the landward side of Aden. We were forever reading reports on the subject when I was in Cyprus. Now the suspicion was that Russian influence was at work in the Yemen, as in other areas of the Middle East, encouraging the Ruler to persevere with, and where possible to increase, his work against the common enemy. *Barrosa* was required to monitor radio traffic in the area and aircraft movements into and out of Yemen; and incidentally to provide radar cover for the colony itself. We could do this – after a fashion. What we could also do was to demonstrate the versatility of sea-power. The usual bitter argument was going on between Navy and Air Force over the use of resources. The Air Force argued that never again would a conflict be fought where the combat zone would be out of range of the V-bomber force. The Fleet Air Arm should wither on the vine and the cash saved could buy more bombers. The Fleet could be protected from air attack with missiles. A few years later the Air Force won their point. The only way the Navy could get its present class of three tiny carriers was to call them 'through-deck cruisers'. Meanwhile the Falklands campaign demonstrated the weakness of the air argument. I could never help feeling that *Barrosa's* return to Aden had as much to do with the inter-Service argument as it did with the need for its radar and radio capability. But we just did as we were told.

After three or four days patrolling quietly up and down outside Aden the powers that be ashore decided that our material confirmed their suspicion of Russian support for Hodeida, and we were allowed into port before continuing our somewhat sinuous passage to Singapore. By then we had steamed an average of two thousand miles during each of the seven weeks that had passed since we left Devonport. At least we'd been kept busy.

Before we left Aden the Army helped us to stage a Ship's Company dance, not the sort of thing one associated with the place, certainly so far as the Navy was concerned. Partners were no problem – Army wives were invited, husbands invited to stay at home. Some people were not too keen on these do's. I have to admit that I never revelled in dances anyway and sometimes one or two of the sailors could be a bit tedious after an hour or so on the hard stuff. On the other hand I got great enjoyment out of seeing an evening when naval life was not all celibacy and bad weather. The dance in Aden went down pretty well and we hoped it would be the first of others during the commission. Unfortunately we never seemed to have an opportunity for any more.

I myself saw the inside of Admiralty House for lunch. I only mention this because it seemed to me to be one of the more captivating official residences. Built on the ruins of an old 12-inch gun emplacement, it was completely circular. Inside it was open plan, except that to allow official entertaining the kitchen had to be kept out of sight. Maybe this was down in a powder magazine. The 'openness' extended right up to the ceiling to give a nice airy feeling, a bull point in that climate; and the bedrooms and offices upstairs opened off a circular balcony running all the way round that second floor. This did or could apparently cause some confusion at night if one needed to visit the bathroom. Unless one took careful bearings before setting out it was not difficult to stray on the return journey. We were not enlightened as to whether the consequent cases of mistaken identity were popular or not. The view from outside, as one would expect from a gun emplacement, was stunning. If the Admiral could sometimes not see a ship entering harbour from his office, his wife certainly could from Admiralty House. My great mistake was not to climb the Peak again on that visit. Sure enough I have not been back to Aden since and do not now suppose that I ever will.

A passage from Aden to Singapore ought, I would have thought, to have included a refuelling stop at Colombo or Trincomalee, but I suppose we were considered to have been on the loose for long enough and were routed only to Gan, our Air Force staging post in the Maldives. We nearly missed the place in a heavy rainstorm which blanked out our navigational radar but a lookout managed to sight some palm trees through the downpour just in time. Gan was at the southern end of the Maldive chain. We had built an airfield there and garrisoned it, and of course the atoll provided a natural harbour. During our time in the Far East there was always some sort of friction over Gan, involving more the locals than ourselves, and the Far East Fleet had to provide a Guardship whenever the friction threatened to strike a spark. The Central Government in Male, the capital, had come to feel that the islanders working on Gan airfield were beginning to be seduced by the fruits of their labours from the less practical and more idealogical attractions of independence. As ever the British ended up as the jam in the sandwich, with Central Government threatening to revoke the treaty by which we used Gan. So a ship had had to be stationed there for the previous six months or so and when the atmosphere became really poisoned had moved up to Male itself. There the only place that the sailors could land for recreation was the tiny islet which was the home of HMG's representative, and the arrangement was not particularly popular with either side.

Almost all the work force at Gan came from neighbouring islets and those 'lucky' enough to live on an adjoining atoll might be seen wading across each day through the shallow water over the reef which joined the two specks of land. To watch them making the journey on a wet day, clothes perched on their heads and the whole topped with umbrellas, was touching on the surreal.

Singapore was two or three days further on down the Malacca Straits. I had a distinct feeling of coming home but was sad to find that a conspicuous palm tree, which I had persuaded the Hydrographer of the Navy to have put on charts some fifteen years earlier as a useful navigational feature on an otherwise featureless stretch of coast, had fallen down and was no longer marked. Change and decay! Singapore did not seem to have changed much though. It was still damp, green, luxuriant and odiferous. Lovely! We had arrived a couple of weeks before Christmas, three months out from Devonport.

Any thought of a quiet Christmas in the Dockyard though hardly seemed to be a starter. The place was full of activity, ships bustling in and out, mostly full of soldiers. The 'Confrontation' with Indonesia in the prelude to Malaysian independence was much on everyone's mind and ten days after we arrived the staff decided that it was *Barrosa*'s turn to do some work as well.

Chapter 26

Confrontation in Borneo

We had just returned to harbour after two or three days' exercises in the Straits outside. Almost as soon as the shore telephone line was brought on board and connected to our system the bell rang and there was the Staff Officer, Operations on the other end. 'Have you ever heard of a place called Tawau?' 'Not yet.' 'Well you'd better find it. We want you to get there as soon as possible. It looks as though there could be trouble with the Indonesians; it's right on the border. How soon can you sail?'

Normally in harbour ships would be at eight hours' notice for steam. Boilers had to be nursed up to a full head. Hurrying things could damage the machinery's health. On this occasion, having just come in from sea the boilers were still warm. 'Give us two hours,' we told the staff. 'We need fuel, a top-up with ammunition to replace what we've just fired and more small arms.' Destroyers were normally complemented to land a platoon of thirty sailors. It looked as though we needed to double that this time.

Two hours later we had what we wanted and were ready to sail. I'm not sure it would be right to say the Ship's Company looked forward to more sea-time but once again it was nice to feel we were wanted. I rang the Staff to ask how soon we were to plan to arrive. 'Full speed,' was the reply, 'but don't overdo it down past Changi. Some other nationals went out in a hurry the other day and washed three people off the beach.' 'Was that a bad thing? Weren't they bathing?' 'Maybe, but they ended up drowned. Not at all popular.'

So off we went, as fast as we dared down to the open waters of the Singapore Strait and then rang down for revolutions for Full Speed. This was rather different than asking for Full Power, which would have meant everything the engines could give. As we had now discovered that Tawau was round on the north-east corner of Borneo and two days' steaming at thirty knots from Singapore we felt that the speed had to be related to the need to arrive in one piece.

The ship took off as the revs built up. The north-east monsoon was

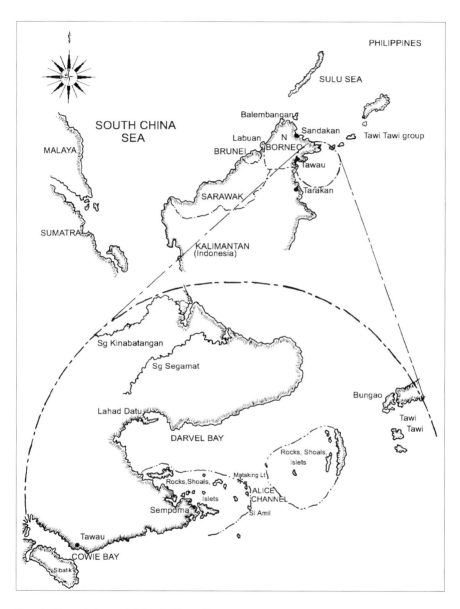

South-East Asia and North-East Borneo

285

just beginning. This would eventually bring quite strong winds and heavy seas down the South China Sea. In December there was still only a slight breeze and swell. At our normal sedate and economical cruising speed of twelve knots we would not have noticed the swell. At thirty knots we were more like a speedboat leaping from crest to crest. The Bridge was soon continually covered in spray. The funnel was turning white from the flying salt. Quite soon the Petty Officer of the Watch on Deck was on the Bridge to report that the forward messdecks were flooding down the ventilator shafts, making the messdecks wet and the sailors unhappy. There wasn't much we could do about it. I seemed to be the only soul on board who was not seasick. This was a complete reversal of the usual situation, when I was always smitten and had to take pills to stay upright. Most others were not bothered normally, so no pills this time!

We ploughed on hanging on to anything that looked immovable. The crockery bills mounted by the hour. We could only try to cheer the troops up with the thought that it was much worse in Arctic convoys.

By the end of the following afternoon we had crossed the worst of the China Sea. A tanker had been organised to meet us off Labuan at midnight to replenish us with fuel; thereafter we would have to wait until someone could reach us off Tawau, having made the passage at a slower and more economical speed. Fuelling at twelve knots for half an hour off Labuan after that mad dash across the China Sea was like stopping bashing one's head against a brick wall. The peace of it! For some reason we also took on nine tons of potatoes – a funny trade to make in the middle of the night.

Then it was back to thirty knots again, flying up the Borneo coast, quite often in rain squalls so heavy that, as when approaching Gan, they completely blanked out our radar. This was tedious as there were not many lights on the coast, but there was not much that we could do about it beyond getting a fix whenever the rain eased sufficiently for the radar to give a picture. Thankfully the swell was a great deal easier on this side of the water and in the early hours of the morning we rounded the north-west tip of Borneo and were in the bathtub calm waters of the Sulu Sea. After that it was a pleasant passage. We slowed down once to investigate a native craft, a *kumpit*, chugging along in the direction of Sandakan. As she was outside the three mile limit we could only peer hard at her and then we both went about our business. By midday we were abreast the lighthouse at the mouth of Darvel Bay, and shortly before tea-time we swung round Si Amil island at the south end of the Alice

Channel between Borneo and the Philippines. We did wonder who Alice was; it seemed an odd part of the world for a lady with a name like that. Sixty nautical miles to Tawau, or two hours at thirty knots. The engines were still turning steadily though the salt on the funnel had by now burned a rather unpleasant shade of brown.

We had already found out that Tawau lay near the head of Cowie Bay and very close to the Indonesian Border. The chart showed Cowie Bay as a large indentation on the north-eastern coast of Borneo. It did not look as though there was going to be much in the way of a sheltered anchorage there and as we swept up the bay we couldn't see much in the way of anything that might be Tawau. To seaward however and just outside the three mile limit we came upon a warship flying the Indonesian flag. Leafing through our books we placed her as a Yugoslav-built patrol craft, probably supplied to Indonesia by the USSR. She hardly seemed to represent a serious threat.

We chased on up the Bay, hoping that we had at least given the Indonesian something to think about. Bearing in mind the urgency of our dispatch from Singapore we felt that we ought to be at Action Stations by the time we arrived, ready for any mayhem that might be under way ashore.

At last we began to make out what must be Tawau. A few houses appeared along the north side of the bay. Gradually they coalesced into what might be called a sea-front. A small jetty came into view with one or two miniscule coasters secured alongside it. A larger fleet of native craft lay at anchor further inshore. It was all very quiet though. I sensed a repeat of Mersing in 1948. Could we get alongside the jetty? It would make it much easier to 'throw' landing parties ashore if we could. There did not seem to be much room though and in any case the chart was rather shy at suggesting how much water there was there. We decided to anchor as close in as we could. There was still no sign of life ashore.

If the locals would not come to us we would have to go ashore and seek them out. Just then a boat nosed out from behind the jetty and soon the Chief Police Officer of the District was on board asking how it was that he had the pleasure of our company. We explained Singapore's concern. 'They're over-reacting again,' he said. 'Of course the situation might well deteriorate. The boundary between us and Indonesia runs slap through the middle of Sibatik island over there on the other side of the bay. No one's entirely clear where it is. I suppose the Indonesians could create an incident there. And of course we have a lot of Indonesian women

287

working the sisal plantations here. Very good looking most of them are too. We did find a heap of Indonesian uniforms in a hut on one of the plantations a few days ago. Maybe that's what's needled Singapore. We're trying to keep the temperature down though. I hate to say so but we'd almost rather you hadn't appeared. Anyway come along to our morning security briefing tomorrow and you can meet the Resident and the Army.' The CPO did his best to be pleasant but his description of the situation did seem a bit of a put-down. Hundreds of tons of expensive fuel oil gone up, literally in smoke. We forgot to ask if he would like any potatoes.

He had just left us and we were putting our ideas into order before bringing the Ship's Company up to date when the Quartermaster appeared. 'Another boat from shore, Sir. Seems in a bit of a hurry.' As he spoke the Quartermaster was being brushed aside. Into the cabin pushed a very angry individual who turned out to be the District Officer of Tawau. He was almost incoherent with fury. 'Who are you? What on earth are you doing here? Why did you have to come up the bay making that damned awful wash? Do you realise we spent the whole of yesterday planting five hundred *nipa* palms along the front and you've washed every single one away?' Hearing of his loss we could only have every sympathy with the DO. We did not normally carry palm seedlings of any sort amongst our stores and could only try to explain. It was not really enough. We did not seem to be very popular.

Relations improved of course. Despite their very understandable concern not to provoke incidents the Chief Police Officer and the Political Resident were keen to send boat patrols up the rivers into the interior. Could we help? Shades of the Brass River and Benin River expeditions of 1895 and 1897 in West Africa in which the previous *Barrosa* had taken part! The First Lieutenant could hardly be contained at the idea and was soon in command of a flotilla of small craft. I seem to remember that some Royal Marines had by now come into the picture and were rather sniffy, as professional small boat people, at being put under the command of a mere naval officer; but we smoothed that one over too. I must admit to having been slightly put out at the reaction of the local European concerns to all this activity. Their security was of course one, but only one, of our prime interests but they appeared to find it difficult to take other than a rather parochial view of the situation. The Bombay Burmah Company for instance who had extensive logging concessions in the forests was at particular pains to make sure we understood that labour relations must not be strained in any way. The Indonesian threat tended to be definitely something for the Government, not for them. I suppose it was ever that way. The First Lieutenant was comprehensively briefed on the subject but I also told him to be sure to fly the largest White Ensigns that the ship could supply.

This slight difference of view in fact melted away under the influence of approaching Christmas. The BBC invited us to take the ship up to their headquarters at the head of Cowie Bay. There we found a neat little hamlet of perhaps six bungalows where the European staff lived; a squash court, tennis courts, probably a village shop/post office. It might have been a 'desirable development' on the bank of the Thames at somewhere like Marlow. We invited them onboard the evening we arrived and chatting to one I asked how they did for leave. 'Well, this time last week I was on the beach in Spain,' came the reply. 'Something of a culture shock?' 'It certainly can be.'

We missed our Christmas there. Early in the morning of Christmas Eve the CPO came on the air with news that the fishing settlement on Si Amil islet, which we had passed on our way in, had been savaged the night before by pirates from the Philippines. Would we take a detachment of soldiers down there at once to cheer them up? We were back in Si Amil by midday and the soldiers were landed, Scotsmen but tact forbids naming the regiment. Twelve hours later we intercepted a message from Si Amil to the police in Tawau: 'Please take the soldiers away. We prefer the pirates.' Oh dear!

We spent the next two days prowling round the area to see if the pirates were going to return. Piracy was a perennial and persistent problem in the area. There were tales of a great battle in the early years of the century between pirates and the Royal Navy on the north shores of Darvel Bay. Seven hundred sailors were said to have been involved. No one seemed too sure of exactly what happened but local lore had it that 'things were then better for many years.'

Piracy really meant raids from the sea on coastal settlements. Philippinos would come over in fast boats, twelve men or so to a boat. The latter might be powered by four outboard motors giving a speed of some forty knots. The risk of being caught was almost nil. The villagers' view of the protection afforded by the British presence in Borneo was of course severely shaken by each raid. The CPO might have been unconvinced that *Barrosa* had a role to play in the context of Indonesian 'Confrontation'. If however we could help against the pirates that would be quite different. The Staff in Singapore took directly the opposite view and I was continually being reminded of our primary role, deterrence of the Indonesian threat.

We were to spend three weeks on this first detachment to Tawau. For two nights over Christmas we chased fleeting radar echoes around Si Amil. Small blobs would shoot across our screens at speeds which somehow matched closely the reported performance of pirate canoes. As the hours passed and blobs appeared and disappeared with some regularity we came to think that we were tracking birds or even gremlins. By Boxing Day morning it seemed that the pirates had had enough for a while and we ourselves went back to Tawau.

This time we got a berth alongside the jetty. The mere allocation of a particular berth as we closed the jetty did not however mean that that was where we could expect to end up. The custom was for a man with a red flag to take station on the jetty at a spot where the Harbour Master wanted a ship to lie. We soon learnt however that this was not necessarily the place which the man with the red flag favoured. As often as not we would be in the act of passing the first wire over to shore when 'Red Flag' would wake up and wander off up the jetty with his flag held high as if to say, 'Follow me or you'll have to move later.' At slack water this did not matter too much. With the tide setting in or out of the bay, when it could run quite strongly, it was rather a tiresome habit.

One afternoon a day or two after our Si Amil excursion the CPO took two or three of us for a tour of some of the plantations outside Tawau. The development of the previous four or five years had apparently been little short of phenomenal. Vast tracts of jungle had been cut for timber and then replanted with hemp, cocoa or rubber. Concessionaires got concessions to cut the jungle for so many yards on either side of the line of a new road planned through the area from Tawau round to Darvel Bay. In return they were required to build a section of the road which was then taken over by Government. Finally someone else moves in to replant the forest with trees or cash crops. I was not quite clear how this admirable rotation seemed to benefit everyone, but apparently it did, and the results were certainly there to be seen. The new road led us past a marvellous waterfall in the depths of the forest, a river dropping sheer for fifty feet or so into a crystal clear pool, a wonderful swim after all that sight-seeing.

We got back onboard to find a heightened degree of bustle. Apparently the Indonesian patrol vessel whom we had passed at the entrance to Cowie Bay on our first and unpopular arrival had been making a nuisance of itself. News had come in that it had boarded and captured two native craft within Borneo territorial waters, had sunk the craft and was holding the crews on board. The Resident was furious, talking of 'the Lion's tail being twisted,' and ordering *Barrosa* to 'do something'. Apparently there had been several other cases of harassment of trading craft within the past month. So far this had always happened outside Borneo territorial waters and there was nothing that the Tawau authorities could do about it, much as they deplored this interference with local trade. Borneo-registered craft were also said to have been terrorised, again outside our limits but reliable evidence appeared hard to come by.

Today the Resident was sure he had real evidence. The lighthouse keeper at the mouth of the bay claimed he saw the incident and was sure that the Indonesian had come inside Borneo waters. An RAF plane flying over the area had also seen if not the incident then at least the consequent wreckage. They confirmed the position as just inside Borneo waters.

I heard the story from the Resident on the telephone but could see only too clearly how meagre the evidence was of just where the incident took place. From Iceland experience I knew well how the difference of a few yards either side of a limit line could be used to sway judgement should a case be brought before an international court. And if we were to take action against the Indonesians here without the very firmest of evidence as to why we were justified in doing so it could be just the spark needed to set off the 'Confrontation' bonfire. I asked the Resident if we could see the RAF log – not that it would have made much difference as the aircraft had only sighted the wreckage sometime after the incident and goodness knows where currents might have carried it by then. And with the best will in the world aircraft navigation could not be expected to be accurate to the standards demanded here. I had no feelings against the lighthouse keeper but his verdict of the position of the incident was by eye only. The Resident would have none of this faint-heartedness, and I could see that at least some sort of action was needed, and even justified though the evidence was flimsy and the outcome likely to be messily inconclusive. So we put to sea as quickly as we could.

We came up with the Indonesian patrol vessel sitting in his by-now usual spot at the entrance to Cowie Bay and just outside the Borneo limit, and closed him looking as determinedly aggressive as we could. He seemed to have a number of 'civilians' huddled on his foredeck, and I asked to come over with our police Interpreter to discuss the situation. The atmosphere onboard was quite friendly but, as I knew it would be, it was impossible to pin the Captain down as to where exactly he had boarded the local *kumpit*. 'The lighthouse keeper says that he knows you were in Borneo waters and one of our aeroplanes confirms that.' 'They are wrong. Look. Here is our track on the chart.' There it was of course, but a track on a chart is only a pencil line, supported perhaps by a few fixes. It can be the work of a moment to cook something up. I tried another tack. 'Can my Interpreter talk to the men you have on board?' 'Certainly.' So the Interpreter went up on to the foc'sle. He was back in a minute or two. 'I do not think these men are from Tawau. I do not know any of them. I think they are Indonesian. Their boat appears to be registered in Indonesia also.' That clarified things a little but of course whatever their nationality the gunboat would have absolutely no right to interfere with a craft if it really had been in Borneo waters. In human terms it had no right to sink it anyway but unfortunately that was outside our remit at local level. So we had made no progress.

About this time the atmosphere took a decided turn for the worse. An officer whom I took to be the First Lieutenant surfaced from the space below the wheelhouse where we had been talking. The Captain had given the impression of being a fairly straightforward seaman. The new arrival was obviously a Party hardliner, the political commissar of the boat. We went over the ground again but of course made no progress. As he made each point the Commissar poked me in the midriff with the sharp points of his dividers, an instrument for measuring distances on a chart. This occasioned no bodily harm but was I thought disrespectful to Her Majesty's representative. What were our options? We could sink the wretched patrol boat any time we chose: we might even manage to do it before they could signal for help and without leaving any trace. Or we could board it and tow it into Tawau. That would please the Resident. Neither option was of course realistic. Either would give the Indonesians a wonderful chance to start whatever they wanted in the way of a proper fight and with themselves as the aggrieved party. Look at things as one might it seemed that we had insufficient grounds to do anything: a messy situation indeed. The Interpreter must have fathomed the way my thoughts were going. 'You know what will happen to those men tonight? They will be pushed overboard, every one.' 'But we can't be sure where the incident took place. Our evidence is not conclusive. If it was outside the limit we can't do anything.' Silence.

We climbed back onboard very discomforted. The gunboat took off for Tarakan just across the border in Indonesia and would no doubt spread a fine tale through the bazaars of how he had seen off the British. I had to tell the other side of the story to the Resident over the R/T. It would be an understatement to say that he was furious. I was instructed to sink the Indonesian at once. I countered that this was hardly sensible, to which the reply was that he was the responsible authority in Tawau and I was to obey orders. This rather acrimonious exchange of views closed with my promising to catch up with the gunboat and try to reason with him again but saying that I was not prepared to open fire without specific concurrence from Singapore.

As in Iceland a Flash message went off, this time of course to Singapore. Off Tawau we had to wait thirty minutes for a reply. It was a slightly tedious wait. It was quite dark by now. The gunboat was high-tailing it for Tarakan with us in hot pursuit. I did not have much idea as to the best gambit when we caught him, if we did so outside his territorial waters. I suppose it was rather like the games one played at school but at the time I did not quite see it that way. Not unreasonably from his point of view the Indonesian was leading us through the shallowest water he could find. We were doing thirty knots across a stretch which our chart showed as last surveyed a hundred years ago and with little circles all over it marked 'less water rep'd' or just 'shallows'. Help! I spent most of the time staring aft rather than ahead watching for the tell-tale enormous increase in our wash, the sinking of the stern which would warn that we were going much too fast in much too little water. At least we were gaining on the gunboat.

I suppose a mile or so separated us when there was a shout from the Wireless Office with a reply from the Commander-in-Chief: 'Do not repeat NOT open fire. Do not give chase.' So that was that. We stayed at sea that night and next morning found the remains of one *kumpit* which we towed up to Tawau. We got a far from friendly reception.

The Resident had already written an angry letter to the Governor of North Borneo which he showed me. Some of the facts were manifestly wrong and I felt bound to protest at his general view. Eventually we got things on to a more even keel and ended up agreeing on a wonderful scheme for physically defining the North Borneo territorial waters in the vicinity of Cowie Bay. A new fish-trap would be built in the area just inside the three mile limit and this would be manned by the police. I should perhaps explain that a fish-trap was a substantial platform built off-shore with 'fences' spreading out from it to guide any wandering fish towards the platform, where they would be netted. Objects would be selected ashore so that the line of sight to them from the platform followed the line of the territorial water limit. It sounded like the work of Heath Robinson and not surprisingly perhaps was never followed up. It would not have been much use at night anyway. For the present however it allowed conversation between the Resident and *Barrosa* to be resumed. In fact relations with the Navy improved from thereon and when it was suggested a few months later that an HM Ship was perhaps *de trop* in those waters the Resident would have none of it.

Chapter 27

To Hong Kong

We had thought that this brush with the Indonesian patrol craft *Bubara* might have warned her off her murderous ways outside Tawau, but apparently not. At the beginning of January 1963 Singapore received intelligence that an important Indonesian activist was likely to attempt to enter Borneo from the Philippines in the next few days and we were ordered up to Darvel Bay to join in measures to stop him. We had just reached our patrol area when a report came through on the police net that *Bubara* had driven a Tawau registered *kumpit* onto a reef not far from Si Amil about five days previously. As ever, could we do something about it? After such a long interval there was not much that anyone could do. In any case it was not beyond the bounds of possibility that the action was intended to draw us away from Darvel Bay, so we stayed put.

According to the intelligence source 'the Leader' was expected to try to reach Borneo from Bungao in the Tawi-Tawi group in the south of the Philippines and roughly opposite Darvel Bay. There was not much in the way of civilisation on the Borneo coast immediately opposite Bungao but it was thought that he might rendezvous there with other activists who would smuggle him in through tracks that were little known and used. Or he might make for the settlement at Lahad Datu at the top of Darvel Bay. Or then again he might try his luck penetrating into the interior of Borneo up one of the big rivers, Segamat or Kinabatangan. The possibilities were legion. A single ship patrolling off the coast would need to cover a line at least forty miles long to take care of only the most likely approach. And then of course if the leader were to put himself in our shoes it would be only too easy for him to reach the same conclusion as ourselves and to make a detour around our patrol line. It seemed we had a somewhat cosmetic exercise on our hands. However, clearly 'something had to be done.' It was 1948 all over again.

The Police in Tawau contributed two launches to patrol inshore along the Darvel Bay coast and another came from Sandakan to cover the more northerly inshore stretch. Our tanker RFA *Eddyrock* which had just arrived from Labuan agreed to join in the game and entered the spirit of things by offering to disguise himself by not flying an ensign. We were not sure who that was going to fool or how it could help, but every little was welcome. And the following day, by which time of course the crossing might well have been made, Captain, 3rd Frigate Squadron, arrived in HMS *Loch Killisport*.

It was something of a surprise to see one of the old Loch class again. *Loch Glendhu* had been on the verge of disintegration when I left her some fourteen years earlier but here was another one, smart and tidy, to take over command. We quickly warmed to Captain(F)3. A senior officer joining is expected to hoist a signal as he heaves into sight: 'I have assumed command.' This is sensible and avoids ambiguity. Some then go on to assume that those they have just taken under their wing do not know what they are about and that all previous plans must be recast. Not so Captain(F)3.

We now had three ships for the offshore patrol and, although we never saw them, the assurance that three launches were doing their stuff along the coast. Our cover was not absolutely watertight but at least we would not be completely wasting our time.

A patrol such as this is, in some ways, like selling insurance. You cannot expect a positive result but obviously must proceed as though you intend to get one. The night after *Loch Killisport* joined we in *Barrosa* sighted a small craft carrying lights as for a minor warship entering Tawi-Tawi bay around the south side of Bungao island. Nothing unusual in this but it was nice to know that someone else beside ourselves was afloat on that empty sea. A little later our 'bedstead' air warning radar picked up an aircraft approaching, and then landing at Bungao. Well, well! Nothing happened the following day but as dark fell that evening we moved in closer to Bungao, showing no lights of course and completely darkened. An hour or so later we picked up the radar echo of a ship, also darkened, leaving the harbour. This was getting exciting; but then she showed no sign of making over towards Borneo and instead turned north up the Tawi-Tawi coast. We discounted, I think rightly, the possibility that if it was the small warship we had seen entering Bungao the night before, she might carry radio-intercept gear and would thus suspect from our radar transmissions that she was being shadowed. So we waited and tracked her on radar, one sweep at random intervals.

An hour passed. By now she had left the coast but was still continuing northwards. Suddenly there was a call from the Surface Warning Radar operator: 'Contact bearing 000°.' 'Plot and report.' A couple of minutes later we had her course and speed. She seemed to be heading to meet our friend from Bungao. Could this be it? It did seem very possible.

But of course it wasn't. Before the two ships met the Bungao boat turned back inshore and the contact hurtling down from the north turned out to be *Eddyrock*, presumably still not flying an ensign. It was an exciting thirty hours though. We never did hear whether 'the Leader' reached Indonesia along another route.

So that was that. *Loch Killisport* departed and we had the place to ourselves again. By now our three weeks in Borneo waters was drawing to an end and we were looking forward to a promised fortnight's self-refit in Hong Kong. We had spent most of our patrol steaming off the coast, mostly at night and with the ship darkened. We were not air-conditioned and the messdecks had been very stuffy. Everyone was looking forward to a spell of fresher weather and a day or two later we turned over to *Brighton*, last seen in the Seychelles, and headed north.

It is only two days' steaming from Borneo to Hong Kong. It took us longer as we were roped in for an Anglo-US exercise to the west of the Philippines on the way. The combined Task Groups (a Task Group is one down the scale of command from the Task Force) were to spend the first day replenishing at sea with fuel, ammunition, stores and anything else that anyone could think of. The weather was not too good and I found it rather tedious. *Barrosa*, although a splendidly sturdy ship, was not as nippy on the rudder as *Russell* had been and we had one or two close shaves. The big aerial on top of the mast seemed to have upset the balance a little.

That phase finished as night fell and the air defence benefit started. Although I well-understood the general principles on which this was to be run it was unlike an anti-submarine action where the Captain or someone in his place had a fairly major role to play in conning the ship. Air defence could only be run by the Direction Officer and his team in the Ops Room. In *Barrosa* they knew what they were doing and were best left to get on with it. I looked in about midnight to keep up to date and to see how much longer it was all going to last. 'How are things?' 'Well, the Americans have had a communication breakdown. We've taken over direction of some of their planes.' 'Do you know what you're doing?' 'Of course, Sir.'

Next morning we all berthed in Subic Bay Naval Base to discuss yesterday's happenings. At least that was the stated plan. *Barrosa* seemed to have the further function of giving the US Navy whisky for breakfast! Then we all went up the hill to the 'wash up'.

Three weeks of fairly hectic day and night activity around Borneo followed by the previous day's replenishment phase had left me just slightly weary. 'Wash-ups' are no doubt very necessary but the warm morning and the repetitive nature of many of the comments on the previous thirty-six hours soon had me dozing. Suddenly I heard the American Admiral who had been in command at sea and who was now on the platform running the 'wash-up' say that the Air Defence phase had been a right mess-up and it was only due to the efforts of HMS *Barrosa* that the whole Task Group had not been obliterated. Would the Commanding Officer of HMS *Barrosa* like to say how his magnificent ship managed this miracle? Our own Admiral, Flag Officer, Second in Command, Far East Fleet, otherwise 'Black' Jack Scatchard, was also on the platform, beaming unusually at this probably unjustified encomium. 'Come on, *Barrosa*.' 'Thank you very much, Sir. We of course did not have to do very much. As ever it has been a great pleasure working with your pilots. I do feel it says a great deal for their training that they were able to mesh so smoothly with our Direction Team when required. If we have the time I would like our Direction Officer here to say a very few words on the nuts and bolts of the operation as we saw it.' Over to you Lieutenant Nalder. Afterwards I asked him, 'What on earth was all that about?' 'Well, after you looked in about midnight the American effort more or less collapsed. We were left running the Air Defence of the Task Force. It struck me that the real honours were with someone on the American Admiral's staff who was a good deal more honest about the situation than I myself might have been.

A day or so later on a bright, clear, fresh morning we reached Hong Kong; and there we stayed for two weeks, our longest spell in port since leaving Devonport. I was lucky enough that my wife had a sister-in-law in Singapore and friends in Hong Kong and being a practical and perhaps even a scheming woman she managed to follow the ship between Singapore and Hong Kong with our two children. This was very nice for me, but it did make me all the more aware of the aches of separation which the other married men had to bear. Whilst the ship was there the Corsons lodged in the YWCA in Kowloon. This did not go down well with Commodore, Hong Kong who 'hoped' that we would be making an early move up-market. This was never really on the cards: even with the enormous help of being able to stay for a time with friends it had been quite expensive enough getting to Hong Kong as it was. Luckily however one or two other ships of the Fleet arrived shortly after us and the Commodore's attention was diverted from *Barrosa*.

Hong Kong in January for the Ship's Company was a life-saver. Petty grumbles were forgotten, in an instant the tropical torpor slipped away, the refitting work which had to be done went ahead with a swing. Less happy it was to consider aspects of life for a section of the local population of the Colony. Take for instance Ah Moy and her little team of Chinese women who came to ask if they could have our rubbish in return for which they would paint our side if we gave them the paint. Painting the side was not particularly hard work and was certainly not an unpleasant job in that sparkling weather. But it was a sad thought to say the least that some people might be in a position where they were glad to do it in return for the ship's rubbish. Yet this was an honourable tradition for ships refitting in Hong Kong, and Ah Moy and her team were a happy little band. One could only hope that there was truth in the old North Country saying that 'Where there's muck there's brass.'

Chapter 28

Pirates

I don't know what the rest of the Far East Fleet did with itself all the time, but I do know that *Barrosa* seemed to keep on drawing the Borneo card. So after our splendid fortnight in Hong Kong it was back to Tawau, where we took over from *Brighton*. We were back home.

We decided to play things differently on this patrol. Last time we had put in a lot of hours at sea but to no very good purpose. As I mentioned earlier we did a substantial amount of prowling round by night, ship darkened, hot and stuffy down below. Whenever we were back in Tawau for a day or two the sailors were very ready for a run-ashore and although there were never any official complaints we heard on the grapevine that the inhabitants had not always appreciated the occasional disturbance. Nor did we for that matter.

On this our second patrol we decided to make opportunities every so often to have a beach picnic or something similar where everyone could let their hair down without causing a rumpus.

We had our first 'banyan' after we had been back for a week or so. We came across a promising-looking beach on the north shore of Darvel Bay, surrounded by jungle and with the nearest habitation a good fifty miles off. We spent a blissful Saturday afternoon there. The sailors swam, built a huge fire, cooked supper and came back in the evening with that delightfully tired feeling induced by a spell of sea, sand and sun. We all felt quite relaxed.

It did not last of course. The Officer of the Day woke me about midnight with a signal from the police to say that Semporna, a small village about twenty miles away on the other side of the Bay, had been ransacked by pirates the previous night and would we please catch the culprits. As it was now twenty-four hours since the raid our chances of achieving anything were plainly nil. I pointed this out to the Officer of the Day and made to switch off the light. He however seemed to feel strongly on the subject. 'Sir, we're here to stop this sort of thing. If we always say it's too late, there's no point in being around.' He was right of course. We raised steam, weighed anchor and ended our lotus-eating break with a brisk night search of Darvel Bay. Predictably we found nothing.

Next day being Sunday we put landing parties ashore on all the little islands that fringe the Borneo coast in those parts. Equally predictably they found nothing either. As the afternoon wore on we began to think about what came next. The only further step that suggested itself was a patrol that night through the channels separating the islands we had just searched in case the pirates should think of returning for a further go at the village. So towards the end of the afternoon we started the first leg of our search. By chance for that first passage, which would be repeated several times during the night, our most experienced Watchkeeper was Officer of the Watch. Even so I found that I had to spend most of the Watch on the Bridge. This was not through any lack of confidence in the OOW. The waters were however extremely narrow, the reefs ever present. I was only too well aware that should we by chance hit some lurking patch of coral, even if it was something not on the chart, it would not look too well if the Captain were found to be relaxing below. More to the point was the realisation that should we ever come across a suspicious contact the latter could easily evade us merely by running across waters too shallow for us to follow. To cap it all the Wardroom was having a film that night which was reputed to be an improvement on our usual rather stolid diet. If possible it ought not be missed. So I altered the patrol line to one down the middle of the Alice Channel between Borneo and Philippine waters, eight miles up and eight miles down. That should require an alteration of course, for which I might want to be on the Bridge, every half-hour. More importantly it would give us sea-room to manoeuvre should we find anything suspicious. It seemed reasonable.

Just after midnight there was a shout down the voicepipe from the Bridge. We had a small radar contact ahead travelling south at six knots. It might be anything but we had seen nothing for two days. It ought to be investigated. We were steaming north up the channel at eight knots so closing speed was fourteen knots. At half a mile we would be illuminating him with our 20-inch signal lantern which doubled as a searchlight. That would be in ten minutes. No point in closing any faster. He would hear our boiler room fans and see our bow wave as well. Meanwhile the Boarding Party was stood to; and suddenly the Bridge seemed to be crowded with people who thought they ought to be there.

It was like a stalk in the jungle. The only noise on the Bridge was the occasional call from the Ops Room giving their latest calculation of the 'target's' course and speed. He did not seem to have noticed us yet, and was still steering slowly south. And then, seemingly quite suddenly, there was only half a mile between us. 'Switch on signal projector.' The brilliant purple light burst out through the dark like a sunbeam through a hole in a thundercloud. Surprisingly it was spot on target. Usually when we tried this, the light would be wandering all round the horizon before it picked out what we wanted. This time it showed us at once a small boat with a sizable number of men in it. Pirates! Who else at this time of night?

But wait! One of the watchers on the Bridge was not so sure. 'They're throwing things overboard. It's cigarette smugglers again.' We had run across the cigarette smugglers on a previous patrol. There was a high tax on cigarettes in the Philippines but none in Borneo – classic conditions for a smuggling operation. But if they were smuggling cigarettes why weren't they steering east for the Philippines instead of south down the Alice Channel? Suddenly the Officer of the Watch shouted, 'They're not throwing boxes overboard. It's the crew jumping in the water.' It must be pirates. Who else would have such a guilty conscience?

This time it certainly was full-speed to close them before they all disappeared. The motor whaler went down with the boarding party and was slipped while we were still creaming through the water. The upper deck lighting and the special floodlights rigged to keep a target illuminated came on and showed an extraordinary scene. We were alongside the boat by now. Men were still jumping overboard. Half a dozen were already in the water, swimming this way and that to get out of the light, anywhere to avoid the whaler. The lights groped down into the translucently clear blue water lighting it up as though it were a film-set swimming bath. Meanwhile the whaler was playing catch-as-catch-can with the would-be escapees. They reported over the walkie-talkie that they had got three. Then, quite quietly, there was a dull plop. No one took much notice. It could have been anything – a bulb going in one of the floodlights.

But it wasn't. Now there was a more urgent message from the whaler. 'Able Seaman X has been wounded.' How on earth could that happen? Had one of the Boarding Party let off a weapon by mistake? No one was supposed to shoot at swimmers in the water or whilst being captured. What had happened? 'One of the pirates has shot him with a pistol while being hauled onboard.' 'Is it serious?' 'Doesn't look too good.' The whaler was ordered back alongside. We could not see any more pirates in the water and it was pointless to continue searching for swimmers further out from the ship and thus in the dark. Meanwhile our wounded seaman was being rushed to the Sick Bay. It took no more than a few moments for the Leading Sick Berth Attendant to decide that we needed a hospital if he was to have any chance of survival. There was nothing more that we could do in the Alice Channel for the moment and none of us wanted to lose a sailor so it was off to Tawau at full speed. We had had a full moon whilst chasing the boat. Now it clouded over and we ran into one of the heaviest of tropical downpours. The rain and the ship's speed removed most of the paint off the front of the Bridge. Somehow it seemed a fitting commentary from above on the events of the night. Unfortunately our Able Seaman died before we could reach Tawau.

For all of us this was a decided shock. These sorts of things did not occur in a well-run ship in the 1960s. The Commander-in-Chief visiting us three or four weeks later whilst we were taking part in a Commonwealth exercise in the Bay of Bengal merely said, 'Well, you've been blooded.' He of course had to see it that way. On my own conscience was the thought that we had not done enough in our training programmes to prepare ourselves mentally for casualties in what was after all meant to be a fighting service. I don't think any other ships had either. It was something of a gap.

Meanwhile next-of-kin had to be told and we all had to agree on the method and place of burial. The man's wife not unnaturally wanted the body brought back to England. This however was going to entail passage through Singapore and the authorities there would not allow this except in a totally sealed and certified lead coffin. Not surprisingly really, this seemed to be quite outside the capability of anyone in Tawau. Eventually the widow agreed to burial in the Christian cemetery in Tawau provided an appropriate headstone was put in place.

All this had to be arranged very quickly, given the tropical climate. But even as we started the process we also had to decide what to do next vis-à-vis the pirates. We thought there had been some thirteen men in the boat. We had captured only three. Where were the other ten? If they had really escaped and lived to pillage another day we had not scored a very famous victory. There was a limit to the amount of time we could now spend around the Alice Channel with a dead man onboard so anything we could contemplate in the way of following up the remaining pirates had to be done quickly.

We decided that we must be back in Tawau that evening, which left the morning to search as many of the islands as we could on the Borneo side of the Alice Channel, as the tide would be carrying any swimmers in that direction. Shortly after daybreak a Landing Party went ashore on the first of the islands on our list and soon came across a fourth member of the gang hiding in a bush. Peaceful persuasion and tear gas both failed to persuade him to give himself up, so mindful of the previous night's events a warning shot was fired into the bush. Unfortunately it hit the man and he later died of his wound. This had in no way been the intention and was most unfortunate. A few weeks later the Commander-in-Chief's Secretary wrote me an official letter asking why we did not send for a Magistrate (from Tawau?) to read the relevant section of the Colonial Law to the man before authorising the firing of a shot. And we had always liked to believe that the staff in Singapore were aware of the realities of life across the Station! The Landing Party returned not very pleased with itself. Its leader, our First Lieutenant, was even less than content with his lot, having been stung by a hornet whilst ashore – no joke at all.

The funeral was next day. We landed as many as could be spared from the ship, everyone very smart in their full white uniforms normally only worn by the sailors three or four times in a commission, and we marched along the shore track to the point where it entered the jungle and where lay the tiny Christian cemetery. We had the good fortune that an Australian priest had his headquarters in Tawau. He got the tone of his funeral address just right. No funeral of a young man with many years otherwise in front of him can be other than sad. This occasion seemed to have a deeper significance as well as we stood there, a hundred of us, Europeans, surrounded on two sides by primary jungle, burying one of our number many thousands of miles from Portsmouth, killed in an encounter with the darker side of the lives of the local people. The priest sensed the mood and put it into perspective.

Next day the man's kit was auctioned on the foc'sle, an old seamen's custom dating from goodness-knows-when and with the object of course of raising money for the dead man's dependants. Ridiculous prices would be paid for the smallest item which would then immediately be put up for sale again.

With the funeral over we began once more to think about the pirates. The Indonesian threat seemed as quiet as ever. The police and civil authorities ashore saw the presence of an HM ship as a God-given opportunity to at least try to achieve results in an area of obvious concern to the indigenous population for whose welfare they were responsible, and we seemed already to have had some sort of limited success. So when we suggested that there ought to be a follow up to the brush in the Alice

Channel we got an enthusiastic response. In essence it was decided to flood the islands along the Alice Channel and offshore of Semporna with as many police and soldiers as could be spared, leave everyone in place for four or five days and see what happened. I suppose it was like setting snares in a number of fairly well-used rabbit runs. Co-operation with the Army was made even easier than usual because the detachment based on Tawau had just changed and was now from the Royal Greenjackets. My wife and I had known the regiment in Cyprus some years earlier at which time it had been named the Oxford & Buckinghamshire Light Infantry. We had always thought them an outstanding lot despite a comment from a visiting Secretary of State for War: 'Here is a battalion resting on its laurels.' Rather unfair we thought. They certainly were not resting on anything in Borneo.

Between us all we put together a small operation. Soldiers from detachments already stationd at Semporna and Lahad Datu as well as Tawau were to be landed on islands fringing the Borneo side of the Alice Channel. *Barrosa* would be up and down the Channel itself and a police launch would prowl around between the islands. We might catch something. It would be no great surprise if we did not.

For once the snares worked. Troops landing on one island almost at once ran into four odd-looking characters and captured all four. Three others were caught on another island but two escaped and could not be recaptured before darkness fell. As the island was otherwise uninhabited and covered with thick scrub which made it difficult to search, it was decided that *Barrosa* would bombard it next day. In the event this proved unnecessary. One of the escapees must have thought out what was likely to happen and gave himself up just as we were about to open fire. The other one remained at large but it seemed somewhat out of proportion to bombard an island just on the chance that one suspected pirate might still be there. Anyway we did not have a Magistrate onboard to read the relevant section of Colonial Law to the chap first.

No more prisoners were taken. Interrogation of those captured however was interesting. One was found to have belonged to the gang we had caught that first night in the Alice Channel. When confronted with his three former companions in prison at Tawau their mutual surprise was so great that much useful information was obtained. He had landed on the island soon after our initial search of the place ten days before and had been living on coconuts ever since. The others all turned out to be members of another gang. They had come over in three groups with a view to armed robbery on the mainland and were thought to be connected with the Si Amil affair just before Christmas. Over the fortnight we had accounted for ten pirates with a further eight known to have set out for Borneo but now missing.

The police and civil authorities in Tawau were delighted and wanted more. We too were pleased at having got a reasonable follow up to our Alice Channel encounter. We asked Singapore if, when a relief arrived in a few days' time to take over from us, we could overlap for a day or two to allow a bigger and hopefully better operation; but not surprisingly the Commander-in-Chief had other ideas. The annual Commonwealth combined exercises in the Bay of Bengal were scheduled to take place shortly and we were judged to have been off the lead for long enough. The Chief Police Officer at Tawau, who by now was a local man, however presented us with a pair of carved tortoise-shells. If you saw them in a shop you might well pass them quickly by, but the thought gave a depth of meaning to otherwise not-all-that beautiful artefacts. On our next visit there we found that the Superintendent had moved on. 'To higher things?' we enquired politely. Er, no, not quite. It was offences with small boys. Oh dear. *Plus ça change* . . .

Our last taste of that operation was perhaps the best. We were back in Tawau for a few hours getting ready to leave to rejoin the Fleet. Reports began to come in from a 'garrison' still on one of the islands that they could see an irregular light winking across the water from time to time. Could it be anything? What direction was it, we asked. They hadn't got a compass but it seemed vaguely north-east. We looked on the chart. Sure enough there was Mataking Lighthouse not more than seven miles away, more north than east, but when you haven't got a compass . . . 'Are you sure it's not the lighthouse?' 'No. We don't think so.' They had been there for several days by now. They must know the lighthouse.

So we stopped off the island that evening, and the Sergeant in command of the outpost came onboard. 'There it is. There's the light', he said, pointing to the lighthouse now flashing out its position. Well, of course the light might have been out of action for their first few days there.

Anyway, now we were visiting, how were they off for stores? Well, they were supposed to have been relieved a couple of days ago so they were a bit low and could certainly use some of this and that. Water? Yes, that certainly was a bit of a problem. They had run out yesterday. 'Well, for goodness sake what have you been living on?' They had, said the Sergeant, been trying to distil sea-water in a kettle. It wasn't really very successful. They would certainly appreciate some water.

Who was resting on their laurels now?

And so we set off to join the Far East Fleet then assembling at Langkawi on the north-west coast of Malaya just north of Penang. It was early March by now and 5 March was the anniversary of the Battle of Barrosa. The long arm of the Royal Irish Fusiliers had some time before reached out to form an association with the First Federation Reconnaisance Regiment, a relatively newly-raised Malaysian unit, and they had invited us to spend Barrosa Day with them at Malacca where they were stationed. I wonder, thirty years and more on, what has happened to this attempt to forge a relationship between the old and the new. At the time the Regiment gave every indication of valuing it and we had a very successful day with them.

Two days later we caught up with the Fleet at Langkawi.

Chapter 29

A Black Mark –
and a Typhoon Avoided

The exercise lasted some six days. It was as much a Commonwealth 'get-together' as anything more serious, Sri Lankan, Indian, New Zealand and Australian ships. Most of us had contacts amongst their Navies and it was good to hear how these had fared over the years. I suppose the exercise went the same way as all others, a replenishment phase, an anti-submarine benefit, air defence and so on; a few memories remain.

One afternoon the Commander-in-Chief arrived almost unannounced onboard *Barrosa* by helicopter saying he had come to find out how we caught pirates whilst others did not. This was flattering but I fear that he may have got an odd impression from this, his first visit. A ship simulating war conditions can itself give a fairly piratical impression. The off-duty watch were sleeping round the decks and we felt disinclined to disturb them. The Coxswain and First Lieutenant took the Admiral round the slumbering bodies and the most that I could add myself as regards the other pirates was that we had without doubt been lucky.

Another curtain is pulled aside. A serial in the programme covered an ingenious little game in which surprise air attacks from the aircraft-carrier in the Fleet would be mounted and ships were to fire a blank round when they had located and locked their gunnery systems on to the attacker. For some reason the guns were to be unmanned until an aircraft was detected. We were attacked one evening around bathtime and those of us on the Bridge were startled and rather pleased to see the turrets being manned by sailors still naked from the shower. All right, they should have been wearing anti-flash gear and overalls, but full marks for keenness.

Then there was the bombardment exercise on a tiny islet in the Nicobars. We were in waters well-known both from wartime attacks on Sabang not far off and from visits in *Loch Glendhu*. We rather prided ourselves in *Barrosa* on our bombarding, having worked out one or two little 'do-it-yourself' exercises to pass the time whilst off Borneo. We thought we had put up quite a creditable performance in this exercise off the Nicobars but the most the Fleet Gunnery Officer would allow was that one or two of our shots had landed somewhere near the target – and he a contemporary both from school days and as Midshipmen in *Queen Elizabeth*!

The exercise over, the Sri Lankans and Indians turned for home and the rest of us set course for Singapore. Instead of taking the usual route into the dockyard which would have passed through the main channel some way out in the Singapore Strait, we steamed in line ahead close in past the Singapore waterfront and thence up via Changi. Malaysian Independence Day was due in a few months' time. Independence for Singapore was not far off. I suppose HMG was saying, 'We're right behind you but take it steady, chaps.'

Barrosa was something of a pretender in this jamboree. We had come to the top of the roster for Guardship duty at Gan and had expected to peel off after the Commonwealth exercise and steam west to the Maldives. When the exercise finished however it was apparently quite quiet there and the Commander-in-Chief reasonably enough wanted our 'bedstead' aerial to lend dignity to the Singapore steam-past so we came with him. That was fine by us but it did get me a day or so later into the classical tug-of-war between family and duty. My wife was in Singapore at the time staying with her sister-in-law. Our wedding anniversary was on 23 March, when we should have been at Gan. That would have been one of those things, just bad luck. But here we were back in Singapore. What a stroke of luck! But then as we settled down in the dockyard the Commander-in-Chief's Social Secretary rang. 'As you're now in Singapore instead of Gan the C-in-C would like you to attend the Commonwealth Exercise Commanding Officers' dinner at Admiralty House the day after tomorrow. All right?' The next telephone call was from the Staff Officer, Operations. 'Gan are worried at not having a guardship. You're top of the roster. If anything happens you may have to sail at short notice over the weekend. All right?' I had just put the phone down when it rang again. My wife. 'We saw you all come in this morning. Most impressive. But there were three sailors hanging about in the middle of the boat in overalls. Was that right? Anyway, now we can have our anniversary dinner. All right?' 'Sorry. We may not be here that long.' The phone was quiet for a few minutes. Then a well-known voice was on the line again. 'If you might be away we'd better have an early anniversary. I've booked a table at the Tanglin for the day after tomorrow. All right?' That of course was the night of the C-in-C's dinner.

Life is much easier at sea. All I could do in Singapore was to toss a coin – family or duty? It came down to family, so I threw myself on the mercy of the C-in-C's Social Secretary, who proved unsympathetic. In the end it was the Staff Officer, Operations, who saved the situation by sailing us at short notice for Gan. The only dinner was at sea. I had certainly earned a black mark though.

It seemed a long way to go just for an eight day stint. By the time we left the RAF Station Commander was murmuring that the situation *vis-à-vis* the 'Central Government' in Male was much quieter and that he thought that if HMG's representative needed to be removed in a hurry, or to have help sent, the Station's Air Sea Rescue launch could do the job. The rest of us felt I think that whatever the 'job' might be, the help of an HM ship might lend a little dignity to a situation which, if it had gone that far, was likely to be something of a shambles.

Back in Singapore my brush with the Social Secretary seemed to have been painted into the background of a busy station. Do Flag Officers though ever forget the rejection of an invitation, almost an order, to attend an official function? No doubt the black mark finds its target somewhere, but I would hope and expect that Admirals would have weightier things to mull over.

Meanwhile after some eight months' fairly hectic steaming half way round the world the ship needed rather more dockyard maintenance than Hong Kong had been able to provide the previous January and with a bit of a creak of an ageing hull she settled into a floating dock in Singapore for a bottom scrape and brush up. The Ship's Company had a week's station leave each watch up in the cool of the Cameron Highlands where perhaps the greatest attraction was a log fire in the evenings. By the latter part of May we were all judged rejuvenated enough to join a Task Group led by the Flag Officer, Second-in-Command, Far East Fleet in his flagship, the cruiser *Lion* on a visit to Japan.

For the sailors this meant the prospect of female company again, noticeably absent since our Hong Kong fortnight. There was rumoured to be a sizable European population in Yokohama, which was the last port on our programme, and there were doubtless other delights as well. On a more elevated level perhaps most of us connected Japan in May with cherry blossom. Others still thought of typhoons. None of us were quite prepared for it to be so drenchingly wet.

The US Navy base at Sasebo in the south of Japan was the first port of call for a Royal Australian Navy Daring class destroyer and ourselves. It was almost under water. 'The rain is early this year.' The cherry blossom had all been washed away, and one's perceptions of a somewhat idealised countryside had gone with it. The jumble of the mud and the rain-soaked country round the base was not particularly appealing; and I made the mistake of being at the outflow end of a Japanese shipyard at knocking-off time. It left something of a sinister impression – an antheap must be quite countrified in comparison. On the other hand here one saw the energetic work force which was catapulting the Japanese economy so forcefully forward. It was quite something.

It was good to have the Australian *Vampire* alongside us for the visit. As a Daring she was newer than we were, slightly larger and faster than ourselves, ten feet longer, a little more in the beam and with fractionally more power. The class was built in the early 1950s. I am not sure what brief the Director of Naval Construction was given but unlike *Russell* and her like they must have come out as expensive ships – six 4.5-inch guns, five torpedo-tubes and an anti-submarine mortar like ours. All this fire-power needed a ship's company twenty-five per cent larger than our own, which was quite a bill in peacetime.

We had thought that it might have been something of a challenge to have such a neighbour. You never know how two ship's companies will rub along together. Pre-War the folklore was that our ships often found great drinking partners amongst the German Nazi fleet whereas with American ships fights and scuffles were more the norm. The only slight awkwardness that might have taken root at Sasebo occurred at a small lunch party that I happened to be having onboard to return hospitality. The guests were of course American but the Captain of *Vampire* was a 'co-host'. One of our guests came up with something like, 'I didn't realise that Australia was still a British colony.' It could have been a clanger but a combined Australian-British team fielded the ball cleanly and we parted friends.

Leaving Sasebo the two ships also parted company. Our own departure was enlivened by our being chased down the harbour by a USN patrol boat returning one of our sailors who had presumably made one too many friends ashore. Our flock always seemed to harbour one black sheep. Having retrieved this one we set off on our own for our next visit, this time to Matsuyama on the Inland Sea. We were going solo for this, and we had been told that Matsuyama would be a completely Japanese environment with no other Europeans about. Help! Or Heaven?

Either way we had time in hand for this one and had to dawdle along at a rather tedious eight knots. Tedious, that is, until we came to make the passage of the Straits of Shimonoseki between two of the main islands of Japan, Kyushu in the south and Honshu. The Straits are narrow and this means that when the tide is running through, either ebbing or flowing, it does so at ferocious speed. In those days travellers between the two islands had to cross the Straits by boat. Because of the current they would wait until slack water, when they would all burst over in a bunch like shoppers on a zebra crossing. Since the Admiralty *Sailing Directions* recommended ships making the passage of the Straits also to choose slack water to avoid the twelve knot tides at other times, one was sure of a quite hectic hour or so. Even at slack water we were cautioned to look out for eddies and whirlpools which could throw ships as large as a destroyer off course. Hong Kong harbour had been equally full of traffic but the ever-helpful Pilot warned that travellers across the Shimonoseki Straits were a deal more hard-nosed and should not be relied upon to give way, rule of the road or no. It was every craft for itself. In the event we had a delightful passage. It had stopped raining and the countryside was looking something similar to what the chocolate boxes suggested it should.

Once through the Straits we were into the rush-hour traffic of the Inland Sea. It was like a maritime Piccadilly Circus. However a little work with the chart gave hope that there must be some quiet route or other through this hectic marine-motorway type environment and sure enough we managed to make an easy night passage to reach Matsuyama next morning.

Was Matsuyama to be the Japan of legend, of picturesque houses with curling roofs and sliding paper doors, of women in kimonos and men in I'm-not-quite-sure-what? This is what we had been led to expect. But no, modern post-War Japan was impressing its mark here too. We anchored a few hundred yards out from what at first glance appeared to be a small and pretty fishing village. The main town was four miles inland so I had quite a trek to pay my courtesy call on the Governor. He turned out to be a venerable and cultivated octogenarian, born into the Shimazi family, one of the old ruling clans of Japan. He told me that he well-remembered the visit of the Prince of Wales in *Renown* just after the First World War. I asked him whether he met the ship's Navigator, my Father. He said, 'No.' But then after lunch he decided that he did remember him, so we must have established a rapport by then! It was sad to hear though of plans for the future of Matsuyama. The pretty fishing village we could see from the ship was destined to become a deepwater oil terminal and the countryside between there and Matsuyama itself was to be developed as a modern city. One cannot help wondering whether it will be too late when Man at last gets to grips with taming this voracious monster called Development.

After our very organised few days in Sasebo the Matsuyama visit was delightfully informal. We were indeed the only westerners in the neighbourhood except for one lone Englishman, ex-Army, who had somehow happened upon the area and decided to make his home there. There were distractions though. We were now just about into the typhoon season and weather reports began to become quite insistent about one storm brewing in the central Pacific, now beginning to head for the Philippines and expected to recurve from there north-east towards Japan. Depending on the direction it took after recurving, we could end up not far from its track. This and the very open nature of the anchorage, where the weather seemed forever to be trying to blow us ashore, did not make for a very relaxed visit despite the apparent warmth of our welcome.

On the morning that we were due to sail to join our Captain (D) in *Caesar* for a two-ship visit to Yokahama, the typhoon report became more ominous. If the storm moved as was now being predicted we looked likely to catch at least the edge of it within the next two days. And of course it might not move as predicted. A small change of direction and we might end up in its path. If you have to meet a typhoon you have to meet it and make the best of what is likely to prove a bad job. If there is no pressing need to do so it is sensible to avoid it. If the storm is recurving north-east from the Philippines towards Japan the Admiralty Pilot recommends, helpfully, that one steams as fast as possible away from it, in this case towards the China coast. The accent is on 'fast'. In *Barrosa* this could, indeed would, take a lot of fuel. We had replenished at sea from the Task Group tanker before reaching Sasebo and now had 75 per cent fuel remaining. On present planning we would be down to 50 per cent on reaching Yokahama. If on the other hand we had to do some high-speed typhoon dodging round the China Sea we could easily end up with empty tanks. The other consideration was that when rebuilt with our huge 'bedstead' aerial *Barrosa* was considerably less stable than when first designed. To compensate we were fitted so that, as fuel tanks were emptied, they could be ballasted with sea-water. This of course could be pumped out before a subsequent refuelling but it was all a bit of a business. To be on the safe side, if there was a typhoon about we needed more fuel.

Was the typhoon coming our way? As we weighed anchor that morning the sky was taking on a dull, leaden, look, not the appearance of a sky charged with rain clouds – a much more menacing warning of something unpleasant. The Pilot writes that 'a vague, indefinable, feeling that all is not well' is often a reliable indication that a typhoon is in the offing.' It's a remarkably accurate description. That is what we felt that morning. A quick signal went off to the Admiral: 'We anticipate a typhoon. Please can we have some more fuel.' Within minutes we had a reply: '*Tidereach* rendezvous with *Barrosa* for RAS (refuelling at sea). *Barrosa* arrange position.'

By then were we heading out from the Inland Sea into the North Pacific at the start of a three day passage to Yokohama and were already encountering a long low sullen swell from the south-east, another harbinger of the storm's approach. In a moment after receiving the Admiral's reply we were in touch with *Tidereach*. She had been visiting somewhere a hundred and fifty miles or so north of us. If we now steamed towards each other at say eighteen knots we would meet in the early afternoon. Having bitten the bullet of arranging for fuel we settled down to make the hours pass quickly.

By mid-morning the swell had increased and was still increasing. The sky was heavier. One bright spot was that both the tanker and ourselves had taken departure from the coast only a few hours earlier so both of us had accurate starting positions from which to make for the rendezvous. Then, with two hours to go before we were due to meet, our Captain(D) in *Caesar* came on the air. He had of course been included in our exchange of signals with the Admiral and had I suppose been working out whether he could do with a topping-up also. She however was down to the south of us, in the opposite direction to *Tidereach* but now, rather than allowing us to meet the tanker as we had already arranged and then fixing her own rendezvous for later, *Caesar* ordered us to shift the rendezvous south and closer to her. That was also closer to the storm's predicted track and, selfishly perhaps, we were not too impressed. No doubt it was a reasonable thing to do but apart from anything else it meant that it could well be dark by the time we all met, the sea could be worse, the wind stronger. *Barrosa* with the topweight of that big aerial was not as handy at RAS-ing as *Russell* had been. Bloody hell!

We were into the afternoon by now. The weather was not getting any better, rather the other way round. It was time with all our sophisticated electronic warfare gear that we should be getting bearings of the tanker's wireless transmissions. We would thus be able to check that we were actually closing each other on the most direct courses. For a good thirty minutes the EW office could get no joy. Wretched sets, completely useless when one could really use them. Then suddenly a triumphant shout on the intercom: 'I'm getting *Tidereach* bearing 350°.' 'Are you sure it's her? How far is she?' 'It's certainly her, Sir. There's no way of telling the range. Signals are fairly indistinct but getting stronger. Probably about fifty miles.'

Hell's bells. We're not closing each other any more after *Caesar's* intervention, both steaming south towards Captain(D). We shan't meet for three or four hours. Dark, and a nasty sea. Bother *Caesar*.

But the EW office was being unduly pessimistic. You cannot measure range with Direction Finding gear, or you couldn't in 1963. Soon the signals were getting much stronger and then there was a call from the Ops Room. 'Surface echo 350°.' A minute or two later, 'Contact steering 180°. Speed 18.' And then the wireless office chipped in, 'From *Tidereach*. Think I have you on radar.'

As the tanker was now going hell for leather for our new three ship rendezvous and we had her only just over the horizon there seemed to be no point in waiting for *Caesar* to arrive before starting to fuel ourselves, so we altered course to the north again and burst up towards her as fast as we could. And there she came, a tiny speck on the line joining that bad tempered swell with the threatening sky, first the suggestion of a mast, then the upperworks and now the hull, creaming down towards us. As we got closer never did a tanker look a more splendid vessel, a huge bow wave ahead, two enormous oiling derricks hoisted upright into position on each side meaning she could take two ships at once and give each two hoses for quick refuelling. A broad speckled wake of foam trailed astern.

In a moment we had agreed a fuelling course and speed and were alongside. The swell, quite high by then, was forgotten and in twenty minutes the Chief Stoker was calling for pumping to stop before the messdecks also were topped up with fuel. As we cast off again *Caesar* hove up over the horizon from ahead.

After all that we just caught the edge of the typhoon. *Caesar* took a bit of a pasting, lost her gyro-compass and so on, but dear old *Barrosa* with a full bottom of oil fuel just ploughed happily along hardly noticing the weather. Onboard one or two of us were reflecting on the versatility of a fleet that can whistle up supplies at the tap of a morse key and can be virtually self-supporting if it has just one or two main bases somewhere round the world.

No doubt that the sailors enjoyed Yokohama. As for the Wardroom, well, the third visit on the trot tends to fall into something of a pattern though if it gave the British business community working there some sense of a link with Home, that was perhaps worthwhile.

Chapter 30

Last Lap

Our passage up to Japan had thankfully been fairly clear of exercises. Full marks to the Staff in Singapore who for once had seen fit to let us concentrate on trying to arrive as washed behind the ears as maybe. We made up for it on the way home though. There were still typhoons ploughing their well-worn track through the Philippines and up towards Japan and we met the fringe of two. After our successful weathering of the edge of the first one on our way up to Yokohama these were no bother to *Barrosa*.

It was more hair-raising when one evening the Admiral suddenly announced that as soon as it got dark he would order us all to switch off radars and navigation lights and he would put the Group through some manoeuvres, as it were blind. On the face of it this was an entirely sensible proposition and should have been well within our capability. Since the War the RN had adopted the USN doctrine of the 'circular screen'. This meant that the anti-submarine screen of escorts for the capital ships of a force were disposed in a continuous circle around the latter. Alterations of course were then a simple matter of all ships turning together when ordered. The circle remained intact and after the turn just moved off in the new direction. We however never seemed to have enough escorts to form a continuous ring so a Group would end up with say a semi-circle of escorts sweeping for submarines ahead of the main body but with nothing in the rear. From the defence point of view this had come to be considered just acceptable: a submarine behind you was a much lesser threat than one ahead. But when it came to altering the course of the main body the escorts had to chase around quite quickly to ensure that they stayed ahead of the latter on the new course. We were now to practise this in the dark with no navigational aids.

The exercise started gently enough. A few turns together, an alteration or two of speed whitened nobody's hair. Our Yeoman of Signals was up on the Bridge thumbing through his signal book by the aid of a drastically-dimmed light. The latter slowed his interpretation of signals somewhat but as he knew most of the book by heart it was no great bother.

Then we became more adventurous. An alteration of 180° was signalled, a complete about turn. All this was being done of course by miniscule signal lamps in order not to alert an 'enemy' by radio transmissions.

A turn of this size required the escorts to increase speed and dash back through water we had just covered in order to get ahead of the main body, in this case our cruiser *Lion*, on the new course. In the dark it was considerably more hair-raising than it sounds when thinking about it in broad daylight. What was *Lion*'s turning circle, her lock if you like when one is thinking of a car? We ought to have known that one. Were all the other escorts turning the right way? How close would one of them pass if by some aberration they turned the wrong way? Ships had started off a mile apart so you might think that everyone had plenty of room but two ships closing at no more than twelve knots each will devour a mile in just under three minutes.

I would not say that there was pandemonium on our Bridge. There was no doubt though that the temperature was rising. Lookouts and everyone else too were being urged to keep an extra-specially keen watch. The Yeoman was being badgered, 'Are you sure we've got that signal right? Are we turning the right way?' The Officer of the Watch was cautioned every half-minute to keep his bloody finger on the bloody Navigation Lights switch. It was getting rather itchy.

Suddenly someone spoke up. 'I think I can hear something.' Not surprising in the certain amount of cross-talk going on. 'Come on then. What is it?' 'I'm not sure. It's a sort of hum.' Hell's bells. Engine room fans and not our own either. Just then the port lookout chipped in, 'Looks like a bit of a wave on the port beam.' 'What do you mean, a bit of a wave?' 'Looks like a bow wave.'

Our nerve broke. Chicken to switch on Navigation Lights. Better chicken than being holed. 'Switch on navigation lights.' Suddenly the Bridge was bathed in the most beautiful and gentle glow from our masthead steaming light, complemented by the wonderful bright red and green of the side lights. There was no time to stare however. Close on our port side another ship switched on a millisecond after us. In an instant both ships were heeling outwards under full wheel and as we passed within feet of each other lights came on all over the Group, and the Yeoman was chanting: 'From the Admiral. Switch on navigation lights and radar.'

Well, it was certainly worth doing. We needed a lot more practice. It would be nice to record that we got it, but there was so much else to do.

Writing some thirty years and more after that stimulating exercise made me recall the British view at the time of Jutland that night action between fleets of any size was as likely as not to be counter-productive. How very true!

By next morning the traumas of the previous night were sidelined for future action and the word went forth that the exercise for this day was that all ships in the Group should practise taking each other in tow. We drew the Flagship, *Lion*, as our partner, and she was to tow us first. Towing is a relatively satisfactory exercise in that it harnesses the activities and skills of a fairly substantial proportion of the ship's company from the Bridge downwards and you can actually see a result quite quickly. You either get your partner in tow or you don't. And of course there's no telling when you might need to do it for real. Either way a prime consideration is to carry the exercise through without either ship having a wire foul a propeller, or collide, or, worst of all, have a sailor tangled up in one of the wires involved and go overboard. The theory is simple. The towing ship passes a wire over to the 'dead' vessel who then shackles the end of it to his anchor cable. The reality has to contend with the tendency of the average wire rope to snag itself round any unsuspecting sailor, or any unprotected part of the ship's structure, whilst running out. Then of course it's all very well practising it in daylight and in relatively good weather. When needed for real, conditions are almost certain to be the exact opposite.

This time I think it was fair to say that we did better than the Flagship. Next time we did it at night and honours went to her without any question. Anyway you can't have a destroyer putting one over on the Flagship.

By the middle of June the Task Group was back in Singapore, twelve days of exercises out from Yokohama. Four months remained of *Barrosa's* first commission in the Far East. It was to seem like the third lap of a three lap race. The first four months had brought us out from Devonport, had seen our first deployment to Tawau and had ended with that bright and shiny fortnight in Hong Kong in January. The succeeding lap had had its excitements and tragedies off Borneo and the diversion of the trip to Japan. We were not running out of steam on this last lap but the course did seem rather familiar.

A high spot however was the arrival of *Duchess* to take over as Captain(D), 8th Destroyer Squadron, which was us. Like *Vampire* she was also a Daring. These big ships might almost have been called light cruisers between the Wars. Designed towards the end of World War Two when the needs of the Pacific were much in mind they seemed to complement that great ocean in their size and performance.

The special appeal of *Duchess* however was that her Commanding Officer was Captain Jack Bitmead, who as a Lieutenant-Commander had had *Broadsword* during that magical spring cruise in 1950. I could hardly believe how things were turning out. Were we to have a repeat of that time during our last lap east of Suez?

I think we might have done had *Duchess* come out sooner and had we spent more time in company. As it was, and true to the way events moved in the Far East, we saw little enough of her. They gave us our Annual Inspection, normally an affair comprising a day in harbour when the ship and her company would have a thorough going over as regards general smartness, paperwork and outlook; and a day at sea to test operational efficiency. This time the ship, in common with the rest of the Fleet, had so many commitments that everything had to be squashed into one day at sea off Pulo Tioman. We started at 0530 and ended twelve hours later. Captain Bitmead being in charge it was done with great thoroughness though with good humour to match. Our skeletons remained in their cupboards: it was just warming to read in the Inspection Report that 'the Bridge Communication ratings carried out their duties efficiently, answering and sending messages like bullets.' They did too. Yeoman Thomas of the old *Broadsword* could have been proud of them.

We did have a little more time under *Duchess's* eagle eye though as we were scheduled to be the principal actors in a film for the Admiralty about replenishment at sea. This was to involve four or five days with *Duchess* and *Barrosa* steaming alongside each other in the limpid waters of the Sulu Sea connected by the various pieces of rope by which transfers of stores and people were accomplished with ships under way. The film crew flew out from England with a very clear brief as to what they were to accomplish together with a script which described in detail the procedures to be filmed. We picked them up in Singapore and spent the time on passage to Borneo and the Sulu Sea rewriting their script to accord with current practice. Somebody at home was plainly right out of touch with what actually happened at sea. Was this anything new though?

In the middle of filming we broke off for a couple of days. I cannot remember where *Duchess* went. *Barrosa* was programmed to visit Sandakan on the north Borneo coast to provide a 'stabilising influence' over Sabah Day. Sabah was the new name for North Borneo, the British half of that huge 'island'. Commonsense was suggesting that in pursuance of their claim to the whole of Borneo the Indonesians would make every effort to create what mayhem they could over the Sabah Day celebrations.

Being by now, in our own estimation anyway, old Borneo hands we took the Malawalli Passage south to Sandakan instead of the open sea route. This was the inshore passage twisting amongst the islets, the reefs and coral heads that fringed the coast; a navigational exercise, not imprudent according to the Admiralty Pilot, good practice for a ship on the Station and with rather more for the sailors to look at after so much open water.

Sandakan was of course the setting for several of Somerset Maugham's tales of life and intrigue in Borneo, an archetypal coastal settlement where in his day a few Europeans lived out a sultry existence of boredom spiced with occasional storms of passion and conflicts with nature and the 'natives'. The Sandakan which we found was not nearly so interesting. It stood on a deep inlet where several rivers joined the sea. These were in flood at the time as was the Kinabatangan further south which was rumoured to be at least sixty feet above its normal level. This was an intriguing thought which we would have liked to verify by personal inspection, but time did not permit.

The town itself could well have used some of these flood waters to wash part of it away and allow a fresh start. Somerset Maugham's romantic-sounding if slightly tragic settlement was caught in the twentieth century malaise of semi-development. A pseudo-sophistication was trying to surface through the mud of the rains and a rather misinterpreted concept of civilisation. Tawau was still a comfortable if rather overgrown village, with or without the *nipa* palms. Sandakan had opted for city status and had lost out in the process.

The District Officer and the Officer Commanding Police Detachment had the security situation as regards Sabah Day well under control. While not unappreciative of the presence of an HM Ship they had already made arrangements to ensure a peaceful celebration of the great day when North-East Borneo became Sabah by locking up all the potential trouble-makers. Was not this a little undemocratic, we ventured. 'Maybe,' they smiled, 'but most people are very happy at not being expected to stage a riot, and the chaps in gaol aren't too worried. They get decent food, no hassling and they don't have the bother of organising unpleasantness. And they'll be out in two or three days. It suits everybody really.' Had Sandakan evolved the ultimate in responsible democracy?

At any rate the District Officer had time to take our First Lieutenant

321

and myself water-skiing on Sabah Day. It was my first, and last, attempt at this. I did manage to stay upright most of the time which was just as well as the river was reputed to be teeming with sea-snakes just then.

After that it was back up the Malawalli Passage to rejoin *Duchess* for two final days of filming and then we were let off the leash again to spend an end-of-commission week up in Hong Kong for early pre-Christmas shopping. I just record here as a matter of fact, no more, that although at the end of our film-making we were perhaps halfway between Hong Kong and Singapore, we were required by the Staff to return almost to Singapore so that we could join another ship also bound for Hong Kong and put in a weekend of exercises on the way. Maybe it was sensible. We weren't quite convinced at the time.

Hong Kong in July was anyway very different from Hong Kong in January. The latter visit had been a wonderful tonic – clear blue skies, crisp almost frosty mornings. July was quite the reverse, hot and very humid. Maybe a week's break was worth it. I don't know. And then it was back to where else than Tawau for a last three weeks' stint.

This time we opted for the more direct route south across the South China Sea instead of our previous more roundabout way following closely the west coast of the Philippines. The charts showed plenty of water although this was interspersed with a good scattering of shoal areas. Many of these were named after ships, sailing ships, which had grounded and been lost on them. You will no doubt recall the lovely treasure of china plates and so forth recovered a few years ago from one such wreck.

Anyway it kept us all on our toes to try something different once in a while. Instead of the radar set whirring away on the foremast we had a lookout as high as he could get to watch for anything resembling a reef or shallow patch and the anti-submarine detecting gear was set to work, adding the protection of technology to the skill of the human eye. It was rather a let-down that we came across nothing new though the Captain of the Foc'sle let it be known some days later that he had found traces of sand on his deck. That might have come from anywhere, mightn't it?

The principal reason for having us back in Tawau was to provide a naval presence over Malaysian Independence Day in mid-September. It was not anticipated that there would be civil disturbances but, as we had heard the previous December, there were a large number of Indonesian temporary workers on the plantations who it was thought might possibly cause some sort of upset. Apparently the Army had chosen that day to make the change-over of units stationed in Tawau and that was taken as ruling them out of the security picture. With hindsight the choice of Independence Day for the change-over might not have been so inappropriate as it seemed to us at the time since it could have meant that double the normal number of troops would be in the Tawau area. Anyway *Barrosa* was told to be ready to man two or three 'vital points' and nearly half the ship's company were organised to land. An unintended bonus of all this preparation was that one of our VPs was the Tawau water tower. Some members of the crew had always apparently wanted to climb this, and now they had the chance 'in the course of duty'. The view from the top did not amount to much!

In fact the Day passed off very well in something approaching the family atmosphere of a village fête. No one from the ship was at the ceremony on the *padang*, the village green, but from all accounts the tenor of the speeches from the Borneo side was: 'Why are you deserting us? Please stay a little longer.'

Effectively that marked the end of our time in the Far East. It was not a bad note on which to go. We stayed around Tawau for another week or so, patrolling the coast to the end and now in company with a patrol boat of the Royal Malaysian Navy. At the weekend we got permission from the owners to use the now-deserted fishing settlement on Si Amil, which had been pirated the previous Christmas Eve, as a holiday camp. The first party ashore met two quite vicious sea-snakes which elected to share the communal dormitory with the sailors but this did not seem to affect its popularity.

And then our relief arrived, signalling while still below the horizon that he had assumed command and required no briefing from us; so, unwanted, we slipped quietly away, made a farewell trip through the Malawalli Passage, and returned to Singapore for the last time. Most of the Ship's Company flew home a couple of weeks later. I had to stay behind for another two or three days. The new Engineer Officer in doing his 'take over' inspection had come to the conclusion that some of the tubes in the boilers had corroded. The presumption was that our commission had somehow, sometime, allowed the boiler feed water to become contaminated; and there had to be a Board of Inquiry. It was a rather unnecessary end to a Commission which had otherwise gone quite reasonably. I never heard the result of the Inquiry: it was strictly Engineers' business. I hope they took into account that in the space of thirteen months the old ship had steamed the equivalent of four circuits round the world at the Equator.

The end of *Barrosa's* first commission east of Suez is the end also of my not very competent attempt to give some sort of idea of what life at sea was like in what I have called 'The Steam Turbine and Rifled Gun' period. As far as *Barrosa* was concerned the story ended with almost breathtaking sharpness. Virtually as we passed the mooring ropes ashore for the last time in the Dockyard it was a question of 'off with the old, on with the new.' It was a low-key finish to our nearly two years together – building at Devonport and service east of Suez. No one seemed sorry to see the 'old guard' go. No one said, 'Well done.' I suppose minds were on other things. Malaysian Independence and its implications, forthcoming independence for Singapore, and 'confrontation' with Indonesia. The main aim was to get the ship going again with a new crew and back into business, and quite right too. In the end the effectiveness of the ship always had to be more important than the affairs of the individual sailor, but in case this doctrine sounds too crude, the ship depended on its sailors. That was right too.

One of my last calls was on the Captain of the Fleet. He was the member of the Commander-in-Chief's staff whose prime interest was morale, and he asked reasonably enough whether the Ship's Company would be going home in good heart. 'Got their tails up have they?' he had asked. For some reason I thought he ought to know the truth. 'They're pretty tired, Sir,' I replied. 'I hope we've always pulled at least our weight and it's been good to have been of some use here. But right now they're very glad to be going home.' It was not the answer he wanted, but it struck me that it would hardly be helpful to say, for instance, that we wished we could stay on for another six months when the Naval Staff themselves were worried about 'overstretch', not enough ships, and too many commitments. And thirteen months was quite long enough for married men to be away from their families.

Perhaps that was too downbeat. I was just leaving *Barrosa* for the last time a day or two later when I found four of the most senior ratings in the ship on deck outside my cabin, the Coxswain, the Chief Boatswain's Mate, the Chief Gunner's Mate and the Chief Electrician. 'Just wanted to say goodbye, Sir. It's been a good commission . . .' We agreed we'd had a good ship, steamed a few miles and by and large had had a good bunch on board. I was very touched. I had never known it happen before. Maybe it had been worth losing a shackle of cable in Campbeltown harbour some twelve years earlier!

That was not quite the end of things though. The film on Replenishment at Sea was released a couple of years later and I was lucky enough to see the first showing in the Admiralty cinema. Outside London was cold and wet, but there on the screen reflecting the sunshine of the Sulu Sea it was heartwarming to see the young men, many of them hardly more than boys when we left Devonport but now burnt by the sun, filled out with a year at sea, going about the job quickly, efficiently and with every appearance of ensuring that it was done well. Even Captain Bitmead must have agreed that there were still seamen left!

I was also amused to see that the Captain of *Barrosa* was there wearing a shirt which had seen better days. I had debated that morning off Balembangan whether I needed a clean one or whether yesterday's would pass muster. I had decided that the Bridge was not going to feature in the footage. Unfortunately it did and the Captain's grubby shirt was there for all to see.

Outline Particulars of Principal Ships Mentioned in the Text

	Built	Dimensions (ft)	Tonnage	Armament	Armour	Power -shp	Speed -kts	Crew
Sutlej	1899	454 × 69	12,000	2 × 9.2" 12 × 6"	6"	21,000 A good steamer. Exceeded design speed.	21	700
Empress of India	1891	410 × 75	14,000	4 × 13.5" 10 × 6"	18"	13,000	17	712
Scylla	1891	300 × 43	3,400	2 × 6" 6 × 4.7"	2–5"	9,000	20 Only 16kts 1909.	273
Fox	1893	320 × 49	4,360	2 × 6" 8 × 4.7"	2–5" Fighting value considered small by 1913	9,000	18	318
Caroline	1914	420 × 41	3,750	4 × 6" 4 × 21" Torpedoes	2¼–3"	40,000	27	325
Invincible Inflexible	1907	560 × 78	17,250	8 × 12" 10 × 4"	3–7"	41,000	25	750
Scharnhorst Gneisenau	1906	450 × 71	11,600	8 × 8.2" 6 × 6"	2–6"	26,000	22.5	765
Renown	1916	794 × 102	28,000	6 × 15" 16 × 4.5"	9"	126,000	32.5	967
Modernised inter-wars								
Heliotrope	1915	262 × 33	1,200	1 × 4" 2 × 2pdr	—	1,800	16	104
Hood	1918	860 × 105	41,200	8 × 15" 12 × 5.5" 8 × 4" & 4 × 21" torpedo tubes	5–12"	151,280	32	1100
Hawkins	1919	605 × 58	9,750	7 × 7.5" 6 × 21" torpedo tubes	1½–3"	65,000	30	712

	Built	Dimensions (ft)	Tonnage	Armament	Armour	Power -shp	Speed -kts	Crew
Valiant *Q. Elizabeth*	1915 1913	646 × 104 Both re-built 1937–9	33,000	8 × 15" 16 × 4.5"	13"	75,000	23	925
Richelieu French	1940	813 × 109	35,000	8 × 380mm 9 × 152mm 12 × 100mm	345mm	155,000	30	1670
Saratoga USN	1927	888 × 105	33,000	12 × 5" 81/90 aircraft	3–6"	180,000	33	2122 inc. Aircrew
Illustrious	1940	753 × 95 (Other Strike carriers of the BPF similar)	23,000	16 × 4.5" 60 aircraft	3"	110,000	31	1600
Norman RAN	1941	356 × 35	1,750	6 × 4.7" 10 × 21" Torpedo tubes	—	40,000	33	220
King George V *Howe*	1940	745 × 103	35,000	10 × 14" 16 × 5.25"	15"	110,000	29	1640
Loch Glendhu	1944	307 × 38	1,345	1 × 4" 2 anti-submarine mortars	—	5,500	19	103
Norfolk	1928	630 × 66	9,925	8 × 8" 8 × 4"	4"	80,000	32	652
Broadsword	1948	365 × 38	1,980	4 × 4" 2 anti-submarine mortars 8 × 21" torpedo tubes	—	40,000	34	230

	Built	Dimensions (ft)	Tonnage	Armament	Armour	Power -shp	Speed -kts	Crew
Virago	1943 Modernised 1951–2	363 × 36	1,710	2 × 4" 2 anti-submarine mortars	—	40,000	32	190
Vanguard	1944	815 × 108	42,500	8 × 15" 16 × 5.25"	14"	130,000	30	1893
Russell	1954	310 × 33	1,300	3 × 40mm 2 anti-submarine mortars	—	15,000	24	111
Barrosa	1947 Modernised 1960–1	379 × 40	2,480	4 × 4.5" 1 × close range guided weapon 1 anti-submarine mortar	—	50,000	31	260
Duchess *Vampire* (RAN)	1952 1959 – Sydney	390 × 43	2,600	4 × 4.5" 5 × 21" torpedo tubes 1 anti-submarine mortar	—	54,000	34	308
Lion	1959	555 × 64	9,550	4 × 6" 6 × 3" (Note 3 below)	1½–3"	80,000	32	800

Notes

1. *Heliotrope* and the four ships before *Caroline* had triple expansion reciprocating engines and were coal-fired. *Loch Glendhu* also had reciprocating engines but was oil-fired. *Caroline* was the first of this list to be turbine-powered and an oil-burner. *Invincible* and *Inflexible* were turbine ships but burnt coal.

2. *Largo Bay* appears in the text but not in the Table since she was identical with *Loch Glendhu* apart from being the anti-aircraft version of the design and thus fitted with 4 × 4" guns instead of the latter's anti-submarine weapons.

3. *Lion*'s gun armament, although seeming light for the 1960s as compared with that of earlier cruisers, was dual-purpose and effective against aircraft as well as ships. The 6" guns fired 20 rounds per minute each and the 3" guns 120 rpm.

4. The aircraft carriers mentioned on page 120 of the text were all built between 1941 and 1944 and were similar to *Illustrious* in offensive capability.